INTRODUCTION TO PHILOSOPHY

Revised Edition

BY

GEORGE THOMAS WHITE PATRICK, Ph.D.

PROFESSOR EMERITUS OF PHILOSOPHY IN THE UNIVERSITY OF IOWA

Revised with the assistance of

FRANK MILLER CHAPMAN, Ph.D.

ASSISTANT IN PHILOSOPHY AT HARVARD UNIVERSITY

HOUGHTON MIFFLIN COMPANY

The Riverside Press Cambridge

The Riverside Press

CAMBRIDGE · MASSACHUSETTS

PRINTED IN THE U.S.A.

TO

MY WIFE

MAUD LYALL PATRICK

PREFACE TO THE SECOND EDITION

THE generous reception which colleges and universities have accorded to the first edition of this *Introduction* encourages now the publication of a fully revised edition. The intimate relation between philosophy and science is more and more emphasized as the years go by, and certain branches of science are changing so rapidly that the new trends must at least be mentioned, even in an elementary book such as this. In the science of physics, where the development has been most rapid — amounting almost to a revolution — it is interesting and heartening to notice that there is a tendency among the physicists to become philosophers, and frankly to acknowledge the philosophical character of some of their writings; while students of philosophy await more and more eagerly the new discoveries in science. For instance, in the case of the Principle of Indeterminacy, some physicists admit that its interpretation must depend upon one's philosophy; and some students of philosophy admit that certain philosophical problems — the freedom of the will, for instance — must await further research in the new physics. From which we may cherish the hope that the last traces of dogmatism are disappearing from philosophy — and the last traces of arrogance from science.

In philosophy, the theory of creative evolution — and of emergence as applied to life and mind — has without doubt become more widely accepted in the new years; while the view that the emergents may be values, or even ideal values — speculative, to be sure — has certainly met with no refutation.

In this revision of the *Introduction*, the number of chapters has been increased from twenty-three to twenty-nine, the increase being due partly to new material and partly to a new arrangement. All the chapters save one have been revised or rewritten — and some new ones added. I wish to acknowledge the valued aid of Dr. Frank Miller Chapman in this edition.

G. T. W. P.

PALO ALTO, CALIFORNIA

PREFACE TO THE FIRST EDITION

THIS book is intended as an introductory text in philosophy for college and university students, and as a guidebook for the general reader who would like to find his way into this interesting field of inquiry. It sets forth no system of philosophy — at least I hope not. The purpose of philosophy is to impel to thought, not to satisfy inquiry with a "system."

Nevertheless, the book is not wholly impersonal. Theoretically, perhaps, one who writes an elementary introduction to philosophy should place impartially before the reader the various theories, reserving any comment of his own. But I doubt whether people like to read a wholly impersonal book. They enjoy an impartial book, but not an impersonal one. Readers usually like to get the viewpoint of the author, if only in a footnote. I have, therefore, not hesitated to indicate my own views, or at least to point out the direction from which the light seems to me to come. In this critical and individualistic age such a method is not likely to lead the reader astray. He will think for himself anyway.

The general standpoint of the book is, I suppose, realistic and pluralistic, and I hope theistic; certainly idealistic, and quite unmistakably optimistic. Furthermore, the validity of the realistic standpoint of the special sciences is quite shamelessly assumed, and it is taken for granted that they deal with realities and not with appearances. In accordance with this plan I have left to a late chapter the whole subject of epistemology, believing that much confusion and discouragement may be avoided by beginning objectively after the manner of the special sciences. Finally, I have dwelt upon the similarities among philosophical systems rather than upon their differences; for while the study of philosophy must stimulate thought, it should not discourage persistent thinking by engendering a cynical scepticism. And, indeed, I think it is quite time to call attention to the agreements rather than the disagreements in philosophy.

The divergence of philosophical systems is a theme dear to the critics of philosophy, ancient and modern. But certainly in these later years a most encouraging *convergence* is beginning to manifest itself, giving promise of a real progress comparable with that of the physical sciences. Rationalism and Empiricism, for instance, as genetically approached by Professor Dewey, are now seen in friendly converse; Mechanism and Vitalism seem about to merge into some theory of creative evolution; while even Idealism and Naturalism, of old the most uncompromising of enemies, no longer appear wholly irreconcilable. If, with Norman Kemp Smith in his recent *Prolegomena* to an Idealistic Theory of Knowledge, we define Idealism as a term covering all those philosophies which agree in maintaining that spiritual values have a determining voice in the ordering of the Universe, and Naturalism as the view that all these values emerge and begin to vindicate their reality at some late stage in the process of evolution, it is only at first sight that these two theories appear contradictory. Why may not spiritual values emerge late in evolution and yet have a determining voice in the ordering of the Universe? If we think of the whole world as a movement in the realization of these values, then the various steps in the evolutionary program would be regarded simply as indispensable stages in this realization.

The differences between Idealism and Naturalism appear still further softened by our newer knowledge of matter and our newer conception of mind. Someone, quoted by Hoernlé, says, "We know too much about matter now to be materialists." Perhaps he should have said, "We know too much about matter now to have any fear of Materialism." If still held, this theory would apparently have lost its reputation for being mechanistic, atheistic, irreligious, or even monistic. And as for Naturalism, we are finding *Nature* to be an immensely more complicated affair than in the innocent days of Herbert Spencer and the early Darwinians, so that there might be room in it for almost anything — for instance, secondary qualities, universals, even Platonic Ideas. Thus, if the antithesis between Naturalism and Idealism has not melted away, at any rate the alleged leanness and meagerness of the former are no longer in evidence.

Idealism, too, is changing its character and losing its harsher aspects. Its subjectivistic forms are harder and harder to maintain. Many now call themselves idealists who claim neither that the world is dependent upon mind, nor the product of mind, nor a manifestation of the absolute, nor made of mind-stuff. It is sufficient to say that spiritual values are the significant things, that is, the *real* things in the Universe, and that perhaps they have a determining voice in its ordering.

I have just been reading the thoughtful article by Professor Urban in the *Philosophical Review* for September, 1923, on "Origin and Value." The author is much troubled by the attitude of philosophical modernism in its dissociation of hitherto faithful connections of ideas, the most serious of which is the dissociation of origin and value, or value and reality; and among modernisms he finds the doctrines of emergents, creative resultants, and epigenesis the most flagrant offenders against these faithful connections.

I agree with Professor Urban that the dissociation of value and reality would indicate the decadence of philosophy, but I cannot agree that the dissociation of origin and value would be equally fatal. The views indicated in this book as promising paths for the reader to explore are certainly sympathetic with the epigenetic and emergent theories — but surely this does not indicate a divorce of value and reality. I cannot believe that all values and all realities are to be packed into origins, nor do I see any reason why the world may not be a blossoming-out process, in which new values are constantly realized. Even if we speak of these new values as novelties, there is no necessary divorce of value and reality. But if there are laid up somewhere in the heavens patterns by which we measure these values, even then there is no reason why they may not emerge in any given local program of evolution.

But I wonder whether there is not some profounder truth than is expressed in either of these views. Could we not think of the world as "biocentric" and "psychotropic," as hungering and thirsting after righteousness, as longing for beauty and truth and goodness, without thinking of these values as envisaged, or willed, or created after any type or pattern? Reflecting much on Aristotle, some such view as this has been often in my mind while writing the pages which follow. Matter is taking on form, and the form is life and mind and social organization **and art** and science and philosophy and religion; and all these are values, and they have a determining voice in the ordering of the world, because all which precedes them is indispensable to them. Hence I do not believe that there need be any divorce of reality and value in the emergent and epigenetic views. In fact I think that S. Alexander and Lloyd Morgan have done philosophy a real service in introducing the word *emergence* to designate the relation in which spiritual values stand to the organization of material elements.

A glance at the footnotes in the chapters which follow will show my indebtedness to many writers. It is a little difficult to single out those to whom I am most indebted, but I am sure that I owe much to Professors John Dewey, S. Alexander, Edward Gleason Spaulding, and Ralph Barton Perry. We all owe so much to James that special acknowledgment is unnecessary save by way of tribute; and I at least owe much to Bergson. I wish to thank Professor J. C. Manry for his painstaking reading of my manuscript and his wise suggestions, and Dr. H. Heath Bawden for his sometimes caustic criticisms, which I have found useful. I am much indebted also to Professor C. F. Taeusch for many suggestions and to Mr. H. J. Phillips for assistance in reading the proofs. J. Arthur Thomson has instructed me with his science and comforted me with his philosophy. I have to thank Charles Scribner's Sons for permission to print the quotation from Santayana on page xiii, and many other publishers for permission to quote from their books.

G. T. W. P.

IOWA CITY, IOWA

CONTENTS

PART I

PHILOSOPHY — ITS DEFINITION, VALUE, AND METHOD

PART II

THE UNIVERSE, ORGANIC LIFE, EVOLUTION

PART III

THEORIES OF REALITY

PART IV

THE NATURE OF MIND AND OF KNOWLEDGE

PART V

THE HIGHER VALUES OF LIFE

O world, thou choosest not the better part!
It is not wisdom to be only wise,
And on the inward vision close the eyes,
But it is wisdom to believe the heart.
Columbus found a world, and had no chart,
Save one that faith deciphered in the skies;
To trust the soul's invincible surmise
Was all his science and his only art.
Our knowledge is a torch of smoky pine
That lights the pathway but one step ahead
Across a void of mystery and dread.
Bid, then, the tender light of faith to shine
By which alone the mortal heart is led
Unto the thinking of the thought divine.
                                        SANTAYANA

PART I

PHILOSOPHY.—ITS DEFINITION, VALUE
AND METHOD

CHAPTER I

INTRODUCTION

A LITTLE girl stood looking out the window, very thoughtful. Presently she turned and said, "Mother, what I don't understand is how there came to be any world." With this reflection she became a philosopher. Most children just take the world for granted; most men and women do also. But some children and some grown-ups are very thoughtful and reflective; they wonder what the world is, how it came to be, what it is made of, and what it is for. When their wonder begins to be serious and systematic inquiry, they are philosophers.

Plato said that philosophy begins in wonder. The Greeks were devoted to philosophy, but as compared with us they were naïve and childlike in their outlook on the world, and free from disturbing doubts; but they were much given to wonder, and their wonder soon became serious and thoughtful.

Doubt and perplexity

But, although philosophy among the ancients began in wonder, in modern times it usually begins in doubt. In our own difficult post-war period, doubt has become a serious and disturbing human ailment.

"There never was a time when so many people were so uncertain about so many things as at present." These were the words of a distinguished speaker at Stanford University recently. Many of us are uncertain about the best form of government, about the best economic or social system, about what things are right and what things are wrong, about the existence of God, and about the soul and its destiny. We are uncertain whether people are better behaved today than they were in the times of our fathers, or whether they were better then than now.

Formerly we were all sure that democracy is the best form of government for all civilized people, and that that form of social

organization is best which provides a full measure of individual freedom and initiative.   We believed that right and wrong were what
our parents taught us.   We believed that God exists because of the
authority of the Church or the Bible.   Now our confidence in all
these old beliefs is shaken, and there is much doubt and confusion.

But we are told that the situation is even worse than this.   There
might be doubt about the fundamental principles of morals or
theology, or about economic and social systems and the theory of
government, but there is still one authority which rests firmly upon
established laws, about which there could be no doubt whatever —
and that authority is science.   But now we begin to hear that the
old foundations of science itself are crumbling.

> At the present time technical scientists find themselves with equa-
> tions which they are unable to interpret, and with theories that they
> cannot make intelligible without statements of a philosophical char-
> acter which certain of their colleagues do not accept.   Stated bluntly,
> this means that scientists do not fully understand their own discov-
> eries because the first principles, which make all technical discoveries
> intelligible, are in a state of flux.   This is the reason why physicists
> like Eddington, and Einstein, and Whitehead, and physiologists like
> Driesch, and Haldane, and Henderson, and pure mathematicians like
> Brouwer, and Hilbert, and Weyl, are writing philosophy.   A new spirit
> and temper is abroad in the world.   The old frame and background
> which contained the contents of the scientist's picture of nature, has
> dissolved in his hands, and he is being forced to shift his attention
> from the constituent details to the general structure, in order to pre-
> vent science from being overwhelmed by its discoveries, and destroyed
> by its very success.   A change which strikes to the very foundation
> of things is upon us.[1]

In a situation like this, what are we to do?   I think there is one
thing which we shall *not* do — and that is to assume the attitude
either of the sceptic or the cynic.   These problems are going to be
solved — and some of them soon.   We happen to live in an age of
transition, when many sciences and many old beliefs are in a state of
flux.   In such a transitional period there is both danger and promise
— and to be living in such a period is, at any rate for the young,
almost an adventure.   There are plenty of things to think about —

[1] F. S. C. Northrop, *Science and First Principles*, p. 2.   By permission of the publishers.
The Macmillan Company.

and there is no greater joy than in this exercise of thought. There are many things to be thought through, and philosophy may be defined as the art of thinking things through — or, if you prefer, it is the habit of trying to think things through.

But just what is involved in this? It involves thinking logically about the subject in hand — as well as systematically and persistently. We must define very carefully the terms which have been used, or which we ourselves are using, and examine their meaning and their implications. The habit of clarification is very much the disposition of the philosopher. To philosophize is to seek clear notions — as it was with Plato. In more technical language philosophy is the critical analysis of concepts and the discovery of relations between them; it thus hopes to integrate our knowledge, to unify and interpret it. So it comes about that logic is perhaps the most essential part of the philosopher's equipment. But the mere critical analysis of concepts would make philosophy a dreary discipline, ceasing however to be dreary when the ideas to be investigated are taken from some sphere of life of great and supreme interest.

Of the principles which are in doubt, there are certain ones which must be cleared up rather soon. I do not greatly fear the disruption of organized society, about which we hear so much, nor the "downfall of our civilization"; but unless we can get some of our moral, social, and economic problems solved, there is grave danger of a rapid decline of our standard of living, if not of social degeneration.

Now it is not the purpose of philosophy to try to solve our social, economic, and political problems; but it is its purpose to think carefully and systematically about certain fundamental questions which concern ourselves, our conduct, and the world in which we live. I have said that a transitional age, such as this, is full both of danger and of promise. I believe that the promise is greater even than the dangers. For instance, what are the facts about the threatened breakdown of science? It may well be that the fruits of science have been less than we expected, but as regards the threatened breakdown of the principles of science, we find upon inquiry that there is nothing very serious about this. So far as those sciences are concerned with things which directly relate to human needs and human happiness, their principles remain unshaken. It is hardly necessary to state this evident truth.

What has happened is this: The whole edifice of the physical sciences, as we have been accustomed to study it, is now found to be part of a larger world of which we had no previous conception. The field of science has been so tremendously enlarged that we are a little dizzy at present. We have to get some new bearings and accustom ourselves to wider horizons. The theory of relativity, the quantum theory, the new Principle of Uncertainty, the discovery that physical laws, as well as social laws, are more or less statistical in character, the fact that we cannot predict how individuals will behave — even individual atoms and electrons — all of these are new discoveries, somewhat startling, and most of them are hard to understand.

But we surmise that the meaning of it is that we are not so much hemmed in by the unrelenting walls of a mechanistic universe as nineteenth-century science taught us. Perhaps there are possibilities in our world that we have not suspected — it might even have a place for freedom. Possibly we have been studying physics and chemistry too much and biology and psychology too little. It may be that biology is not just a branch of physics — nor psychology a branch of biology. The mathematicians also are doing strange things. They appear to be able to fathom depths not revealed by physical measurements and instruments of precision. Equations seem suddenly to have acquired unsuspected possibilities.

Thus our new world is full of promise and rich in possibilities; but in respect to human relations it is a period of great confusion. Evidently it is a time for reflective thinking — and this is just what philosophy is.

Now we must think

Under the title, "Now We Must Think," Chester Rowell discusses the advantages and disadvantages of periods of uncertainty.

> Who does not long for the static times, when men did not need to think?
>
> The ages of Roman peace, for instance, when there was no more war because all the world was subdued; when there was plenty for the favored of Rome, and misery only for voiceless slaves. Or for the thirteenth century of Europe, when religion was the main concern of

mankind and all its doctrines and institutions were settled. Or the later nineteenth century, when liberal democracy in government and individualistic capitalism in business had arrived in the advanced nations and were on their way in all others. Or even the era of Coolidge, to which we now vainly dream of returning, when all was for the best in this best of possible worlds.

Things were settled then. We knew what was true or false, what was right or wrong. Our thinking on the background of things had already been done for us; we had only the smaller task of adjusting ourselves to that fixed background. There were certainties, by which we could measure things. We did not have to inquire, to examine, to weigh. We knew. Even the future was certain, since the essentials were all fixed, and there could be nothing to change but the details. It was a finished world we had arrived at, in which we could busy ourselves with our personal affairs, with no need to reconsider fundamentals.

Now we find ourselves in a whirlpool, in which nothing is fixed, not even the direction of the current in which we are floating.

After all, are we not fortunate to live in the age of unsettlement? The times of certainty are also the times of stagnation. When we know what to think, we cease to think. When conditions of life are fixed, we merely tramp the treadmill in them. The great periods are the new ones, when, because everything is undone, everything has to be done. The *Pax Romana* froze into Byzantine lethargy in the Eastern Empire, and was only prevented from doing so in the West by the invasions of the barbarians. The theological fixity of the thirteenth century gave way to the ferment of the Renaissance and the Reformation, when nothing was sure, but also nothing was torpid.

Our misfortune is not that we are thrust into a time when thinking must be done, but that we do not do it. It was a thousand years after the Roman Empire fell before men realized that they were no longer living in it. Many of us still imagine that we are living in the world that died forever on August 1, 1914. Recent events are shaking us out of that illusion. The process is painful, but it may be salutary. It challenges us to think new thoughts. The first and the hardest step in that process is to unthink the old ones. Or, perhaps, for some of us, to think at all. This is no time for the slothful.[1]

In times past there have always been certain established authorities, such as custom, tradition, and the religious beliefs of the group, to answer our hard questions, to settle our doubts, to guide our conduct. We have discovered that all these authorities are in sad need

[1] Chester Rowell, Editor *San Francisco Chronicle*, in the *Chronicle*, August, 1934.

of revision — and the revision has not yet been made.   For the moment, the only authority which all men trust is the authority of science — and despite the limitations of science which we have just mentioned, our faith in it has been fully justified.   But the trouble is that science does not attempt to answer the urgent questions about values, life, and conduct which press upon us.   Science can tell us a great deal about air and sea and land, about the stars and their size, distance, and constitution, about the rocks far beneath the earth's surface, about the atoms and the light-waves, about plants and animals and our own bodies.   But beyond the physical realm the voice of science is very hesitant.   Most of us have only a limited interest — perhaps a kind of scientific curiosity — in the structure of the rocks, the distance of the stars — or even in our own bones and muscles; but we have a profound and persistent interest in things human, social, economic, political, moral and religious.   It is about life that we want to know — its meaning, its future, its conduct.

What then are we to do?   These questions lie beyond the present field of science, and we have become sceptical of the authorities upon which our fathers relied to answer them.

We are living in a very singular moment of history.   It is a moment of crisis, in the literal sense of that word.   In every branch of our spiritual and material civilization we seem to have arrived at a critical turning-point.   This spirit shows itself not only in the actual state of public affairs but also in the general attitude towards fundamental values in personal and social life.   Many people say that these symptoms mark the beginnings of a great renaissance, but there are others who see in them the tidings of a downfall to which our civilization is fatally destined.[1]

In a crisis like this, there seems to be one thing at any rate which we can do.   There is still one authority to consult — and this is *reflective thought*.   It is man's peculiar power and prerogative to think.   Most of the real progress which the world has made in every field has come through the medium of reflective thinking, especially the thinking of the great men of all times.   When it becomes serious, sustained, and logical, and directed towards questions of life and values, it becomes philosophy.   As Professor James said, Philosophy is an unusually persistent effort to think clearly.   I do not see that

[1] Max Planck, *Where is Science Going?* (W. W. Norton and Company, Inc., New York), p. 64.

there is anything else that we can do in the situation which now confronts us except to think our problems through, weighing carefully the opinions of the leaders of thought, both those of the present and those of the past, and testing our conclusions by experience and experiments. To do this is to extend the methods of science into the fields of human relations and human problems.

Concretely, I should say that the urgent need of the present is to widen the scope of the natural sciences to take in all the subjects of human interests. This will be to extend the field of science further into that now taken by philosophy. Philosophy has usually been occupied with borderland problems, lying beyond the field of the natural sciences, and yet occupying almost the center of human interests. When these problems are solved, they become a part of scientific progress — and philosophy moves on to the new fields which always lie beyond.

Some would go further than this, and urge that science should not only extend its scope, but should shift the focus of its inquiries from the physical world over into that of human relations. Possibly we have found out all that we need to know for the present about space and time, ether waves, neutrons and electrons. At a meeting of the British Association for the Advancement of Science not long ago, the suggestion was made that science should take a ten-year holiday; and there have been recurring expressions of the view that scientific effort should now be turned more in other directions than the furthering of our knowledge of our physical environment — and our control over it. Our acquaintance with the physical world has outstripped our knowledge of ourselves; and our control of the forces of nature has outstripped our powers of self-control. Our social, economic, moral, philosophical, and religious problems must now receive more of the attention of science, and the tremendous intellectual power exhibited in scientific thought and research must be turned more into these other directions.

What we need now is to have life itself, its meaning and relative values, interpreted for us. This has always been philosophy's task, which has sometimes been defined as the cultural study of meanings and values, or as the interpretation of life. Matthew Arnold said of the tragic poet Sophocles that he saw life steadily and saw it whole.

In this telling phrase both the aim and the method of philosophy are given. The aim is to see life as a whole, not with the slant of the business man or the clubman or the artist or poet or preacher or the university professor, nor with any slant at all; but to see it as it would be seen by "the spectator of all time and all existence"; [1] and the method is to see it steadily, with neither prejudice nor bias nor half knowledge.

A world view

Again, philosophy has been defined as *the attempt by use of scientific methods to understand the world in which we live.*

This attempt to understand the world, to combine the results of the special sciences into some kind of consistent *world view*, has always been the aim of philosophy from the days of Thales, the first Greek philosopher, to the present. But just what do we mean by *the world*? Among the Greeks it meant the *Cosmos*, or, as we should say, the *Universe*; and philosophers of all ages have courageously set themselves to this tremendous task of getting a theory of the Universe, its extent and duration (space and time), its creator (God), its purpose, its primary stuff or material, its relation to man and to his soul and destiny. To this end labored Democritus and Plato and Aristotle and Saint Augustine and Bruno and Descartes and Spinoza and Kant and Hegel and Herbert Spencer and others of the great "philosophers," and these immense world problems still haunt us and must be studied.

But at the present time this astronomical meaning of "the world" is less in our thoughts. With our modern individualistic, human-istic, and romantic moods we turn more to immediate interests, and "the world" means something else to us. With our northern climate, our indoor living, our big cities, our crowded populations, and our social life, the world we live in is not an astronomical world; it is rather a social, political, literary, moral, and religious world.

The ancient Greeks were much troubled by the problem of permanence and change; but by change they meant physical change, the motion of material atoms and particles and the phenomena of

---

[1] Plato said that the philosopher is the spectator of all time and all existence, and that he is one who sets his affections on that which really exists. — *The Republic*, VI, p. 486.

growth and decay.   These questions are still unanswered; but our interests now are with another kind of changing world — changing social customs, changing political relations, changing morals, changing religion, and changing literary standards.   But this kind of "world" is quite as much in need of interpretation as the other — and so philosophy remains with us; only now it becomes the interpretation of *life*, its value and meaning, its source and its destiny. Hence, evolution, progress, knowledge, the ways of the mind, problems of conduct and society have come into the foreground; but it is as true as ever that philosophy is an attempt to understand the world we live in.

Despite the rather strenuous life that we lead now, busied as most of us are with athletics and social activities, with books and magazines, with college routine, with recreations and amusements, I believe that we are more thoughtful and inwardly serious than in former times; and that the philosophic impulse dawns earlier in our lives.   Old philosophies and established traditions are no longer received without question.   The spirit of fresh inquiry is everywhere; but the trouble is that, owing to our intensely social life, time is lacking for careful and persistent study of the life problems.   In the study of philosophy we simply take time to think some of our problems through.

Probably there are very few of us who have not seriously asked just such questions as these: Is the Universe a universe of thought, or just of dead matter?   Is it under the rule of mechanical laws, or does it embrace some plan, purpose, and goal?   Can we any longer hold a religious view of the world?   Is there any God at all, or is there nothing but matter and energy?   What is matter made of?   Is my mind, which is now thinking and wondering, something different from matter, or is it just a grouping of atoms or a function of my body?   I am alive.   What is life?   Sometime I shall die.   What is death, and where do I go from here?   Tomorrow I shall do many things.   Some of them will be right and some wrong.   What is right and what is wrong?   All about me I see men striving for money and fame and pleasure.   Are these really the highest values, or are there other values that are higher and better, such as peace, simplicity, faith, love, work, the enjoyment of art, the pursuit of science?   What is most worth while? I can ask all these questions. Is it possible to find an answer to them? What are the limits of knowledge?

Again, objects of beauty surround us in nature and in art. Some of the buildings in our city or on our college campus are beautiful and some are ugly. Just what is beauty? What is it that we enjoy in classical music and what is it that we admire in the old masters, in the Gothic cathedrals, in the Greek temples? I admire the sunset, the moon seen through the clouds, the wild flowers, the autumn leaves. Would nature be beautiful if there were no eye to see it or no mind to appreciate it? I walk through the crowded city and see men striving and straining for wealth, position, power. Some of them are loudly declaiming against injustice, and I long to know what justice is and why men struggle and strive. All these are philosophical problems. To *ask* these big questions, to *reflect* upon them, to *study* them in a scientific way and to *try to answer* them — this is philosophy.

The search for unity

Herbert Spencer defined philosophy as *completely unified knowledge*, contrasting it with science, which is partially unified knowledge. His notion was that philosophy tries to unite the several sciences into a unified system, just as each special science tries to unite the particular facts within its own field into a unified system. This was a very ambitious conception of philosophy; we do not hope now to realize it. But it was defective in another way. It was formulated in the last century when our hopes were bright that the natural sciences, physics, biology, psychology, sociology, would solve the world riddle. These hopes have been somewhat disappointed. There is an unexplained residue — a romantic element in life, even an element of tragedy — which must be taken account of in any true philosophy. And, besides, philosophy is something far more than the unification of the special sciences; it must satisfy not only our scientific interests but our moral and religious needs, our longings and aspirations; these too are facts, which any system of thought must consider. If we could take *all* these facts and *think them together*, that would be philosophy.

Wisdom

Finally, philosophy has been defined as *wisdom*. The word *philosophy* is from the Greek word *sophia*, wisdom, and the verb *philein*, to love. It is just the love of wisdom. Socrates disclaimed having wisdom, but said he had the love of it. But wisdom is precisely what he seemed to his contemporaries to have; he is the typical wise man and the world philosopher. It might prove troublesome to try to explain just how wisdom differs from knowledge; we can feel the difference, but we cannot express it. Perhaps taste and appreciation are involved. Is philosophy something like intellectual good taste? And is intellectual good taste something which enables us to appraise rightly the various *values* which are offered to us so freely in this rich and wonderful modern world of ours? We have become pretty well convinced that neither wealth nor pleasure is the highest value; and we are trying to find out what the highest values are. Everyone seems to be pursuing something — but why? We seem to need a key to this puzzle of the relative worth of things — work, play, amusement, study, eating, drinking, love-making, science, art, music, poetry, social service, politics, business, and all the rest.

Metaphysics

In recent years this humanistic aspect of philosophy, this attempt to interpret life, to see things in the large, to gain the right perspective, has been emphasized much more than the older metaphysical problems, such as the nature of reality, of God and the world, of purpose, of causality, of mind. The term Philosophy is a wider term than Metaphysics, including all these subjects and also Epistemology, or the theory of knowledge, as well as such subjects as Logic, Ethics, and Aesthetics.

Poetry and philosophy

In this connection **Perry's** distinction between the philosopher-poets and the poets who are not philosophers is illuminating. [1]This will help us still further to understand what philosophy is, especially in its newer aspects. Some of the great poets seek merely to describe

[1] Ralph Barton Perry, *The Approach to Philosophy*, chap. II.

life; others seek to interpret it.   The latter are the philosopher-poets.   One thinks of Lucretius, Omar Khayyám, Dante, Goethe, Wordsworth, Browning, and the Greek dramatists.   Consider Aeschylus, Sophocles, Euripides, or even Aristophanes, the comic poet.   These men were dreadfully in earnest.   They were moralists, thinkers, prophets, reflecting the national consciousness of their people.   The prophet is a man who brings a message; and if the prophet is a poet, he is a philosopher-poet.   Aeschylus, for instance, depicts in majestic language the tempestuous power of fate against those who disregard the ancient laws of morals and religion.   The immutable moral law and the fateful suffering of men constitute the burden of Sophocles' exquisite dramas; while Aristophanes in comic vein upholds the old traditions of Greece.   Lucretius in Rome wrote a long poem in hexameter verse to set forth a materialistic theory of the world and save men from the fear of the gods; he would still be celebrated as a philosopher, had he written only in prose.   Omar Khayyám in his exquisite quatrains presents a distinct philosophy of life.   It is partly the felicitous form of his stanzas as translated by FitzGerald that makes Omar so popular; but it is partly his strange philosophy and his conclusions, so repugnant to our reason, so agreeable to our fancy.

> Into this Universe, and *Why* not knowing,
> Nor *Whence*, like Water willy-nilly flowing;
>   And out of it, as Wind along the Waste,
> I know not *Whither*, willy-nilly blowing.
>   .   .   .   .

> Strange, is it not? that of the myriads who
> Before us pass'd the door of Darkness through,
>   Not one returns to tell us of the Road,
> Which to discover we must travel too.
>   .   .   .   .

> Ah, Love! could thou and I with Fate conspire
> To grasp this sorry Scheme of Things entire,
>   Would not we shatter it to bits — and then
> Remould it nearer to the Heart's Desire?

It is Dante, however, who is the supreme philosopher-poet.   He tells us in the *Divine Comedy* of the very shape and substance of the universe, of the origin of man and his destiny, and of the beginning of evil and its cure.   In the beautiful lines of the *Paradiso* we read that from the very heart of the universe there streams forth the dazzling brightness of divine love, whose purpose is the redemption of man from sin. Goethe also is a thinker and a philosopher. The redemption of man is likewise his theme; but it comes now from experience, not from sacrifice and obedience. Wordsworth is burdened with "the heavy and the weary weight of all this unintelligible world," and Browning, "the soul dissector," comforts us with his belief in God and truth and love.

The wonderful appeal of all these philosopher-poets reveals the eternal demand in the human heart for a solution of the riddle of the world. We have our lyric and our epic moods and our dramatic and romantic moods, in which we delight in Sappho and Homer and Virgil and Horace and Shakespeare and Shelley and Keats and Byron and Swinburne; but perhaps over all prevail our philosophic moods, in which we turn to the philosopher-poets for light and consolation.

It is significant, in illustrating the philosophical tendencies of the present time, to notice how even the drama has become philosophical. The modern dramatist wrestles with the problems of life. Ibsen is the fountainhead of this new drama, in which the poet and painter have given place to the thinker and the teacher. Emancipation from outgrown and offensive traditions is Ibsen's theme and the feelings which he awakens in the reader or spectator are not so much those of aesthetic enjoyment as of thought and protest.

In the so-called problem plays, the author takes advantage of the prevailing philosophic mood to awaken interest in his play. Finally, in Bernard Shaw the aesthetic attitude is reduced to its lowest limits and there is little left but a preachment. The feverish interest with which we read the plays of Ibsen and Shaw and Galsworthy and the Russian school of writers reveals the longing we feel to have our doubts settled and to penetrate life's mysteries, even though we recognize that the beauty of poetry and the drama is somewhat dulled when they become too heavily laden with thought. But this philosophic tendency of poetry is one of the signs of the deep and prevailing interest in philosophy.

It was in the time of Socrates that the word *philosophy* first came into general use. With Plato and Aristotle the word assumed the more technical meaning of real knowledge, or knowledge of ultimate reality, somewhat like the German word *Wissenschaft*, or our own word *science* when used in its broader meaning. In later Greek times, among the Stoics and Epicureans, the word came to have a narrower meaning, as the guide of life. In periods of political turmoil or religious perplexity, such as those preceding the Christian era, men have little time or taste for pursuing deep philosophical speculations; but they need a philosophy as a guide of life and usually adopt some philosophical system which seems suited to this end. Philosophy thus becomes the art of living; to the Stoic the art of living wisely, to the Epicurean the art of living happily. Even now the word is often used popularly in this sense, as when we speak of "a philosophic attitude," or of taking anything, particularly any calamity, "philosophically"; calm or fortitude is evidently what is meant. Philosophy in its true meaning, as the search for unity and truth, may well lead to such calm and fortitude.

To turn for a space of time from intense absorption in particular needs and to let one's mind range freely over the mysteries of existence is to return to one's absorptions a different person. It is hard to describe precisely what happens, but we all know that it does happen. There is a kind of enlargement of oneself, a new power to see things in wider relationships, a calmness and an openness.

This is what one finds in all the master spirits of the ages. One is rather glad that Socrates wasted time on the street-corners of Athens. One rather suspects that something of value came because Spinoza took time off from his grinding of lenses to contemplate the universe. One feels similarly about all the great artists — Dante, Leonardo, Goethe, Shakespeare, Beethoven, Brahms. These men went beyond the food and shelter needs. They were facing life, death, courage, love, hate, frustration, devotion....

That is why poetry, drama, science, and philosophy have endured through all the ages. In them man has risen to his more essentially human interest. In them he has emerged from mere animalhood. As Aristotle expresses it, "Nor is it right to follow the advice of people who say that the thoughts of men should not be too high for humanity or the thoughts of mortals too high for mortality; for a man, as far as in him lies, should seek immortality and do all that is in his power to live in accordance with the highest part of his nature." [1]

---

[1] Overstreet, H. A., *The Enduring Quest* (W. W. Norton and Company, Inc., New York), pp. ix, x.

In connection with this chapter read:

Wm. Pepperell Montague, "Philosophy as Vision," *International Journal of Ethics*, 44, 1–22. Oct., 1933.

Further references:

Ralph Barton Perry, *The Approach to Philosophy* (Charles Scribner's Sons), chaps. I, II.

William James, "Philosophy and Its Critics," *Some Problems of Philosophy* (Longmans, Green and Company), chap. I. Also in Everyman's Library, *Selected Papers in Philosophy*.

C. D. Broad, *Scientific Thought* (Harcourt, Brace and Company), Introduction.

Mary Whiton Calkins, *The Persistent Problems of Philosophy* (The Macmillan Company), chap. I.

H. A. Larrabee, *What Philosophy Is* (The Vanguard Press, 1928).

Susanne K. Langer, *The Practice of Philosophy* (Henry Holt and Company, 1930).

STUDENT'S REFERENCES

Dictionaries.

J. M. Baldwin, Editor, *Dictionary of Philosophy and Psychology.* 3 vols. (The Macmillan Company.)

Encyclopaedia Britannica.

Encyclopaedia of Religion and Ethics

Histories of Philosophy.

J. Burnet, *Greek Philosophy: Thales to Plato* (The Macmillan Company.)

E. Zeller, *Outlines of the History of Greek Philosophy* (Henry Holt and Company).

W. T. Stace, *A Critical History of Greek Philosophy* (The Macmillan Company).

H. E. Cushman, *A Beginner's History of Philosophy*, 2 vols. (Houghton Mifflin Company).

T. Gomperz, *Greek Thinkers* (Charles Scribner's Sons).

A. Weber and R. B. Perry, *History of Philosophy* (Charles Scribner's Sons).

W. Windelband, *A History of Philosophy*, translated by J. H. Tufts (The Macmillan Company).

H. Hoffding, *A History of Modern Philosophy*, translated by B. E. Meyer, 2 vols. (The Macmillan Company).

F. Ueberweg, *History of Philosophy*, translated by Morris (Charles Scribner's Sons).

J. E. Erdman, *History of Philosophy*, translated by Hough, 3 vols. (The Macmillan Company).

G. P. Adams and W. P. Montague, Editors, *Contemporary American Philosophy: Personal Statements*, 2 vols. (The Macmillan Company).

A. K. Rogers, *English and American Philosophy since 1800* (The Macmillan Company).

J. H. Muirhead, Editor, *Contemporary British Philosophy* (The Macmillan Company).

W. R. Sorley, *A History of English Philosophy* (Cambridge University Press).

Edward L. Schaub, Editor, *Philosophy Today* (Open Court Publishing Company).

Harvey Gates Townsend, *Philosophical Ideas in the United States* (American Book Company).

Source books.

B. Rand, *Modern Classical Philosophers* (Houghton Mifflin Company).

C. M. Bakewell, *A Source Book in Ancient Philosophy* (Charles Scribner's Sons).

D. S. Robinson, *An Anthology of Modern Philosophy* (Thomas Y. Crowell Company).

R. B. Perry, Editor, *Scribner's Philosophy Series* (Charles Scribner's Sons).
A. E. Avey, *Readings in Philosophy* (R. G. Adams and Company).

Philosophical Journals — English and American.

The Journal of Philosophy, fortnightly (Columbia University).
The International Journal of Ethics (The University of Chicago).
The Philosophical Review, bi-monthly (Longmans, Green and Company).
The Monist. A Quarterly Magazine devoted to the Philosophy of Science (Open Court Publishing Company, Chicago).
Mind. A Quarterly Review of Psychology and Philosophy (The Macmillan Company).
The Hibbert Journal. A Quarterly Review of Religion, Theology, and Philosophy (Williams and Norgate, London).
The Personalist. A Quarterly Journal of Philosophy, Theology, and Literature (The University of Southern California, Los Angeles).
Philosophy of Science (The Williams and Wilkins Company, Baltimore).
The Journal of Philosophical Studies (The Macmillan Company).

CHAPTER II
PHILOSOPHY AND SCIENCE

SO INTIMATE is the relation between science and philosophy that some knowledge of the special sciences, especially of the more generalized branches, such as mathematics, physics, chemistry, biology, and psychology, is indispensable to the student of philosophy. The ever-widening fields of these sciences make it more and more difficult for the philosopher to be in mastery of them. This is conducive to a healthy humility. Ready-made systems constructed without due regard to the results of observation and experiment are held in less and less respect. Therefore philosophy is at the present time tending rather in the direction of the critical analysis of concepts and the study of meanings and values — in a word, to logical and humanistic studies. Nevertheless, the ideal philosopher must be master of all the special sciences.

What is science?

The word *science* comes from the Latin word for knowledge and is derived from our old familiar friend in the First Latin Book, *scio, scire*. Science is knowledge. But there are different kinds of knowledge, and by scientific knowledge we mean that which is certain, exact, and fully organized: real knowledge, well organized, is scientific knowledge.

Since philosophy, too, seeks a knowledge of the world, the two subjects would seem to have the same aim; yet there is a difference. Sometimes it has been said that science *describes* while philosophy *interprets*. Mr. J. Arthur Thomson, whose little book entitled *An Introduction to Science* is recommended to the reader, following Pearson and many other modern scholars, defines science in this way:

> *Science is the complete and consistent description of the facts of experience in the simplest possible terms.*

The scientist in his study of any group of phenomena first collects his facts, analyzes and classifies them, studies the conditions under which they occur (that is, their causes), ascertains their uniform modes of behavior (that is, their laws), and sets all of this down in the form of a systematic treatise. Here his work ends.

Now, of course it *is* a kind of explanation of a thing to show the conditions under which it occurs — that is, its causes — as when we explain typhoid fever by calling attention to the invariable presence of a certain kind of bacillus; and it *is* a kind of explanation of a thing to show that it is an instance of a general uniformity or *law*, as when we show that a pendulum, constantly falling to its lowest point, is an instance of the general law of gravitation, all natural bodies, like the pendulum and the earth, tending to move toward each other. But still it is true that science really attempts no ultimate explanation of things; it only analyzes and classifies them, determines the conditions under which they occur, and formulates their modes of behavior.

The work of science, then, is as follows: [1]

I. The acquisition of facts
II. The description of facts
    1. Definition and general description
    2. Analysis
    3. Classification
III. Explanation of facts
    1. Ascertaining causes (invariable antecedents)
    2. Formulation of laws (uniformities of behavior)

Philosophy and science

Now, philosophy is like science in seeking knowledge which is certain, exact, and well organized. But it is not satisfied with this; it seeks knowledge which is also *comprehensive*. The human mind is not content merely to determine the invariable sequences of phenomena and to formulate their manner of behavior. It craves some ultimate explanation of things — their first cause, their moving cause, their purpose, their meaning, their value. It is this attempt to *interpret* the world, then, which is one of the tasks of philosophy; while science classifies, formulates, and describes. *The object of philosophy is*, as Mr. Broad says, *to take over the results of the various sciences, to add to them the results of the religious and ethical experiences of mankind, and then to reflect upon the whole. The hope is that, by*

[1] Compare Jared Sparks Moore, *The Foundations of Psychology*, p. 97.

this means, we may be able to reach some general conclusions as to the nature of the Universe, and as to our position and prospects in it.[1]

It is no doubt this *ambitious* enterprise, this hope to get a synoptic view of the work of the special sciences, and then to find some *meaning* in the whole that has in the past led to the unfavorable criticism of philosophy by scientists. But of course neither the attempt to gain a synoptic view of the whole nor the attempt to interpret its meaning could be in itself an occasion for criticism; for the human mind has a primary interest in both these things, and any object of human interest whatever is a legitimate subject for scientific inquiry, provided scientific methods are used. The critical attitude could only arise from the use of wrong methods in the work, or from the alleged hopelessness of the undertaking. The latter criticism would be a very weak one, and could have been made at any stage of the progress of thought against the possibility of the achievements of science itself. As regards method, it is of course true that in the past logical methods have not always been used in the study of philosophy, just as they have not in science.

Let us defer till a later chapter the question of method and get well fixed in our minds the subject-matter of philosophy. I think we may say that it has two distinct tasks, both of which differ from the work of science, and both of which are clearly legitimate fields of human thought. The first, then, is the conscious reflection upon the world as a whole, particularly as to its meaning, purpose, and value. The second is the critical examination of the concepts made use of both by science and common sense. The first has been called speculative philosophy, the second, critical philosophy.[2]

As regards the first of these two fields, let us notice again that it is one of the profound cravings of the human mind to get just this synoptic view of life which philosophy attempts. It is not merely a quantitative view of the world that we desire, its mathematical relationships, its predictability; we want and we must have some knowledge, or at least some theory, of its *"intrinsic qualitative character."*

[1] C. D. Broad, *Scientific Thought* (Harcourt, Brace and Company, 1923), p. 20. The original not italicized.
[2] Compare C. D. Broad, *Scientific Thought* (Harcourt, Brace and Company), Introduction. In a later chapter we shall see what is meant by the word "speculative."

Science today is quantitative rather than qualitative. It expresses the relationship of the intensities of two phenomena — as, for example, the intensities of the electric current and of the illumination of an incandescent lamp — and compensates for its inability to answer the question "how" by its wealth of data as to "how much." Research monograph and textbook alike emphasize the observable quantitative relationship and rarely venture far into the speculative hinterland where "how" must precede "how much." As we teach science today in our schools the effort of learning the quantitative relationships too frequently leaves neither the instructor nor the student leisure for fruitful inquiry or speculation as to the mechanism itself.[1]

The scientist is forever measuring, weighing, computing, and making sketches of details. "This," says the philosopher, "is all useful and necessary work; but I would like to get a picture of the way the house is going to look when it is done — or at least a glimpse of it. I am truly grateful to the scientists for all their laborious work, but I am — at times anyway — a little weary of studying all these details — and I long for some picture of the whole."

Philosophy tries to put this picture-puzzle of a hundred curiously shaped bodies of knowledge together, to see what sort of universe they make. This is the sense in which philosophy, as Bacon so audaciously said, "takes all knowledge for its province." It does not — it should not — presume to supersede, or to short-circuit, the laborious work of the scientists, the psychologists, the historians; it aims to synthesize their work and focus it upon man's ultimate needs. *Philosophy is the integration of knowledge, the synthesis of the sciences.*[2]

The mechanic will tell you the meaning of every part of the machine; but what is the meaning of the machine itself? The botanist will tell you the meaning of root, branch, leaf, and stem of the tree — and perhaps he may tell you the meaning of the tree itself in the economy of plant life; but what is the meaning of life itself? Has life any meaning? Has nature any meaning? Has the world any meaning? Has consciousness any meaning? Perhaps none of these has any meaning, value, or purpose; *but such a conclusion could be reached only after reflective inquiry — and such reflective inquiry would be philosophy.*

The demand that science should be supplemented by philosophy

[1] John Mills, *Within the Atom* (D. Van Nostrand Company), p. xi.
[2] Durant Drake, *Invitation to Philosophy* (Houghton Mifflin Company), p. ix.

is becoming more and more urgent as science itself withdraws more and more into the mysterious background of symbols and mathematical equations, and forces itself to be indifferent to what lies behind the symbols. "To understand the phenomena of the physical world," says Sir Arthur Eddington, "it is necessary to know the equations which the symbols obey but not the nature of that which is being symbolised. It would be irrelevant here to defend this change, to make clear the intellectual satisfaction afforded by these symbolic equations, or to explain why the demand of the layman for a concrete explanation has to be set aside." [1] But the philosopher might reply that the same intellectual satisfaction which the scientist gets from his equations and symbols the philosopher gets from his hypotheses of what the reality behind the symbols really is. It is as a philosopher that Eddington goes on to say that it is to the background of phenomena that our own personality and consciousness belong.

The analysis of concepts

The critical examination of concepts referred to above is philosophy's second task. In logical order it should be the first, but to most students it is second in point of interest.

All the sciences use certain concepts and make certain assumptions which require critical examination. There is need of some general science to undertake a critique of these concepts and assumptions and to carry the examination of them further than the special sciences find necessary for their purpose. As examples may be mentioned such concepts as matter, mind, energy, space, time, cause, law — that is, natural law — order, quality, quantity, series, individuality. It is the task of philosophy to undertake this examination.

But it is not alone the concepts of science that need critical analysis. Those used in philosophy as well as in daily life are in equal need of study. As illustrations we may mention such concepts as truth, purpose, knowledge, good, evil, God, beauty, happiness. Here again the distinction between science and philosophy

---

[1] Sir Arthur Eddington, *Science and the Unseen World*, p. 30 (Allen and Unwin Ltd. and The Macmillan Company). By permission of the publishers.

should not be stressed too much. Both are eager to know the exact meaning of the concepts they use, and to use them accurately.

This need of analysis may be illustrated by reference to two concepts constantly employed both in science and philosophy. They are *cause* (including causation and causality), and *law* (that is, laws of nature).

Cause

All the sciences are engaged in the search for causes, not only for the sake of the knowledge itself but because, if causes are understood, the forces of nature can be controlled and the future predicted. So the scientist seeks for the cause of crystallization, of rust, of the souring of milk, of the failure of crops, of malaria and typhoid fever and cancer, of business depression and good times, of strikes, of war, and of the decline of social morality. In daily life we are all in search of causes; the cause, for instance, of the leaking of our fountain pen, of the fading of our complexion or our falling hair, of the success of our neighbor's son, of athletic defeats.

In the study of the concept of cause there are two problems: 1. What *is* a cause? 2. Does every event in the world have a cause — or are some happenings completely free? As regards the second of these questions, the physical sciences assume the universality of the law of causality. Nothing happens without a cause — and an adequate cause. The present is wholly the product or outcome of the past — and the future will be the outcome of the present. Whatever phenomenon presents itself to our view, we may with absolute confidence seek for a cause. It happens because of some previous happening. All scientific research depends upon this postulate and would be meaningless without it. In assuming the law of causality at the very beginning of his research, the scientist, as Max Planck says, takes a jump into the metaphysical sphere, for the law of causality is not given in any sensuous experience.[1]

But now philosophy must make this a subject of inquiry. *Is* causality a universal law? Are there not exceptions in the sphere of human action? Is not the human will free? Can the law be universally applied in ethics, in psychology, in sociology, or even in biology? Is life in any sense free?

[1] Max Planck, *Where is Science Going?* p. 158 f.

Just lately a new interest has been awakened in the old problem of freedom and determinism. This is owing to a new law which has appeared regarding the behavior of those infinitesimal units of matter which are studied in micro-physics. Knowing the position and velocity of a body, we should be able to predict where it will be the next instant; but the particles in question do not behave in this way, as sober bits of matter should. Statistical laws governing their behavior we can safely formulate but not the behavior of the single particle. Hence there has arisen in science something very new and startling — namely, the so-called principle of uncertainty, or Heisenberg's *Principle of Indeterminacy*. This seems to have a bearing on the old problem of freedom of the will. Those who have a firm faith in this have hailed the discovery as lending a new support to the doctrine of indeterminism, a support coming directly from the field of science itself. But this matter needs careful study. We shall return to it in a later chapter.

But if we could settle the question of the universality of the law of causality, we should still have another on our hands. What is a cause? Science, although largely engaged in the search for causes, is not concerned with the metaphysics of the question. Of course it has to have a working basis for the determination of causes, and it has a very simple rule. A cause is an invariable antecedent. If we are seeking the cause of a certain thing, say typhoid fever, and invariably find a certain bacillus present, this is called the cause of the phenomenon. Armed with this conception of cause as mere *sequence*, and with the assumption of the Uniformity of Nature, the scientist is in possession of all that he needs to control phenomena and predict the future. Armed with the simple knowledge of sequence, he can go on to prevent typhoid fever, to avert the failure of crops, to secure good health and the success of his children.

But still we do not know what a cause really is. There must be, so it seems to us, something more in causality than mere sequence in time; there must be some inner connection between cause and effect. This connection philosophy seeks.

The untrained mind looks upon the relation between cause and effect as if the cause *produces* the effect. The cause is a kind of *agent*; it does something to the effect; there is a process of *enforce-*

ment between the cause and the effect. In the case of mechanical causes, it is very hard for us to believe that this is not true, and it would be very hard to prove that there is not something like mechanical necessity uniting the effect with the cause; but science knows nothing of any such necessary connection and philosophy hesitates to affirm it, for, as Hume pointed out, the only necessity in the case may be a necessity of thought. We know nothing of objective necessity, and the conception of cause as an *agent*, which does something to the effect, no doubt is a kind of analogy carried over to nature from our own experience as agents. When I put forth effort and use strength in overcoming obstacles, as in moving physical objects, there is a feeling of *enforcement*, a feeling of myself as an agent effecting changes. When we do things or suffer things done to us, there is the feeling of *power* or *force*; and so, when we see things happening in nature, we carry over this inner experience of effort, or agency, which we think causes things to happen in our own lives, and assume that causation in general is just such a case of power or enforcement. This is called an *animistic* or *anthropomorphic* explanation of causation, explaining things in nature by our own feelings and experiences. And it is wholly unnecessary for science to make assumptions of this kind, since its ends may be fully served merely by the observation of uniformities as seen in the mere routine of experience. There is regularity and uniformity in the happenings. Furthermore, we are learning that the laws of nature are largely statistical in character, based on observation of averages. "It appears," as stated by Conger, "that our scientific knowledge at its very foundations is indefinite and loose, based upon selection of certain radiations with accompanying neglect or ignorance of others. And our laws of causation must then carry with them something of this initial defect." [1]

But after all this has been explained to us, we still believe that there must be some other connection or relation between events than mere routine, and so philosophy, going beyond science, has attempted various theories of causation which shall explain this relation. Perhaps the world is a timeless process in which the principle

---

[1] G. P. Conger, *New Views of Evolution*, p. 213 (The Macmillan Company). By permission of the publishers.

of causality is reducible to the principle of logical ground.   Perhaps
the world is an organism in which every part is in sympathetic
vibration with every other part.   Perhaps the world is a dynamic
unity in which there is interaction among all the parts.   Perhaps
there are no separate bonds uniting individual things, God being the
bond that unites all things in himself.   Perhaps all individual things
are parts of one unitary being, giving apparent order and connection between things, the unity in things being that kind of unity
called personality.   Perhaps — and this may be the most profound
interpretation of all — cause is really just what in popular thought
it is supposed to be, namely, *productive activity, creative power*, and
perhaps the scientific use of the word *cause*, as a mere antecedent in
time, points to cause as just a sign useful in the prediction of events.[1]

First cause

Again, since science rests quite content in the belief that every
event has a cause and finds the assumption fully justified by its
fruits, the student of philosophy will insist upon inquiring about the
first cause.   Going back over an infinite series from effect to cause,
and then to another cause, does not satisfy his demand for some kind
of a *whole* or completed system.   So we say naïvely that in the beginning God created the world, and thus complete the picture, only
to introduce other perplexities which we long to solve.

Furthermore, we may ask — Anyway, is it quite certain that
every event has a cause?   May it not be that things just happen
without any cause?   And, furthermore, am not I myself daily,
perhaps hourly, conscious of acts of freedom, in which my choice is
not determined by any antecedent event?   Am I not myself a free
creative *source* of happenings — and may there not be other such
sources?

Final cause

But still another aspect of the cause problem shows the limitations

---

[1] For a discussion of the problem of causality see:
  Hume, *A Treatise on Human Nature*, bk. I, part III.
  Karl Pearson, *The Grammar of Science*, 3d ed., part I, chap. IV.
  John Stuart Mill, *Logic*, bk. III, chaps. III, IV, V, XXI, XXII.
  Bertrand Russell, *Principles of Mathematics*, I, chap. LV.
  W. T. Marvin, *A First Book of Metaphysics*, chap. XI.

of science and the need of philosophy.   What shall we say of final causes?   The expression *final cause* was used by Aristotle in a special sense.   The word *final* here does not refer to any first or last cause, but to the *end* or *purpose* of an action, like the Latin, *finis*.   In human affairs the end or purpose of an action, or a product of action, is spoken of as a cause, as when the observation of an anticipated eclipse of the sun is the cause of setting up a telescope in a certain place.   So the question arises whether in nature, quite outside human affairs, there are ends to be gained which may be regarded in any way as determining all structures or processes; that is, whether final as well as efficient causes exist in nature.   Science is not concerned with final causes, but the student wonders, nevertheless, whether things in nature are not in some way determined by ends to be attained.

Laws of nature

Next consider another fundamental notion in science, that of *law*. What is a law of nature?   Science is very largely engaged in finding out these laws and formulating them, such, for instance, as the laws of chemical valence, or the laws of thermodynamics, or the laws of falling bodies.   We speak of things *obeying* the laws of nature and of the world as being *governed* by natural laws.   There is much confusion here in the popular mind, and the student should understand just what a law is in science, and what the limitations of the scientific view are.   The word *law* is used in two wholly different senses, and it would be better if we had two words for the two ideas.   In morals and in jurisprudence a law is a command, or rule, or injunction, which some authority imposes upon intelligent beings and which they are supposed to obey.   In science the word has no such meaning; it means an observed uniformity in the behavior of things. Strictly a law of nature is a mere formula, or shorthand expression, for certain observed uniformities of behavior in natural objects.   It is, as Pearson says, the *résumé* or *brief expression* of the relationships and sequences of certain groups of perceptions and conceptions, and exists only when formulated by man.[1]

So we see that laws of nature are not forces or powers or commands at all.   They are nothing but shorthand statements of cer-

---

[1] Karl Pearson, *Grammar of Science*, 3d ed., part I, p. 82.

tain uniformities in the behavior of things. Therefore, the universe is not "governed" by the laws of nature; neither do things "obey" these laws. We shall have to look elsewhere for the *government* of the world, for laws of nature are impotent.

Thus it is that science does not explain *why* things act as they do, only *how* they act; what their *habit* of acting is. When we study the behavior of atoms in their chemical combinations we find that they behave in very definite ways, but we do not know why they behave so. They seem to have what we used to call *affinities* for one another, so that, for instance, two atoms of hydrogen combine with one atom of oxygen to form a molecule of water. But the word *affinity* seems to point to a theory drawn from human analogy and probably no chemist would countenance such a theory. He is content merely to record observed uniformities.

The law of gravitation first formulated by Newton does not explain why bodies gravitate toward one another, but only how they do so. The law says that "every particle of matter in the universe attracts every other particle with a force directly as their masses, and inversely as the square of the distance which separates them." [1]   It occurred to Newton, watching the fall of an apple, as it is said, that all bodies throughout the universe — such, for instance, as the earth and the moon — tend to move toward one another, just as the apple tends to move toward the earth. The law expresses the manner of their movement, but it says nothing about the cause. Newton did not know why bodies move together, nor does anyone know now. Even the word *attract* has a technical sense as it occurs in the law, for it is not implied that there is any "attraction" in the human sense between material bodies. They may be driven together; or, as Einstein thinks, their behavior may be due, not to any force acting between the bodies or upon them, but to the nature of space.

We see, therefore, that from the point of view of science, a law of nature is not only not a force or power, but that it tells us nothing as to the nature of the forces that are at work or even whether there are any forces. But the mind of man is so constituted that he longs to know not merely how things act, but *why* they do so. Hence the need of supplementing science by philosophy.

[1] Simon Newcomb, *Popular Astronomy*, 6th ed., revised, p. 81.

Before we leave the subject of law, there is another question that may come up. Even granting that a law tells us nothing about the forces which make things go and behave as they do, is it quite true to say that a law of nature is nothing but a formulation of an observed uniformity, and further that it is man-made, and has no existence until formulated by man? Pearson, as we have seen, makes this statement. So it would appear that Newton did not *discover* the law of gravitation, but created it. Surely, you say, the heavenly bodies behaved precisely in this manner before Newton observed them or indeed before any man ever existed. Well, while Pearson might make a logical defense of his position claiming that the law *is* the formulation of uniformities which are observed and hence imply an observer, and that in nature there are only certain sequences and relations, nevertheless there are many philosophers who would not agree with him wholly in this matter.

There are other positions which might be taken. One might say the laws of nature are *decrees* of God, and hence resemble human laws as we use the word in jurisprudence. Or, if this position seems too naïve, one might say with Plato that laws are eternal realities, altogether transcending individual things, and that things behave according to the laws; or one might undertake a logical examination of the concept of law, tracing it back to the more general notion of the uniformity of nature, and that back to the still more general notion of *Order*, which latter concept is involved in the very notion of a universe or a cosmos.[1]

I have referred to two concepts, namely, that of *law*, and that of *cause*, which are constantly used in every science and which nevertheless are not defined by science in such a way as to satisfy the inquiring mind. The same is true of many other common terms used in science, such as *space, time, energy, matter, mind*. Thus it becomes apparent that some general science like philosophy or metaphysics is needed to examine these terms.

[1] For a clear treatment of the subject see Marie T. Collins, *Some Modern Conceptions of Natural Law*, and the profound discussion by Bernard Bosanquet in *The Principle of Individuality and Value*, as well as Josiah Royce's essay on "The Principles of Logic" in the *Encyclopedia of the Philosophical Sciences*, I, pp. 67–135.

Facts of experience

There is one such term particularly in need of critical examination and this is the term *fact* or *fact of experience*.

If science is a complete and consistent description of the facts of experience, the question will arise, What is a fact of experience? Of course science has to have some definition of a "fact." It is usually defined as something immediately observed and not inferred, and the medium of observation is usually one of our organs of sense, such as the eye or ear or hand; but sometimes a fact may be something internally observed; for instance, a feeling or emotion. In general we may say that *sense-data* are the facts upon which science is built.

But now the philosopher is not satisfied with this disposition of facts; he wishes to know much more about them. Are the facts of science, then, nothing but groups or bundles of sensations combined into percepts? I thought, the reader will say, that science had a firmer foundation. I thought that science is the one thing in the world that is built on solid objective realities, not on "sense-data." If science is built on sense-data, on the perceptions of human beings, why then its whole fabric is in a way subjective. I supposed that science tells us about objective things as they really are, and as they were before ever man existed.

But when we come to think of it, how is science going to get at these solid objective realities except through the sense organs of the scientist? So the problem arises, just what are these sense-data and how are they related to the real things of the world, or are *they* the real things? Thus we are forced into philosophy — into that particular branch of it called Epistemology, the science of knowledge.

Thus in the end we see something of the relation of philosophy to science. They have the same spirit and the same purpose — the honest and laborious search for truth. In this search for truth, science imposes upon itself a certain peculiar task and this task involves certain limitations. But the inquiring, wondering human mind chafes at these limitations and insists upon penetrating into regions lying beyond the field of science — and thus philosophy arises.

Applied science

In thus revealing the close companionship of science and philosophy, I have been using the word "science" in its broader and more dignified sense, as a certain kind of knowledge; namely, that which is exact, certain, and fully organized. It is hardly necessary to add that this is not the popular idea of science, which is apt to emphasize its practical side. Sometimes we think of science as a kind of wizard that is going to fight the next war. It is something of almost uncanny power, personified in our Edisons and Burbanks. It suggests *mastery* of the forces of nature. It is something which wrests from Nature her secrets in order to use them for practical ends. We immure ourselves in our laboratories and dig out the gold of science in order that we may exchange it for happiness in the form of labor-saving and time-saving devices, means of rapid transportation over land or water or through the air, instantaneous communication by the ether waves, cinematographic devices to afford us amusement and instruction, and subtle inventions of every sort to provide us with comforts and conveniences. Or science is conceived as a powerful ally of man, to which we may turn in time of want to learn how to increase the fertility of our soils, or in time of war to provide us with instruments for annihilating our enemies, or in time of sickness to discover X-rays to diagnose our diseases, or antitoxins to prevent them, or serums to cure them.

In other words, science to many people is just an *instrument* to be applied to increasing man's power over nature, not something intrinsically good in itself. It is applied science which they have in mind. It is interesting to know, however, that the great discoveries in science, even those which have led to these practical applications which are prized so highly, have usually been made by those who had no immediate interest in the practical applications, but were actuated purely by their scientific interest, by the love of knowledge for its own sake. It is, of course, this theoretical science which is so closely related to philosophy. And even the most practical people, those who are always thinking of the practical applications of knowledge, are not always in a "practical" mood. Sometimes we all thirst for knowledge for its own sake. Then we turn to science in the broader sense, as love of exact knowledge. Sometimes we are in

a mood of wonder, musing whether the whole world has any meaning, purpose, or value. Then we turn to philosophy. Or, perhaps,
we are in a mood of doubt or even of despair, oppressed by the weight
of our perplexities and cares — and then we turn to religion.

In connection with this chapter read:

J. Arthur Thomson, *Introduction to Science* (Home University Library,
Henry Holt and Company).

Further references:

Ralph Barton Perry, *The Approach to Philosophy* (Charles Scribner's Sons),
chap. v.   *Present Philosophical Tendencies* (Longmans, Green and Company), chaps. III, V.

James Ward, *Naturalism and Agnosticism* (The Macmillan Company), part I,
lectures 2–5.   (The classical discussion of recent years on the meaning of
law).

C. D. Broad, *Scientific Thought* (Harcourt, Brace and Company).

L. T. More, *The Limitations of Science* (Henry Holt and Company).

Karl Pearson, *The Grammar of Science*, 3d ed. (Adam and Charles Black),
chaps. I–V.

Max Planck, *Where is Science Going?* (W. W. Norton and Company), chaps.
II, III.

Ray H. Dotterer, *Philosophy by Way of the Sciences* (The Macmillan Company), chap. I.

Henry Margenau, " Meaning and Scientific Status of Causality," *Philosophy
of Science*, I, no. 2.

F. S. C. Northrop, *Science and First Principles* (The Macmillan Company).

CHAPTER III
RELIGION AND PHILOSOPHY

THE relationship between philosophy and religion is very intimate, but is of a different kind from that between philosophy and science. Philosophy tries to gain a more unified and complete understanding of the world than does science, but religion attempts a still more perfect unity. While philosophy tries to get some unifying conception of the world which shall enable us to grasp its meaning in our thought, religion attempts nothing less than the securing of an actual unity or harmony between the individual and the world. In religion we attempt to adjust ourselves to the world, or the world to ourselves. It is not concerned so much with the knowledge of God, for instance, as it is with the gaining of God's favor, or the coming into friendly and harmonious relations with him.

Many religions, to be sure, have lengthy creeds dealing with the world as a whole, its creation, constitution, and its final destiny; but the center of religious interest is not in any of these as objects of knowledge, but in our relation to them. Thus a theistic religion presupposes a knowledge of God — but this is not its center of interest, which is the worship of God — or the gaining of his favor and protection.

Professor Ladd wrote an essay entitled, "Is the Universe Friendly?" [1] This is evidently a religious problem. To make the universe friendly is one of the aims of religion. Primitive man believed himself surrounded by hostile forces which he could not control — the sun and the sea, winds and tempests, lightning and pestilence. By means of offerings, sacrifices, and prayers, he hoped to render all these forces friendly. Under the influence of religion, the world became peopled with kindly and beneficent spirits, being in sympathetic relation with man, commanding awe and reverence and worship and obedience, yet protecting and befriending him.

[1] George T. Ladd, "Is the Universe Friendly?" *Hibbert Journal*, 10, pp. 328–43.

So it was in ancient India with Indra and Varuna and Soma.   So in ancient Greece with Zeus and Poseidon and Apollo and Athena.   So among the Hebrews with Jehovah.

It has been said that the function of religion is to make man feel at home in the world.   But philosophy and science also make us feel at home in the world, by widening our knowledge and giving us the keen joy of comprehension; while religion does this in a more direct and human manner by introducing a personal relation between man and the powers of the Universe.   Science, philosophy, and religion are all alike in this, that their aim is to understand the world; but the purpose of the understanding is different in each.   In science the purpose is frequently pure theory, or knowledge for its own sake, but more commonly it is knowledge subordinated to practical economic ends.   In philosophy the purpose is the love of wisdom and the resulting mental peace and satisfaction.   In religion the purpose is peace, harmony, adjustment, salvation.   Philosophy and religion thus deal often with the same ideas, such as the soul, its origin and destiny, God and creation; but the interests are different in the two fields.   In the former, they are theoretical and intellectual; in the latter, emotional and personal — practical in a sense different from the practicality of applied science.

What is religion?

If anyone who has not reflected much about such things should be asked what religion is, he might find it difficult to say.   Perhaps he would take refuge in the remark that all definitions are unsatisfactory, and that religion especially is something which must be experienced, not defined.   This is true, but nevertheless the word *religion* means something and it is well to know what it means.

When we think of religion, probably a group of things will come to mind, such as churches, prayers, sermons, songs, collections, creeds, and rituals, people sitting quietly together.   But evidently these things are not religion.   If we study all the religions of the world, ancient and modern, and try to abstract the elements common to all, we should arrive at some kind of definition.   Perhaps it would be something like this:

"Religion is a feeling of dependence upon the unseen powers which control our destiny, accompanied by a desire to come into friendly relations with them."

Religion is a belief in "a power not ourselves which makes for righteousness" and a desire to come into harmonious relations with that power.

"Religion is the consciousness of our practical relation to an invisible spiritual order."

Religion is the love of God. It is communion with the Oversoul. It is loyalty to the highest within us. "I, the imperfect," says Emerson, "adore my own perfect." Thus religion is based on a deep, instinctive feeling of higher values. It is the divinity within us reaching up to the divinity above. It is looking up very high to ultimate values and being drawn to them by sympathy and recognition. "Ideas and feelings are religious," says Wundt, "which refer to an ideal existence." Thus the names, symbols, and persons of religion are sacred, holy, because they are supreme values transcending common things. Hence the religious attitude is one of loyalty, devotion, reverence, humility.[1]

Philosophy is forever searching, inquiring, questioning; religion is an attitude — an attitude of faith, faith that the world is something worth while, that the universe is not just a great machine, that there are values — perhaps eternal values, which the mind of man can partly know, that there is after all a moral right; that wrong is wrong and never right.

Spirituality

In religious writings the word *spirit, spiritual, spirituality,* are ever-present. Perhaps the student has been confused by these words. They suggest hazy, ghostly things, the existence of which he has come to doubt. But these words now have a definite meaning neither ghostly nor mysterious. They refer to the things of highest worth. Spirit is nothing different from mind, but it is mind seen under the aspect of value. To be spiritual, says Santayana, is to live in the presence of the ideal. The meaning of spirituality and

[1] On the definition of religion, see James B. Pratt, *The Religious Consciousness,* chap. i. Pratt defines religion as the serious and social *attitude* toward the Determiner of Destiny.

its relation to religion are best expressed by Drake in these words:

> This disposition of the heart and will, through which a man comes to care for the highest things and to live in gentleness and inward calm above the surface aspects and accidents of life, we call, in its inner nature, Spirituality; when it is embodied in outward forms and institutions, and spreads among whole communities, we call it a religion.[1]

Thus religion loses its mysterious and dogmatic and oracular character and becomes the instinctive response of the soul in need. It is not something the "truth" of which we have to question and argue about and seek evidences for. It rests upon the recognition of a realm of higher values and a kind of instinctive sympathy with them and longing for them. Since the task of philosophy is to study the meanings and values of the world, we see how intimate is the relation between philosophy and religion.

Influence of philosophy upon our religious beliefs

One is often asked what effect the study of philosophy is likely to have upon our religious beliefs. At first the study of philosophy may be disturbing, especially if one's religious creed is rather narrow and uncompromising. But if it is broad and simple, philosophy will strengthen it. "What doth the Lord require of thee, but to do justly, and to love mercy, and to walk humbly with thy God?" Sympathy, righteousness, and humility are not likely to encounter much criticism from philosophy. As Bacon said, "It is true that a little philosophy inclineth Man's mind to atheism; but depth in philosophy bringeth men's minds about to religion." [2] Indeed, philosophy should help us to put our fundamental religious beliefs on a solid intellectual foundation and so relieve us of much perplexity and doubt. Sometimes our religious beliefs are held timidly and with trembling doubt. We have a subconscious dread lest "profane" science should come in and dissipate our beliefs. Philosophy takes us up into the mountain-top and allows us to look over into this valley of uncertainties. In this, as in many cases, knowledge ban-

---

[1] Durant Drake, *Problems of Religion* (Houghton Mifflin Company), p. 244.
[2] *The Essays of Lord Bacon*, XVI, "Of Atheism."

ishes fear. Having seen the worst and found it not so very bad, thereafter there is greater peace.

Ethics and religion

Religion should not be confused with ethics, which is a normative science dealing with the standards of right conduct; nor should it be confused with right conduct itself. Religion is a powerful motive to righteousness, but it is more than righteousness. Its essential note is reverence and its peculiar aim is harmony and adjustment; and harmony with the highest involves righteousness of conduct. History shows us how hard it is to *compel* men to do right, but in some great *cause* their energies may all be enlisted and the best in them drawn out; it is love rather than fear that is really effective. The motive of loyalty makes the most powerful appeal to men. "The spirit of religion," says L. P. Jacks, "is that of uncompromising loyalty to the highest."

The comparative study of religions

Nothing has done more to vitalize the interest in religion in recent times than the study of the history of religions. Some good book on this subject should be in the hands of every student, and he should become familiar with the religions of ancient India, of Greece and Rome, of Scandinavia, of the Mohammedans, of the ancient Hebrews, as well as with the history and meaning of Christianity. Common to all will be found the belief in unseen powers which rule the world and make for righteousness; and a desire to come into harmonious relations with them, with perhaps always the feeling of unity and the certainty of response.

The social character of religion

In recent literature on the origin and nature of religion, much emphasis has been put upon its social character. This movement is apparently a part of the general emphasis upon the social nature of man which characterizes this century. The nineteenth century called attention to the evolution of man and his relations to the lower animals. The twentieth century has the more attractive task of investigating his social nature and social relations. The study of religion from this point of view has thrown much new light on the whole subject.[1]

It is pointed out by this modern school that religion is social in its origin, a kind of expression of group consciousness. Early religious rites and ceremonies were performed by or on behalf of the whole group, and an important function of early religions was evidently that of social control. Religion, in its real meaning, is the emotional expression of the collective spirit of the group and has its purpose in cementing the group into a closer and more effective union. The teaching of Jesus is pre-eminently social, emphasizing love, sympathy, co-operation, and righteousness. Particularly at the present time we are living in a positive, scientific, and social age. Our religion, if it is to survive, must likewise be positive, and social, having as its end the more perfect socializing of humanity, emphasizing love and sacrifice and community of interest. Just now, as it is pointed out, with the massing and crowding of populations throughout the world, there is instant and imperative need of religion as a socializing power. To this end a reconstruction of religion is necessary, recognizing its social origins and the social needs of the present.

The social aspects of religion have been expressed in a different way by Dewey in his recent Terry Lectures at Yale, published under the title, *A Common Faith*. Dewey believes that the gradual emancipation of religion from the dominance of the idea of the supernatural will vastly enhance its social value, since that idea has had the effect of diverting religious activity from its original social aim.

Dewey distinguishes between the noun, *religion*, and the adjective, *religious*, making the religious attitude a quality of our experience. Religious experience is not a special kind. On the contrary the religious quality belongs to many of our experiences, its characteristic quality being that of faith in ideal ends or values; a harmonizing of ourselves with actual conditions through faith in

---

[1] Compare:
> Emile Durkheim, *The Elementary Forms of the Religious Life.*
> Jane Ellen Harrison, *Themis; A Study of the Social Origins of Greek Religion.*
> Charles A. Ellwood, *The Reconstruction of Religion.*
> E. S. Ames, "Religious Values and the Practical Absolute," *International Journal of Ethics,* XXXII, no. 4.
> George Willis Cooke, *The Social Evolution of Religion.*

these ideals. Thus religion becomes the unification of the self through allegiance to ideal ends. To these we respond as worthy of controlling our desires and choices. "The ideal ends to which we attach our faith are not shadowy and wavering. They assume concrete form in our understanding of our relations to one another, and the values contained in these relations." [1]

If religion be defined as "emotion felt in the presence of something deemed *supremely* worthy of our attention and devotion," [2] it would seem, in these times of social uncertainty, that our attitude must become more and more religious as our attention and devotion are directed more and more to social ideals.

Dewey's attempt to arrive at a conception of religion that shall make it adaptable to an industrial and social age — and a very critical one — is interesting and valuable. But such attempts at the reconstruction of religion lie outside the province of philosophy, which is the attempt to understand the world in which we live and to evaluate, not religion itself, but the concepts involved in our discourse about it. From this point of view, religion is not primarily a social attitude, however much its reverberations through the group may have integrated and socialized the group itself. Religion seems sometimes like a grateful escape from society. It suggests solitude and prayer and communion, not with other people, but with God. It suggests a feeling of dependence upon some being in whose hands our destiny lies, whose favor we would like to win. It suggests worship, reverence, adoration, faith, love, hope.

If we think of religion in this way, we may understand how it has come about that it has a lesser place in the life of today than at other times. The present age has placed its reliance upon certain newfound gods — science, invention, industrial and commercial expansion, social reconstruction, new forms of social organization, labor unions, clubs, fraternal societies, and organizations of a thousand kinds.

Just at present, our trust in these things, especially our trust in science and its practical benefits, and in the new control which we have gained over nature's forces, is becoming less confident. There

---

[1] John Dewey, *A Common Faith* (Yale University Press, 1934), pp. 33, 87.

[2] Durant Drake, *Invitation to Philosophy* (Houghton Mifflin Company, 1933), p. 475.

are indications that these things may fail us as a source of peace and happiness. We hear of possible social and political revolutions, of increased friction between classes and between nations, and even of a possible collapse of our civilization.

When doubts begin to assail our hitherto self-confident age, the outlook for religion becomes brighter. Religion does not flourish in a cocksure, self-glorying era, such as that preceding the Great War. Something of humility is essential to the religious attitude. So long as the ever-advancing discoveries of science were being applied to lessen our discomforts and remove our fears and anxieties, we did not so much feel the need of religion. But when, as may happen, we make the discovery that our wonderful inventions, our warships and airships, as well as our countless organizations, are powerless to bring us peace and fulfilment and may not even avert social disaster, and that our materialistic civilization has done little to promote the things of higher value — art, literature, morality, peace, and social stability, then perhaps the mood of religion will return. We shall need the fruit of the spirit, such as love, peace, kindness, faithfulness, temperance.

At all events, we see that the relation between religion and philosophy is most intimate. If we define religion as *the cultivation of the spiritual values which are ever-present, but sometimes dormant, in the human soul*, it belongs to philosophy to scrutinize these values, determining their source and their objective equivalents. If, again, religion is the response of the soul to the divine forces of the universe, philosophy must tell us about these divine forces and whether any such exist. If, as one writer says, it is indispensable to the religious attitude to believe that somehow there lies behind things a power or essence that has something in common with our own nature, something that can without abuse of language be called personal, then philosophy must determine whether there is in science or metaphysics anything to prevent our believing in such a personal power; and what reason, if any, there is in science or metaphysics for so believing.

Perhaps then it will be discovered that the old conflict between religion and science has disappeared with our better understanding of what science really is and our fuller understanding of religion.

The supernatural

We have seen that Dewey believes that the fruitfulness of religion has been lessened by the intrusion of the idea of the supernatural. This discussion does not belong to the task of philosophy. It is, however, within its province to analyze the meaning of the term. Such an analysis would be one of the services of philosophy to religion. Here it is necessary only to call attention to the effect upon this concept of our rapidly changing scientific attitude. In historic cultures, and still to some extent in that of our own times, the word " supernatural " has meant something outside the domain of natural law. Supernatural beings, such for instance as the gods of ancient Greece, are not controlled or limited by the ordinary laws of nature; and supernatural events are not explained by known laws. It is probable that the logical analysis of the term would now lead in a quite opposite direction. The imagination is constantly at work creating ideal ends and values, transcending the whole domain of nature, as it is known to us; and these *super*-natural ends are not only pictured but actually and constantly realized. For instance, mankind is now creating a social conscience which never existed before in nature or any of nature's manifestations. In remote geological time, there was no life upon the earth — and when it came it was super-natural. So of mind, and moral feeling, and social organization, and art, and science. It is useless to affirm or deny the existence of the supernatural until we fix upon whatever particular connotation we choose to give to "nature." Just now physicists are trying to find some law which may explain the "supernatural" behavior of the electron as it circles in its orbit about the nucleus of the atom, since it appears to disobey every known law of physics.

Whether this "hunger for cosmic support," to use Professor Otto's phrase, has its origin in "the groping of a lonely-souled gregarious animal to find its herd or its herd leader in the great spaces between the stars," or, whether it is a kind of instinctive longing of a homesick soul for some friendly union with a far-off world of ideal values is just one more philosophic "problem." Plato held the latter view.[1]

---

[1] Compare M. C. Otto, *Things and Ideals* (Henry Holt and Company), p, 287. The quotation is from Gilbert Murray.

If the term "supernatural" is not in very good standing in present-day science, this could not be said of the term "mysterious." "The most beautiful thing we can express," says Einstein, "is the mysterious. It is the source of all true art and science. He to whom this emotion is a stranger, who can no longer pause to wonder and stand rapt in awe, is as good as dead: his eyes are closed.... It is enough for me to contemplate the mystery of conscious life perpetuating itself through all eternity, to reflect upon the marvelous structure of the universe which we can dimly perceive, and to try humbly to comprehend even an infinitesimal part of the intelligence manifested in nature." [1] In this connection it is significant that a recent book of science by one of our most distinguished scientists, Sir James Jeans, is entitled *The Mysterious Universe*. And J. W. N. Sullivan, writing in the *Atlantic Monthly* for January, 1935, says: "Perhaps today is the first time in the history of science when the universe has really become mysterious.... That the universe is now so mysterious is due, it appears, to the way we think about things. But it may well be that we shall never hit on a way of thinking about things that will abolish that mystery."

Possibly we cannot define religion, nor fully describe our religious experiences and emotions; but its meaning to us is profound and significant. This is well expressed by Mr. Will Durant, writing in the *Saturday Evening Post* of January 26, 1935. This is what he says:

> In our youth we think of religion as an assemblage of ideas; in our old age we perceive how subordinate these ideas are to the functions that religion fulfills in the individual and the state. To the individual it offers, first of all, an answer to his questions; it gives him some mental stability and peace by enabling him to complete, through hypothesis and belief, a world picture left irritatingly uncertain, fragmentary and uncomforting by science and philosophy. It solaces his solitude, and reassures him in his fear of the unknown; it enlists the universe on his side, and satisfies his mystical longing for union with the ultimate force and meaning of the world. It redeems the hard prose and dull routine of his earthly existence with the drama of ritual and the poetry of faith; it conceives a divine epic of creation and salvation, through which the individual career, otherwise so trivial and so brief, takes on

[1] Albert Einstein, "What I Believe," in *The Forum Magazine*, October, 1930.

cosmic proportions and endless significance; it gives to life a meaning that can survive death, and takes from death and poverty some share of their terror and their sting. But more than that; it deepens conscience by giving to morals an emotional and supernatural basis of divine surveillance and solicitude; it strengthens, by threats of punishment and promises of reward, the social instincts against those individualistic impulses which, unhindered, would tear a society to pieces. It has given to nations — sometimes, as in the Middle Ages, to continents — the social unity of a common creed and a common moral code. Hence statesmen have courted and favored it, lavishing wealth upon it like Rameses, attributing their victories to it like Ashurbanipal, building perfect temples for it like Pericles, allying themselves with it like Charlemagne; and even proud rebels like Ashoka and Akbar, Constantine and Peter, Napoleon and Mussolini, have made their peace with it, lest the order forged by their arms should be undone by the loosening of morals and the clash of faiths.

In connection with this chapter read:

Edgar S. Brightman, *Introduction to Philosophy* (Henry Holt and Company), chap. x.

Further references:

W. K. Wright, *A Student's Philosophy of Religion* (The Macmillan Company).

Arthur C. McGiffert, *The Rise of Modern Religious Ideas* (The Macmillan Company).

William James, *The Varieties of Religious Experience* (Longmans, Green and Company).

Richard Cabot, *What Men Live By* (Houghton Mifflin Company).

Josiah Royce, *Sources of Religious Insight* (Charles Scribner's Sons).

G. A. Barton, *The Religions of the World* (The University of Chicago Press).

Edwin D. Starbuck, *The Psychology of Religion* (Charles Scribner's Sons. Contemporary Science Series).

James Bissett Pratt, *The Religious Consciousness* (The Macmillan Company).

John Dewey, *A Common Faith* (Yale University Press, 1934).

J. H. Leuba, *A Psychological Study of Religion* (Open Court Publishing Company, 1923).

Salomon Reinach, *Orpheus* (Liveright).

Kirsopp Lake, *The Religion of Yesterday and Tomorrow* (Harvard University Press).

G. Galloway, *Philosophy of Religion* (Charles Scribner's Sons), chap. iv.

H. S. Coffin, *What is There in Religion?* (The Macmillan Company).

CHAPTER IV
IS PHILOSOPHY WORTH WHILE?

ONE taking up philosophy for the first time is probably impressed, and possibly frightened, by the magnitude of the subjects under discussion. It seems quite presumptuous to study such immense questions as the nature of reality, the meaning and purpose of the world, and the value of life. The scientist, who devotes himself to a snug little corner of reality — for instance, animal morphology, geological strata, or political organization — is perhaps inclined to criticize the philosopher for the largeness of his field.

The scientist, however, whatever his domain, soon finds that it is anything but a snug little corner. It is revealed as so immense and has so many interrelations, and reaches out to so many other sciences that he is almost forced into philosophy himself — or ceases, at any rate, to criticize the latter because of its largeness.

Nevertheless, there have been schools of thinkers who, frightened or repelled by the vastness of the problems of philosophy, have refused to enter upon their study. Two such schools may be mentioned here, the Positivists and the Sceptics.

Positivism

The Positive Philosophy is a technical term applied by the French philosopher, Auguste Comte (1798–1857), to his view of the world. Comte believed that the search for first causes, ultimate reality, and all such things, is wholly vain. The human mind must confine itself to actual facts, to *phenomena*, as we call them; that is, to things as they appear in our actual experience. It is useless to try to find out what lies back of phenomena, about things in themselves. Philosophy must limit itself to discovering the relationships between phenomena and their invariable modes of behavior.

Comte's interests were in sociology, a science of which he claimed to be the founder; and he thought that scientific methods might be applied to the study of society to the end of greatly increasing human welfare. Positivism, therefore, really amounts to this: Science is the final stage of human thought. It deals with what is certain, useful, positive, especially with what is useful for perfecting our social institutions. No one would care to disagree with Comte in his emphasis upon the value of science, nor would many, perhaps, question his opinion regarding the supremely important position of the social sciences. Few possibly would agree with him that the study of wider philosophical problems is vain. In the next chapter we shall see what Max Planck thinks of Positivism.

Scepticism

Another school which would discourage us from approaching the mount of philosophy is that of the Sceptics. Scepticism first appeared in ancient Greece in the time of the Sophists. Gorgias, for instance, said that nothing exists; if it did, we could not know it; if we could know it, we could not communicate our knowledge to others. Later, in the Graeco-Roman period, Scepticism took the form of a "school" of philosophy led by Pyrrho. Although these thinkers came after the brilliant age of Socrates, Plato, Democritus, and Aristotle, and the many Greek triumphs in the fields of mathematics, logic, metaphysics, and ethics, nevertheless, they despaired of gaining knowledge. They were fond of pointing out the contradictions in the opinions of philosophers and of asserting in quite a dogmatic fashion, unbecoming, as one would think, in a Sceptic, that knowledge is impossible. The conclusion which they drew also seems strange to us. They thought it better to suspend judgment on all the questions that the philosophers had discussed about God and the soul and the world, and thereby attain for themselves mental poise and tranquillity. This was a characteristic Greek attitude. The Greeks, especially of the later period, wanted to live in a tidy, well-ordered, and circumscribed world. It disturbed and perplexed the Stoics, Epicureans, and Sceptics to labor with the unending problems which philosophy offers. All the Greek schools, therefore, after Aristotle, sought for some philosophy of life which should free their minds from fear and afford equanimity and peace.

In modern times, Scepticism in the Greek sense has almost passed away. The most distinguished Sceptic of modern times was David

Hume (1711–76), but even his scepticism is not the radical slashing kind of the Greeks, but rather a critical inquiry into the actual limits of knowledge. Faint-hearted resignation does not commend itself to our modern genius. A resolute and hopeful facing of every problem with persistent and undaunted efforts to solve it — this is the modern spirit. Philosophers may differ, human judgment may be fallible, our senses may deceive us; but we will find out which of the philosophers is right, how wrong judgment may be righted, and how the deception of the senses may be corrected. The modern spirit is one of courage and adventure. Hardship and death attended the discovery of the Antarctic pole; but all difficulties were surmounted and the pole was visited. Two students were discussing their courses of study. One said, "I am going to specialize in organic chemistry." "Why?" asked the other. "Because," said the first, "I believe it offers more *problems* now than any other subject." There is plenty of doubt in modern thought, but it acts, not as an anodyne to lull us into equanimity, but as a spur to drive us to further and more persistent inquiry. Hence doubt has an important function in our philosophizing, not only spurring us to action, but discouraging dogmatism. Bertrand Russell speaks of "liberating doubt." "Philosophy," he says, "removes the somewhat arrogant dogmatism of those who have traveled into the region of liberating doubt and it keeps alive our sense of wonder by showing familiar things in an unfamiliar aspect."

> "Rather I prize the doubt
> Low kinds exist without,
> Finished and finite clods, untroubled by a spark."

Browning would surely have little sympathy with one who should say that the questions of philosophy cannot be answered; therefore, we should not raise them. To him life is an eternal adventure, an endless process of development, in which

> "We fall to rise, are baffled to fight better."

Doubt and even bewilderment beset the student in the pursuit of philosophy, but to raise the doubt, pursue the truth, and hope to attain it — this is the great adventure of the human spirit.

We hear more now of Agnosticism than of Scepticism. The term was first used by Huxley, but has usually been associated with the name of Herbert Spencer. In its Greek origin it means "without knowledge." Spencer believed that absolute knowledge is impossible. All knowledge is relative and cannot go further than such facts as matter, motion, force, and consciousness, and all these are merely symbols or modes of the Unknowable. Spencer's Agnosticism is thus only a form of Positivism, and not of the extreme type, since he goes further in his assertions about the Unknowable than a positivist would feel entitled to do.

Huxley used the word in a religious sense to indicate his belief that, though we may not deny the existence of God, we can know nothing of his real nature. This is the more common meaning of the word *Agnosticism* now. In philosophy it is generally used in its Spencerian sense, indicating that human knowledge is relative and limited, so that knowledge of ultimate reality is impossible. There would seem to be little to criticize in such a guarded Agnosticism as this, but in general Agnosticism is too apt to emphasize the limitations of knowledge, sometimes having a flavor of dogmatism, confidently affirming that the kind of knowledge which philosophy seeks is unattainable, thus going beyond the more modest attitude of doubt. It is therefore contrary to the spirit of philosophy, which is that of persistent, unwearied inquiry. One writer speaks of the agnostic as a quitter.[1]

Some world view inevitable

The fact is that the whole discussion as to whether we shall or shall not enter upon the study of philosophy was settled long ago by Aristotle when he said, "Whether we will philosophize or whether we won't philosophize, we must philosophize." Wisely Edwin Wallace said, "Consciously or unconsciously every man frames for himself a theory of the relation of the individual to the universe, and on his attitude to that question his whole life and conduct, public and private, depend."

Most people who decry the study of philosophy have a system of their own often quite complete. Some theory of God they have, if only it is to deny that there is any God. Some theory of the universe

[1] Scudder Klyce, in his *Universe*, p. 9.

they have, if only the three-story view of "Heaven above, Hell below, and the Earth in between." Some theory of values they have, if only that personal gain is the highest good. Since, then, we are all to have some theory of life and the world, it will be well to have as intelligent a theory as possible, formed after a critical and historical study. It will be well to study the great world views of the great world thinkers, of Plato, Aristotle, Saint Augustine, Spinoza, Kant, Darwin, Royce, and James. We shall be surprised to find, if we follow the history of philosophy down to the present, how great has been the progress in really solving many of the difficult problems, and how idle is the complaint that they cannot be solved.

There is a general impression that metaphysical inquiries are especially baffling, and that the history of philosophy is a history of speculative theories, quite in contrast to the steady and triumphant progress of the physical sciences. It is true that tremendous progress has been made in the physical sciences in the last hundred years; but it is also true that the history of science is a history of discarded theories. Recently some of our most cherished beliefs respecting the Euclidean geometry, the Newtonian physics, and the Darwinian theory of evolution have been called in question, and in late years our theories of the constitution of matter have been revolutionized. Nevertheless, there has been a steady and brilliant advance. Precisely the same is true of philosophy. I should say that in the last twenty-five years progress in philosophy has been quite as rapid and quite as brilliant as progress in science, if, indeed, we wish to make any sharp contrast between them.

In some respects, indeed, "science" has made less progress than "philosophy" — its most general conceptions would astonish neither Aristotle nor Descartes, could they revisit our earth. The composition of things from elements, their evolution, the conservation of energy, the idea of a universal determinism, would seem to them commonplace enough — the little things, the microscopes, electric lights, telephones, and details of the sciences, would be to them the awe-inspiring things. But if they opened our books on metaphysics, or visited a philosophic lecture room, everything would sound strange. The whole idealistic or "critical" attitude of our time would be novel, and it would be long before they took it in.[1]

[1] William James, *Some Problems of Philosophy* (Longmans, Green and Company), p. 24. See also the article by James Ward on "The Progress of Philosophy" in *Mind*, 15, no. LVIII, carrying the same thought.

Science not to be confused with applied science

I suppose the reason that the advance in science seems so much greater than the advance in philosophy is because our attention is usually fixed on the brilliant results of the special sciences in the mechanic and industrial arts.   It is not science, but applied science, that is meant.   We have become accustomed to swell with pride when we think of what science has done for man.   Every school-girl knows by heart the long list of benefits which it has conferred, the wireless telegraph and telephone, the ocean greyhound, the limited express, the automobile, the aerial mail, the long list of time-savers and labor-savers adding to our daily comfort; the con-quest of disease through public sanitation, antiseptic surgery, and preventive medicine; the application of chemistry to agriculture, and the shortening of the hours of labor by the invention of ma-chinery.

Lately, however, and especially since the Great War, one hears less about the benefits conferred upon humanity by the mechanic arts.   The social crisis through which the world is now struggling has led many to question, not the value of the physical sciences, nor even that of applied science, but the direction in which science has been applied.   Perhaps the most conspicuous of the " triumphs " of applied science has been in the art of war, which actually threatens the destruction of our civilization.   One muses also on our count-less time-saving devices, wondering whether they have given us any more time for things really important.   Are labor-saving in-ventions a benefit to humanity unless they are accompanied by a knowledge of how to use the new leisure?   Has the moral and in-tellectual and aesthetic education of man advanced at equal pace with the progress of the mechanic arts, so that he can be trusted with his suddenly acquired wealth and leisure?   Is it possible that our method of combating disease by protecting us from infective agencies may have the effect of weakening our *resistance* to disease?   Is it true, as Todd says, that a pasteurized and sanitized society is not necessarily progressive or dynamic?

All these questions set us thinking.   It is just possible that too much attention has been given to applied science and not enough to applied philosophy.   Or perhaps science has been applied in the wrong directions. Possibly, instead of applying it with such dazzling success to the arts of war, to the increase of wealth, and to the accumulation of externalities, it should have been applied more to education, and to the conservation of racial, moral, and economic values. We have acquired too much wealth and not enough wisdom.

By virtue of the advancement that has long been going on with ever accelerated logarithmic rapidity in invention, in mathematics, in physics, in chemistry, in biology, in astronomy, and in applications of them, time and space and matter have been already conquered to such an extent that our globe, once so seemingly vast, has virtually shrunken to the dimensions of an ancient province; and manifold peoples of divers tongues and traditions and customs and institutions are now constrained to live together as in a single community. There is thus demanded a new ethical wisdom, a new legal wisdom, a new economic wisdom, a new political wisdom, a new wisdom in the affairs of government. For the new visions our anguished times cry aloud but the only answers are reverberated echoes of the wailing cry mingled with the chattering voices of excited public men who know not what to do. Why? What is the explanation? The question is double: Why the disease? And why no remedy at hand? The answer is the same for both. And the answer is that the so-called sciences of ethics and jurisprudence and economics and politics and government have not kept pace with the rapid progress made in the other great affairs of man; they have lagged behind; it is because of their lagging that the world has come to be in so great distress; and it is because of their lagging that they have not now the needed wisdom to effect a cure....
At present the future of mankind is dark. "Stop, look, and listen" — the prudent caution at railroad crossings — must be amended to read "stop, look, listen, and THINK"; not for the saving of a few lives in railroad accidents, but for the preservation of the life of humanity.[1]

Students of philosophy, therefore, need no longer be frightened away by a comparison of the meager fruits of philosophy with the richer fruits of science. If by philosophy we mean not systems of metaphysics or futile discussions about the Absolute, but rather the search for wisdom, the appraisement of values, and the careful logical analysis of concepts, it seems to be just what the world needs now.

[1] Alfred Korzybski, *Manhood of Humanity* (E. P. Dutton and Company), pp. 20, 21, 30. By permission of the publishers.

But after all it is not what we *need* which interests us, but what we *want*. One of the deep impulses of the human mind is the craving to know. Curiosity is a characteristic instinctive reaction; scientific curiosity has always been a powerful incentive to scientific research. We love to pry into nature's secrets; we wish to understand the world around us — its source, its meaning, its probable future.

Part of the value of science is intellectual. It would be a dull mind that could see the rich variety of natural phenomena without wondering how they are inter-related. Quite apart from all questions of practical utility, the modern mind feels strongly urged to synthesize the phenomena it observes, to try to combine happenings in the external world under general laws.[1]

We recall the words of the poet Lessing: Did the Almighty, holding in his right hand *Truth* and in his left *Search After Truth*, deign to tender me the one I might prefer — in all humility, but without hesitation, I should request *Search After Truth*.

In connection with this chapter read:

Cassius J. Keyser. *The Human Worth of Rigorous Thinking* (Columbia University Press), chap. I.

Further references:

J. H. Muirhead, *The Use of Philosophy* (Harvard University Press, 1929).
T. V. Smith, *The Philosophic Way of Life* (University of Chicago Press), chap. I.
M. C. Otto, *Things and Ideals*, "Hast any Philosophy in Thee, Shepherd?" (Henry Holt and Company), chap. I.
Gamertsfelder and Evans, *Fundamentals of Philosophy* (Prentice-Hall, Inc.), chap. II.

[1] Sir James Jeans, *The New Background of Science* (The Macmillan Company, New York, 1934), p. 50. By permission of the publishers.

CHAPTER V

METHODS OF STUDY

THREE hundred years ago, a Frenchman, René Descartes, called the founder of modern philosophy, sat down to think. He was tired of the subtleties of the scholastic philosophy — and he believed that by adopting a few simple rules to guide his thought, he might unaided think out the great problems of existence. He would use the same rationalistic method which had led him and his contemporaries to such brilliant results in mathematics and the science of mechanics.

Descartes' four rules

Here are his four famous rules:

The *first*, never to accept anything for true which I did not clearly know to be such; that is to say, carefully to avoid precipitancy and prejudice, and to comprise nothing more in my judgment than what was presented to my mind so clearly and distinctly as to exclude all ground of doubt.

The *second*, to divide each of the difficulties under examination into as many parts as possible, and as might be necessary for its adequate solution.

The *third*, to conduct my thoughts in such order that, by commencing with objects the simplest and easiest to know, I might ascend by little and little, and as it were, step by step, to the knowledge of the more complex....

And the *last*, in every case to make enumerations so complete, and reviews so general, that I might be assured that nothing was omitted.[1]

Since Descartes' day thousands of searchers for truth have found his four rules helpful in the conduct of their own thinking. But modern science is empirical — emphasizing the importance of experience, observation and experimental research; and adds other rules to those of Descartes. The result is what we call scientific method — and philosophy claims no exemption from the rigorous

[1] Descartes, *Discourse on Method*, part II, pp. 15, 16. Translation by John Veitch. Everyman's Library. By permission of E. P. Dutton and Company, publishers.

rules which scientific method prescribes. Sometimes, however, the claim has been made that philosophy does have a kind of esoteric method by which it can approach more directly to the portals of truth — at least some kinds of truth — than through the laborious method of logical research. This is the method of intuition, or immediate insight. It is the method of the mystics.

Mysticism

All through the history of thought there have appeared from time to time philosophers who have laid claim to a special and exclusive method. These were the Mystics. Mysticism is an interesting chapter in the history of thought; some of the finer spirits are found in this company. Perhaps their claim to a peculiar and direct insight into truth should not be hastily rejected.

The Mystics believe that certain kinds of knowledge, particularly the knowledge of God, come not through the labored efforts of reflective thinking, but through direct insight and intuition. The powers of reason may sometimes be transcended and we may have a direct approach to God, or an immediate union with reality, so that truth is felt, apprehended, or grasped in a single pulse of the soul life. Something like moments of ecstatic contemplation bring us face to face with reality.

Such was the view of Plotinus (A.D. 204–69), the Neo-Platonist, and something like this has been held by a great company of Christian Mystics, such as Saint Teresa, Saint John of the Cross, Meister Eckhart, Jacob Boehme, and George Fox; while mystical views may be found in the poetry of Shelley, Wordsworth, Tennyson, and Whitman, and in the *Essays* of Emerson. Indeed, Bergson, one of the most widely known and widely read of the philosophers of the present day, a psychologist, biologist, and evolutionist, teaches a kind of mysticism; for with Bergson, intuition is superior to intellect. Intuition is almost synonymous with life itself, leading us, at any rate, to the very portals of life. It is a kind of divining sympathy, like animal instinct, only become self-conscious and capable of reflecting upon its object.

There is a certain *rapport* between nature and mind, which in our purely intellectual and scientific moods we cannot gain, and through which there comes to us a peculiar insight into the innermost secrets of life. This is not, in Bergson's view, like a revelation which comes to the mind from without, as in the older Mysticism. It is rather due to the fact that the mind itself is a part of the very current of life, which is more real than matter. This does not necessarily mean that philosophy has any esoteric method of discovering truth which science does not have; it means rather that the particular task which confronts the scientist in his dealing with the world of matter makes the intellect his instrument. But if the scientist in his philosophical moods were to go in search of reality, he would find himself in possession of another avenue of approach through direct intuition. The work of the philosopher here is somewhat like that of the artist, who *identifies* himself with the object, "putting himself back within the object by a kind of sympathy." It is as if, when we approach nature by means of the intellect, a certain "barrier" exists between nature and the mind, which intuition breaks down through sympathetic communication.

If this be Mysticism, surely the word should connote no quality of error, as it commonly does. It should rather be considered an interesting "lead" to follow up in our further search for the sources of knowledge. Just at present we may neglect this wider question, for we are now concerned not so much with the sources of truth as with the methods we may use in our study of philosophy.

Scientific method

But let us return to what is known as scientific method as used today in scientific investigation — and indeed in the reflective thinking of our daily life. Later we may ask whether this method can be used in philosophy, and if so whether it is the best or the only method. Dewey, in his little book *How We Think,* has given us a clear account of the procedure of reflective thinking.[1] Reflective thinking begins when there is some problem to be solved or difficulty to be met, as when, following a strange road, a traveler comes to where it forks; he will have to do some thinking then if he has never

---

[1] A further detailed description of the processes of thought as applied to science and philosophy may be found in an excellent book entitled *An Introduction to Reflective Thinking,* by Columbia University Associates in Philosophy.

done any before. Deciding which road to follow is a little problem, philosophy offers us big problems, but the method of solution is the same.

First, we must analyze the situation carefully and collect all the facts bearing on it that we can; and we must be fair and impartial and unprejudiced in our observation of the facts. This elimination of the personal equation, of our tastes and preferences, of our likes and dislikes, and of our traditional and religious systems, is exceedingly difficult, and the failure to observe this has been the source of mischief in countless cases of philosophizing in the past. Prejudice leads us astray in the reflective thinking of our daily life and has been the cause of abundant error even in science. No progress in science or philosophy can be made, if we commit ourselves in advance to some fond theory. In daily life, when some problem suddenly presents itself, we are apt to fall back upon habit or custom in deciding it. Most of us have some ready-made "system," some favorite collection of ideas, which we have gotten from tradition or social inheritance, or from our political party, or our church, or perhaps from some book which has impressed us deeply, or from some new "movement" in poetry or popular fiction, or even possibly from an impressive picture on the screen, and we solve the troublesome intruding problem offhand by reference to this system. And it is very probable that in our solution of the question we shall be strongly influenced by our personal feelings, our wishes, and desires. Some "emotional complex" will decide the question for us.

But in philosophy and science our reflective thinking must be freed from these errors of "systems" and subjective interests, those "idols" of the theater and the cave, as Bacon called them. This freedom from prejudice is an ideal which is very difficult to realize. In the physical sciences it has been realized in a remarkable fashion by a great army of patient, persistent, and unprejudiced workers, and the rich contributions which they have made to knowledge attest the fruitfulness of this method. In philosophy this wholly impartial attitude is even more difficult than in science, and few of us attain it. But so far as it is possible, every problem whether in philosophy or in science must be approached in the spirit of genuine scientific interest, whose motive is a keen desire to know, a real scientific curiosity.

The hypothesis

The second step in philosophical method, after the preliminary observation of facts, is the proposed solution of the problem. This is what Dewey calls the "suggestion." It is also called the hypothesis or provisional theory. Oftentimes it comes as a flash of insight — a kind of intuition of the solution of the problem. It ranks in importance with the patient observation of facts which precedes and follows the suggestion. It may come after a preliminary observation of a few of the facts in the situation. It may come after years of laborious investigation, or after weary months of careful cataloguing of observations. It may even come at the very beginning of the investigation. It furnishes the clue to work from, and adds immense zest to the research. Our minds function in such a way that we have to have a theory to work on. The theory may be wrong and will have to be discarded when experiment and further observation have failed to verify it. But it *must* be verified when the nature of the problem makes verification possible; and where some kind of verification is not possible, research soon loses its interest. In verification the logical process involves deductive reasoning. We assume for the moment that our theory, our "guess," is true and we deduce its consequences, and then rigorously compare the implications of the theory with the actual facts. It is an *If — then* process of thought; *if* the theory is true, *then* such and such things would follow. Do these things square with the facts?

Midway between stations your motor car stops. You anxiously seek the cause. To find it is "the problem." Someone makes a "suggestion." Probably each member of the party makes one. The gas is out, a connection is broken, a piston has jammed, a feed-pipe is clogged. You take the most promising suggestion and try it out. "Trying it out" means deducing the consequences of the theory and comparing them with the facts. If not verified, you try another.

A physician is called to see a patient who is ill. To find the cause

of the trouble or the character of the disease is his "problem."
He makes a few preliminary observations of the facts, asks questions,
tests pulse and temperature. Then a suggestion comes to him —
typhoid fever. *If* it is typhoid, *then* certain hidden symptoms will
be present. He makes these decisive tests and verifies his hypothesis, or disproves it.

This is the method of reflective thinking in our daily life; it is
the method by which great discoveries have been made in science;
it is a method which must commonly be used in philosophical
inquiries.

But the question will present itself whether it is possible to use
this method in philosophy. How can we apply it to the great life
problems about God and the world and the soul? Is not verification the all-important part in the method, and is verification
possible in these large world problems? Is not philosophy in danger
of becoming speculative just because verification is impossible?

In answer to this I think we may say that the method in question is merely the method of reflective thinking, and no matter
how stupendous our problems, we must reflect upon them. We do
not mean that philosophical inquiry is limited to this method.
We shall notice presently other ways of studying, such as logical
analysis, analogy, and the historical method. But in that constructive part of philosophy in which we are most interested, after
we have made full use of critical analysis and the study of the history
of our subject, we must still continue to reflect upon it, and the
success of our reflection will be in proportion as our observations
are careful and impartial, our experience wide and varied, and our
intuitions profound.

A very peculiar importance attaches to that part of scientific
method which we call the *suggestion*, the flash of insight into the
solution of the problem. This is where brains count — and experience. When our motor car stops, a lot of foolish suggestions
may be made. Someone in the party will make the useful suggestion, and this person will be the *wise* one, and his wisdom will
consist partly in his experience with motor cars and partly in —
brains. The great discoveries in science and philosophy have been
made by great men. Anybody can see an apple fall. A few may

ask why it falls. Only the great brain of a Newton can project a theory of gravitation. Nowhere is the almost uncanny power of mind seen so clearly as in the recent investigations of physicists into the electrical nature of the atom, or the investigations of mathematicians into the theory of relativity. It is the creative power of thought, sometimes called the creative imagination. In its higher forms, it seems like a special endowment of genius — a kind of vision or inspiration. *Sagacity* is what James called it.

But the vision of truth does not come from sagacity alone; or, if it does, sagacity must include experience. The "wise" man in philosophy and science is not merely the "seer"; he is the man who knows, as well as the man who sees. The one who is quick to detect the trouble with your motor is the man who has had experience with motors and their ways. The great scientist is, to be sure, the great-brained man — but he is also usually the man versed in the whole lore and history of his science. So the great philosopher will be the man not only of deep insight, but a man of rich experience and profound knowledge of life.

Thus the method of philosophy is empirical. Our theories must spring out of experience and be tested by experience. A crucial test in the physical laboratory may not be possible, but in the laboratory of life the hypothesis must find its verification. The failures in the history of philosophy — and they have been many — have been partly due to the neglect of that close touch with life which is essential. A philosophical theory that comes into conflict with no accepted principles of science or philosophy, that is self-consistent, and that has been formed only after the most careful and impartial analysis of all the factors involved and after the widest appeal to human experience, is to that extent verified. Its wide appeal, its satisfactory working, even the prestige which it may have because of the successful scientific achievements of its proponent, are all steps in the process of verification.

This method of reflective thinking, as we have just outlined it, is the method by which constructive work in philosophy is done. But perhaps the student will say: "I do not hope to do constructive work; I am only anxious to know about philosophy, to have my questions answered and my doubts resolved." But to study philosophy is to philosophize. In a lecture room in a certain American university there is a motto which says, οὐ φιλοσοφία, ἀλλὰ φιλοσοφεῖν, "not philosophy, but to philosophize." It is the thinking about the great questions of life that does us good, rather than the study of the thoughts of other men.

Planck's description of scientific method

In Max Planck's recently published book, *Where Is Science Going?* there is a chapter on scientific method.[1] It is interesting to know what method is pursued by the distinguished founder of the new quantum physics, which has done so much to revolutionize physical science. In the first place, Planck flatly rejects the theory of the Positivists that we know nothing of the world beyond our own immediate sensory experience, and that we have no concern with any such world. To the Positivist any object, such as a house or a tree, is just a complex of our immediate sensory perceptions. It is meaningless to say that back of this sensory experience there is a real object.

Planck rejects this positivistic theory and believes that science today rests on a broader and more stable foundation. It makes the postulate that there is a real external world existing independently of our knowing processes, although this world is not directly knowable. But it is indirectly knowable and the complete knowledge of it is a goal ever to be approached but never to be fully attained. The means through which the scientist comes to know the nature of the physical world around us are *measurements*. In making these measurements and in all our observations and experiments we must use every effort to eliminate all sources of error arising either from our instruments of research or from subjective tendencies of our sensory organs. These measurements and observations constitute the raw material which the scientist uses in constructing a picture of the external world.

But how is this picture gained? Here the all-important thing is the constructive work of the scientist himself. He must make some hypothesis. "He may give rein to his own spirit of initiative, and allow the constructive powers of the imagination to come into

[1] Max Planck's *Where is Science Going?* (W. W. Norton and Company, Inc.), chaps. II and III.

full play." He must try to organize into one law the results of his experiments and his experience. The hypothesis must be free from inner logical incoherence, and the deductions from it must agree with the research measurements and experiments. Many a promising theory fails to survive these tests and must be rejected and a new one found.

Thus we see from Planck's description of scientific method how largely science springs from the mind of the scientist. The great laws of physical science have come from great men. The recent revolutionary discoveries in physics and microphysics have been made possible not only by the new and wonderful instruments of precision and patient experiments and observations but through the genius and brilliancy of such men as Planck, Einstein, Niels Bohr, Heisenberg, Hertz and Schroedinger.

And yet it is not brilliant intuitions alone which make great scientists philosophers. Patience, industry, honesty belong also to their equipment.

> The philosopher should be a man willing to listen to every sugges-tion, but determined to judge for himself. He should not be biased by appearances; have no favorite hypothesis; be of no school; and in doctrines have no master. He should not be a respecter of persons, but of things. Truth should be his primary object. If to these quali-ties be added industry, he may indeed hope to walk within the veil of the temple of Nature.[1]

Illustrations of method

Sir James Jeans, in a chapter on "the Methods of Science,"[2] illustrates these methods by the great historical theories concern-ing the motions of the heavenly bodies. The sun appears to rise in the east and set in the west. The fixed stars do the same. The moon, and those "wanderers" called the planets, also rise and set but irregularly. How shall all this be explained?

Previous to the advent of the Greek scientists, mythological explanations satisfied the minds of the ancients. The Greeks themselves wrestled with the problem for several hundred years.

---

[1] Faraday, in Sir Richard Gregory's *Discovery, or the Spirit and Service of Science*, p. 12.

[2] Sir James Jeans, *The New Background of Science* (The Macmillan Company, 1934). Revised edition, chap. II. By permission of the publishers.

Finally, Ptolemy of Alexandria, about A.D. 150, undertook a complete scientific explanation. He offered an hypothesis or theory to explain all the motions of the stars. This affirmed that the earth is fixed and stationary at the center of the system, the sun, moon and stars revolving around it, a complicated system of cycles and epicycles explaining the peculiar motions of the planets.

This theory, called the Ptolemaic System, seemed to explain the facts fairly well and prevailed throughout the Middle Ages, furnishing finally the cosmological foundation for Dante's great poem, *The Divine Comedy*. But, with the increase of astronomical knowledge in the sixteenth century, Copernicus became dissatisfied with this theory and made another hypothesis, resulting in the new Copernican system. He proposed to consider the sun as the center of the solar system, the earth and the other members of the system revolving around the sun in circles. This new theory fitted the facts better — but not perfectly. Kepler, studying the motion of Mars, substituted ellipses for circles as the paths of the planets. This explained still more facts, but left others unexplained. Then Newton came and proposed a wonderful and far-reaching law for all the heavenly bodies, namely, the law of gravitation, according to which every object in the universe attracts every other object with a force varying inversely as the square of the distance. This new law was found at once to explain in a marvelous way all the motions of all the heavenly bodies — even the motions of those mysterious and erratic bodies called comets. It explained also the falling of objects upon the earth, the trajectories of balls and bullets and the movements of the tides.

With the coming of Newton's great law, the scientific world was satisfied. The secret of the motions of bodies celestial and terrestrial was laid bare. Not until the present century did any doubts arise. But our increasingly accurate instruments finally detected something wrong with the planet Mercury. Leverrier observed that it does not move in accordance with Newton's laws. Its elliptical orbit itself turns in a manner bewildering to the Newtonian physics.

So then another revision is made and now Einstein comes forward with his famous theory of relativity, explaining not only the erratic behavior of Mercury but also a great number of other facts difficult hitherto to understand.   The part played by deduction in scientific method is illustrated in the verification of Einstein's law.   *If* the relativity theory is valid, *then* the light of a distant star passing near the sun should be deflected from its straight-line course.   Astronomers waited for a total eclipse of the sun and the deflection was shown to occur in accordance with Einstein's law.

As we review these several theories on the motions of the celestial bodies, it might appear that science is a history of discarded theories; but, as Jeans comments, such a conclusion would be that of a novice, for what really happens is that science is "ever progressing through a succession of theories, each of which covers more phenomena than the predecessor it displaced, towards the goal of a single theory which shall embrace all the phenomena of nature."

The history of philosophy

Owing to the abstract and difficult character of philosophical inquiries, their study is usually approached historically.   The history of philosophy is perhaps the best approach to the whole subject.   No matter how large the problems are, we may at any rate quite modestly approach them by historical inquiry.   We may read what Plato and Aristotle, what Descartes, Spinoza, Kant, and Royce have written about them.   We may associate for a while with the great men of the past.   The history of philosophy is only the history of reflective thought on subjects peculiar to this study.   The great philosophers have been among the great thinkers of the world, and their thought may for that reason be in the nature of visions.   If one were to enumerate the philosophers from Democritus to William James, one would find that they have been men who have powerfully impressed themselves upon their own and subsequent times.   Plato was a literary genius whose Dialogues have charmed readers of every age.   Aristotle made great discoveries in logic and science and wrote profound works on ethics and politics.   Descartes was the founder of analytical geometry, and the discoverer of important laws in physics and optics.   Leibniz was a mathematical genius giving us the infinitesimal calculus.   Francis Bacon was Lord Chancellor of England.   Locke was an influential statesman in the reign of

William and Mary, and one of the sources of modern educational ideas. Hume was probably the most profound thinker that Scotland has ever produced. Kant anticipated the nebular hypothesis. Herbert Spencer was a contributor to many branches of science, and one of the sources of evolutionary thought. James almost revolutionized the science of psychology. When men of this type speak on the profound questions of philosophy, they command our attention. In the end, however, we shall not be satisfied to rest in their opinions; we shall subject them to critical analysis and complete them by our own reflective thought.

Introduction to philosophy

Finally, there is a still more modest method of studying philosophy than that of its history. Preliminary even to this is the definition of terms and the mere statement and exposition of the various problems, with the mention of the different theories about them. It is to this preliminary task that the present book is devoted. We may define terms and explain theories and perhaps to some extent examine critically the concepts used. Possibly we may find that the divergence among the various systems of philosophy — a divergence much exploited by the critics — is not so great after all. This would seem to be the ideal way to take up the study of philosophy: first, through an "Introduction," to get the terms, problems, and typical theories before us; second, through the study of the history of philosophy, to gain a knowledge of the opinions of its great men; third, to apply to all the problems the method of critical analysis and reflective thought.

In connection with this chapter read:
John Dewey, *How We Think* (D. C. Heath and Company).

Further references:
J. Arthur Thomson, *Introduction to Science* (Home University Library, Henry Holt and Company), chap. III.
Columbia Associates in Philosophy, *Introduction to Reflective Thinking* (Houghton Mifflin Company).
T. P. Nunn, *The Aim and Achievement of Scientific Method* (The Macmillan Company).
A. N. Whitehead, *The Organization of Thought* (Williams and Norgate), chap. VI.

Douglas Clyde Macintosh, *The Problem of Knowledge* (The Macmillan Company), chap. xx, " The Problem of Scientific Method."

Bertrand Russell, *Our Knowledge of the External World* (*Scientific Method in Philosophy*) (The Open Court Publishing Company). See also his more concise chapter "On Scientific Method in Philosophy" in his *Mysticism and Logic* (Longmans, Green and Company), chap vi.

Sir James Jeans, *The New Background of Science.* Revised edition (The Macmillan Company, 1934), chap. ii.

CHAPTER VI

PHILOSOPHICAL THEMES

IN WHAT order shall we pursue our philosophical inquiries and with which ones shall we begin? Will they group themselves into some definite plan, so that we can get a bird's-eye view of them at the beginning? When the little girl looked out the window and asked her mother how there came to be any world, I think she taught us where to begin. What is the world, how did it get started, and how has it grown to its present estate? The ancient Greeks, who first studied philosophy in a systematic way, began also with these questions. They called them *cosmological* inquiries.

Cosmological inquiries

We may, then, adopt this plan and begin with the study of Cosmology, inquiring first about the Cosmos, or the Universe, and about the nature of Space and Time. Then we may ask about the Earth and the first beginnings of Life upon its surface. Then will follow easily the study of the Evolution of life, and this will suggest the problem of its Purposiveness, if it have any. Teleology is the name given to the study of purpose or design in nature.

This first group of problems we may put in tabular form as follows:

$$
\text{I. Cosmological Inquiries} \begin{cases} \text{The Universe, Space, Time} \\ \text{The Origin and Nature of Life} \\ \text{The Philosophy of Evolution} \\ \text{Is there Purpose or Design in Nature?} \end{cases}
$$

Ontological inquiries

Very early in the history of philosophy, thinkers began to ask about the stuff the world is made of. Can everything in the universe be resolved into some elementary form of being, some ultimate reality, such, for instance, as matter, or energy, or mind? This is the ancient problem of Reality, or the problem of Being. The technical term for it is *Ontology*, from two Greeks words meaning the science of being.   It represents the search for the "First Principle."   We love to reduce everything to some final unity or elementary "stuff"; and if we believe that we have found such a final unity, we call our theory of reality a *monistic* view, or just *Monism*, from a Greek word signifying alone or single.   If now we believe that there is only one ultimate reality and that this reality is matter, we may call this view *Materialistic Monism*, or just *Materialism*.   On the other hand, if we come to the conclusion that the one ultimate reality is not matter, but Mind, or Spirit, we may call this view *Spiritualistic Monism*, or *Spiritualism*.   Sometimes it has been called *Idealism*.

But perhaps we shall not succeed in resolving the whole world into one elementary substance and shall find that in the very last analysis there are two ultimate forms of being, such as Mind and Matter.   If so, we may call this theory *Dualism*, from the Latin word for two.

Or, finally, it is just possible that reality cannot be reduced even to two ultimate forms, but that there are more than two, possibly many.   Then our theory of reality will be called *Pluralism*.   These Ontological problems we shall find difficult to solve and the various answers not quite satisfactory; but men have always wondered about ultimate reality and we can at least study the various views of the philosophers.   This second class of inquiries we may also put in tabular form.

$$\text{II. Ontological Inquiries} \begin{cases} \text{Monism} \begin{cases} \text{Materialism} \\ \text{Spiritualism or Idealism} \end{cases} \\ \text{Dualism} \\ \text{Pluralism} \end{cases}$$

The philosophy of mind

Next will come a series of inquiries of the most urgent and intimate kind — inquiries about the Mind.   We should like to know what the Mind is and whether it is different from the Soul, or the Spirit, and we are curious to know about Consciousness and Self and Personality, and how the Mind is related to the Body, and whether the old problem about the Freedom of the Will has been settled, and whether, finally, the Soul is or can be, immortal. All these would seem to be psychological inquiries, since they relate to the Psyche or Soul. But the study of the mind is of such immediate interest that it has become the subject of a special empirical science devoted to the investigation of mental processes and the term Psychology has been appropriated for this science. So in philosophy those larger and more ultimate questions which the science of psychology has not yet approached we may include under the general name, The Philosophy of Mind. In tabular form these inquiries will appear as follows:

III. The Philosophy of Mind
- The Search for the Soul
  - Historical
  - Reconstructive
- The Relation of Soul and Body
- The Freedom of the Will

The theory of knowledge

Even before we reach this point in our philosophizing, we shall encounter so many difficulties and find our doubts so hard to resolve that we shall begin to wonder whether the human mind is capable of real knowledge and whether the best avenues of knowledge are through the sense organs or through some "faculty" of reason. So we shall be forced into the study of the Theory of Knowledge, or Epistemology, as it is called. Perhaps some readers will think that we should have begun with this — and that, no doubt, would be the logical order. But the Theory of Knowledge is a difficult subject, and if presented first might frighten us away from the study of philosophy — and we may assume tentatively that the human mind does have the power of real knowledge, and that such real knowledge is offered us in the special sciences. In general, faith is better than scepticism as a point of departure. Later we may ask about the sources and the validity of human knowledge. This inquiry will cover the following special subjects:

IV. The Theory of Knowledge or Epistemology
- The Sources of Knowledge — discussing the rival theories called Rationalism and Empiricism
- The Validity of Knowledge — as seen from the standpoint of Realism and Idealism
- Pragmatism — its theory of knowledge and of truth

The higher values of life

A quite distinctive field of philosophy is that of *values*. What are values and how do they differ from facts? Are they objective in nature or subjective in the human mind? There are three kinds of values which might be studied in philosophy, namely, religious values, moral values and aesthetic values. Preliminary to the study of religious values, we shall wish to inquire about God and the meaning of God in human experience. If God is good and created the world, how shall we explain the presence of evil in the world? Then the study of moral values will open a subject of the most extreme interest, and especially at the present time, when there is so much confusion about morals. Finally, aesthetic values, or the study of beauty, as exhibited in nature and the fine arts, should engage our attention.

So our fifth division will be as follows:

$$V. \text{ The higher values of life} \begin{cases} \text{Religious values} \\ \text{Moral values} \\ \text{Aesthetic values} \end{cases}$$

The following table, combining these several groups of problems, will show at a glance the road we have to travel:

I. Cosmological Inquiries	The Universe, Space, Time The Origin and Nature of Life The Philosophy of Evolution Is there Purpose or Design in Nature?
II. Ontological Inquiries	Monism { Materialism Spiritualism or Idealism Dualism Pluralism
III. The Philosophy of Mind	The Search for the { Historical Soul { Reconstructive The Relation of Soul and Body The Freedom of the Will
IV. The Theory of Knowledge or Epistemology	The Sources of Knowledge — discussing the rival theories called Rationalism and Empiricism The Validity of Knowledge — as seen from the standpoint of Realism and Idealism Pragmatism — its theory of knowledge and of truth
V. The Higher Values of Life	Religious Values Moral Values Aesthetic Values

PART II

THE UNIVERSE, ORGANIC LIFE, EVOLUTION

CHAPTER VII
THE UNIVERSE

By the Universe is meant the totality of Space and all it contains. More accurately it may be defined as the totality of Space, Time, and Matter, or again as the Space-Time-Manifold.

In very recent years our knowledge of the physical Universe has been vastly extended through the co-operative achievements of the sciences of astronomy, mathematical physics, and astrophysics, assisted by the arts of photography and spectroscopy, and by our marvelously perfected modern telescopes. The great telescope on Mount Wilson in California with its 100-inch reflector is soon to be supplemented, as we hope, by the new super-telescope with its 200-inch reflector. The new telescope will enlarge the observable region of space about one thousand times, and the observable distance of objects about ten times beyond the power of our present instruments; and our largest telescopes now enable us to see photographically objects so distant that light traveling 186,000 miles a second requires 500,000,000 years to reach us.

This rapidly accumulating knowledge of the physical Universe ought to satisfy the demands even of the wondering student of philosophy. Many of the things about which we have wondered are even now in the very process of being explained. Though the answers are sometimes hesitating and tentative, and though no finality is claimed for them, still our progress toward the understanding of the physical world both in its macroscopic and microscopic aspects is so rapid as to be almost bewildering. Some of the riddles of the Universe are being answered.

In the present chapter we shall refer to certain of the answers to the questions which most perplex us about the Universe as a whole. What most impresses us when under the guidance of astronomy we begin to think about the Universe in this way is its incredible vastness; and yet at the same time we are told that it is possibly finite — not infinite. We have usually thought of it as infinite; and perhaps we shall recall an ancient argument designed to prove that the Universe is infinite in extent. It was said that if it is finite and we could go to its outer rim and hurl a javelin outward, it must either go on or be thrown back by some obstacle. In either case there must be something beyond the outer margin, however far we assume that to be.

But the mathematician of today is not impressed by this reasoning. The javelin may go on — but it will *go on around*. The Universe may be finite — but unbounded. A ray of light sent out from our sun may go on to infinity, but will return sometime to a point near its place of starting. The earth, for instance, is a finite sphere; but if a body should start from a point on the equator and travel around in a spiral, it could go on forever around the sphere. If, furthermore, it moves in a spiral with infinitesimal change of latitude, it could go on forever without returning to its point of departure. Verification of the theory that the Universe is finite though unbounded belongs to the future. Einstein has believed that it follows from the theory of relativity that space is finite, turning back upon itself. Its curvature, furthermore, is said to depend upon the matter which it contains — and the more matter there is, the greater the curvature. In the vicinity of great masses of matter, like the sun or some other star, the curvature would be greatest.

But if the Universe is finite, surely we shall ultimately know something of its actual size. Estimates, of course, have been made. One of the largest is that proposed by Hubble of the Mount Wilson Observatory, who thinks it may have a diameter of six thousand million light-years. This means that a ray of light traveling at the rate of 186,000 miles a second would require nearly twenty billion years to go around the Universe. Thus it would appear that if any one has felt at all cramped at the thought of living in a finite universe, he need worry no longer. The finite Universe is "infinitely" larger than the infinite Universe of our earlier imagination.

Other Universes than our own

But what is contained within this unthinkable vastness of space? In the study of the stars, it may be well to begin with our own little Earth. But evidently in the Universe such terms as little and big are just relative. Our Earth may be little but it is about eight thousand miles in diameter, having a solid core composed, perhaps, largely of iron and nickel with a thick outer crust of basaltic rock and a thin outermost crust of land and water swarming with living things. If we have ever felt any childlike wonder why the Earth does not fall into the sun by the enormous "pull" of gravity, we can now see that such a mass of solid iron has considerable momentum as it rushes about our central luminary at the rate of about one thousand miles a minute

The Earth is one of nine planets revolving around the sun, constituting with the asteroids, comets and satellites our Solar System — and the Solar System is a little colony in an immense group of stars, which we may call Our Universe, but which astronomers call the Galaxy, or the Galactic System. This Universe has perhaps a hundred thousand million stars. They are suns like our own, although many are vastly larger — and are in various stages of development. Presumably they should have planets revolving around them like our own. It is generally believed, however, that few if any of them have. Much is known about the laws of evolution of the star-suns; and their normal life history does not presuppose or even admit of planetary systems.

The stars of our Galaxy are not arranged in a sphere, but are in the form of a gigantic disk, likened sometimes to a revolving cartwheel, whose outer rim is the Milky Way — the latter composed of stars too distant to be resolved by the eye. Its longer diameter is now thought to be about 100,000 light-years and its shorter diameter 20,000 light-years, remembering that a light-year is about six million million miles. Our Solar System is nearly two thirds the way out from the center, and is moving in the direction of the star Vega.

Although our Solar System is so large that a rocket starting from its center and traveling at the rate of two miles a minute would require 3650 years to reach our outer planet, Pluto, nevertheless the chances of a collision with other stars are negligible, so vast are the stellar distances. All the stars are in incessant motion, yet because of their distances from us they appear to us as "fixed stars." Hence the constellations remain the same to our view as they were to the ancients who named them. Not only are the stars within the

Galaxy all in motion, but the Galaxy itself is moving through space at an estimated rate of two hundred miles a second.

Vast as our Galaxy is, the inquiring mind moves still farther out and asks again what there is beyond. Only a few years ago no answer could be given to this except the answer of empty and infinite space. But now we know that space out there is not empty — and perhaps not infinite. There are other galaxies than ours, resembling our own in form and substance but many of them enormously larger. We call them spiral nebulae or island universes. There are 100 million of them within the sphere of our telescopes and it has been estimated that there are 500 million million in the whole Universe. The distances between these island universes are of the order of a million light-years; and they are in all stages of development, from star dust to distinct and individual suns.

The emptiness of space can be faintly realized when we are told that if the matter in all the stars in all the nebulae lying within the observable portion of space were equally distributed in this space, the density of the material could be "visualized as corresponding to a grain of sand in each volume of space equal to the volume of the Earth." [1]

Cosmic evolution

Another great problem about which we wonder when we think about the Universe as a whole is its past and future. Was it created or has it existed forever? If created, how and when? Will it continue to evolve or change forever, will it sometime be destroyed, or will it sink into a state of absolute stability and death? Here science has made less progress than in studying the depths of space and the movements and relations of the stars. We have no instruments for peering into the past and future of the world, as we have for piercing the depths of space. And yet we do know something of the past and the probable future of the earth and the sun and the stars — and our knowledge in this field is rapidly increasing.

Concerning our own solar system we have recently gained a new insight into its origin and history — even into its probable destiny. As regards its origin, the old *nebular hypothesis* gave way to the so-

[1] Dr. Edwin Hubble in the *Scientific Monthly*, September, 1934, p. 197.

called *planetesimal theory*, and the latter has recently been greatly modified. What happened we may picture somewhat as follows: A long time ago — let us say 5000 million years — our sun was pursuing its silent and solitary way through space. Incidentally it is interesting to note that the sun has aged but little in the last 5000 million years and will continue to radiate light and heat as it is now doing into a future too remote to estimate in years. Sir James Jeans has estimated the age of our sun at a round eight million million years, an estimate very problematical.

Except for its own slow aging, it is rare indeed that anything ever happens to a moving star; but at the time mentioned, let us say five billion years ago, something did happen to our sun, something which had never happened to it before, and will probably never happen again. Another star came near it; not very near — but near enough to affect it. The gravitational pull of the passing star set up a monstrous tidal action in the gaseous substance of the sun, until finally filaments shot out from it toward and away from the other star, extending out farther than the distance of our present outer planet, which is 3700 million miles from the sun. As the visiting star departed, these filaments began to condense into great masses, which ultimately became our present planets, revolving endlessly around the sun. The planets were smaller at first, gradually increasing in mass as they gathered in the surrounding debris from the original outpouring of the sun's substance. This they are still doing, as in the case of the meteorites which are drawn to the earth's surface.

This theory, called the Tidal Theory, was first developed by Sir James Jeans. Concerning this, he says in the last edition of *The Universe Around Us* (1934) that he believes a large proportion of astronomers now accept it " as giving the *most probable* origin of the solar system; it can of course make no claim to finality or certainty."

We may thus estimate the age of the earth as around 5000 million years and its probable future will be far greater in length. We need not, therefore, any longer worry about a freezing planet destroying all living things. There is little doubt but that the earth will be habitable for very many millions of years. For the next million years it has been predicted that the climate will be favorable for life and man.

"Fair and mild" is the weather forecast for the next few thousand years. Civilizations may fall or rise, but if man is destroyed it will be through his own folly or ignorance — not by the failure of the beneficence of Nature.

Is the Universe running down?

For many years there has been a theory current among mathematical physicists that the Universe is running down. This arises in connection with a famous law called the second law of thermodynamics. According to this law there is in any material system a continual loss of available energy due to the fact that in all transformations of energy some of it becomes unavailable for doing further work by passing into the form of diffused heat and is radiated into space. We may transform the latent energy of our forests, coal-beds and deposits of oil into kinetic energy to drive our cars or carry our messages — but some of it is always lost in every energy transformation. The Universe must, therefore, be running down and tending to equilibrium. Even if untold stores of energy are locked up in the atoms and might possibly be utilized, nevertheless with fateful certainty they will be used up and the world must sometime come to a standstill. But curiously enough since we are not allowed to think of a beginning in time, it must follow that in infinite time the Universe must long ago have run down and become dead and motionless. It seems, however, to be teeming with life and energy — to be very much "a going concern." Presumably, therefore, there must be some creative energy at work; perhaps even a continuous creative process.

Mr. John Langdon-Davies in an article entitled "Was There a Creation?" in the *Forum* for February, 1934, discusses a naturalistic explanation of the " Creation," based on the theory of the expanding universe. The distant nebulae and island universes seem to be rushing away from us at incredible speeds, leading to the belief in some gigantic initial explosion which signaled the beginning of the creation. But the theory of an expanding universe is itself based on the shifting of the dark lines of the spectrum toward the red end when viewing those distant stars, a phenomenon indicating retreating sources of light. Since many believe that this phenomenon may be explained in other ways, it is too soon to draw these inferences regarding the explosion theory of the creation.

Jeans in his book, *The Universe Around Us*, thinks that we must assume the creation of the material Universe at a time not infinitely remote — say 200 million million years. Several naturalistic explanations of this creation have been proposed; or, if we choose, we may get a concrete picture of it if we wish to think of "the finger of God agitating the ether." Such crude pictures, however, may be avoided if we cease to regard space, time, and matter as if they exist separately. When we think of them as merely aspects of one fundamental reality, the whole picture changes, and we come, Sir James says, "very near to those philosophical systems which regard the Universe as a thought in the mind of its Creator, thereby reducing all discussion of material creation to futility." But, he concludes, the decoding of the messages of astronomy is at best filled with uncertainties.[1]

But suppose we are not able to think of space, time, and matter in this way, but are constrained to believe that the Universe will finally come to an end, would such a conclusion warrant any sense of limitation or depression? I think we may safely dismiss any trouble of this kind by reflecting on the probable age of the Universe when finally its race is run. In order to get some faintest notion of the stupendous time that the stars will endure, consider that our own sun has already existed for something like eight million million years and that its diameter is only 865,000 miles. There is a star in the lesser Magellanic cloud, seen in our southern hemisphere, which, when viewed through a telescope, shines with a glorious and effulgent brightness, although it is at such a distance that our own sun at the same distance could not be seen even with the largest telescope. It is estimated to be 1000 million miles in diameter. If we remember that the slow aging of a star is proportional to its size, we may understand how difficult it would be to get any idea of the probable duration of this super giant sun in our southern skies. It becomes apparent that a universe existing for a finite time has no actual meaning to us different from one existing for an infinite time. Our world will continue in being "infinitely" longer than the infinite time of our imagination. We must not forget, however, that all this argument relating to the running-down of the Universe applies only to the conception of the Universe as finite. If it is infinite, it would have an infinite amount of energy and could run down only in infinite time.

Other habitable worlds than ours

One of the things about which we wonder when, in a philosophic mood, we study the Universe as a whole is this: Are there other planets or stars on which there is life — possibly even higher forms of life, with human beings like ourselves who write poetry and study science and philosophy and wonder about the World? We noticed above that the laws of star development leave little ground for believing that of all the countless millions of suns in all the universes there are many which could have planets revolving around them, on whose cooling surfaces life could exist warmed by the rays of their central luminary. Our own solar system, we discovered, was the outcome of a kind of cosmic accident when two stars came near each other; and space is so large and the stars by comparison so small that this could rarely happen in the case of other stars — perhaps might never happen elsewhere. Illustrations showing the relative smallness of the stars compared with the immensities of Space seem to show that collisions or even near approaches are improbable.

But just how valid is this argument? It would appear that Time is as long as Space is empty; and the number of the stars as impressive as the emptiness of Space. What has happened once may happen again — or may have happened in the "infinite" past — and there seems to be plenty of time for anything to happen. Planetary systems like our own in the past, present or future certainly are not out of the question.

But if there are other planetary systems than our own, is it probable that they offer conditions which make life possible? Or if the cosmic conditions are favorable, are the internal evolutionary conditions favorable for the beginning of life? Of our own nine planets, only three, the Earth, Mars, and Venus, seem to offer any promise of life, past, present or future. Venus is shrouded in perpetual clouds, so that we cannot know what these conceal, but the most powerful spectroscopes reveal the presence of no oxygen in its atmosphere. Mars reveals little free oxygen. It is doubtful if life as we know it exists on either. The Earth was the fortunate one among the planets. Its size, distance from the sun, period of revolution, the length of the year, and the inclination of its axis were all most propitious. Its surface conditions also were most favorable. There was just the right proportion of carbon, oxygen and hydrogen. The peculiar thermic qualities of water, the ample rainfall, the nearly constant temperature of the oceans and the favorable proportion of water and land — all favored the appearance and evolution of life. If the first simple germs of living matter were due to those chance configurations of atoms and molecules which form its basis, the conditions for such an event were in the highest degree propitious. When and where could all this take place at other times and other places?

Thus we are confronted with the startling possibility that nowhere in the Universe except in our own solar system are there any forms of life, and that nowhere else except upon the Earth has there been an evolution of life culminating in the creation of human beings who can contemplate the beauty and the vastness of the starry heavens and wonder about their origin and destiny. Thus, the Earth, far from being "an insignificant planet of a mediocre star," or an "inglorious speck" in the vast ocean of Space, has achieved the only truly glorious destiny of all the stars.

We laugh at the ignorance and arrogance of the philosophers of the Middle Ages, who, following Aristotle, taught the geocentric theory of the Universe — and believed that the sun and moon and all the stars existed only for the edification of man; but now it would almost seem that present-day science is not altogether inconsistent with this. And yet, as it is hardly necessary to add, any such assumption carries with it again both the danger of ignorance and the suspicion of arrogance. The argument drawn from the almost miraculous convergence of conditions favorable to life on the surface of the Earth again overreaches itself. For as Henderson [1] pointed out some years

[1] Lawrence T. Henderson, *The Fitness of the Environment* (The Macmillan Company).

ago, there are too many adaptations in the picture to make it the work of chance, and if it were some kind of plan, then, the plan might have become effective at many other times and in many other places.

In connection with this chapter read:

Sir James Jeans, *The Mysterious Universe.* Revised Edition (The Macmillan Company, 1932).

Sir Arthur Eddington, *The Nature of the Physical World* (The Macmillan Company, 1928), chap. VIII.

Further references:

W. F. G. Swann, *The Architecture of the Universe* (The Macmillan Company, 1934).

Harlow Shapley, *Flights from Chaos*, chaps. XII, XIII.

Sir Arthur Eddington, *The Nature of the Physical World* (The Macmillan Company, 1928).

J. A. Thomson, *The Outline of Science* (G. P. Putnam's Sons, 1922), I.

Sir James Jeans, *The Universe Around Us.* Revised Edition (The Macmillan Company, 1931); *The Stars in their Courses* (The Macmillan Company, 1931); *The New Background of Science* (The Macmillan Company, 1933).

Lewis Guy Rohrbaugh, *A Natural Approach to Philosophy* (Noble and Noble, 1934).

CHAPTER VIII
SPACE, TIME, AND RELATIVITY

Space

SOMETHING of the extent of Space and the duration of Time we have learned; but it seems as if we had missed the essential point, as far as philosophy is concerned. What *is* Space and what *is* Time? Have they any real objective existence independent of the thinking mind? What was there between the stars before ever there was a mind of man — or was there anything at all? It would seem at any rate that the stars must have had distance, direction, and position in their relation to one another. Are these relations objective and real or are they products of the mind of man?

Commonly we think of Space as a great void, in which, however, bodies may exist and through which they move. We think of it as extending in all directions and as having no limits, hence infinite. The heavenly bodies move through it, and if they moved in a straight line could go on forever. Science sometimes speaks of it as filled with the ether. It seems to exist in three dimensions, right and left, up and down, forward and backward. It seems to be infinitely divisible, since any portion of it could be divided into two portions, and so on forever. Furthermore, Space, as we think, is not dependent upon the bodies in it and would continue to exist if all such bodies were destroyed, like a kind of immense receptacle or, shall we say, a great emptiness. Think of an empty box with six sides; then let the sides expand, move away into the distance and disappear. This is Space.

But when we begin to reflect upon the Space idea, all this seems less certain. We find that empirical Space — that is, the Space of our actual experience — is something quite different. To try to understand just what Space is, let us start with the simple facts of sensory experience. If I take a pair of compasses and touch the back of your hand, you get a perception of two steel points. But you get more than this: you get the perception of a certain relation between them, a relation which you call distance or position. There is evidently a unique kind of *relationship* between the two perceived points, and this relationship of distance or position is perceived just as much as the points themselves are perceived. If a silver dollar is placed upon the back of the hand, it is not perceived merely as something heavy and cold, it is perceived as something *spread out*, or *extended*. Likewise the sense of sight gives us, besides color and light, the spread-out or extended quality of objects, their *voluminousness*. From our various senses, therefore, we get immediate perception of certain relations between objects, which we call *spatial relations*, and these seem to be of three classes, which we describe as right and left, up and down, forward and backward. Thus perceptual Space is said to have three dimensions.

It would be possible, of course, to say that the spread-outness of objects, their extensity, is not really any external reality at all, but a peculiarity of the mind, a special form of our sensibility. This view was held by the great philosopher, Kant, and in this opinion he has been followed by many other thinkers. Nevertheless, it is probably an incorrect view, and we may believe that not only are objects of experience real, but that Space itself is objectively real. But the reality of Space, when reduced to the final analysis, is found in a certain kind of relationship between bodies, namely, the relations of position, distance, and direction. The student of philosophy, therefore, who is confused by the strangeness of Space and the difficulty of understanding it, may think at first only of position, distance, and direction, and may consider Space as merely the name for all such relations as these; but he may think of these relations as real and, therefore, of Space as real.

Conceptual space

Having thus considered Space as meaning the real objective position, distance, and direction of objects, we may now go a step further and distinguish another slightly different meaning of the word, as it is used in both philosophy and mathematics. Sometimes this is called conceptual Space, as distinguished from perceptual or sensational Space, as described above. We have been speaking of the Space which we perceive, but now the Space that we *think about* is a little different. The Space that we think about, conceptual Space, is not simply the perceived relations between objects; it is a kind of plan of all possible relations of this kind. We perceive the eight corners of the room in which we are working, and at the same time we perceive the relations among these eight corners — and this is actual perceived Space. But now in imagination we think of other rooms above this, one upon another, and so we picture a world of ideal Space extending indefinitely in every direction. This is conceptual Space, and it seems to us like a void or receptacle; and it seems infinite in extent, which means nothing more than that we cannot think of any limit to these possible spatial relations. Conceptual Space thus appears to be a construction of the mind, and to lack that kind of reality which is possessed by the Space of our perception.

Mathematical space

Now, it is this conceptual Space which is the Space of mathematics, but mathematicians ascribe to it certain qualities which even the conceptual Space of the plain man certainly does not have. Euclidean Space, for instance, is infinite, homogeneous, continuous, isotropic, and is in three dimensions, a conception resulting from the complete abstraction from the qualities of sensuous perception except in extension in three dimensions. Mathematics thus deals with ideal Space, which, of course, is based upon real or perceptual Space, but goes far beyond it. Mathematical Space is thus a construct, like the points, lines, and surfaces constituting the basis of the science of geometry. This does not mean that points, lines, and surfaces are fictions, or even purely mental things, or mental creations. They are real in their own way, but not as sensible particulars. When we say, therefore, as is now customary, that mathematics is not an existential science, but rests upon certain assumptions such as axioms and definitions, this statement is liable to be misinterpreted. The fact that geometry gives us results which fit the physical world in which we live reveals a closer connection with "reality" than might be inferred from its purely logical character.

Time

Now, there is another kind of relation existing in our experience than the relation of extension, which as we have seen gives us the experience of right and left, up and down, far and near. We have also the experience of *before* and *after*, or *succession*. This we call *Time*. Suppose, again, that the two steel points of the compasses be placed upon your hand. You have, in addition to the touch and temperature sensations, the experience of extension. Suppose, now, that the same points be presently laid again upon precisely the same parts of the hand; you have now an additional experience of *after* or *later*. That peculiar kind of relation which we call *before* and *after*, or the relation of *succession*, is thus also a unique kind of experience, and to this we give the name *Time*. It is the relation, not of spatial coexistence, but of temporal succession, and has, not three dimensions like Space, but only one.

Time seems to flow on like a stream, and in this stream we distinguish three parts, which we call the *present*, the *past*, and the *future*, the present being real in experience, the past constructed in memory, and the future anticipated in imagination. The present, however, as James has shown, is not a "knife-edge," or instant; it actually has a certain duration. In this moment of duration there is, indeed, a before and after; but, for the most part, our before and after, our yesterday and tomorrow, are ideal constructions like conceptual Space. Conceptual Time, again, is a little different from perceptual Time. It is the abstract Time we think about. In this ideal Time the present is a knife-edge, having no duration, or zero duration — and the past and future stretch away to infinity.

Space-Time

Now, I fear that some of us will not be satisfied with this "empirical" description of Space and Time. The notion of an *absolute* Space, infinite in all directions, in which things exist and move, and the motion of an *absolute* Time which will go on forever and had no beginning, seems more natural and comforting. Indeed, Newton himself believed in such an absolute Space and Time, and only recently have they been questioned. It is probably what the words Space and Time mean to most of us, and certainly we have no right to say dogmatically that nothing corresponding to this meaning exists.

In fact, during the early years of this century there was a school of investigators trying to find out what the reality is which in some way corresponds to conceptual Space and Time. Einstein in Germany, Eddington, S. Alexander, and C. D. Broad in England, and many other collaborators began peering into this obscure region of reality. And the interesting thing about these studies is that they are no longer pursued as psychological problems, but as problems in physics and mathematics. We are in search of the actual objective entity, which, so to speak, is the mother of Space and Time.

The first result of these profound and mathematically rather intricate researches has been to show that Space and Time are themselves more closely related to each other than we supposed. Or perhaps Space, Time, and Matter, all three, may have a common matrix. Even starting with our own experience, what we seem to have is not Space and Time as separate elements in experience, but rather four sets of relations, namely, up and down, right and left, forward and backward, and before and after. All events are space-events and all points in Space are point-events. It has been suggested, therefore, that the reality which we seek is neither Space nor Time but Space-Time; and that which really exists is not Space with three dimensions and Time with one, but Space-Time with four dimensions.

Now four-dimensional being is hard for us to understand, but mathematically it presents no serious difficulty. Take a lead pencil and lay it on a table. If we consider it as representing a line, it has one dimension, which we call near and far. Now, take a second pencil and lay it on the table at right angles to the first. We have now two dimensions, near and far, and right and left, determining a surface. Now, take a third pencil and place it at right angles to the other two. It will stand upright on the table. We have now three dimensions, determining a solid. Now, take a fourth pencil and try to place it at right angles to all the others. This we shall find impossible to do; nor can we think of such a figure. This is because the physical world in which we live, and to which our bodies belong, is the three-dimensional world of Space. But it does not follow from the fact that we cannot picture a four-dimensional reality, or build it up with pencils, that such a reality may not exist.

Not only do mathematicians feel quite at home dealing with the fourth dimension, but even we ourselves find three dimensions insufficient as soon as we cease speaking of points in Space and begin speaking of *events* in Space. Such events require four dimensions to determine them. Suppose it is a case of an accident which happened in New York City. If I say it happened on Broadway (one dimension), you will ask where on Broadway. When I say that it happened at the corner of Broadway and Ninety-Sixth Street (two dimensions), you will ask whether it happened on the surface streets or in the Subway. When I say that it happened in the Subway at that intersection (three dimensions), you will ask *when* it happened. If I reply that it happened in the Subway at that intersection on Tuesday noon (four dimensions), then the event is fully determined.[1]

The theory that Time is the fourth dimension of Space, or more strictly that the world in which we live is a four-dimensional space-time continuum, was first proposed by Minkowski, but more fully elaborated by Einstein.

> The non-mathematician is seized by a mysterious shuddering when he hears of "four-dimensional" things, by a feeling not unlike that awakened by thoughts of the occult. And yet there is no more commonplace statement than that the world in which we live is a four-dimensional space-time continuum.[2]

Instead, therefore, of thinking of an "absolute" Newtonian Space of three dimensions, and an independent Time of one dimension, it is possible to think of an original "space-time manifold" of four dimensions, in which Time is the fourth dimension. At this point, however, Einstein's General Theory of Relativity passes beyond the mere solution of the problem of Space and Time and approaches a metaphysical theory of reality; for it supposes that the space-time continuum is, so to speak, the ultimate physical reality of the Universe. If this be true, it immediately becomes of great interest to the student of philosophy; for it appears that it can be shown mathematically that such a four-dimensional manifold under the relativity theory is not a homogeneous affair, but tends to inequalities, or "singularities," and, so it is said, *such singularities are what we call matter.* Matter, as it were, is a kind of kink in the time-space manifold, and where these kinks occur, Space is warped or distorted.

---

[1] Compare Edwin E. Slosson, *Easy Lessons in Einstein*, p. 31.

[2] Albert Einstein, *Relativity*. translated by Robert W. Lawson (Henry Holt and Company), p. 65.

This makes it possible for Einstein to offer a wholly new theory of *Gravitation*, throwing new and needed light on this obscure subject. We remember that Newton formulated the *law* of Gravitation, telling us *how* all material bodies tend to move toward one another, the stone to the earth, and the earth to the sun; but he did not tell us *why* they behave in this way. We have usually thought of Gravitation as a kind of *force* "pulling" bodies together. Newton himself thought of it as a "force" "drawing" material bodies out of the straight line in which they would naturally be moving, and toward other material bodies, the forces being proportional to the inverse square of the distance between the bodies. But no one knows about any such force, nor how it could "pull" things together; hence it is of great interest to learn from Einstein and Eddington that it may be possible to explain Gravitation in a simpler way by the supposition that it is due to the nature of Space itself; that Space is distorted or puckered or curved in the region of masses of matter, and that the behavior of any particle when it enters this gravitational field is due, not to any mysterious "force," but to the puckered character of Space in such a field, which determines the path of the particle.

A recent writer in the *New York Times* puts this in strong language as follows:

The Newtonian universe, with its foundations, Aristotelian methods of thought and Euclidean space, has been completely shattered and the fragments swept into the limbo of obscurity, along with the geocentric system and the flat earth of the Zetetics. In its place we have a relativistic cosmos, a four-dimensional space-time manifold, built of lines of force and a network of intervals, with events instead of objects and wave-packets of energy instead of points. Most of our basic ideas, such as identity, causality and simultaneity, are illusions due to ignorance and faulty mental processes; all knowledge is (in the ultimate) verbal, and its only possible content is structure. Our language, having descended to us from early days of humanity, carries primitive and animalistic implications, and is of a structure not corresponding to the structure of the human nervous system or to that of the universe, and therefore not only prevents us from accepting and assimilating the new methods and discoveries in mathematics, but is positively injurious and increasingly destructive to our mental health and our social progress.[1]

___

[1] George Moreby Acklom reviewing Alfred Korzybski's book, *Science and Sanity* in the *New York Times Book Review*, February 11, 1934.

All this, as the author adds, sounds rather terrible. But it means that we must revise our language to fit the new conceptions of nature and we "must introduce a new non-elementalistic terminology." It presents to us apparently the hopeful prospect of looking forward to a larger universe in which the human spirit will find itself less confined than in the mechanistic world of the nineteenth century.

The ether

For a long time it was supposed that there is a mysterious something called the Ether which fills Space — if we may still use this expression. It had long been known that light travels at a definite rate, about 186,000 miles a second. Since it did not seem possible that light is composed of particles actually traveling at that rate, it was concluded that light is a form of wave motion.

With the undulatory theory of light it was necessary to have some medium for the transmission of the waves — something to undulate. It was assumed, therefore, that the whole Universe is filled with a stationary medium called *Ether*, and that light waves are waves in this Ether. To serve its purpose, such a medium must have certain qualities. It must be frictionless, solid, immovable and admitting of strains and stresses. Some of these qualities, however, involved contradictions. Such a medium could hardly exist; and yet some such medium there must be.

When the electromagnetic theory of light was proposed by Maxwell, a whole series of phenomena was unified. It was a grand discovery to learn that light waves and heat waves and the long wireless waves and the short X-rays were all alike except in length, having the same rate of propagation and being subject to the same laws. But the Ether as a medium for all these waves was more indispensable than ever, and yet the Ether itself was a bundle of contradictions. It was nothing but the substantive of the verb "to undulate"; and finally it was said to have no qualities at all except extension in three dimensions, being thus equivalent to space.

Some years ago Michelson and Morley carried out a celebrated experiment to determine whether the Earth is moving through a stationary medium, such as Ether. Since the Earth is moving

nearly twenty miles a second in its path around the Sun, if there is a
stationary Ether through which it is ploughing, this would cause an
ether wind, or ether drift, on the surface of the Earth. Since now,
by hypothesis, light is caused by the wave motion of the Ether, it is
evident that it would take longer to send a ray of light a given distance forward against this ether wind than it would to send it backward with it, just as it would take longer to send your voice against
the wind than backward with it; and it would take longer to send a
ray of light forward and back a given distance than it would to send
it out at right angles to the line of flight the same distance and back.[1]
The latter could be tested by means of a delicate instrument devised
by Michelson and Morley, but the results were wholly negative.
Light was found to travel in all directions at the same rate. At first
sight these strange results would seem to disprove the existence of
the Ether, but presently it was learned from the principle of relativity that even if there were an Ether, it would be impossible to detect
our motion through it. This is because of a principle first enunciated
by Fitzgerald and Lorenz to the effect that bodies set in motion are
slightly shortened in the direction of their motion. Later experiments, however, not involving this principle have similarly given
negative results. There seems to be no evidence that the Earth is
moving through a stationary Ether or any Ether at all.

The theory of an Ether, therefore, has been largely dropped from
the language of science. The chief function of the Ether was to
serve as a fixed frame of reference. But Einstein has shown that all
motion is relative, and that it is meaningless to say that any one
thing is fixed, while other things move in it or past it. If you are
sitting in a railway car looking at the train on the next track, it is not
easy to say which train is moving. Both may be moving in opposite
directions, or in the same direction at different rates, or either one
may be still and the other moving. You glance down to the ground
to get a fixed standard of reference. But suppose there is no third
object for comparison — only two objects having apparent movement in respect to each other. It is meaningless to say that one is

[1] A swimmer knows that it is easier to swim across a stream of a given width having a current
of a given velocity and back to his starting-point than to swim the same distance upstream and
back to the point of starting, even though he has never tried to show the reason for this mathematically. See Eddington, *Space, Time, and Gravitation*, chap. I.

still, the other moving. If we accepted the theory of the Ether, we would have to say that the Earth is at rest in it.

We cannot speak of the newer ontologies as being a revolt against the mechanical philosophy of the nineteenth century and the early years of the present century.   It is not a revolt, but a new direction forced upon us by the advances in science. Whether we are studying the microscopic or the macroscopic world, whether we follow the researches of the biologist or the chemist, whether we study the atom and the subatomic structure, we find a tendency away from the older mechanistic views.

The new field into which we are led is often strange and puzzling. It is perplexing at first to hear that the old familiar Newtonian Universe with its infinite space and everlasting time has been called in question; strange to learn that time, space, and motion are only relative; that such ancient and well-established principles as identity, simultaneity, and causality could be doubted; that the Heisenberg principle of indeterminacy has threatened the old determinism; that the flow of energy and the flood of light are not continuous but proceed by little jumps; that the ultimate units of matter may not be after all our new-found friends, the negative electron and the positive proton, but also neutrons and positrons; and finally that the Universe is not eternal but may be undergoing cyclic changes.

It may be confusing — but some of it is rather comforting. It may after all turn out that Nature is not a monstrous machine grinding away forever under the rule of necessity without end or purpose — and that there is still something to be said for freedom. And the Universe itself seems a bit more tidy and livable, if it is finite — even if it is so frightfully large; and it was always tiresome to try to think of Time going on forever.

Some will find comfort also in the final suggestion of Sir James Jeans, when he says that in the last analysis the Universe is a universe of thought — and its creation an act of thought.   In similar vein, Eddington, after reducing our knowledge of the material world to pointer-readings, says "it is not foreign to our view that the world-stuff behind the pointer-readings is of nature continuous with the mind." [1]

[1] Sir James Jeans, *The Mysterious Universe*, p. 154.   Sir Arthur Eddington, *The Nature of the Physical World*, p. 331.

In connection with this chapter read:

Sir James Jeans, *The New Background of Science.* Revised Edition (The Macmillan Company, 1934), chap. III.

Further references:

A. S. Eddington, *The Nature of the Physical World* (The Macmillan Company, 1929).

Victor F. Lenzen, *The Nature of Physical Theory* (John Wylie and Sons, 1931).

Robert A. Millikan, *Time, Matter and Value* (The University of North Carolina Press, 1932).

Sir James Jeans, *Through Space and Time* (The Macmillan Company, 1934).

W. F. G. Swann, *The Architecture of the Universe* (The Macmillan Company, 1934), chaps. IX, X.

Roy Wood Sellars, *The Philosophy of Physical Realism* (The Macmillan Company, 1932), chap. XIII.

C. D. Broad, *Scientific Thought* (Kegan Paul, Trench, Trübner and Company), chaps. III, IV.

James MacKaye, *The Dynamic Universe* (Charles Scribner's Sons).

CHAPTER IX

ORGANIC LIFE — ITS NATURE AND ORIGIN

IN THE last chapter we found that the Universe, as known to us, consists of Space, Time, and Matter. It was hinted, to be sure, that these are probably not the absolute ultimate realities; for they seemed rather to be just those aspects of reality which we can apprehend. Beyond them there was believed to be a kind of mystical universe of mathematical realities — with perhaps a hypothetical mind beyond it all.

If, however, as we shall learn in a later chapter, we approach the quest from another point of departure, namely, the analysis of the physical world around us, we find that we are led ultimately to some form of electric or radiant energy. Are we then to conclude that such ultimate concepts as electricity, energy, or space-time are to stand for us as the final *realities* of the world?

This would be an easy inference — and a very hasty one. When we close our books of science and turn to our own experience we discover another and wholly different universe. It is a world of living things — a veritable wonderland of Life and Mind; a creative world of new forms, new species, new inventions; a world of growth and development, of conscious self-acting beings capable of thought and feeling, of memories of the past and anticipations of the future, of emotions and aspirations; a social world of co-operating individuals; a world of reflective thinking, of science, art, philosophy, and literature; a world of ends, purposes, and values. Instantly we ask, Is this world of our experience, this world of living things, less real than that of space and time and quivering energy?

Evidently then if we are to be philosophers or even beginning students of philosophy we must direct our inquiry now to the Universe of Life. What is Life?

The origin of life

The origin of life on the Earth's surface has become a very interesting and serious question since the discovery that all living germs come from other living germs.   The Roman poet, Lucretius, in his book, *De Rerum Natura*, solved the difficulty very easily, as did others of the ancients, by the theory of spontaneous generation. Clods of earth, he said, when warm and wet, soon bring forth living forms.   In modern times, also, it was at first thought that spontaneous generation could be demonstrated in a test tube.   If you take a little water from a pond and expose it to light and warmth, it will soon swarm with living things.   If, now, you first sterilize it by the application of heat and again expose it to light and warmth, it will still after some time show evidences of life.   If, however, you repeat the experiment, taking the precaution to close your test tube with a little cotton wool, so as to exclude the living germs which may be floating in the air, no life can be made to appear.   So the controversy of the nineteenth century over spontaneous generation ended; and under the leadership of Pasteur a new and fruitful science was born, the science of bacteriology, with its wonderful contributions to our knowledge of germ diseases and to the arts of sanitation, aseptic surgery, and even agriculture.

Incidentally, we see again how results of great practical benefit flow from purely theoretical investigations.   These investigators were not working in the interests of applied science, searching for new knowledge of disease and its cure.   They were scientists, seeking knowledge for its own sake.

But now it is in the same mood of wonder and desire to know that we ask, Where, then, did the first living germs come from on our planet?   Since there was a time when conditions were such on the Earth that no life was possible, while now its whole surface swarms with living beings, we wonder how the first living germ arose. *Omne vivum ex ovo*, says the biologist — all life comes from an egg. Given, perhaps, one germ cell, through evolution we can people the Earth.   But whence came the first one?

As regards the first appearance of living things upon the Earth, there are three traditional views: (1) The first germs of life may have come to the Earth from some other planet, traveling through space. (2) Life came to Earth by the creative act of the divine will.   God created life upon the Earth.   (3) Life arose upon the Earth by a natural process, being slowly evolved from inorganic matter.

Concerning the first of these three theories — theoretically it is not impossible that life should be transported through space from some other planet or star, either as ultra-microscopic living germs driven by light radiation, as was proposed by Arrhenius,[1] or hidden in the cleft of some meteorite dropped upon the Earth's surface. Eminent scientists have proposed this solution of the problem. But it does not really solve the problem; it merely transfers it to another world.   And the view seems unnecessary.

The second proposal, that life is the result of a divine creative act, depends for its value on the way it is interpreted.   Our impulse would be to think of God at some moment of time and some point in space issuing a decree or fiat, creating life.   As thus interpreted, this solution of the problem would not appeal to scientists, who are accustomed to look for order and continuity in all the work of nature.   If, however, we think of God as the creative agency, or the Creative Will, continually at work throughout nature, this view might commend itself as the best of the three.

The third theory, that of the gradual evolution of the organic from the inorganic, is the one generally accepted by biologists today. Although there is as yet no undisputed evidence of any generation of the organic from the inorganic, and although our laboratory experiments seem to indicate unequivocally that all life proceeds from previous life, yet it does not follow that conditions may not have been such at some time, or at some times, that life could arise from non-life.   One cannot say that in the warm terrestrial waters millions of years ago the organic could not have been evolved by natural processes from the inorganic.   We are almost compelled to believe that just this did happen.   It may have happened once; it may possibly be taking place daily somewhere now.

It seems, then, that we cannot look for the origin of life either in interstellar migration, a divine creative act, or in spontaneous generation.   It is more in accordance with the thought of the day to believe that life originated in some process of evolution, which means slow, orderly, progressive change.   But when in the course of evolution some *novelty* appears, unique, decisively different,

[1] See *The Life of the Universe*, by Svante Arrhenius.   Translated into English by H. Borns, vol. u, chap. IX, pp. 250 ff.

representing a higher level, showing new and hitherto unknown qualities, escaping perhaps from the mechanistic treadmill of the ages, it is legitimate to use the word *created*. By some kind of creative process, therefore, life came to Earth — let us say by *creative evolution*. We have to thank M. Bergson for this enlightening phrase. Every student should read his masterly book, *Creative Evolution*.

The nature of life

If, as we must believe, every form of life — plant, animal, man, with all that the latter term implies of the human mind, human history, human institutions, even art and science — has arisen by a process which we call evolution from very early and simple forms of life — say from unicellular organisms — it becomes of the utmost importance to the student of philosophy to understand not only the origin but the meaning of life itself.

The key to the problem of life is found in that magic word, organization. A living body is an *organism*, and the peculiar feature of a living organism is the possession of a group of unique properties, of which the two most conspicuous are *irritability* and *reproduction*. Living organisms are responsive to stimuli and they have the power of self-perpetuation. But organic bodies possess also other distinctive properties, such as growth by the assimilation of food, adaptation and self-adjustment to the environment, self-maintenance, and self-protection.

The above properties are possessed by all living organisms, but when the organization proceeds further and we arrive at very complex and highly integrated living bodies, still other properties appear, such as sensibility, instinct, selective choice, memory, intelligence, and consciousness. To the sum of the first set of properties we may give the name *Life*; to the sum of all these properties we may give the names *Life* and *Mind*.

The biologist and the psychologist, now, will be satisfied to study the behavior of these organisms and to describe, classify, and relate all their peculiar properties. But not so the student of philosophy. He must inquire more about the very nature of Life and Mind, how and why they arise, and whether they are new kinds of reality, or whether they are merely combinations of the simpler forms found in the inorganic world. In the latter we have atoms and molecules, and molecules are combined into numerous chemical compounds according to certain peculiar affinities. But how and why do the chemical compounds get "organized" into living bodies, and how do all those wonderful properties, such as reproduction and self-maintenance, arise? Is it due to some *vital principle* that has been *added* to inorganic compounds? Is life a kind of entity, which exists in addition to the atoms and molecules, or is it just a function of atoms and molecules, or is it a function of a certain *form* or *structure* which atoms and molecules take on?

It has been held many times in the history of philosophy that life is due to a vital principle, a special factor, which is to be distinguished sharply from all forms of mere matter and from all mechanical forces. The name *Vitalism* has been given to this view. Something like this was held by Aristotle and is held by eminent biologists at the present day. But on the other hand many thinkers in all the centuries and many biologists both of the past and of the present, strenuously deny the existence of any such thing as a vital principle, or special life force, and believe that life is due to the action of ordinary physical and chemical forces. To this view we usually give the name *Mechanism*. It is closely related to that theory of the world which we have learned to know as Naturalism, and has often been associated with Materialism.

Mechanistic conceptions of life

Mechanism stresses the purely mechanical character of all processes, organic as well as inorganic. In explaining life, whether of micro-organisms, plants, animals, or man, it is necessary to assume no other materials and no other forces than those exhibited in inorganic nature, as, for instance, in the movement of the spheres, or the formation of rocks and soils, or of chemical compounds. Physical and chemical laws are sufficient to account for all forms of life and perhaps even of mind; they can all be described in terms of matter and motion. They are all, in the last analysis, *movements of mass particles in space*. The so-called higher forms are distinguished by greater complexity of structure; but they involve no new materials and no new forces. The human body with its marvelous brain and nervous system, as well as the whole kingdom of plants and animals, can be analyzed into the same carbon, oxygen, hydrogen, nitrogen, calcium, and other chemical elements, as the soil, the rocks, and the water. Nor are any other forces at work in them than are present in the inorganic bodies. "A living organism is a complex system of physical-chemical mechanisms." Continuity prevails in nature from the simplest to the most complex forms. There is no sharp line of cleavage between the organic and the inorganic. In the chemically complex inorganic colloids we have an easy stepping-stone to the organic colloids and thence to higher forms of life.

It is not necessary, according to this view, to assume any mysterious vital forces to account for life, nor is it necessary to suppose that evolution is purposive or teleological. We should not gratuitously import into the processes of nature any mental concepts, or spiritual or psychic forces, or any notions of ends, purposes, or values. Thus the world scheme is immensely simplified.

Historically, the mechanical theory of living organisms originated with the atomists in ancient Greece. It received encouragement through the work of Copernicus, Galileo, Descartes, and Newton. It was amplified in Herbert Spencer's law of evolution, expressing the manner of the redistribution of matter and motion. It was immeasurably strengthened by Darwin's discovery of the law of natural selection, explaining the origin of new animal species. It found a vigorous defender in Huxley, in his *Physical Basis of Life*. In this century it was expounded by Professor Loeb, in his *Mechanistic Conception of Life*. It is the view adopted by many biologists at the present time, as a working hypothesis—by no means regarded as a final philosophy. In accordance with the law of parsimony,[1] they do not wish to assume other forces than physical and chemical ones, unless such other forces should prove to be necessary. It is a direct violation of this law, it is claimed, when the vitalists

---

[1] The law of parsimony was first formulated in the fourteenth century by the scholastic philosopher, William of Occam. The Latin form of the law reads: "*Entia non sunt multiplicanda praeter necessitatem*" (Entities, principles, or forces should not be multiplied beyond necessity). This has been called Occam's razor, lopping off the heads of many unnecessary scholastic principles or hypotheses.

affirm the presence of a vital force to explain life, a procedure ridiculed by Molière, who compared it with the attempt to explain the sleep-producing effect of opium by the circular argument that opium possesses a " dormitive property." It is just this tendency to explain things by words that has been the bane of philosophy from the beginning. Goethe says:

> Denn eben wo Begriffe fehlen
> Da stellt ein Wort zur rechten Zeit sich ein.

But mechanism goes further. It attempts to explain not only life, but mind as well, on purely mechanical principles. The speculations of a philosopher reasoning about the universe and its realities are as much a product of mechanical and naturalistic laws as are the workings of a giant locomotive. Man and society, science and art, philosophy and religion, are all the product of mechanical forces and all are subject to mechanical laws. The human realm is a part of the physical realm. Psychology is included in physiology. Thought and feeling are forms of motion, and physics and chemistry are the prerogative sciences. A clear statement of this thoroughgoing application of mechanical principles to mental and social processes may be found in a book by A. P. Weiss, entitled *A Theoretical Basis of Human Behavior.*

Difficulties

At first sight the mechanistic explanation of life seems quite convincing. Certain rather serious objections have been urged against it, however, which we must now consider. If these objections seem to offer almost insuperable difficulties to the acceptance of a mechanistic interpretation of life, we must not hastily infer that a vitalistic interpretation will offer fewer difficulties. Possibly we may be able to get down below both of these theories and find some common ground for a reconciliation.

The first difficulty that we encounter is that when we try to explain life, growth, reproduction, mind, morals, society, and, indeed, the very fact of evolution itself, by means of a few concepts found useful in physical and chemical science, we are in danger of importing into these concepts a wealth of meaning which they do not have in their respective spheres.

The number of concepts which we find at our disposal from the physical sciences is very limited, while the realities to be explained are very intricate. The concepts which we have at hand are such as cause and effect (interpreted either as mechanical equivalence or as mere sequence), mass particles in motion, action and reaction, the reaction being quantitatively determined by the impact of material particles. Strictly it would seem that we cannot even speak of attraction and repulsion. These are figurative terms imported from the world of mind.

These mechanical concepts, now, seem a wholly inadequate equipment for the interpretation of the rich content of life. They are the concepts which we have found useful in describing the behavior of material bodies. It is not quite clear why we must be limited to these concepts in describing the phenomena of life and society. It is not even clear how we shall explain or even describe the fact of evolution itself by means of them.

Herbert Spencer defines life as "the continuous adjustment of internal to external conditions." It seems difficult to explain life mechanistically on this definition; and whether this is a sufficient definition or not, the power of adjustment indubitably belongs to life. Life is self-adjusting, self-maintaining, self-preserving, and self-perpetuating. There is nothing like this in the mechanical world. Machines do not adjust, maintain, preserve, or perpetuate themselves. Mechanistic philosophers are very fond of considering certain concepts, such as matter, motion, energy, electricity, as ultimate. They enable us to describe quantitatively many phenomena in the physical world. But there are certain other concepts, such as *life* and *mind* and *struggle* and *will* and *impulse* and *appetency* and *purpose* and *interest* and *value* and *creative evolution*, which are equally useful in explaining other great areas of existence, and apparently indispensable in explaining them. It seems a little like dogmatism to say that we must not consider these, or some of them, as ultimate, but that we must reduce them to the other list of mechanistic concepts.

I think there is a marked tendency at the present time to question the assumption, so common at the close of the nineteenth century, that the concepts of physics and chemistry have any peculiar prerogative in explaining life and man and mind. Indeed, J. S. Haldane, the English physiologist, directly reverses this order.[1] "The idea of the physical universe," he says, "as a world of self-existent matter and energy is only a temporary working hypothesis by means of which we are able to introduce a certain amount of order and coherence into a large part of our experience." "This hypothesis breaks down in connection with the phenomena of life." "The phenomena of life involve another and radically different conception of reality." "The idea of life is nearer to reality than the ideas of matter and energy, and therefore the presupposition of ideal biology is that inorganic can ultimately be resolved into organic phenomena, and that the physical world is thus only the appearance of a deeper reality which is as yet hidden from our distinct vision, and can only be seen dimly with the eye of scientific faith." Haldane thinks that biological conceptions may soon be extended to the whole of nature.

J. Arthur Thomson believed that "the formulae of physics and chemistry are inadequate for the re-description of the everyday bodily functions, or of behavior, or of development, or of evolution." They "do not suffice for answering the distinctively biological questions." In biology "we need new concepts — such as that of the organism as a historic being which has traded with time, and has enregistered within itself past experiences and experiments, and which has ever its conative bow bent towards the future." [2]

In fact, none of the unique qualities which distinguish living from non-living matter has been explained. We can only say that living things *grow*; they *choose* things suitable for food and reject other things; they *adjust* themselves to the environment; they are *sensitive* to stimuli; they *protect* themselves and reproduce themselves; but we have no explanation of these powers in terms simpler than the powers themselves. We have learned a good deal about the *manner* of reproduction and the *laws* of heredity. We can describe by means of Mendel's laws how certain characters, which we call unit characters or genes, are distributed in the off-

---

[1] See especially his *Mechanism, Life, and Personality* (John Murray, London), pp. 101, 104.
[2] *The System of Animate Nature* (Henry Holt and Company), I, pp. 143–60.

spring.   We can discern through our powerful microscopes the minute divisions of the cell.   We can count the chromosomes in the nucleus, and even the chromomeres, and can watch their division.   We can make the supposition that there are separate "factors" or "genes" in the germ cell, which stand in definite relations to the several future parts of the organism.   But transferring the mystery to very minute structures does not make the mystery any the less; we can watch the division of a cell into two cells, but we do not understand either why it divides or how the daughter cell inherits all the peculiar forms of the parent cell.   "The study of the cell has on the whole seemed to widen rather than narrow the enormous gap that separates even the lowest forms of life from the inorganic world." [1]

But other serious difficulties with the mechanistic scheme confront us.   One thing, for instance, which is not generally appreciated is that mechanism has at its disposal no *organizing* or *directive agency* which will make the evolutionary process intelligible. Mechanism, at least in its extreme form, involves the explanation of living beings, from the simple speck of protoplasm to the complex human body, as due to the chance assemblage of mass particles in space.   We could not even say that vital processes are due to the peculiar character of the motions of the mass particles, for all motions must conform to the usual mechanical laws.   But the particles get into peculiar relationships, and these peculiar relationships constitute life, and these peculiar relationships or constellations of atoms and molecules are accidental.   Life, therefore, is a mere incident, or, worse still, an accident, in cosmic evolution. Indeed, it would seem inconsistent even to use the phrase *cosmic evolution*, for the word *evolution* implies some orderly progressive change or unfolding.   We should have to speak merely of cosmic change.   It would not be consistent with the mechanistic conception to think of the world of organisms as an unfolding of something wrapped up or potentially present in the original matter or energy; neither would it be consistent to think of it as working or progressing either consciously or unconsciously toward any end, purpose, or goal.   It would seem that the consistent mechanist must hold that

[1] E. B. Wilson, *The Cell in Development and Inheritance*, p. 434.

the world of living forms has all come about by the accidental groupings of molecules of matter.

And this indeed is what the extreme mechanist does maintain — and with much apparent reason. We have to remember, he says, the immensity of time which has elapsed since the earth's crust first became fit for living organisms, permitting every chance combination to be tried, those only surviving which were fitted to their environment.

At first thought this seems wholly incredible. If we recall the marvelous complexity of the chemical formulae of the molecules of which the living cell is composed, it would seem impossible that such groupings could ever have taken place by chance. It is as if one should take the bulkiest of Sunday newspapers, cut all the words into letters, and make separate cuttings of the spaces, punctuation marks and capitals, shuffle all thoroughly, then draw out the slips one by one at random and place them in rows, to find after repeating this through unlimited time that the original order has been reproduced, every letter, capital, punctuation mark and space being in its original place. But the mechanist accepts this illustration and affirms that by the logic of chance every possible combination must occur and that this very thing would happen. So in nature through the immensity of geological time the combinations of atoms and molecules found in living germs must have happened — a view much encouraged by the fact that geologists are continually enlarging their estimates of the length of each of the geological periods. Apparently there has been plenty of time for almost anything to "happen."

But the problem cannot be so easily solved as this. It may be possible to imagine that a speck of protoplasm, however complex its chemical formula, might have arisen in the course of time by the fortuitous grouping of inorganic particles; but the difficulties in this explanation seem to weigh too heavily upon us when we begin to reflect upon all its implications. If the mere grouping of the inorganic elements present in a living cell could have taken place by chance, would the group be a *living* thing? Would it have the power of reproduction, self-preservation, discrimination and spontaneity? Would it ultimately in its further complex groupings attain to sensibility, thought and feeling, and to the power of control over the very forces of nature? Does that peculiar *urge* which is found throughout the entire realm of living things suggest something more primeval than a quality arising through the accidental grouping of elements?

It is an accepted view among our biologists that the organic has arisen from the inorganic by a slow process of evolution; but I believe it is not a generally accepted view that this has come about by chance. Probably most biologists would hesitate to affirm this; many would hold just the opposite view. Benjamin Moore, for instance, says, "It was no fortuitous combination of chances and no cosmic dust which brought life to the womb of our ancient mother Earth in the far distant Palaeozoic ages but a well-regulated, orderly development, which comes to every mother earth in the Universe in the maturity of her creation when the conditions arrive within the suitable limits." [1]

A somewhat similar conclusion is drawn by Henderson, Professor of biological chemistry in Harvard University, in two much discussed books. His argument seems to show that however we may explain the coming of life upon the Earth, it could not have been the result of chance, but of some deep pervading law or tendency, the character of which is unknown to us. The world, he thinks, is *biocentric*, centering about the production of life. [2]

The autonomy of life

We see how difficult it is to describe living processes in terms of matter and motion when we consider such striking facts as the restitution of function and the regeneration of lost parts in animal bodies. When one part of an organism is injured, another part having normally a different function may take over that of the injured part. In the case of the starfish, when one arm is cut off, the living organism successfully undertakes the restitution of the lost part, the living cells evidently assuming foreign duties. The animal has to meet an emergency to the end of self-preservation and proves equal to it.

[1] *The Origin and Nature of Life* (Henry Holt and Company, Home University Library), p. 190.

[2] Lawrence J. Henderson, *The Fitness of the Environment* (by permission of the Macmillan Company, publishers), and *The Order of Nature* (The Harvard University Press).

Thus it comes about that the vocabulary of the mechanical sciences does not fit the behavior of living organisms. Life is autonomous, having its own laws and its own vocabulary. Life is insurgent, pressing with patient and never-tiring persistence into every nook and corner of the Earth's crust, into the depths of the seas, under thick antarctic ice, in hot springs, on mountain-tops, in arid plains. Life is struggle. It has this capacity — to persist and struggle with the environment, to adjust itself to conditions. It is the will to live, the continuous adjustment of internal to external conditions. "Tactics and strategy are its instruments." It is inventive, and, as Bergson says, "remains inventive even in its adaptations." Life is selective, seeking its appropriate food and rejecting that which it does not find fit.

Try, for instance, to explain the scratch-reflex of the dog by means of the elementalist theory, by referring it to the physico-chemical elements at the basis of the act. Marshal them all together, but in the end you find that there is an element lacking. Something has intervened between the simple elements and the reflex — and that something is *the dog*. In other words, there is something else that is real besides the material elements and the physical and chemical processes, namely, the organism itself, involving structure and organization and integration.[1]

Vitalism

Is there now any way in which all these puzzling difficulties in the mechanistic theory of organic life may be met? Is the theory called "Vitalism" any better? Let us now consider this proposed solution of the problem.

Vitalism in its crudest form is the doctrine that life is due to a non-material force or entity called a "vital principle." This theory goes back to Aristotle, who thought of the soul as the vital principle, or the seat and source of life. Plants have a vegetative soul, animals have a vegetative and sensitive soul, while the soul of man is vegetative, sensitive, and rational. During the Middle Ages, following Aristotle, it was generally believed that there is a source of life quite distinct from matter, usually some psychical or spiritual principle.

[1] W. E. Ritter, *The Unity of the Organism*, chap. XXI, see especially pp. 198 ff.

Descartes, however, taught that plant and animal bodies are machines pure and simple, actuated only by material forces. The body of man is no exception to this rule; only in the case of man there is a spiritual soul, which acts upon the body. After Descartes it was easy to extend the principle of mechanism to man's whole personality, omitting the soul; and in scientific circles it became customary in many cases to ridicule the notion of a vital principle or any spiritual entity residing in plant or animal bodies. This mechanistic attitude has become traditional in scientific circles, so that in biological laboratories at the present day it is no doubt considered good form to smile at the notion of a vital principle. Such a principle could not be subjected to any experimental tests and would not lend itself to scientific demonstration.

Under these circumstances, the recent revival of vitalism in scientific circles is significant. The leader in this "neo-vitalism" is Hans Driesch, a German biologist. Driesch, whose conclusions are based upon experimental evidence, is fully convinced that life cannot be explained on a mechanistic basis. He says:

> No kind of causality based upon the constellations of single physical and chemical acts can account for organic individual development; this development is not to be explained by any hypothesis about configuration of physical and chemical agents.... Life, at least morphogenesis, is not a specialized arrangement of inorganic events; biology, therefore, is not applied physics and chemistry; life is something apart, and biology is an independent science.[1]

Driesch, further, believes that life is due to the presence of a non-material factor, to which he gives the name *Entelechy*, and sometimes the name *Psychoid*. The first of these terms is taken from Aristotle and means a perfecting principle; the second indicates the author's belief that the vital principle is mental in its nature. While many biologists — probably a large majority of them — regard the revival of vitalism as a recrudescence of mysticism, nevertheless, a surprising number of biologists, zoologists, and palaeontologists have adopted more or less fully the neo-vitalistic position.

[1] Hans Driesch, *The Science and Philosophy of the Organism* (Gifford Lectures, 1908), p. 142. Compare also his recent chapter entitled "The Breakdown of Materialism," in *The Great Design*, edited by Frances Mason (The Macmillan Company, 1934).

The newer vitalism

For the most part, however, neo-vitalism takes a somewhat different form from that of Driesch and his successors. The use of the word vitalism is avoided, suggesting, as it does to many, outworn mystical theories. But the necessity of an initial urge or impulse in organic matter, which shall account for the onward movement of organic evolution, is recognized by an increasing number of biologists.[1]

Sometimes this takes the form of a conative principle operating within the sphere of organic life, such for instance as Darwin's "struggle for existence," Nägeli's "internal factor tending towards perfection,"[2] or Geddes and Thomson's "originative impulse."[3] The "struggle for freedom" is what it is called by Albert P. Mathews. The tree of life, he says, is "psycho-tropic," tending upwards toward mind. In the primeval slime from which all life has proceeded there is a *capacity* which the mechanistic philosophy has overlooked. It is the capacity of struggling against the environment. This is the very essence of life. Life is struggle.

> While the fact of evolution has been established... there still remains unexplained, or not adequately explained, the great onward rolling tide of life, which bears man riding like Neptune on its crest.... Considered as a process rather than as a road, evolution is the struggle of life with its environment, a struggle for freedom, leading to the triumph of the mind and the winning of individuality; it is the struggle of the spirit within us to be superior to matter, to escape the trammels of matter, to secure a fuller individual life and a larger freedom.[4]

John Burroughs used to say that we have to assume in the organic world something which he calls an organizing principle. "Natural selection," he says, "is not a creative, but a purely mechanical process." "Chance, or chance selection, works alike in the organic and the inorganic realms, but it develops no new forms in the inorganic, because there is no principle of development,

---

[1] Compare the writings of J. S. Haldane and J. Arthur Thomson. See above, p. 102.

[2] His *Vervollkommnungsprinzip*.

[3] "We feel compelled to recognize the persistence of some originative impulse within the organism, which expresses itself in variation and mutation and in all kinds of creative effort and endeavor." — *Evolution*, Home University Library, p. 202.

[4] Albert P. Mathews, "The Road of Evolution," *Yale Review*, January, 1922, pp. 340, 344, and 346.

no organizing push. But in organized matter there is, in and behind all this organizing, a developing principle or tendency; the living force is striving toward other forms; in other words, development occurs because there is something to develop. An acorn develops, but a quartz pebble only changes." [1] Sometimes also we hear of a special force or energy, comparable with other recognized forms such, for instance, as the "biotic energy" accepted by Benjamin Moore and J. M. Macfarlane. All these remind us of the "inherent growth force," such as Goethe believed in, or the "life force" repeatedly referred to by Bernard Shaw.

Again, this inner urge, force, or principle is referred to as something like mind, or at least rudimentary mind, as when Ernest William MacBride, professor of zoology, Imperial College of Science, London, writes "In the last resort, therefore, we may endorse a view expressed by a leading physicist. 'In every living thing there is a nucleus of mentality enclosed in an envelope of matter which obeys the laws of matter.' Even if we express the 'mentality' on the lowest plane as memory and striving, the mystery of its origin remains the same." He believes that all living matter is "endowed with something that strives to meet adverse circumstances and can control its own growth." [2]

And yet all these views, vitalistic or neo-vitalistic, are vigorously contested by many biologists, who cannot accept any force, principle, or primeval urge, not fully explicable on mechanical principles. Are we then to continue to have two opposing schools of biologists on this serious question of the nature and origin of life? Possibly there is a *via media*, which will recognize the truth in both vitalism and mechanism.

The theory of levels

Let us make the supposition that the secret of living organisms is found in the process of organization — in structure. Life then would be the outcome of a certain kind of organization of non-living elements. Living bodies are highly organized, highly com-

---

[1] John Burroughs, *Accepting the Universe* (Houghton Mifflin Company), p. 209.

[2] "The Oneness and Uniqueness of Life" in *The Great Design*, edited by Frances Mason (The Macmillan Company, 1934), pp. 133–58.

plex and highly integrated forms of simple inorganic elements. A living body contains no mysterious entity called a vital principle, or vegetative or sensitive soul. It is not a soul or vital spark in living organisms which causes life — or gives rise to the power of growth and reproduction. These properties are the outcome of organization and structure.

Organic evolution would thus proceed by the method of *creative synthesis*. Creative synthesis means nothing more than that a synthesis takes place, and thereby new processes, powers, or activities appear — that is, are created. The *theory of levels* has thrown much light on the problems of life and mind. Electrons and protons are organized into atoms, atoms into molecules, molecules into cells, cells into living bodies, and at each new level of organization new qualities appear, which are in the nature of new creations, since they cannot be inferred by adding together the qualities of the elements which are organized. Oxygen and hydrogen are organized into a molecule of water, which possesses properties that do not belong to oxygen or hydrogen, and that could not be predicted from the completest knowledge of these two elements. Water will refresh the thirsty plant, and will freeze at a certain temperature. Not so the oxygen or hydrogen of which it is composed. There is something more in the water than oxygen and hydrogen; there is structure. A molecule of water is comparatively a simple structure, but other molecules, such as those of the colloids, are remarkably complex and possess remarkable qualities. Finally comes that wonderfully complex structure of complex molecules which we call living matter, and then there emerges a whole series of new qualities, such as growth, assimilation, irritability, adaptivity, and reproduction. These remarkable qualities are not the sum of any qualities belonging to the elements of which the structure is composed. Two plus two do not make four in this case. The new created qualities arise from the organization.

What we see all the way up the ladder of evolution is *matter* taking on *form*, taking on structure and organization, and, as the outcome of these new forms, we see the creation of new and "strange" powers. At each new level of reality we have new powers and new capacities and new qualities. It is a flowering-out process, wholly different from the mechanical sequences which we see in the world of physics. New realities are born at each new level. *Life* is one of these realities.

Instead, then, of seeking to interpolate a new agency — non-material and not perceptual — we express the fact that living is not explicable in terms of matter and motion by saying that all organisms — known to our senses as collocations of protoplasm — reveal new aspects of reality, transcending mechanical formulation.[1]

What is to come in the future is not predictable from what is now present, for we do not know what will be the rules of action, the laws of motion, when other mental states shall have come into being, when there are other sensations, purposes, ideas. The universe produces new things; produces sensations, emotions, ideas, where none existed; produces new mental states as time passes. And with these it produces new methods of action. It is not true that the thing that has been is the thing which shall be, that the thing that has been done is the thing that shall be done, and there is no new thing under the sun. On the contrary, new things and new methods of action come forth in the process that we call evolution....

The laws of action, the laws of motion, we conclude, are different when specified mental states are present, as compared with the methods of action when those mental states are not present or when other mental states are present. This is one of the fundamental principles for our biological outlook on the world. It affects all our further conclusions.[2]

Thus life is not due to the presence in the living organism of any mystic "vital principle," or "life force." It is the evolutionary product of organization. The original inorganic elements were not alive; but they were brought into new relations or patterns of an organic kind, resulting in organic wholes or unities, from which there arose new and strange qualities and capacities, such as the power of growth, of the assimilation of foods, and of reproduction — and eventually the epoch-making capacity to feel, to become aware, and to think and reason.

It is evident that the theory of levels throws a new and revealing light upon the relation which exists between life and mind on the one hand and the world of inorganic matter on the other. It

[1] J. Arthur Thomson, *The System of Animate Nature* (Henry Holt and Company), i, p. 168.
[2] H. S. Jennings, *The Universe and Life* (Yale University Press, 1933), pp. 47, 48.

directs our attention upon the whole evolutionary process, rather than upon the motions of particles of matter in their physical and chemical relations.   In the theory of levels we are introduced to the whole subject of evolution, which we shall study in the following chapters; and particularly to those forms which are called creative or emergent evolution.   In the same connection our attention is called to the organic or organismic theory of nature, as contrasted with the elementalist theory.   The student should read the original sources of this movement as found in the writings of Bergson, Sellars, S. Alexander and C. Lloyd Morgan.   Critical reviews may be found in McDougall's *Modern Materialism and Emergent Evolution*, and in Drake's *Invitation to Philosophy*.[1]

In its very simplest form, emergent evolution means simply this: that in the evolutionary process new qualities, new modes of action, and qualitatively new entities arise when physical structures become more complex and integrated.

Aristotle thought of the world as a great *process*, in which matter is taking on form, or structure; and the *reality* is always found in the structure — or as we should say, in the organism — not in the elements.   We can go back from living organism to cell, and from cell to molecule, and from molecule to atom — and finally to a mere wave-packet; but we are getting away from reality — not toward it.   The *real* things are organisms and their characteristic reactions and their peculiar qualities and capacities.   The organismic view of nature is at the present time gaining favor over the

---

[1] On the theory of levels, compare Roy Wood Sellars, *Evolutionary Naturalism* (Open Court Publishing Company), chap. xv, and *The Principles and Problems of Philosophy* (The Macmillan Company), chap. xxiv, and George P. Conger, "The Doctrine of Levels," *Jour. Phil.*, xxii, no. 12.

On creative evolution, compare Henri Bergson, *Creative Evolution* (Henry Holt and Company).

On emergent evolution, compare C. Lloyd Morgan, *Emergent Evolution*.   Read also two interesting little books from the standpoint of the biologist and zoologist.   First, William Morton Wheeler, *Emergent Evolution and the Development of Societies* (New York, 1928).   Second, H. S. Jennings, *The Universe and Life* (Yale University Press, 1933).

On the theory of emergence and its logical aspects, compare Arthur O. Lovejoy, "The Meaning of Emergence and its Modes," *Jour. Phil. Studies*, ii, no. 6, and "The Discontinuities of Evolution." *Univ. of Cal. Pub. in Phil.*, v, pp. 173–220.

Compare also S. Alexander, *Space, Time and Deity*, C. D. Broad, *Mind and its Place in Nature*. W. E. Ritter, *The Unity of the Organism, or The Organismal Conception of Life*.

The subject was discussed by the present author in his book, *What is the Mind?* (The Macmillan Company, 1929), chap. v, and in his chapter entitled "Idealistic Confessions of a Behaviorist" in the symposium *Has Science Discovered God?* (New York, 1931).

older mechanical theories. "Science," as Mr. Whitehead says, "is taking on a new aspect which is neither purely physical, nor purely biological. It is becoming the study of organisms. Biology is the study of the larger organisms; whereas physics is the study of the smaller organisms." [1]

Life is thus the characteristic reaction of an organism of a high degree of complexity. The result is to minimize or perhaps to eliminate the old controversy between the mechanist and the vitalist — or even between the materialist and the idealist. Matter itself arises as an outcome of the organization of protons and electrons, which themselves are below the level of matter. At a vastly later period in evolution, mind arises as the ideal expression of a living organism of an exceedingly high degree of complexity. Matter and mind both represent stages in evolution, not antithetical forms of being. We may say that Nature climbs up to life and mind through the organization of matter.

Mechanism and vitalism are also transcended in the theory of creative evolution. Mechanism serves as a useful hypothesis at a certain stage of evolution, but its operation is superseded when life and mind are realized, since life and mind themselves become effective in determining in part the course of future events. At the other end of the scale we have recently learned through the science of microphysics that subatomic structures are not wholly subservient to mechanical laws. The electrons and protons behave in a manner shocking to the strict mechanist. Vitalism is equally superseded in creative evolution, since life is regarded as an outcome of organization.

The organizing agency

Since in creative evolution organization plays so prominent a part, the question naturally arises — What are the causes or agencies of organization? This is a philosophical question — and the various answers which have been given to it are deeply interesting. Some of these we may now discuss; but it should be kept in mind that the value of the theory of levels does not depend upon the determining of the source of organization. Organization is a fact before our eyes;

[1] *Science and the Modern World*, p. 145.

and the remarkable new powers which arise in organisms are also observed facts. There was a time when living organisms did not exist upon the flaming surface of the earth; they exist now. Hence the causes of organization become a problem of profound interest. What we seem to need is some kind of power or force wholly different from mechanical forces and just the opposite of those gravitational forces which tend to drag the world down to an equilibrium. We need some kind of power to organize elements into wholes, to direct and integrate physical energies — to marshal them into order, so to speak. Some creative agency seems to be required. It should not, of course, be overlooked that the hypothesis of the chance grouping of inorganic atoms and molecules into organic wholes is a legitimate hypothesis. Some of the difficulties of this theory we have already studied. Are there other theories which escape these difficulties?

At first sight this seems to be the old philosophical problem of *the moving cause*. In the Hebrew philosophy we read — "In the beginning God created the heaven and the earth." In Aristotle, it is the *Primum Mobile*, or *First Mover*, or *God*. In Plato, it is the *Demiurgus*, or *World-Builder*. In Anaxagoras, it is *Nous*, or *Mind*. And so we could go through the history of philosophy, recalling the *Natura Naturans* of Bruno and Spinoza, the *Absolute Idea* of Hegel, the *Absolute Ego* of Fichte, the *Pure Creative Energy* of Schelling, the *Absolute Will* of Schopenhauer, the *Will to Power* of Nietzsche, the *Unconscious Will* of von Hartmann, the *World Soul* of Fechner, the *Universal Will* of Wundt, the *Unknowable* of Spencer, the *Power that Makes for Righteousness* of Matthew Arnold, the *Absolute Self* of modern idealists, and simply *God* in many and many philosophies.

For the moment we may not be interested in these philosophical theories of a creative agency. We wish to hear from the scientists — particularly from the biologists. Is there from the biological point of view any initial *agency* which may serve to explain the constructive work of nature and which we may think of as the cause of those structures whose functional activity is life?

With Bergson, the *élan vital* is a primordial world-principle, the basic reality of all being, the source and ground of evolution, a vital impulse, or push, or creative ground, pervading matter, insinuating itself in it, overcoming its inertia and its resistance, determining the

direction of evolution as well as evolution itself. This ever-chang-
ing, expanding, free activity is life itself. The earliest animate
forms, tiny masses of protoplasm, were possessed of a tremendous
internal push, "that was to raise them even to the highest forms of
life." The evolution of life is a creation that goes on forever by
virtue of an initial movement.

Whether we will or no, we must appeal to some inner directing principle in order to account for this convergence of effects. Such convergence does not appear possible in the Darwinian, and especially the
neo-Darwinian, theory of insensible accidental variations, nor in the
hypothesis of sudden accidental variation, nor even in the theory that
assigns definite directions to the evolution of the various organs by a
kind of mechanical composition of the external with the internal forces.[1]

C. Lloyd Morgan, in his book entitled *Emergent Evolution*, says
we must acknowledge an original *Activity* which is the *nisus* or urge
making actual the whole evolutionary movement. In many passages in this book he interprets this activity as mind or spirit, but he
prefers to call it simply God, and even suggests that it acts from
above as a *drawing* force.

Within us, if anywhere, we must feel the urge, or however it be
named, which shall afford the basis upon which acknowledgment of
Activity is founded. What then does it feel like? Each must answer
for himself, fully realising that he may misinterpret the evidence.
Without denying a felt push from the lower levels of one's being — a
so-called driving force welling up from below — to me it feels like a
drawing upwards through Activity existent at a higher level than that
to which I have attained.[2]

Sometimes again the agency in question is thought of as some
cosmic impulse more fundamental even than life itself. The "creative agency" that Patten tells us about seems somewhat like the
vital impetus of Bergson. There is in nature, he says, an abiding
compulsion

which is cumulative, or progressive, producing that increasing architectural organization that we call nature-growth, or evolution.... Progressive union and stability, progressive co-operation, organization,
service and discipline are, therefore, inherent properties of life and

[1] Henri Bergson, *Creative Evolution* (Henry Holt and Company), p. 76.
[2] C. Lloyd Morgan, F.R.S., *Emergent Evolution* (Henry Holt and Company), p. 208.

matter.... The ceaseless flow of creative services is evolution, and evolution is serial creation.... In this broader concept of nature-growth, light and gravity, vitality, genes, and gemmules, heredity, intelligence, "selection," social conduct, and all the rest of the growth-machinery of life portrayed by the physicists and biologists may be regarded merely as local, or special manifestation of a common creative agency.[1]

There have been few attempts to determine more exactly the nature of this evolutionary urge, this inner directing force, this primordial direction and co-ordination of energies. Of course, it is easy for us to interpret it as Mind. It is perhaps too easy for us to do so, reading back into nature, as the power which makes things go, that which makes them go in our little human world. And yet Hobhouse says, in the preface to the second edition of his important work on *Mind in Evolution*, that he has been led to "raise the question whether mind (in the infinitely varied form of its activity, from the groping of unconscious effort to the full clearness of conscious purpose) may not be the essential driving force in all evolutionary change."

In a somewhat similar strain, A. S. Eddington, at the end of his chapter "On the Nature of Things" closing his striking book on Space, Time, and Gravitation, comes to the conclusion that something of the nature of consciousness forms the essential content of the world.

The theory of relativity has passed in review the whole subject-matter of physics. It has unified the great laws, which by the precision of their formulation and the exactness of their application have won the proud place in human knowledge which physical science holds today. And yet, in regard to the nature of things, this knowledge is only an empty shell — a form of symbols. It is knowledge of structural form, and not knowledge of content. All through the physical world runs that unknown content, which must surely be the stuff of our consciousness. Here is a hint of aspects deep within the world of physics, and yet unattainable by the methods of physics. And, moreover, we have found that where science has progressed the farthest, the mind has but regained from nature that which the mind has put into nature.

We have found a strange footprint on the shores of the unknown. We have devised profound theories, one after another, to account for

[1] William Patten, *The Grand Strategy of Evolution* (R. G. Badger), pp. xii, 28, 29, 47

its origin. At last, we have succeeded in reconstructing the creature that made the footprint. And lo! it is our own.[1]

William Morton Wheeler of Harvard University, writing as a biologist, thinks that organization is the work of the components of the organism, and that it is not directed by extraspacial and extra-temporal "entelechies," or organizatory factors, or *élan vital*, or any metaphysical agency. The organizing agency or tendency is immanent — not transcendent. Wheeler himself is an ardent defender of the theory of emergence and it is interesting to learn that this view does not necessarily presuppose the existence of any transcendental agencies. But *why* do the components of a unitary complex have a tendency to organize themselves? Wheeler believes that they are by nature *social*. They have "an irresistible tendency to cohere and organize themselves into more and more complex emergent wholes," so that "association may be regarded as the fundamental condition of emergence." [2]

This is a highly interesting theory. Apparently Wheeler would attribute the social impulse not only to living cells but to the electrons and protons which organize themselves into atoms, and to atoms which organize themselves into molecules. Since the ultimate constituents of the atom behave sometimes like waves and sometimes like particles, there seems to be no reason why we should not ascribe to them also social tendencies. This would seem to make our electrons less rather than more "delirious." But have we escaped a *meta*-physical theory? The electrons were scarcely physical before; with a social quality they appear even less so.

Of course, we must not forget that other eminent biologists deny the existence of any organizing agency in nature other than the old established physical and chemical forces. Possibly the mechanistic theory would be regarded as the "orthodox" belief among a very large number of our biologists. Many others would simply leave this matter undetermined. The question is unsolved and becomes a "problem" of the highest interest to students of philosophy. How do protons and electrons get organized into atoms; and atoms into molecules; and living cells into plants and animals and human beings?

[1] *Space, Time, and Gravitation* (Cambridge University Press), pp. 200–01.
[2] William Morton Wheeler, *Emergent Evolution and the Development of Societies*, pp. 39, 40.

On the whole, the new physics tends to soften the old controversy between the vitalists and the mechanists. In the older theory there could be no discontinuities in nature. All that happens in the world belongs to a determined chain in the cause-and-effect sequence. If we could gain a perfect knowledge of the present, we could predict the future to the last minute detail. Discontinuities, to be sure, do appear in nature, such as that between the inorganic and the organic, or between matter and mind; but, so it is said, they are not really discontinuities, because we have been taught that such things cannot exist. The connecting chain of events must be there, could we but detect it.

But many physicists are now losing faith in this a priori reasoning. The tendency is rather to face the facts themselves, even if our beloved major premises have to be restated. Among such facts are the principle of uncertainty, illustrated by the erratic behavior of the electrons in their paths within the atom, the discovery of the statistical character of the laws of nature, the growing importance of mutations in organic evolution, displacing the older doctrine of small variations, and, finally, the renewed distrust of the nineteenth-century attempt to spread the mechanistic net over the whole universe of life and mind and matter.[1]

In conclusion, what shall we say in answer to this difficult question concerning the origin and nature of life? The problem itself is momentous, for if we can find the key to the mystery of the origin and the nature of the first living cell, we shall perhaps have found the key to the whole "grand strategy of evolution," which has culminated in human life and human consciousness and human history. Both the current theories of life, that of Mechanism and that of Vitalism, we have found to be disappointing. There is no sharp line of cleavage between the organic and the inorganic. There are no new *materials* and perhaps no new forces at work in the living cell. But it seems as though there are present in nature's depths "formative influences struggling up to freedom," impulses and urges toward organization — and toward relations which for want of a better word we may call *social*; from these new relations — this new "to-

---

[1] Compare W. F. G. Swann, *The Architecture of the Universe* (The Macmillan Company, 1934), chap. xi, "Vital Processes."

getherness" — there spring new qualities and values, making evolution truly creative.

Perhaps we may think of nature as a whole as a process of serial creation, of which the momentous outcome was to be, first, Life — then Mind, Consciousness, Society, History, Art, Literature, Science, Philosophy, and Religion.

In connection with this chapter read:

Gamertsfelder and Evans, *Fundamentals of Philosophy* (Prentice-Hall, Inc.), chap. XI.

Further references:

John B. Watson and Will Durant, "Is Man a Machine? A Socratic Dialogue," *The Forum*, November, 1929, pp. 264–70.

J. S. Haldane, *Mechanism, Life, and Personality* (John Murray).

Jacques Loeb, *The Mechanistic Conception of Life* (The University of Chicago Press).

Henri Bergson, *Creative Evolution* (Henry Holt and Company).

R. F. A. Hoernlé, *Matter, Life, Mind, God* (Harcourt Brace and Company), pp. 97–107.

Hans Driesch, "The Breakdown of Materialism" in *The Great Design*, edited by Frances Mason (The Macmillan Company, 1934), pp. 231–303.

—*The Science and Philosophy of the Organism*, The Gifford Lectures for 1908. 2 vols. (Adam and Charles Black).

Ernest William MacBride, "The Oneness and Uniqueness of Life," in *The Great Design*, edited by Frances Mason (The Macmillan Company, 1934).

W. F. G. Swann, *The Architecture of the Universe* (The Macmillan Company, 1934), chap. XI.

Henry Fairfield Osborn, *The Origin and Evolution of Life* (Charles Scribner's Sons).

Roy Wood Sellars, *Evolutionary Naturalism* (Open Court Publishing Company), chap. XV.

CHAPTER X

THE PHILOSOPHY OF EVOLUTION

IN THE last chapter we discussed the origin of life upon the earth and theories of its real nature. Life has existed on the earth's surface for nearly a thousand million years — at first in the form of simple unicellular organisms; finally in myriad types of plants and animals of almost infinite complexity, culminating in the human species, which is itself an integral part of the whole pageantry of life, and yet the possessor of mental powers such that it can survey its own entire history and speculate upon the origin and meaning of life.

How has this miraculous transformation come about? We have invented a name for the whole age-long process — and we call it *Evolution*. It is one of the most absorbing problems of philosophy — of interest to everyone who does any scientific or speculative thinking. Not long ago people who do not usually do much serious thinking became interested in evolution, and it sprang into front-page notice in every country and city newspaper. This was because certain theories of evolution seemed to conflict with certain views of religion — and people are very sensitive about their religion.

Thus it happens that evolution has become almost a mystic word. To many it seems to answer a thousand hard questions; to others it is just a problem. Even the word "evolution" — as someone has said — like its German equivalent, *Entwickelung*, is euphonic, gliding from the tongue with delightful ease. In a card catalogue of a large university library I found nearly eight hundred cards under the word "Evolution." It is questionable whether any other single subject has so large a number.

What then *is* evolution? What interest has the student of philosophy in this subject? That the world is in a constant process of change is evident enough. Society changes, customs change, our environment changes, races and animal species change, the earth's surface changes, star clusters change. As Heraclitus said in the beginning of Greek philosophy, everything moves and changes. *That it changes in a gradual and orderly manner is the doctrine of evolution.*

There would certainly appear to be nothing very *revolutionary* about *evolutionary* philosophy. It is what we should expect. Since philosophy is an attempt to understand the world, our interest in evolution will depend upon the extent to which it adds to such understanding. It will be our purpose, then, in this chapter to see to what extent the doctrine of evolution will help us to understand the world.

General theory of development

When we use the word "evolution," we usually have in mind organic evolution, or the theory that animal species are descended from other animal species, and that all species of plants and animals have a common ancestry; and we usually attribute this theory to Darwin. There are several errors in this popular conception. Evolution is a broader term than organic evolution, and refers to the general theory of development by orderly, progressive changes. By progressive changes we usually mean those in the direction of greater complexity and a higher degree of organization. In this wider sense we may speak of the evolution of stellar systems, the evolution of the earth's surface, or societal evolution. It is now believed that even our chemical elements have evolved from something simpler.

When evolution is defined as orderly progressive change, the definition is far from accurate — certainly if we wish to include under it all the gradual changes which are taking place on the earth in the onward march of time. The definition is merely a general one covering the most apparent changes taking place in the various phases of organic life. Such changes appear to be in the direction of greater complexity of structure and greater differentiation of function. As for the use of the word "progressive," this is just a problem. The word implies a goal toward which something or someone is striving. It is very tempting to think of Nature as striving toward or aiming at the production of life and its higher and higher forms, and of mind, reason, and intelligence. But we have no right to assume this in a definition of evolution. We may make it as a philosophical or even a scientific hypothesis.

Many attempts have been made to arrive at a strictly scientific definition of evolution.[1]   Sometimes it has been described simply as "a system undergoing irreversible change"; or as "genetic continuity."   Conger says that evolution implies three fundamental notions: 1. Change in time. 2. Serial order. 3. Inherent causes. To these he would add a fourth, namely, creative synthesis, if the inherent causes are to be described.

Organic evolution, on the other hand, refers to the development of living forms from simpler living forms and ultimately from the simplest micro-organisms.   It teaches that all forms of living matter, all plant and animal species, and all races of mankind are descended by gradual changes from the first primordial living germs. The theory of organic evolution was proposed long before Darwin's time and is not synonymous with Darwinism.   Darwinism is a theory or set of theories subordinate to the general doctrine of organic evolution and serving to explain the method of such evolution. While the evidences for organic evolution are now complete, the evidences for Darwin's theory are not so complete.   The following table will represent the relationship of the different kinds of evolution:

$$\text{Evolution} \begin{cases} \text{Cosmic or General Evolution} \\ \text{Organic Evolution} \begin{cases} \text{Darwinism} \\ \text{Lamarckism and other theories} \end{cases} \end{cases}$$

Evolution and religion

When the doctrine of organic evolution was brought prominently before the world by Darwin in the middle of the last century, two misconceptions arose, which in our own time have been largely corrected.   The first was that there is some kind of *conflict* between

---

[1] Such an attempt has been made by H. W. B. Joseph in his small monograph entitled *The Concept of Evolution* (Oxford, 1924), and by A. E. Taylor in chapter XII of the collective work, *Evolution in the Light of Modern Knowledge.*   Compare also Alfred J. Lotka in his *Elements of Physical Biology*, chaps. II, III, IV, and G. P. Conger in his *New Views of Evolution* (The Macmillan Company, 1929), chap. II.

The word "evolution" was little used by Darwin.   He was content to propose a theory to account for the origin of species.   In the early part of the eighteenth century, certain anatomists proposed a "theory of evolution" or preformation, according to which all the parts of a full-grown animal were present in microscopic form in the embryo, so that they had only to grow or evolve.   This theory, which was indeed a theory of unwrapping, was later given up, but the word *evolution* was resuscitated by Herbert Spencer, who proposed a grandiose theory of inorganic and organic development, to which he gave the name evolution, although etymologically the word did not fit his theory.

evolution and religion, and the second was that evolution has explained the world. As regards the first, we have come to learn that the religious attitude has been greatly strengthened by the enlarged vision which evolution has brought us. We have become accustomed now to the idea of development, and we understand its immeasurable superiority over the old spasmodic theory of creation. We see evolution everywhere about us — in nature, in society, in the mechanic arts. In recent years we have witnessed the evolution of the automobile from its crude beginnings not many years ago. Our pride and admiration in the latest smoothly perfect product is not lessened by the fact of its gradual development; neither is our admiration of man lessened by his history of growth and struggle, as he has fought his way upward from lower animate forms, overcoming every obstacle.

Perhaps much of the unhappy and needless antagonism to the theories of evolution in the last century could have been avoided, if Darwin had spoken, not of the *descent* of man, but of his *ascent*. It all looks quite different when we think of man as the crowning masterpiece of nature's evolutionary methods. The theory of evolution lends at once a new charm to the world, if we think of it as a process of realization, as the progressive creation of higher and higher values.

In Watson's beautiful poem, *The Dream of Man*, man, undaunted by the picture of his humble origin, says:

> This is my loftiest greatness
> To have been born so low.
> Greater than Thou the ungrowing
> Am I that forever grow.
>
> . . . . . .
>
> From glory to rise unto glory
> Is mine, who have risen from gloom.
> I doubt if Thou knew'st at my making
> How near to Thy throne I should climb,
> O'er the mountainous slopes of the ages
> And the conquered peaks of time.

It would be hard to exaggerate the extent to which the evolutionary or genetic method of study has enriched every department of knowledge. Evolution has given us a new method, the genetic method, by which we learn to understand things by studying their growth and development. Every science is now studied genetically, and we have come to understand that no branch of human knowledge can be understood apart from the knowledge of the way the subject-matter of that science has grown or developed. It is safe to say that both ethics and religion have participated richly in this new method and that both these subjects have been immeasurably clarified.

Evolution as a method only

The other misunderstanding that arose about evolution was almost the opposite of the first. It was that evolution had explained the world, including man and his mind, and that no other philosophy or religion was necessary. This curious error probably came about because of a confusion between evolution as a method or law of change, and evolution as a force or power. There is a popular belief that evolution is a kind of creative force, something that can do things. On the contrary, it is a mere description of nature's method. We see in evolution that nature behaves in a certain uniform way, or, if you choose, that God creates by a certain uniform method. The student of philosophy, who has already learned that natural laws are not forces nor powers, but merely observed uniformities, is not likely to fall into the mistake of making a God of evolution.

One of the surprises for us in the study of evolution is the discovery of how little of the world it has explained. It has given us a valuable method of study, by which we are able to understand the meaning of many forms and functions in relation to their historical setting; but on the deeper problems of life and mind it has thrown little light. We soon discover great gaps in its story of life, which we supposed, of course, had long since been bridged by science, but which we now find have not been bridged at all. We find that evolution has not explained what life is or how it began, or how it reproduces itself, or how growth and assimilation take place, or why there is a struggle for existence, or why or how variations occur, or even how species change into one another; nor has it explained that which is most important of all, the origin and nature of consciousness.

This disappointment, which we are sure to feel in the failure of evolution to explain our great philosophical problems, must not, however, be laid as a fault at the door of science.   It is due rather to a popular misunderstanding of the purpose and claims of evolution. The evolutionary scientist, like any other scientist, is the very last to make rash claims about solving the problems of the world.   He is, rather, a patient worker, content to point out, if he can, some of the steps in the method by which nature is working.

Herbert Spencer

One of the most important figures in nineteenth-century evolutionary philosophy is that of Herbert Spencer (1820–1903).   Spencer's *First Principles*, in which his theory of evolution is fully developed, was published in 1862, three years after the publication of Darwin's *Origin of Species*.   It does not appear that Spencer was indebted to Darwin even for his belief in organic evolution, for this had been proposed by many writers before Darwin, and Spencer merely accepted it.   Spencer's significance, indeed, does not lie in this direction, but rather in his outline of a general system of cosmic evolution.   What he gives us, therefore, is an actual system of philosophy, while Darwin was merely working on the problem of the origin of plant and animal species.

To Spencer, therefore, the whole world is a great evolutionary process.   The materials of this process are found in Matter, Motion, and Force, which are not themselves ultimate realities, but represent merely the limits of our knowledge.   He calls them *modes* of the *Unknowable*.   The world as we know it results from the redistribution of Matter, Motion, and Force.

Now, it seemed to Spencer that it is the task of philosophy to find some formula which will explain the manner of the redistribution of these three ultimate knowables, or the manner of evolution.   This formula is as follows.   It sounds rather formidable, but if carefully studied will be found to be significant of the manner in which evolution proceeds.   Evolution, then, is "an integration of matter and concomitant dissipation of motion; during which the matter passes from an indefinite, incoherent, homogeneity to a definite, coherent, heterogeneity; and during which the retained motion undergoes a parallel transformation."

Robbed of its forbidding aspect and put in simple language, this means that all changes represent a process of integration and differentiation.   In the beginning the world was a fiery mass, all alike and highly diffused.   It began to be solidified, integrated, and different. Planets were separated from the sun; land and water, mountains and valleys appeared and represented further differentiation.   Anyone can see how this process of integration and differentiation was carried on in every phase of development.   In living beings there was first the undifferentiated mass of protoplasm.   Step by step the all-alikeness is changed into manifold differences.   Certain organs are set apart for digestion, others for locomotion, others for perception. A single phase in the process may be illustrated at an advanced stage of evolution when the four-footed animal becomes erect, using his forward limbs no longer for locomotion, but for climbing and manipulation of food.   Another phase later appears when the thumb is opposed to the other four digits and a new differentiation takes place. In society the same process is seen in the division of labor; even at the present time labor is becoming more specialized daily.   Changes in language illustrate the same law.

Spencer was rather carried away with the possibilities of his favorite formula, and if not with him, at any rate with many of his disciples, it has passed for an explanation.   In later years, however, numerous exceptions were found to Spencer's law and some critics have gone so far as to ask, If it be true, what of it?   We may call this process "Evolution," but we are little wiser than we were before. We desire to know more about that mystic trio with which Spencer starts and we are unreasonable enough to ask to know more about his Unknowable.   It pleased Spencer to write this word with a capital U, and it was a convenient abyss in which to sink all the hard questions as to origins and productive and creative forces.   But this kind of Agnosticism does not appeal to the modern student, because philosophy springs from a desire to know, so that Agnosticism becomes the negation of philosophy.

On the whole, although Spencer throws little light on the philosophy of evolution for us, nevertheless he had an immense influence in the nineteenth century in extending the idea of evolution itself and applying it to every branch of knowledge.   It was this as well as his valuable contributions to special subjects, such as ethics, religion, psychology, education, that made him an outstanding thinker of the nineteenth century.

Organic evolution

The history of the doctrine of organic evolution goes back to the ancient Greeks. Aristotle not only taught the doctrine of evolution, but he had, what Darwin lacked, a theory of its *causes*. Lucretius, the Roman poet, gives a somewhat complete picture of the gradual development of animal life from the simple first beginnings and even anticipated the theory of the survival of the fittest.

In modern times evolutionary views were freely advanced in the latter half of the eighteenth century and the first half of the nineteenth. In these years a long list of writers, among whom was the poet Goethe, anticipated the theory of organic evolution, that animal species have a common ancestry and have arisen by a process of gradual change from simpler animate forms. The theory was held by Darwin's grandfather, Erasmus Darwin, before the close of the eighteenth century.

Lamarck

It was Lamarck, however, the famous French naturalist, who at the opening of the nineteenth century first formulated a complete theory of species transformation. But Lamarck's *explanation* of the origin of new species was radically different from that which afterwards became famous as Darwinism. Lamarck's view is both interesting and important, because it has to some extent been revived in our own time, when the difficulties in Darwin's theory have become recognized. Furthermore, it seems to be the more natural and easy method for explaining the changes which have taken place in plants and animals. Lamarck supposed that the environment modifies individual organisms and that the modifications thus produced are transmitted by the organisms to their offspring. In the case of animals he recognized also the modifying effect of use and disuse of bodily organs and the influence of effort and desire on the part of the animal. Since, now, the modifications which result from the action of the environment and from use and disuse are said to be passed on by inheritance, his theory involves the *inheritance of acquired characters*, a phrase which has become famous, leading to a century-long dispute. If we may suppose that such changes take place in animal bodies and may be passed on to the offspring by inheritance, the whole plan of evolution becomes much simpler.

Thus suppose, to take the classical instance, that giraffes, or the ancestors of the giraffe, once did not have long necks. The constant stretching of the neck to get the tender leaves at the tops of the trees would elongate it. This elongation would be inherited by the next generation. In this way changes of all kinds might take place in the bodily structure of animals or in their habits, even to the forming of new species.

We could easily see how, for instance, the peculiar structure of the hind legs of the cat, admirably fitted for jumping upon her prey, and of the shorter, stiffer forelegs, fitted for receiving her weight after the jump, has come about simply by modifications due to the practice of jumping; and the new practice of jumping might itself be explained by a change in the conditions in which the cat lives, such as a necessitated change in the food supply. But Lamarck seems also to think that there are deep desires or "needs" in the organism resulting from internal forces tending toward development.

To the beginner in these studies Lamarck's theory of evolution seems very natural and convincing. It seems reasonable that the action of the environment should constantly be modifying habits and structure, and that an animal or man could, according to his desire, by use or disuse of any organ, gradually change its structure or function, and, furthermore, that these modifications could be transmitted to the next generation, thus perhaps finally effecting radical changes, even to the production of new species.

The inheritance of acquired characters

But it will be seen that Lamarck's theory, captivating as it is, rests upon a certain assumption, and herein lies the difficulty. It rests upon the assumption that modifications of structure acquired during the life of an individual can be passed on by inheritance to his offspring. This inheritance of acquired characters has in modern times come to be doubted, both because it is impossible to explain theoretically how it could occur and because there is very little actual evidence that it does occur.

If, then, modifications in the structure and habits of animals cannot be passed on by inheritance, how in the world can we explain evolution? Animal species would seem to remain unchanged from generation to generation; as indeed outwardly they appear to. Now, although Darwin himself did have a limited belief in the inheritance of acquired characters, nevertheless his theory of evolution gets along without it. Presently we shall see how Darwin thinks this wonderful thing is accomplished — by small chance variations and natural selection.

But first a word more ought to be said about the inheritance of acquired characters. At first sight it appears wholly reasonable that such characters should be inherited and even to be borne out by daily observation. Are not the sons of blacksmiths sturdy and the sons and daughters of musicians musical, and are not these and many other qualities inherited from parents who have acquired them? If by diligent and persistent effort through the years of my youth and manhood I strengthen my muscles, heart, or lungs, increase my skill of hand or foot, improve my voice, cultivate my taste, purify my morals, may I not hand these acquirements on to my children? Yes, but it will be by social inheritance, not by biological inheritance. Biologically the physical and mental equipment of the child is the same as that with which his father started, not the same as that with which his father ended, save only by such individual differences as are due to what are called *variations*, coming, it is believed, from internal causes. If at first it seems rather discouraging to learn that our dearly earned virtues cannot be handed on to our children, we may at least take some comfort from the fact that our acquired vices are not handed on either; but in either case this is only a half-truth, for in such matters social inheritance is of the utmost importance. We may be very sure that our children and our grandchildren will inherit by imitation, association, and instruction both our acquired virtues and vices, but at birth they will start where their parents started. If the sons of blacksmiths are sturdy and the children of musicians musical, it is because these qualities run in these families, not because the parents have acquired them by practice or exercise.

It should be said, however, that biologists are not now wholly agreed about the non-inheritance of acquired characters, and the subject is again under investigation, the interest in it being renewed owing to the difficulties which have arisen in the alternative Darwinian hypothesis. Ingenious researches are being made in many laboratories in the attempt to unravel this knotty and puzzling problem, with results which by no means confirm us in the old belief that bodily modification can have no effect upon the germ-plasm.

Darwinism

Charles Darwin was born in 1809 and died in 1882. His *Origin of Species* was published in 1859 and his *Descent of Man* in 1871. In the history of science Darwin's work ranks in importance with that of Copernicus, Galileo, and Newton, in giving new direction to human thought and stimulating scientific research. It is true that nearly all the fundamental principles of Darwin's new science had been anticipated by other workers, but it was his patient and painstaking research and the clear formulation of his theory, which launched it upon the world as a new scientific view. It is perhaps true that Darwin's method is more valuable than his theory of evolution, being a perfect example of the inductive method, coupled with inexhaustible patience in research and experimentation, and associated with the utmost candor, honesty, and mental grace. After an initial draft of his theory in 1842, Darwin deferred its publication for seventeen years, during which time the theory of natural selection was independently proposed by his friend, Alfred Russel Wallace. Acrimony, however, and jealousy were qualities unknown to these searchers after truth.

The mere machinery of Darwinism, though familiar to everyone, may be briefly summarized. Every species of animal is enormously prolific, tending to increase in geometrical ratio. There is a certain kind of codfish which produces two hundred million eggs. It has been estimated that a single dandelion plant, should all its seeds mature, would in the fourth generation produce plants enough to cover a land area 245 times greater than that of the United States. A single bacterium might produce a million bacteria in a day,[1] and

[1] See William M. Goldsmith, *The Laws of Life*, p. 186.

Linnaeus said that three flies and their offspring could consume the carcass of a horse as speedily as a lion could.

Since, then, plant and animal species are so prolific, there is neither room nor food enough for all. Hence there follows a *struggle for existence*, in which there will be a *survival of the fittest*. Who are the fittest? Those individuals best adapted to the environment. Why should there be any difference in this respect between individuals? Because of slight *variations* in structure or function between individuals of the same species, even those born of the same parents. Like begets like, but not just like. Those having favorable variations will be selected and preserved. This is called *natural selection*. They will live, thrive, and propagate, probably transmitting their favorable variations to their offspring. The less favored ones will perish. Gradually, in this way, there will be a modification of structure and in time a modification so great as to result in a new species. The sharp tooth, the tearing claw, the horny hide, the warm fur, all are useful in the desperate battle of life with enemies and elements, and all have arisen by slight accidental variations selected and preserved by heredity. Among birds that did not migrate, some individuals accidentally migrating would find more abundant food, would live and thrive and transmit this new peculiarity to their offspring. Thus instincts arise. Even the human eye, the greatest wonder of adaptation, might so arise from a single group of cells sensitive to light, thus warning the fortunate possessors of this variation of danger or prey.

If the difference between Lamarck's theory and that of Darwin is not entirely clear to the reader, it will become so if we use again the illustration of the peculiar structure of the hind legs of the cat. With Lamarck, individual cats actually change the structure of their legs by constant jumping after their prey, and these changes are passed on by inheritance and added to by the next generation. With Darwin the change is not due to practice, but is an accidental one, having its origin in internal causes in the germ-plasm of the individual. Some cat was born with a variation in the structure of the legs favorable to jumping. In the struggle for existence such an individual would have an advantage over others of its kind owing to this modification. While its competitors in the struggle might die, such an individual would live and prosper and pass on to its off-spring this favorable variation, since it was due to an inner factor and would be heritable.   Thus Nature selects.

This, then, is the celebrated Darwinian theory of the evolution of plant and animal species.   The theory is ingenious — even fascinat-ing.   It will be noticed that it does not depend upon the modifying action of the environment, nor upon the modifying effect of use and disuse, nor does it involve the inheritance of acquired characters. It assumes only the occurrence of small variations, which might be accidental, and the preservation of the favorable ones by natural selection.   Certainly such variations do occur and surely natural selection would seem to preserve them.   What the student of phi-losophy wishes to know, however, is whether the theory will really work.   Will it explain the origin of new species and will it explain the progressive development of species from the simplest micro-organisms to the wonderful complexity of the human body, and, most important of all, will it explain the coming of intelligence and the human mind?   And finally, *if* Darwin's theory *will* explain all these, then just what assumptions are involved in it?   What does Darwin take for granted and what does he explain?

In connection with this chapter read:

Darwin, *Origin of Species* (D. Appleton and Company).
Gamertsfelder and Evans, *Fundamentals of Philosophy* (Prentice-Hall, Inc.), chap. x.

Further references:

Sir J. Arthur Thomson, *Riddles of Science* (Liveright Publishing Company, 1932), chap. XLVI.
James Ward, *Naturalism and Agnosticism* (The Macmillan Company), I, Lectures 7, 9, 10.
H. H. Lane, *Evolution and Christian Faith* (Princeton University Press).
Creation by Evolution, Frances Mason, Editor (The Macmillan Company).
G. Watts Cunningham, *Problems of Philosophy* (Henry Holt and Company), Part IV.
Geddes and Thomson, *Evolution* (Home University Library, Henry Holt and Company).
J. Arthur Thomson, *The Gospel of Evolution* (G. P. Putnam's Sons).

CHAPTER XI
EVOLUTION SINCE DARWIN

Controversies

UPON the publication of Darwin's two books, *The Origin of Species* and *The Descent of Man*, a storm of controversy burst forth in England on the subject of evolution. Darwin had included man, both body and mind, in the long history of development, so that his views came into apparent conflict with religious beliefs. It must be remembered that there was a twofold content in Darwin's teaching, one relating to the *fact* of evolution, the other to its *method*. Only scientists were interested in the second; the world at large and particularly the religious world was deeply interested in the first.

Darwin's health, which was never good, did not permit him to make public defence of his position; but he found a zealous and able defender in Thomas H. Huxley, who wrote and lectured in vigorous and effective defence of evolution. Long before the close of the century it had become an accepted theory not only in England but in other civilized countries. If there is still any opposition to it, even in religious circles, this is found only in certain communities in America. Evolution is no longer a theory but a law.

But what about Darwin's own particular theory of organic evolution? How has that fared among scientists since Darwin's time? Is it still believed that the secret of evolution is found in the natural selection of small, chance variations? Here the agreement among scientists has been much less unanimous. Difficulties began early to appear in Darwin's theory, and succeeding years witnessed a gradual divergence from it.

Weismann

First, a mechanistic interpretation of organic evolution was encouraged by Huxley, Tyndall, Haeckel, and others, an interpretation not contemplated by Darwin himself. This was still further promoted by the Neo-Darwinians, following Weismann. Furthermore, Weismann's very important discoveries concerning the continuity of the germ-plasm and the immortality of the germ-cells completely changed Darwin's theory of heredity.   Probably nothing since the publication of *The Origin of Species* — excepting only de Vries' theory of mutations — has done so much to influence the course of evolutionary science as August Weismann's discovery that heredity depends solely upon the transmission of the germ-cells, which are not affected by changes in the body cells and which are transmitted from generation to generation subject only to their own variations or mutations.   This discovery transformed Darwin's theory of the origin of evolutionary changes, for he supposed them to originate in modifications of the body cells, whereas Weismann showed that the germ-cells are unaffected by such changes.

> In development a part of the germ-plasm (i.e., the essential germinal material) contained in the parent egg cell is not used up in the construction of the body of the offspring, but is reserved unchanged for the formation of the germ-cells of the following generation.[1]

Heredity, therefore, works in such a way that every individual springs not really from the parent but from the "immortal" germ-cells safely stored and preserved by the parent.   This discovery, made by Weismann though anticipated by Galton, does not weaken Darwin's theory of descent; it merely enriches it, since evolution is made more than ever dependent upon the principle of natural selection.   The inheritance of acquired characters was made more improbable than ever.

Notwithstanding the increased emphasis upon natural selection by the Neo-Darwinians, it began to be apparent that although natural selection is an indispensable factor in evolution, it cannot in any sense be called a *cause* of evolution.   Indeed, the cause or causes of evolution remain unknown today, as they were when Vernon L. Kellogg wrote as follows ten years ago:

> Since Darwin's day much has been added to our knowledge of the facts about the manner and the effect of evolution, but only two important new alleged causal factors have been presented for consideration as primary causes of evolution; these are mutations and Mendelian inheritance.   Neither has had any general acceptance as sufficient

---

[1] Geddes and Thomson, *Evolution* (Henry Holt and Company), p. 114, quoting Weismann.

explanation of either species-forming or adaptation, which are the co-ordinate fundamental problems of organic evolution. In this same post-Darwinian period, also, the two most important explanations of evolution current in Darwin's time, namely, Lamarckism, or the inheritance of acquired characters, and Darwinism, or natural and sexual selection, have been weakened rather than strengthened as sufficient causes of evolution. Hence we are in the curious position of knowing now much more about evolution than was known fifty and sixty years ago, but of feeling much less confident that we know the causes of evolution.[1]

Mutations

De Vries' epoch-making discovery took place in 1900. From that time to the present more and more attention has been given to mutations in the study of evolution and less to variations. Heredity says that like produces like. The theory of variations says that like produces like but not just like. The theory of mutations says that like usually produces like, but sometimes something wholly different is suddenly produced — at least something so different that it may be called a new variety or a new sub-species — possibly even a new species. Darwin had tried to explain the origin of species — but de Vries in his experiments with the evening primrose actually saw something like this right before his eyes. He found that new types suddenly appeared, these types breeding true. To these sudden, decisive changes he gave the name "mutations," to distinguish them from the slight "variations," which Darwin had emphasized. Incidentally, it should be noted, that the mystery of evolution was greatly increased, not diminished. Why should mutations happen?

Palaeontologists have found evidence that in former geologic times mutations were more frequent and more extreme than at present, thus helping to explain the vast separation of plant and animal species. Austin H. Clark, in his book, *The New Evolution*, says, "Unbroken continuity of descent coupled with abrupt discontinuity or change in bodily form is a common, striking and well known phenomenon in all types of animal life. It is far more striking among the invertebrates than it is among the vertebrates."[2]

[1] Vernon L. Kellogg, "Where Evolution Stands Today," *The New Republic*, April 11. 1923.
[2] Austin H. Clark, *The New Evolution, Zoogenesis* (Williams and Wilkins Company, Baltimore, 1930), p. 188.

Mr. Clark goes further and brings forward the astonishing theory that the major groups of animals have existed from the very beginning:

> There can be only one interpretation of this entire lack of any intermediates between the major groups of animals — as for instance between the backboned animals or vertebrates, the echinoderms, the mollusks and the arthropods.
>
> If we are willing to accept the facts, we must believe that there never were such intermediates, or in other words that these major groups have from the very first borne the same relation to each other that they have today.[1]

This sounds like creationism, a theory which Mr. Clark hastens to repudiate, the explanation being apparently that in the earliest stages of organic life discontinuities were found more abrupt than even our modern mutations.

Mutations breed true; but how do the new varieties or species survive? The answer is, by natural selection. So it has come about that Darwinism survives even in this altered form — and is perhaps stronger today than at any time since its threatened collapse in the early years of this century. Darwinism has evolved as everything does; and Darwin himself would be the first to expect and to welcome new discoveries and new developments.

Unexplained factors

Just how much have Darwin and his brilliant successors contributed to our real understanding of the world of living things? How far have they helped us to understand man — his wonderful body and his even more wonderful mind? If we grant certain things, let us say the first living cell, heredity, variations and mutations, the struggle for existence, and natural selection, then we see how there might be a gradual development from the simplest organisms to the most complex. But as soon as we begin to examine these presuppositions critically, we find that we know little about them. Evolution has been so much exalted as the discovery of one of Nature's great secrets that the student of philosophy is somewhat confused to find how little it explains and how much depends upon the postulates with which it starts.

[1] *The New Evolution*, p. 189.

The theory of organic evolution is based upon three postulates — or shall we say, three mysteries. They are the struggle for existence, heredity, and variations or mutations. Of course, the value of a scientific theory concerning the origin and diversification of species is not weakened because of these unexplained postulates, since the struggle for existence, heredity, and variations and mutations are facts which nobody disputes. The trouble arises when the casual reader infers that a Darwinian theory of evolution explains more than it attempts to explain. The scientist no doubt would rejoice to understand all about the struggle for existence and heredity and the deep causes of mutations; but for the present he may, like Darwin, be content to take these for granted and try to work out a theory of descent.

Consider, for instance, the struggle for existence. The careless reader of Darwin might think that the struggle for existence is explained by the fact that more individuals are born than there is room or food for; but, of course, this explanation assumes the activity, insurgency, and spontaneity which belong to all life. If, then, one would really seek for an explanation of evolution, if one would hope to understand the progressive unfolding of living forms and functions culminating in the supreme intelligence of man, the secret would seem to lie rather in the insurgency of life than in the action of a negative principle like natural selection. One would say, "Right here lies the secret and the explanation of evolution — in the very nature of life, in the will to live, in the primordial impulse, push, appetency, desire, aspiration, or whatever it is, which is life itself." Granting this, the mere machinery of evolution, Darwinian or other, is of less interest.

Heredity

Many people seem to think that evolution has explained the world of living things, although no biologist dreams of making any such claim. Let us consider the matter of heredity, so fundamental in the Darwinian theory. To what extent has it been explained by Weismann's theory of the continuity of the germ-plasm, by the Mendelian laws of inheritance and by the discovery of the marvelous structure of the germ-cell with its chromosomes and genes?

The fact of heredity is so familiar to us that we forget the amazing wonder of it. Think of those tiny bits of matter, the seeds of our common garden flowers. Many of the different kinds look much alike. Some of them are so small that they can hardly be distinguished by the eye. In each one is a germ-cell, and from that cell springs a new plant, repeating in a thousand minute details the mother plant from which the seed came. And then the plant produces a flower just like the flower of last summer; and then from the flowers come a host of tiny seeds, each one again possessing the same marvelous potencies. Does the seed "remember" the form of the parent flower? How does it all happen?

If this is hard to understand, think of the human body with its almost infinite complexity. Think of the details of one single organ like the eye or the marvelously complicated structure of the brain; and then recall that the human organism springs from a tiny egg-cell, which has the potency, when properly fertilized by a still more minute sperm cell, of producing another human form, slowly maturing during a score of years, resembling when mature the parent form in all its wonderful details, and even repeating a host of little habits and mannerisms belonging to the particular individual or family from which it sprang. Language fails to give any adequate idea of the miracle of biological inheritance.

When we first hear about the continuity and immortality of germ-plasm, we might almost think that heredity has been explained. For if the germ-cells are actually continued from parent to child, then the child would be like the parent. But there are two difficulties easily overlooked. Though the germ-cells were the same as those of the parent, how does it come about that the body cells and all parts of the body of the child are like those of the parent? We do not know. But *are* the germ-cells of the child the *same* as those of the parent — or are they just similar?

An illustration will make this clear. Put a pair of mice in a granary. Each mouse has a certain amount of germ-plasm in its organism. Some of this may be transmitted to the offspring. But in a short period there will be one hundred mice from the pair and each of these will have as much of this germinal material as the original parents. Evidently the original amount of germ-plasm has been multiplied by fifty, the new parts "inheriting" all the peculiarities of the original. Put in this way, we can see that heredity is not explained by the theory of the continuity or immortality of the germ-plasm.

When we come to think of it, nothing *could* be continuous from generation to generation except the process and the form; and to say that the form is continuous is just to say that the child resembles the parent. In other words, heredity is transmission. The theory of the continuity of the germ-plasm makes it easier for us to understand how successive generations remain essentially the same, because they spring from *similar* germ-plasm — not from the *same*; but when we say similar germ-plasm, we are assuming the whole mystery of heredity. What we are apt to forget is that in both parent and child the amount of germ-plasm is constantly increased by the division of the germ-cells, and in this division the fundamental mystery of heredity is packed.

Neither should we allow ourselves to think that the new knowledge of the structure of the germ-cell has explained the wonder of heredity. The *gene* theory, proposed and elaborated in America by T. H. Morgan and his associates, has vastly extended the scientific knowledge of the germ-cell. It appears that the latter is a veritable wonder-box of amazing marvels. Mendel has shown that in biparental inheritance the various traits and characters of the parents are distributed in the offspring as specific units, not mixed or blended, and always according to very definite laws. It is now known that the source of this peculiarity of inheritance is found in the structure of the germ-cell. Each cell contains a definite number of minute masses of chromatin, called chromosomes. There is a definite and characteristic number of chromosomes in the cells of each species of plants or animals. The microscope fails to resolve the chromosome into its parts, but we know that it is made up of a large number of separate particles called *genes*. The genes are distinct individuals, each one different from the others and each one standing for some distinct trait of inheritance in the generation to follow. Genes are "the highly varied and highly specific discrete units, perhaps the ultimate units of life." [1]

[1] H. H. Newman, *Evolution Yesterday and Today* (The Century of Progress Series), p. 145.

Concerning the actual constitution of the genes we know little. We must believe that they exist, for only in this manner can the facts of inheritance be explained. Heredity and diversity can only be due to the fact that the genes are sorted and distributed in certain ways. It does not really help us in the understanding of heredity to say that there is a mechanism called mitosis, which "attends to the equitable passing on from cell to cell of the units of heredity." Nor does it help us to understand the diversity factor in inheritance to be told that there is another "mechanism," called meiosis "that shuffles the maternal and paternal genes of each parent and deals out a great variety of assortments of the ancestral genes present," [1] thus furnishing material for the operation of natural selection.

Even the use of the word "mechanism" has a certain question-begging aspect. What we seem to have in the germ-cells is a series of marvelous *contrivances* for the carrying on of a plant or animal species by means of heredity. Machines are, to be sure, contrivances — but contrivances of some agent to gain some end. It all seems as if some inherent intelligence, or some impulse or push, were striving toward some goal, the goal being both the continuation and the diversification of the species. We might, of course, personify Nature and think of her as the directing agency; or we might introduce some "entelechy" or an *élan vital*; or finally we might just introduce the word "mechanism," without explaining how a mechanism could do such wonderful things. We do not know that there is any guiding agency such as the *élan vital*, nor do we know that there is anything in the germ-cell which might answer to a mechanism. The things that happen in this whole complicated process which we call heredity would seem to be best described by some such terms as struggle, ingenuity, invention, purpose, planning, strategy, or desire for self-perpetuation and self-expression. We have, of course, no right to assume the presence of anthropomorphic forces such as these terms imply, nor have we any right to call the whole process mechanical. The genes are believed to be the very units of life. We know nothing of their inner being. They may be organisms as complex as are the cells themselves. We may call them tiny bits of chemicals or, if we please, we may call them the divinities within us. Judging

[1] *Idem*, p. 122.

from the marvelous manner of their combinations and the stupendous results emerging therefrom, we might well say that the genes behave like genii.

I have referred to the excellent little book by Professor Newman in the Century of Progress Series. His description of the processes of heredity is strictly scientific, and yet he uses somewhat naïvely such expressions as "guiding factors" in evolution, a mechanism that "attends to the equitable distribution of the units of heredity." He speaks of some mutants as being "better than" others, and of tissues and organs that "work together in unity and harmony." [1]

Evidently it is not easy to describe in mechanistic language what goes on in the germ-cell. At any rate the secret of evolution seems to center here. It is here that mutations originate and at the present time the key to organic evolution is sought more and more in mutations. Wisely Tennyson said of the flower in the crannied wall that if we could know it all in all we should know what God and man is. But biologists are teaching us that it is in the germ-cell of the flower that the secret really lies.

While it is no doubt true that biologists have discovered the abode of the secrets of heredity, we must await with great interest further studies in this direction. In particular we must await the effects which the new discoveries in physics may have upon these researches in genetics. Professor Whitehead refers to this in the following quotation:

This general deduction from the modern doctrine of physics vitiates many conclusions drawn from the applications of physics to other sciences, such as physiology, or even such as physics itself. For example, when geneticists conceive genes as the determinants of heredity. The analogy of the old concept of matter sometimes leads them to ignore the influence of the particular animal body in which they are functioning. They presuppose that a pellet of matter remains in all respects self-identical whatever be its changes of environment. So far as modern physics is concerned, such characteristics may, or may not, effect changes in the genes, changes which are important in certain respects, though not in others. Thus, no a priori argument as to the inheritance of characters can be drawn from the mere doctrine of genes. In fact, recently, physiologists have found that genes are modified in

[1] H. H. Newman, *Evolution Yesterday and Today* (Williams and Wilkins Company, 1932), pp. 104, 107, 123, 156.

some respects by their environment. The presuppositions of the old common-sense view survive, even when the view itself has been abandoned as a fundamental description.[1]

Natural selection

What is the philosophical significance of natural selection? What light does it throw upon the apparently upward trend of evolution, upon the successive steps in increased complexity of organisms, upon the growing differentiation of parts, upon the appearance of instinct and intelligence? It is necessary for the student of philosophy to understand, if he can, just what natural selection is, for in the successive revisions of Darwin's theory which have taken place since the beginning of this century, the importance of natural selection in organic evolution has been emphasized more rather than less. This will be understood if we attempt a brief statement of the present biological doctrine of organic evolution, as follows: Evolution takes place through heritable variations, that is, mutations, in the germ-plasm, specifically, in the genes, the cause of these variations being unknown. When these variations are of such a character as to result in favorable adaptations of the organism, they are preserved by natural selection. These changes accumulating, new varieties and even new species may arise.

The reason that the full difficulties in the Darwinian hypothesis have not been appreciated is that the popular mind is prone to *personify* natural selection, to think of it as some kind of intelligent direction of affairs, to think of it as using *strategy*, so to speak, as selecting, nursing, encouraging, promoting; in other words, to think of it, as many people do of natural laws, as some kind of *force* or *agency*, by which evolution is accomplished. "What is called Darwinism," said John Burroughs, "is entirely an anthropomorphic view of Nature — Nature humanized and doing as man does. What is called Natural Selection is man's selection read into animate nature." [2]

When we come to realize that natural selection is not an agency of any kind, that it is merely the name of a certain sifting process in

[1] A. N. Whitehead, *Nature and Life* (The University of Chicago Press, Chicago, 1934), pp. 13, 14. By permission of the publishers.

[2] John Burroughs, *loc. cit.*, p. 242.

nature which checks the insurgency of life, then we begin to understand how little enlightenment has come to the student of philosophy from this source. Someone has said that natural selection is really natural rejection; but the trouble is that either word, selection or rejection, implies to the uninitiated some sort of intelligent *inspection, appraisement,* and final *decision.* Now that the whole evolutionary process does imply some appraisement of values, at least some strategy seems the more evident the more we study it; but let us get out of our minds the notion that natural selection is such an appraising or strategical agency. Natural selection merely sifts out those individuals who are not so peculiarly fitted to the environment as to survive in the struggle. If we could think of natural selection as a kind of policeman who guards the door of evolution and knocks on the head all who do not present themselves with a new and better equipment for the strife, even then the secret of evolution will be found, not in the obstructing policeman, but *in the genius of the individuals who devise the new equipment.* But we may not even think of natural selection as such an intelligent *sorter* of the fit from the unfit, as we have in artificial breeding of domestic animals. *All* the individuals pass through the gate and the unfit die of starvation. Evidently we must look elsewhere than to natural selection for the springs of progress and the source and secrets of evolution.

And that is all there is to Natural Selection. It is a name for a process of elimination which is constantly going on in animate nature all about us. It is in no sense creative, it originates nothing, but clinches and toughens existing forms.... What I mean to say is that there must be the primordial tendency to development which Natural Selection is powerless to beget, and which it can only speed up or augment. It cannot give the wing to the seed, or the spring, or the hook; or the feather to the bird; or the scale to the fish; but it can perfect all these things. The fittest of its kind does stand the best chance to survive.[1]

To the student of philosophy, therefore, keen to know something of the real secrets of evolution, the principle of natural selection is a distinct disappointment. His interest turns away from this negative blocking process to the force or the genius or the strategy which provides individuals with the *new equipment,* enabling them to elude the destructive power of competition. Neither is any help promised

[1] John Burroughs, *los. cit.,* pp. 246–47.

from the principle of the survival of the fittest, a phrase first used by Herbert Spencer, since this is merely another way of expressing the action of natural selection. It does not mean that those individuals who are absolutely the fittest — that is, the best — survive, but those whose qualities best fit their possessors to the immediate environment.

An overworked word

On the whole, all the theories of organic evolution, including Darwinism, are somewhat disappointing to the student of philosophy, who is trying to understand the world of living things. There are more gaps and unexplained factors than we supposed — and they are found in very critical places. Most disappointing of all is the complete failure of any accepted theory to determine the causes of evolution itself. The fact is that evolution is a very much overworked word. At the close of the last century and in the beginning of this one, the idea of evolution held almost undisputed sway. It was extended far beyond its original application and applied quite universally.

We began to hear of inorganic, cosmic, astral, geologic and atomic evolution. Even the "delirious electrons" evolved into atoms, and matter itself was the product of a process of development. Social evolution had already made its appearance, and we learned that the new law applied also to the development of language, ideas, beliefs, the family, the church and the state, and to social and political institutions. In fact, in those days of first enthusiasms it occurred to no one that there is any realm of reality at all excluded from the field of evolution. Nothing is fixed or final; nothing is created; everything just grew and is growing.

Out of these enthusiasms there did indeed spring a wonderful new impetus to scientific study, as the fruit of the genetic method began to be evident to us. Our understanding of all things was amazingly increased by the knowledge of their genetic relations. But lately the limitations of the evolutionary philosophy have begun to appear. Spencer's identification of progress and evolution first was called in question. Recent post-war history has sobered the optimism which was the heritage of nineteenth-century enthusiasm for the future of humanity, encouraged by the Spencerian-Darwinian philosophy. Sociologists now have less to say about societal evolution.   Society changes, but seldom in an orderly manner.   Sometimes its changes are sudden and disastrous.

Again, the hypothetical evolution of matter, according to which the chemical elements may have arisen from some simple proto-element, like hydrogen, turns out when examined to be anything but an evolutionary or unwrapping process.   It would be decidedly a building-up process, more like an architectural enterprise in human affairs.   We may question whether either the word evolution, or the word development, is the proper one to apply to the series of changes studied by Darwin in the world of living organisms, or to the succes-sive steps by which life and mind have appeared in the world. Evolution means unwrapping, unrolling, or unfolding.   It indicates a process in which the implicit is becoming explicit, the potential, actual.   There is no evidence that organic evolution is in any sense an unwrapping process.   On the contrary, it is distinctly of an epi-genetic or upbuilding character.   Even the simplest Darwinian va-riation, much more a mutation, is a real increment, a novelty, a new creation, a veritable plus.   The whole movement so brilliantly de-scribed by Darwin and his predecessors and successors could more correctly have been called an *epigenesis*.   But this word is forbid-ding — and besides has a technical meaning in biology debarring it from general use.   It conveys, however, the meaning of growing *upon, not out of.*

Neither is evolution a process in which the potential is becoming actual.   We speak of the evolution of the automobile — but the latest skilled product of this art was not potential in the first crude machine.   Every improvement has been a new creation, a new thought.

Tyndall said that in matter he saw the promise and potency of all life.   This was mere rhetoric, fitted to stir a nineteenth-century audience.   Since we do not know the causes of evolution, we do not know of any developmental potency in matter.   The only way to support this proposition would be to argue that since all life has come out of matter, it must have been contained potentially in it, where the only authority for the major premise is the etymological meaning of the word evolution. One might as well say that one sees in oxygen and hydrogen the promise and potency of water and all its forms, or in the behavior of apes the promise and potency of the infinitesimal calculus. Water satisfies thirst, and revives the drooping plant, and freezes at zero Centigrade. But certainly there is no promise of any of these qualities in oxygen and hydrogen. There is something more than oxygen and hydrogen in a molecule of water, namely, a certain peculiar organization with the accompanying characteristic qualities of water.

Briefly, then, the meaning of evolution is that it is a creative process, something new appearing at every step of the developmental history. Every change is a transformation. The French word *transformisme* is a happier word than the English *evolution*, or the German *Entwickelung*. The word *development*, which has been defined as "the revelation of the successive phases of something in which there is a manifest unity," is better than *evolution*, since it does not connote an unwrapping process; but it fails again to carry the notion of a plus or increase. What we call evolution is neither an unwrapping of something, nor is it the mere revelation of a unity. It seems more like a series of surprises, like the invention of air transports, or telephonic speech with Europe.

Evolution is a history of new forms and functions. Every new form is a plus — a new creation. Since Wundt introduced the notion of creative synthesis, the word *creation* is coming into general use both in science and philosophy. Creation does not mean the production of something out of nothing. The architect creates a Gothic cathedral, but not the stone and mortar. The promoter creates a new organization, but he does not create the men that compose it. Creation means just this — the production of something distinctly new and unique. Reality is found, as Aristotle told us long ago, in structure, form, organization, and function — not in the mere stuff which happens to compose the material. Organic evolution is essentially constructive and creative.

Thus Darwinism has nothing to teach us concerning either the origin or the nature of life and mind. It records only the unexplained appearance of an unending series of new events, one of which is the great event of mind. If we seek to know the origin of life and mind, we must go beyond Darwin in some deeper analysis of the process called evolution. It is not an unrolling process. It is not a movement from the potential to the actual. It cannot be defined as a series of orderly changes, for as far as the changes are evolutionary, they are disorderly. To define it as a system undergoing irreversible change is accurate but not illuminating. Spencer's definition of evolution as a process of integration and differentiation touches one of its peculiarities, but tells us nothing of its inner nature; and Spencer's celebrated formula, supposed to describe, if not to explain, the whole evolutionary process in nature in all her departments, is now generally believed to be "empty." We know that evolution is integrative, expansive, constructive, epigenetic, creative, formative. It seems like a work of creative imagination. It reminds us ever of the work of the artist. "If we personify Animate Nature, it must at least be as an artist with inexhaustible imaginative resources, with extraordinary mastery of materials." [1]

However attractive it may be to compare evolution with the work of the artist or to think of it as the product of creative imagination, this is going beyond our present knowledge. So far as we can now see, evolution is a process of organization, the formation of new unitary complexes, the characteristic reactions of which issue in the new qualities, new functions and new activities which mark the steps of evolutionary progress. Provisionally, evolution may be defined as a process of organization, tending to increased complexity and integration, and to increased definiteness and stability, issuing in new structures, each with its characteristic reaction, thus giving to the world new qualities, new powers and new modes of action, all leading to increased control and enlarged freedom. The human body is such a new structure; and the human mind is such a new power and mode of action.

The evolution of man

About thirty thousand years ago, there lived in central Europe a race of men called the Cro-Magnons. They were tall and straight and handsome, with brains as large or larger than our own. They left paintings on the walls of their cave dwellings indicating high

---

[1] *The Outline of Science*, edited by J. Arthur Thomson (G. P. Putnam's Sons, New York), III. p. 705. 4 vols.

artistic skill.   Mankind seems to have changed little anatomically
or physiologically since their time.

But if we go further back in geologic history, the story is different.
Fossil remains dating from a period nearly half a million years ago
show a low-browed, brutish being possessed of cunning so superior
to the ferocious animal of that time that he could survive among
them.   Has the cunning of the *Eoanthropus* developed into the human intelligence of today?

The controversy which has raged over the question of human
evolution has made the search for the so-called "missing link" between man and ape highly interesting; and this interest has been
stimulated from time to time by the discovery in ancient geologic
deposits of skulls or parts of skulls and certain bones and teeth strik-
ingly similar to those of man.   The oldest of these finds was that of
the Java man, or the *Pithecanthropus erectus*, found in Java in geological deposits laid down half a million years ago.   Then came the
Heidelberg man, and then the numerous remains of the Neanderthal
men who are believed to have lived in Europe fifty thousand years
ago.   These men were short and immensely strong, with beetling
brows and low foreheads.   They shambled along or squatted around
their primitive campfires and carved beautiful flints.   Other discoveries were those of the Piltdown man who lived in England possibly two hundred thousand years ago, and the Rhodesian man and
the very ancient Pekin man found in China in 1929.

It is now generally recognized by anthropologists that none of
these were the ancestors of *Homo sapiens*, the man of today.   They
were the so-called "tentative men," side branches off the main ancestral line leading to modern man.   They were not among nature's
successful experiments; they became extinct.

> The dimly descried history — for the inquiry is still young — gives
> one the impression of tentative apes and tentative men, of ages of
> experiment and sifting, of a candelabra-like branching of the genealogi-
> cal tree.   All who envisage the facts clearly must resent the vulgarity
> of the half-truth that "man sprang from monkeys."   To many, who
> are willing to pass beyond scientific description, to philosophical or
> religious interpretation, it is impossible to shut out the idea of an in-
> herent purpose as the core of the evolution process.[1]

[1] J. Arthur Thomson, *The Gospel of Evolution.* (By permission of G. P. Putnam's Sons. New
York, 1926.)

Recent theories of evolution

In recent philosophical theories the belief in formative influences or formative forces at every evolutionary stage is very common. Bergson's *Creative Evolution*, referred to in the preceding chapter, has been a fruitful source for later thought. General Smuts of South African fame has written a book called *Holism and Evolution* [1] in which he sets forth the view that there is an operative factor in the world which organizes, integrates, and synthesizes. The world tends toward *wholes*. The world is not a collection of aggregates — but a system of units, wholes and organisms, such as the atom, the molecule, the cell, the plant, the animal — and finally human personalities.

General Smuts's view is closely related to the organismic theory of nature, which has done much to reconcile the old differences between mechanism and vitalism. "Science," as Mr. Whitehead says, "is taking on a new aspect which is neither purely physical nor purely biological. It is becoming the study of organisms. Biology is the study of the larger organisms; whereas physics is the study of the smaller organisms." [2] The emphasis upon configuration by the Gestalt psychology reflects a somewhat similar view, as does also the general theory of emergence.

Cosmic evolution

Boodin, in his *Cosmic Evolution*,[3] has presented a carefully worked out theory of evolution based on the principle that nothing happens without a cause, and systems like Darwin's do not reveal the causes even of organic evolution. Evolution, he believes, has its cause in the "creative adaptation of life to the energy patterns of the cosmic environment." Evolution is creative synthesis — but a synthesis "for which all the necessary conditions are supplied," and they are supplied by the energy structure of the Universe. Intelligence, creative imagination, the sense of beauty have developed as creative responses to the energy structure of reality. If "there is to be advance in nature towards higher levels, these levels must exist." As

[1] Hon. J. C. Smuts, *Holism and Evolution*. (The Macmillan Company, 1928.)
[2] *Science and the Modern World*, p. 145.
[3] John Elof Boodin, *Cosmic Evolution*, chaps. II, III.

Aristotle taught, things do not spring from Night and Chaos. Evolution on Earth is guided by a "pre-existent cosmic structure."

All this is highly interesting and enables us to view evolution from the standpoint of a lofty idealism. It carries us back to Plato and his eternal ideal types.

Creative evolution

In Chapter IX attention was called to the much discussed and relatively new theory of Emergent Evolution. Here it is only necessary to refer specifically to the book of C. Lloyd Morgan entitled *Emergent Evolution.* Evolution, he says, is a series of stages, in which there supervenes at each new level a new form of "relatedness" — or, as we should say, perhaps, a new structure or organization — and from this new form of relatedness something new "emerges," which is *effective* in determining the "go of events" from that stage on. Thus, from matter emerges life — and from life, mind. The world is a pyramid with ascending levels.

> Near its base is a swarm of atoms with relational structure and the quality we may call atomicity. Above this level, atoms combine to form new units, the distinguishing quality of which is molecularity; higher up, on one line of advance, are, let us say, crystals wherein atoms and molecules are grouped in new relations of which the expression is crystalline form; on another line of advance are organisms with a different kind of natural relations which give the quality of vitality; yet higher, a new kind of natural relatedness supervenes and to its expression the word "mentality" may, under safeguard from journalistic abuse, be applied.[1]

But what causes the emergents to emerge? What is the *agency* which lifts the world, so to speak, from one level to the next? Here Morgan definitely takes his stand on the necessity of affirming a power which he calls Activity, or Mind, or God.

> For better or worse, I acknowledge God as the Nisus through whose Activity emergents emerge, and the whole course of emergent evolution is directed. Such is my philosophic creed, supplementary to my scientific policy of interpretation.[2]

[1] C. Lloyd Morgan, F.R.S., *Emergent Evolution* (Henry Holt and Company), p. 35.
[2] *Loc. cit.*, p. 36.

It should be observed that *Emergent Evolution* is merely another name for *Creative Evolution* — or rather it is an attempt to reduce to scientific language the manifest truth that evolution is creative. It is based on the fact that organization takes place, and as the outcome of such organization new things appear with new properties and powers — making new laws necessary, not abrogating others. Old things, such for instance as chemical elements, or more elementary things like atoms or protons and electrons, get into new relations and combinations — more specifically, into that particular kind of combination called organisms — and then something new appears a novelty, a new creation, possessing its own characteristic reaction. These new things, furthermore, become thereafter effective in determining the course of future events. As thus stated the theory of emergence would seem to be free from logical difficulties and may be considered as one of the most important contributions of recent philosophy. Its significance may be seen when we realize that entities of such supreme importance as *life* and *mind* may be thus explained as to their origin.[1]

Many biologists welcome the theory of emergence on the ground that it elevates biological laws to an equality with those of physics and chemistry. For instance, Jennings says:

> The doctrine of emergent evolution makes the biologist loyal to experimentation and observation in his own field of work, whatever is found in other fields. Courage and defiance sprout from his soul in place of timorous subservience to the inorganic. No longer can the biologist be bullied into suppressing observed results because they are not discovered nor expected from work on the non-living parts of nature. No longer will he feel a sense of criminality in speaking of relations that are obvious in the living for the reason that they are not seen in the non-living. Biology becomes a science in its own right — not through rejection of the experimental method, but through undeviating allegiance to it. The doctrine of emergent evolution is the Declaration of Independence for biological science.

[1] For references on emergent and creative evolution, creative synthesis, and the theory of levels, see above, p. 112. For a penetrating study of the logical principles involved in emergence, see Arthur O. Lovejoy, "The Meaning of Emergence and its Modes," in *Jour. Phil. Studies*, II, no. 6. Compare also his paper on "The Discontinuities of Evolution," *Univ. of Calif. Pub. Phil.*, v. A criticism of emergence may be found in Wm. McDougall's *Modern Materialism and Evolution* and in *Proceedings of the Aristotelian Society*, Supplement, VI, pp. 39–68. Compare also Drake's *Invitation to Philosophy* (Houghton Mifflin Company, 1933), p. 305.

In sum, acceptance of the doctrine of emergent evolution would, probably, work out to the benefit of science and of humanity. It combines the advantages of mechanism and vitalism, though missing the ineptitudes of each. It offers no obstacles to the continued progress of science, nor to its formulation. At the same time it sets no limits as to what science shall discover. It recognizes that science is never finished, that it must continue to develop as long as evolution continues.[1]

Evolution as strategy

The tendency to approach the study of evolution with a wholly new set of concepts is illustrated in a book by William Patten, Professor of Biology in Dartmouth College. It is entitled *The Grand Strategy of Evolution*. Certainly evolution has all the appearance of being some kind of "strategy," but hitherto it has been customary to use all such words in a figurative sense, it being understood, of course, that it looks like strategy, but is really just mechanism. But in this book such terms are used in quite other than a figurative sense. In fact the view of evolution here set forth completely reverses our older ideas about it. The author sets out with a wholly different set of concepts, so different that it is hard at first to adjust ourselves to his new views — so habitually has our thought run in mechanistic Darwinian channels.

In the first place, Patten thinks that the

concept of a creative drift from the futile conflict of chaos toward a more stable structural organization and unity is the central idea of evolution, and the general recognition of this phenomenon is the distinguishing characteristic of the scientific and intellectual thought of modern times.[2]

Back of all evolutionary processes lies a universal compulsion to constructive action.[3]

But it is not this notion of evolution as a creative movement toward structure and organization which is the striking feature of Patten's view; it is rather his further belief that this creative movement proceeds by the action of certain fundamental properties of

---

[1] H. S. Jennings, "Diverse Doctrines of Evolution," in *Science*, January 14, 1927, pp. 21 ff., 25.

[2] William Patten, *The Grand Strategy of Evolution* (R. G. Badger), p. 44.

[3] *Loc. cit.*, p. 129.

all life and mind — yes, even of all reality, namely, *self-preservation, self-sacrifice,* and *co-operation.* This is what he says:

> Natural selection and the survival of the fittest are perhaps the broadest terms used in the biological sciences, but the processes so designated have no creative value. The terms merely imply that a definite sequence of products ensues, or affirm the self-evident fact that something already created is selected for survival, or that it endures. They do not suggest how it was created, why it survives, or wherein its fitness lies.

> I shall try to show that there is but one answer to all these questions; that there is but one creative process common to all phases of evolution, inorganic, organic, mental, and social. That process is best described by the term co-operation, or mutual service.[1]

"Creation is the birth of new things through the mutual services of pre-existing things." Egoism, altruism, and service (co-operation) are, therefore, ultimate concepts through which alone we can understand evolution. It is always the investment of self in a purpose beyond self which determines the evolutionary movement — that is, progress. Evolution consists in just this — that things brought together in a definite time and space relation act together co-operatively; and as a result something new appears, which could not otherwise exist, having new qualities. An atom, an organic body, an animal, or a state, is essentially a co-operative system, which endures only so long as an inner co-operation endures and so long as co-operation with the environment endures.

All this seems to be very instructive and suggestive. It illustrates what seems to be a prevalent tendency in biology now, a tendency to place less emphasis on matter, motion, and force, and more upon life itself and its concomitant creation of values. We have tried without much success to interpret heredity, variation, and the struggle for existence in terms of chemistry and physics, in terms of masses of matter in motion, in terms of that mysterious something called "energy," and to explain evolution as a process of natural selection of chance variations. Perhaps we should reverse this and explain variation in terms of evolution, and explain heredity and the struggle for existence in terms of self-expression and co-operation. Perhaps, as Patten suggests, even growth, as in plants and animals,

[1] *Loc. cit.,* pp. 32, 33.

is a kind of "self-enlargement," which is a fundamental property of matter.

Instructive also is his belief that evolution means a progress in *discipline* rather than in *freedom.* "Progressive union and stability, progressive co-operation, organization, service, and discipline are, therefore, inherent properties of life and matter." Owing quite to incidental historical circumstances, we are now living in an age in which it has become customary to exalt freedom to the skies. This is due to a passing social situation, the revolt from a stage in social evolution in which authority had developed into tyranny. The love of freedom has become a kind of mania with us.[1] In a way, of course, evolution *is* in the direction of greater freedom. True freedom arises through co-operation, the freedom to grow, to develop, to create. There is no conflict of ideals here; it is only that we have for inevitable reasons come to emphasize freedom too much and discipline too little. If, then, as Patten thinks, freedom belongs to the original chaos, while discipline and co-operation characterize all growth and organization, the biological view seems here to strengthen the ethical view. It may give a new direction to our freedom-intoxicated age to learn that discipline and co-operation are fundamental in the evolutionary method. It may also give us new light as to the place of the doctrine of the survival of the fittest in social organization.

After the triumph of Darwinism in the last century some European statesmen justified the ruthless rivalry of nations by an appeal to the law of struggle for existence, and the law of the survival of the fittest, as fundamental laws of nature. This was owing to their failure to recognize that the law of co-operation is more fundamental than the law of competition; and it is just because of this short-sightedness that we witnessed the threatened collapse of European civilization after the Great War. When we can introduce into political and international relationships some of that co-operation which is shown in the body of a plant or an animal, or even in the structure of an atom, then we may hope for a social stability comparable with the stability which we find in nature.

From another point of view Edwin Grant Conklin has developed the same thought in his book, *The Direction of Human Evolution.*

[1] Eleutheromania, Irving Babbitt called it.

The evolution of the human body and brain is at an end, but not so social evolution, and the direction which it must take is that of increased group specialization and co-operation. Without this no further progress for the human race is possible. If democracy means a loose social organization and greater freedom of the individual, it is doomed. If it means specialization and co-operation, it is the road to social welfare.

Life and mind as achievements

In conclusion, evolution seems to be a process of *achievement*, in which, step by step, higher values are won. Life itself is one of these values; mind is one; science is one; social organization is one. Dare we go further and say with Hegel that philosophy, art, and religion are the final values toward which the world is striving, or shall we say that consciousness itself is the highest round of the ladder?

I do not think we can answer these questions yet; but if it be true that evolution is a process of achievement, a great movement in the realization of values, then it becomes no longer a gospel of despair, as it has so often been, but a gospel of hope.

In connection with this chapter read:

H. H. Newman, *Evolution Yesterday and Today* (Century of Progress Series, Williams and Wilkins).

Further references:

Darwin, *The Descent of Man* (D. Appleton and Company).
Vernon L. Kellogg, *Darwinism Today* (Henry Holt and Company).
C. Lloyd Morgan, *Emergent Evolution* (Henry Holt and Company).
J. G. Boodin, *Cosmic Evolution* (The Macmillan Company).
William Patten, *The Grand Strategy of Evolution* (R. G. Badger).
Edwin Grant Conklin, *The Direction of Human Evolution* (Charles Scribner's Sons).
General J. C. Smuts, *Holism and Evolution* (London and New York).
Austin H. Clark, *The New Evolution* (Williams and Wilkins).
William Morton Wheeler, *Emergent Evolution and the Development of Societies* (New York, 1928).
George P. Conger, *New Views of Evolution* (The Macmillan Company, 1929).

CHAPTER XII

IS THERE PURPOSE IN NATURE?

IN THIS chapter we discuss a very old philosophical problem, that of *ends* or *purposes*. Is there *purpose* or *design* in nature? Does the world have a *goal*, or *end*, or *purpose*? *Teleology* is the name applied to the study of these questions. It is from two Greek words meaning the science or study of ends.

Purpose in human affairs

It is very evident that human beings work toward ends. Theoretically, whatever we do, we do for a purpose. You have a purpose in reading this book, perhaps to gain a knowledge of philosophy, perhaps to prepare for an examination. If you make anything, it is made for a purpose; and each part of it has its own purpose. The motor car has a purpose. Every casting in it, every bolt, spring, pinion, rod, gasket, bushing, flange, or ball has its purpose. It is natural for us to think teleologically; that is, as if everything had a purpose, just as it has in human affairs. It is natural for us to think that every part of the human body has a purpose. The child seems instinctively to be a teleologist, for he is always asking the question, What is this for? He seems to take it for granted that everything in the world has a purpose, just as he assumes that everything which man makes has a purpose.

But when the child grows up and begins to reflect, he sees that the subject presents difficulties. He sees clearly enough that human beings, who can think and look forward and make plans, act purposively. But is it so certain that there is any purpose outside the human mind? Science seems to teach that everything in nature acts not purposively, but mechanically. Whatever happens in nature, the falling of a stone, the erosion of a continent, the formation of a snowflake, happens mechanically; that is, its action is rigorously determined by preceding physical conditions. Every phenomenon in nature is fully accounted for by the sum total of physical conditions preceding it. A physicist, as soon as he stops to inquire what things are *for*, deserts his scientific standpoint; for the latter always presupposes that the complete explanation of things is found in the chain of physical sequences which conditions them.

Take the automobile again. Its parts do not act purposively — they act blindly and mechanically, following definite mechanical laws. The horn honks, not to warn of the approach of the car, but because a current of electricity has been turned into a certain circuit and mechanically causes the vibration of a certain diaphragm. A wheel turns, not to propel the car, but because a certain amount of physical energy has been communicated to the axle; and if anything goes wrong with the mechanism, no part of the car can adjust itself in an adaptive way to the new situation, but grinds itself out according to fixed mechanical law. So also of the tree or human body. The sap in the tree is stirred to action, not to attain any end, but because of the mechanical influence of the sunlight. The muscles of the body contract, not in order to deliver a blow, but because of the inflow of muscular and nervous energy.

Pursuing this line of thought the reader may say: I think I see through the riddle. The parts of the motor car, of course, all act mechanically according to fixed physical laws; but it is still true that every wheel, valve, and washer has a function to perform, and this function may be regarded as a purpose, if we think of the whole machine as *planned* or *designed* by an inventor or a mechanic. The *purpose* is outside the machine in the *mind* of the man who designed it.

Apparent purpose in nature

And now, he continues, let me think about the tree and the human body. All the parts *must* act mechanically, and yet there seems to be a purpose in them, just as in the parts of the motor car. Certainly the purpose of the eye is to see, and of the thumb to grasp, and of the teeth to bite and chew; but since they are physical objects governed by physical laws, the purpose must reside outside the body in some world-builder, or God. In other words, the tree and the human body must have been *designed* by someone having the mental power of vision to see an end to be accomplished, and then to adapt the instrument to the end; for it is quite clear — to take the case of the tree — that there is a plan or purpose in its parts — the leaves to serve as the lungs of the tree taking up the carbon dioxide from the air, the rootlets to absorb the moisture from the earth, the strong trunk to resist the winds, the rough bark to protect the vital parts beneath. Likewise the warm fur of the musk ox and the sharp tooth of the tiger have their purpose.

In other words, the various parts of the body or the tree or the flower or the blade of grass are *instruments* for accomplishing certain ends, just as the parts of a motor car are instruments, each for a certain purpose; but, like the parts of the motor car, none of these instruments acts purposively. They blindly follow mechanical laws.

All this sounds very reasonable, and it seems to imply that animal bodies and plants and trees are in some way the product of intelligence and design; and, since they are not the product of human intelligence, they must be the work of a cosmic intelligence, or God.

But it is just an analogy

As we think about the matter more carefully, we begin to see that our reasoning was nothing but analogy. The parts of animal bodies and of plants have a striking resemblance to the parts of an automobile in this only, that they perform certain functions in such a way as to contribute to a final result, speed on the part of the motor car, and life or activity on the part of the animal. By analogy we infer that, since the motor car is the product of an outside intelligence, the plant and animal body must be also. What we really see in plant and animal bodies is a very wonderful *adaptation*. There is an adaptation between the parts of the tree and the environment, the latter consisting of sun and soil and air. There is an adaptation between the fur of the polar bear and the climate.

Adaptation

Now, just what *is* adaptation and what does it imply? Does it imply a mind which has thought of the adaptation and designed it; or is it nothing more than a relation of fitness or adjustment to the conditions under which an organism lives? Does adaptation imply a purpose? Could it not have been attained by organisms through the method of trial and error? Has not Darwin explained it by the action of natural selection operating on small chance variations? If so, is not our whole analogy between the motor car and the tree a fallacious one? Furthermore, do we have in nature any such perfect adaptations as we have in human machines? Are there not countless cases of maladaptation, such as the city and the earthquake, or the migratory instincts of the birds and the late storms of spring which kill them by thousands?

But, if we reject purpose as an explanation of adaptation, what is the alternative? Is *chance* the alternative? Are we, then, to suppose that all the world of beauty and order came fortuitously into being? Did the order which we see in the movements of the heavenly bodies just happen? Did it just happen that there is a moon to light our way at night? Did the grateful alternation of sunshine and rain just happen? Did it just happen that the air is fit to breathe and that the Earth brings forth fruits and grains fit to serve as food? That this orderly world has come about by the chance collisions of atoms of matter is more difficult to believe, as someone has said, than that Shakespeare's plays should happen from an explosion in a printing office.

What, then, are we to do? That the world has come about by chance seems impossible to believe; at any rate, we will not believe it until we have exhausted all other hypotheses. On the other hand, that the world is a great machine, designed and created by some transcendent world-builder for some definite purpose, as the mechanic creates a motor car, seems like a childish analogy having little scientific value.

But are there not other possibilities? Are chance and purpose the only alternatives? And if there are no other alternatives, might we say that the world is purposive without going so far as to think of it as a kind of manufactured article, planned and executed by some anthropomorphic god? Clearly the problem needs a great deal of reflective thought. A glance at the history of the subject will first be helpful.

Historical

There was an old Greek philosopher named Anaxagoras, who discovered that the world is made out of a vast number of little atoms.

Atoms, he thought, would serve as the *material* of the world, but what imparts to the atoms their original *motion*? Anaxagoras needed a *moving cause*, and, therefore, affirmed that *Mind* was this moving cause. But we can hardly say that Anaxagoras was a teleologist, for he considered mind to be merely an initial cause of the world, not a designing intelligence.

Next came Socrates, who said that Anaxagoras did well to introduce mind as the cause of the world movement, but that he did not make enough use of this principle, for he, Socrates, saw evidences of benevolent intelligence and design in all the works of nature, instancing the beautiful adaptations seen in the human body, such as the protection of the eyes by the bony ridge above them and by the eyelashes and eyebrows. Socrates, therefore, is a representative of that view, already referred to, according to which the world is conceived somewhat after the manner of a machine, but a machine which is designed and planned by an outside intelligence. This view is sometimes called the carpenter theory of the Universe, or the watchmaker theory, giving us a static rather than a dynamic purposiveness.

Plato was no less confident than Socrates, his teacher, that the world is purposive, but he held the theory in a less anthropomorphic and mechanical form. The world, Plato believed, is through and through rational and orderly. It is a "cosmos," not a chaos. Its ultimate realities are Ideas, and the world becomes real in proportion as crude "matter" takes on these ideal forms. In Plato's philosophy the eternal Ideas are *types* or *patterns*, of which individual things are imperfect copies. The Good and the Beautiful are, for instance, eternal values which are to be copied. With Plato the world has a meaning and its meaning is to realize the perfection of the eternal Ideas. A philosophy which speaks of cosmic values, ideas, patterns, and types is thoroughly teleological. Surely, we have here in Plato, right at the beginning of the controversy, a wonderful conception of the Universe, which is quite different both from the crude theory of chance and the mechanical watchmaker theory of Socrates. Plato, to be sure, did not work out this part of his philosophy with great clearness or consistency; but it was certainly an epoch in the history of thought when it was first proposed that the world is a movement in the realization of values.

Following Plato, Aristotle also held a world view thoroughly teleological. In some passages he speaks of design quite after the manner of Socrates. Everything in the world has what Aristotle calls a "final cause," or purpose. The end for which a thing exists is a true cause of the existence of that thing, just as much as any efficient or mechanical cause. These ends Aristotle called *final causes*, a phrase which has become classical in the discussion of the problem of purpose. We must not ever confuse final causes with first causes or with ordinary mechanical causes.

As we get into the spirit of Aristotle's philosophy, however, we discover that it is a kind of immanent dynamic purposiveness which he advocated. The world was never created, but is an eternal process or movement or development, in which the potential is always passing on into the actual, and the actual is the ideal. We may say that animal species, human beings, states, institutions, and justice are ideas which nature is realizing, or as we might almost say, which nature is striving to realize.

But, Aristotle continues, what is the initial force or prime mover of the great world-development process? It must have some cause. Here Aristotle offers a suggestion very rich and provocative of our thinking, for he says that the Prime Mover, or God, moves the world by attracting it. The final ideal reality is *good*, hence desired. This daring conception of the Universe as a great process of realization drawn onward by the vision of an ideal end almost takes one's breath away. Could it be true? Could it be reconciled with our modern evolutionary philosophy?

Meanwhile, another great Greek thinker, Democritus, utterly denied the existence of any cosmic intelligence, plan, purpose, goal, or ideals. The Universe is a concourse of material atoms, themselves in eternal motion, whose mechanical configurations constitute all objects of experience. Epicurus and Lucretius, representing the later Epicurean school, developed this anti-teleological view, denying that nature has ends or purposes or any goal — denying also that ends or purposes do in any way act as causes determining the course of events. During the Middle Ages, it was the world view of Plato and Aristotle, rather than that of Democritus and the Epicureans, which found general acceptance. The tendency increased,

however, to go back to the form of statement held by Socrates. God
designed and created the world. It was even thought that the Earth
is the center of the Universe and was especially planned as a residence
for man. This view finds its crowning exposition in Dante's *Divine
Comedy*, where the whole Universe is a grand and mighty drama,
existing for man and his redemption.

General purposiveness in nature was supported by Bruno, Newton, Leibniz, Voltaire, and later by Goethe, John Stuart Mill, and
many others. In scientific circles, however, a teleological view
of nature was opposed from the time of Descartes. Plant and
animal bodies and even the human body, as Descartes taught,
were machines pure and simple. The introduction of final
causes, said Francis Bacon, has done much to retard the progress
of science, which is concerned only with physical causes. Spinoza
and Hobbes likewise excluded all teleological notions from their
philosophy.

Parenthetically we may remark here — and this should throw
light on the whole subject — that the conception of the world as a
mere mechanical sequence of events, in which each step is determined and fully explained by the preceding ones, was a conception
perfectly fitted to Francis Bacon's purpose, which was not to *understand* the world, but to *use* it, to *control* it, to *exploit* it. The world is
"explained" by a knowledge of its mechanical sequences, if by explanation you mean that kind of understanding which enables us to
make *use* of natural forces. One of the objects of the natural sciences
is to gain acquaintance with the *chain of sequences* which are observed in nature and the *uniformities* which we see, *in order that*,
desiring any particular kind of behavior, we may know how to get it.
Such knowledge is highly useful in the practical arts, in commerce,
and in industry. Our tremendous success in predicting events, in
controlling the forces of nature and in bending them to our material
needs is due to Bacon's method. Philosophy, however, is an attempt to *interpret* the world, and no mere observation of sequences
leads to such interpretation. Possibly the world has no *end* or *purpose* just in the human sense of the word *purpose;* but it undoubtedly
has a *plan*, if by plan is meant a pattern, or a determinate order,
rather than a design. Indeed, we may even say that it has a *design,*

if by this word is meant not something designed, but something of which the unity and meaning can be discerned.

Returning to the history of the controversy, although Descartes himself applied the mechanistic conception only to the materially extended world, not including the free activity of thought or the purposes of God, yet it was easy after his time to extend the conception to the whole Universe, utterly denying any kind of cause except efficient or material causes. It seemed, however, a little difficult for the mechanists to account for adaptation in nature, especially in the organic world. Paley, a theologian of the eighteenth century, wrote a work whose purpose was to prove the existence of God by the evidences of intelligent design in the world; and he used the now well-known comparison of the watch and the human eye. The manifold parts of the watch and their adaptation to one another and to the purpose of keeping time are no more evidence of an intelligent designer than are the equally manifold and wonderful parts of the human eye, which was clearly made for the purpose of sight. Instances of adaptation in nature, such as the wonders of the human body and the marvelous instincts of animals, may be heaped up until the non-scientific reader is easily persuaded that nature is crammed with evidence of intelligent and conscious purpose.[1] It would seem to be impossible to account for such adaptations by chance, and it was assumed that conscious design was the only alternative, an argument that was rather ineffectively met by the opponents of teleology instancing the many cases of maladaptation in the world, and of sin and death and suffering. But with the coming of the Darwinian theory of natural selection interest in this kind of argument lapsed.

Darwin's contribution

But while the citing of cases of maladaptation may not weaken the old argument for design, this argument was immensely weakened by the coming of the theory of evolution in the nineteenth century, and especially by Darwin's theory of natural selection. These cast

[1] A collection of such instances and a modernized form of Paley's argument may be found in a book by J. N. Shearman, entitled *The Natural Theology of Evolution*. A more modern treatment may be found in the recent symposium entitled *The Great Design* edited by Frances Mason (The Macmillan Company, 1935).

a wholly new light on the old puzzle of adaptation and greatly strengthened the position of the mechanists; for it was now thought possible to explain adaptation in the organic world otherwise than by either chance or design, namely, by gradual small variations and natural selection of the fittest.   Even the human eye, or any other marvel of adaptation, or any of the wonderful animal instincts, could be explained in this way.   Given only plenty of time, variation, heredity, and the struggle for existence, and a single group of cells on the surface of the body fortuitously sensitive to light might develop into such a complicated organ as the eye, quite on mechanistic principles.

Hereupon the old watchmaker theory of the Universe propounded by Socrates, nourished by Dante, developed in a childish form by Paley, fell into complete disrepute.   Science explains all things by simple mechanical causation, and it is unnecessary to call in any designing God, or even any mystic vital force

Purpose in inorganic nature

That purposiveness in some sense prevails in the world of living organisms seems to be unquestionable, as we shall see presently; but is there any evidence whatever that it prevails in the sphere of the inorganic?

Long ago the Hebrew poet wrote that the heavens declare the glory of God and the firmament showeth his handiwork.   Other poets, philosophers, and religious teachers have expressed the belief that the order and beauty of nature are evidences either of an intelligent creator or of an immanent indwelling intelligent mind.   But the modern reader is not greatly impressed by their inferences, since he believes that science, for which he has a sort of reverential ardor, teaches otherwise.   Although perhaps the man of today is inclined to place too much confidence in the opinions of scientists on matters lying outside their special fields, nevertheless it would be very interesting indeed to find out, if we could, their opinions regarding purpose in nature.   This might be somewhat difficult, since the scientist, if questioned on this subject, would probably say that his interests lie within a certain group of phenomena, and that within this group his aim is to give an accurate and complete description of the facts, and to explain these facts as far as he is able. By explanation, he says, he means the noting and recording of the causes and conditions under which things arise and the laws of their changes, growth and development — and by cause he means efficient cause, not final cause or purpose. As a scientist he is not concerned with purposes and ends in nature.

But suppose the scientist were pressed for his own personal opinion as regards ends and values, or intelligence manifested in nature. Only a straw vote, no doubt, could gather the opinions of scientists on this question. Such a vote, if it could be taken, would probably reveal that their opinions are much divided. Many would say that they can see no evidence of purpose, plan, or ends in nature. Many others would express their belief in an immanent soul or intelligence. Others would accept a belief in a first intelligent cause, and still others would say that back of all and perhaps identical with all is something which may be called Mind.

Many attempts have been made to gather the opinions of scientists on this subject. Two of these, made in recent years, lie on my desk. One is edited by Frances Mason and is entitled *The Great Design*,[1] with an Introduction by the late Sir Arthur Thomson. The chapters are written by fourteen eminent scientists, among whom are Robert Grant Aitkens, James Arnold Crowther, C. Lloyd Morgan, Sir Oliver Lodge, and Hans Driesch. The articles as a whole indicate the belief of the authors that when we "contemplate the order in Nature, the system of the spheres, the universality of law, we seem to see a great design" — "a pattern in the whole," and that the world exhibits "evidence of an Infinite Intelligence that holds the worlds in order." This work does not profess to furnish any cross section of scientific opinion on design in nature, but gives the views of a certain number of eminent scientists. The second book is entitled *Has Science Discovered God? A Symposium of Modern Scientific Opinion*.[2] In this work are gathered the views of sixteen men of science. It includes chapters by Millikan, Mather, Eddington, Conklin, Einstein, Julian Huxley, McDougall, Pupin, Jeans and others. In summation the editor says:

---

[1] *The Great Design*, edited by Frances Mason (The Macmillan Company, 1934).

[2] *Has Science Discovered God?* Gathered and edited by Edward H. Cotton (Thomas Y. Crowell Company, 1931).

The conclusion of some of the best scientific minds civilization has produced, as stated in this discussion, proving that we are not living in a mechanistic dispensation, but in a universe of order and design responding perfectly to the nicety of mathematical law, and of beneficent purpose also, is not only *one* of the most important facts that confronts us — it is *the* most important. It may be the human appeal of Huxley, the mysticism of Eddington, the reverence of Mather, the convictions of Millikan or the simple faith of Einstein. Whatever its form, it is sending men's minds rapidly forward to belief in the "vision splendid."

Although this book also does not profess to represent a cross-section of scientific opinion, it is interesting as setting forth the views of men whose names have become so well known.

Mention was made in a previous chapter of Henderson's study of purposiveness in inorganic nature.[1] Such studies as this are interesting for the reason that, since natural selection has so long been relied upon to disprove purposiveness in the organic world, and since it can have no application to the inorganic world, the presence of purposiveness in the latter would be a real evidence of some fundamental purposiveness in nature generally. Henderson finds that before life appeared upon our planet there was a peculiar *fitness* of the environment for it, which appears to be in the nature of a preparation. We may not be justified in speaking of it as a preparation; but the fitness is apparent and needs an explanation.

Among remarkable illustrations of this fitness, Henderson mentions the presence upon the cooling surface of the Earth of the necessary proportions of carbon, oxygen, and hydrogen, and the peculiar character of their compounds; the great quantities of water and carbonic acid; the nearly constant temperature of the ocean; the ample rainfall; the unique expansion of water at the freezing point, preventing our rivers and lakes from freezing solid in winter; the thermal qualities of water, together with its high specific heat moderating the summer and winter heat of the Earth; and the latent heat and solvent power of water. All these and many other peculiarities of the environment illustrate its unique and remarkable fitness for *life*. "Water, of its very nature, as it occurs automatically

[1] Lawrence J. Henderson, *The Fitness of the Environment*, and *The Order of Nature*. Henderson is Professor of Biological Chemistry in Harvard University.

in the process of cosmic evolution, is fit, with a fitness no less marvelous and varied than that fitness of the organism which has been won by the process of adaptation in the course of organic evolution."

These are only a few of the noteworthy instances in inorganic nature anticipatory, as it would seem, of life and its requirements. What conclusions are we to draw from such a situation as this? Only one conclusion is possible, as Henderson believes. There is a hitherto unrecognized *order* in nature, whose exact laws we are as yet unable to fathom. It is almost infinitely improbable that the unique totality of properties of the physical elements which provide the maximal fitness for organic life should be the result of accident.

> The connection between these properties of the elements, almost infinitely improbable as the result of contingency, can only be regarded, is in truth only fully intelligible even if mechanistically explained, as a preparation for the evolutionary process. By this I mean to say that it resembles adaptation....
>
> Hence we are obliged to regard this collection of properties as in some intelligible sense a preparation for the processes of planetary evolution.... Therefore the properties of the elements must for the present be regarded as possessing a teleological character.[1]

Mechanism rules throughout the world, but does not rule supreme. There is an organization and order independent of mechanism. Not only is life itself something transcending mechanism, but the tendency toward life is also something transcending it.

But now, how are we to interpret this tendency, this teleological character of the inorganic world? Shall we say that it indicates a purpose, or design? Henderson does not take this further step. His aim is not to interpret in any human terms the order which he finds in nature, but rather to limit himself to the necessary implications of the actual facts which science discerns. He does, however, go so far as to compare the primeval tendency which is discovered through the whole process of evolution to the work of an architect who designs a house.

But perhaps the most interesting of his conclusions is that the Universe is "biocentric." Since, now, there was a time when no life existed on the Earth, this statement can mean nothing else than that

[1] *The Order of Nature* (Harvard University Press), pp. 190, 192.

the world in its inorganic stage looks forward to the coming of life, is adjusted to it, is in some sense a preparation for it. At any rate, "the properties of matter and the course of cosmic evolution are now seen to be intimately related to the structure of the living being and to its activities." [1] As Whitehead says, "It is the essence of life that it exists for its own sake, as the intrinsic reaping of value." [2]

The biological point of view

When we begin to study the simplest living organism, we find that there is something which eludes the mechanical scheme; and this is *life*. A full description of the physical and chemical processes in a living organism does not give a complete understanding of it; there is something else which can only be expressed by the introduction of teleological concepts. We are up on another level of reality and we need new categories to explain what happens there.

The cause-and-effect relation, so fundamental in the mechanical sciences, no longer furnishes the key to the world of living organisms; a new relation appears, namely, that of *means* and *end*. It does not, of course, replace the relation of cause and effect; it supplements it. With the coming of life, something appears which we must designate as *value*. Life is a good; and whatever contributes to it is an instrumental good; for instance, food, air, water, sex, exercise.

In physics the data are taken as external to and independent of each other. That is of the essence of the procedure of the mathematical physicist. His symbols take no cognisance of behaviour as exhibited in life or purposive action. But when we are observing a living organism this is just what we must take account of. We cannot get at the meaning or the reality of our data if we take them as if existing in isolation from each other. It is characteristic of the phenomena with which we are here concerned that the details of form, movement, and chemical composition which we distinguish in them are essentially and not accidentally connected with each other. "We are accustomed to the fact that a limb, or even a bone, of a certain build is associated with a whole body of a certain build. We know also that if an animal is breathing we may expect to find its heart beating and all its other organs in a state of more or less evident activity. We associate together the details of structure and activity as those of a living animal;

---

[1] *The Fitness of the Environment* (The Macmillan Company), p. 312.
[2] Alfred North Whitehead, *Nature and Life* (The University of Chicago Press, 1934), p. 9.

we think and speak of it as alive, and we regard its structure and activities as the expression or manifestation of its life. What I wish to maintain is that in so regarding a living organism we use an hypothesis which is for biology just as intelligible, just as elementary, just as true to the facts known, and just as good a scientific working hypothesis, as is the hypothesis of the indestructibility of matter for physics and chemistry." [1]

When biological science speaks of conditions as "beneficial" or "harmful" for the organism; when it calls some chemical substances "foods," others "waste-products"; when it speaks of the "function" of an organ, or through the concept of "organization" interprets the parts in the light of the whole; when, in dealing with "growth," "behavior," "reproduction," etc., it applies the concept of the maintenance or development of each characteristic type of living structure — its language is full of the kind of teleology which the term "value," or, if it be preferred "objective value," is here intended to cover. Wherever, broadly speaking, the facts challenge us to say, not merely that B is the effect of A, but that B is the *reason why* or *that for the sake of which* A exists or occurs, there we have the *immanent purposiveness* of living things.

When we ask what character in natural objects, or in nature as a whole, exhibits this immanent purposiveness, this "design," most clearly, the answer must surely be that it is *organization* — not merely in the static sense of a systematic structure of differentiated parts, but in the dynamic sense of this structure at work and functioning as a whole, responding through its organs (which are very literally "instruments") to its environment, adapting that environment to itself and itself to it. A purposive structure, in Kant's famous phrase, is one in which parts and whole are reciprocally means and ends. The subordination of the parts to the whole lies precisely in that delicate mutual adjustment of the parts which, in respect of their functioning, we call *regulative*, and which in form as well as in function yields the characteristic individuality — one might almost say, using the word in the artistic sense, "the effect" — of each living thing. Aristotle went straight to the heart of the matter when he compared this organization of each living thing to the order of a commonwealth. "And the animal organism must be conceived after the similitude of a well-governed commonwealth. When order is once established in it, there is no more need of a separate monarch to preside over each several task. The individuals each play their assigned part as it is ordered, and one thing follows another in its accustomed order. So in animals

[1] Viscount Haldane, *The Philosophy of Humanism and of Other Subjects* (Yale University Press), pp. 208–09. The quotation is from Viscount Haldane's brother, J. S. Haldane, *The New Physiology* (1919), p. 31.

there is the same orderliness — nature taking the place of custom and each part naturally doing its work as nature has composed them." We have here clearly what in the language of modern biology is expressed as "the conception of the living thing as an autonomous unit in which every part is functionally related to every other and exists as the servant of the whole." [1]

Non-mechanical concepts

In the realm of organic life we need have no hesitation in using the word *purposive*. It is a concept as useful in the study of life and mind as is that of motion in physics. Try to understand a political institution, or a social organization, or a commercial enterprise, without the concept of purpose; then see whether you have any better success in understanding the functions and structures of the human body, of the bird's wing, or the instincts of the ant or bee, without this concept. Even the simplest organism *selects* certain things for food and *avoids* other things because they do or do not serve its purpose. Also in the primary division of the cell there is a selective process, by which, when the chromosomes divide, a selection is made from the material in the cytoplasm suitable to its use. The rootlets of the plant select from the soil those elements which serve its purpose. There is purpose in the nest which the bird builds, namely, the hatching and rearing of the young. We can give a detailed account of the mechanism of the bird's movements, the physical forces involved, just as we can of the behavior of the men conducting a political campaign; but these movements and forces do not tell the whole story. Concepts such as matter, motion, cause and effect are good and wholly pertinent — only they are not sufficient. No doubt such concepts as purpose, means, end, value, do not tell the whole story either; but they are quite as necessary as the concepts of mechanics in coming to an understanding of the facts of life. In organic bodies *the part is for the sake of the whole and the integrity of the whole is a value;* and this is all that is necessary to give us the teleological or purposive character of nature.

In the organism there is manifest a development from birth to death, a development, too, controlled in the interests of the species

[1] R. F. A. Hoernlé, *Studies in Contemporary Metaphysics* (Harcourt, Brace and Company), pp. 159, 160. The quotations are from Aristotle, *De Part. An.*, 645a, 20, and Henderson, *The Order of Nature*, p. 21.

to which the individual belongs. The end governs in these respects also, just as it supersedes the relationship of externality. Here the end is no external force or event. It is simply the fundamental character of the phenomenon, a character which endures through succession and change and is present throughout their course, moulding the development to its own purpose. There is apparent discontinuity at moments, there is accident, there is the contingency inseparable from externality. But the tendency remains unfaltering.[1]

Many of the new views of evolution, which have been mentioned, imply the notion of an end or purpose. Orthogenesis, in whatever form it is held, is teleological. When we say that evolution has a *direction*, when it is spoken of as *creative*, as *a struggle for freedom*, as a process of *realization*, as having a *drift*, as *strategical*, as consisting essentially of *co-operation* or *mutual service*, as comparable to the work of an *artist*, as proceeding from the *needs* of the organism — then a teleological world view is implied. It is implied also by all such expressions as *an inner directing principle, an evolutionary urge, a primordial direction and co-ordination of energies*. Even the phrase *struggle for existence* implies the notion of an end.

The interpretation

If, then, nature even in its inorganic stage shows evidence of order, structure, organization, harmonious unity; if in the realm of living organisms it shows values, ends, and purposes; if evolution is selective, showing direction and co-operation, how finally is all this to be interpreted? Is the world purposive in the sense of being *purposed*? Has it a design in the sense of being *designed*? If so, we must introduce the notion of *mind*, and think of the world movement as something planned or designed by a mind which can imagine in advance an end or purpose, and in some way *will* it, or create it, or cause it to come into being. The world would exist, then, first as *idea*, and our tendency would be to think of the idea as a kind of efficient cause, or at least as one of the conditions or antecedents of the coming of the world into being.

If we introduce mind as a world cause, it would not, of course, be necessary to think of it in a crudely anthropomorphic form, as if a

---

[1] Viscount Haldane, *The Reign of Relativity*, p. 324.

world-builder, working upon plastic or resistant material, planned, contrived, designed, or manufactured the world after the manner of the old watchmaker theory. We should think of the world as the expression or manifestation of an infinite or absolute mind or self; or we should think of mind as immanent in the world, an indwelling spirit or intelligence working through evolution and the laws of nature in a spiritually ordered world. Practically all our modern idealistic, personalistic, theistic, or pan-psychic systems of philosophy have this great thought in common: The world is essentially rational, purposive, and teleological, being the manifestation or expression of an infinite, absolute, or indwelling mind, consciousness, self, spirit, or God. So taught Fichte, Hegel, Fechner, Lotze, Wundt, Paulsen, Bradley, Royce, Bowne; and so are teaching at the present time many of our leading American, French, German, and Italian philosophers. It is not necessary to suppose that the indwelling cosmic mind, the world soul, the divine presence, must work just as our minds do, if we are to call its action purposive. As Bosanquet has pointed out, we may still speak of an action as purposive without considering the "end" as the completion of a serial process in which means and end have a temporal relation. Consider, for instance, any organic product, say a flower.

It is ridiculous to say that such a product arises by accident; that is, as a by-product of the interaction of elements in whose nature and general laws of combination no such result is immanent, as though we were dealing with the insight of a human contriver, by which the more complex developments and combinations were not anticipated.... On the other hand, we must not say that "purpose is operative" in the flower or the wave, if that is to mean that we ascribe them to an end or idea, somehow superinduced upon the course of their elements by a power comparable to finite consciousness, operating as it were *ab extra*, and out of a detached spontaneity of its own. If the former notion spelt accident, this spells miracle.[1]

The evidence is rather strong, as we have seen, that the world *is* purposive in the sense of exhibiting order, pattern, "design," organization, structure, value, ends; and certainly the most natural, if not

---

[1] Bernard Bosanquet, *The Principle of Individuality and Value* (copyrighted by The Macmillan Company. Reprinted by permission), pp. 147, 148, 149.

the most logical, explanation of this fact is the presence of mind immanent in the world. That the action of the "divine mind" is ideational, volitional, actuated by desire, like the finite human mind, is not necessarily implied in a purposive world. It is not even implied that such a mind is conscious, if by consciousness we mean that awareness and togetherness of thought which characterizes finite minds. The question of the attributes of creative mind is not, however, before us now; the only problem that concerns us here is whether any better hypothesis is possible to explain the evident purposiveness of the world than the presence of mind either external to and transcending nature or immanent and indwelling in nature. It is significant, indeed, that so careful a scholar and scientist as L. T. Hobhouse says that his later investigations have led him to believe that something of the nature of mind is to be carried further down in the organic world than he has previously believed; and even to raise the question whether mind may not be the essential driving force in all evolutionary change.[1]

The new teleology

Is there, however, any other possible way of explaining teleology than by the assumption of a mind in nature realizing ends through a process of envisagement? No doubt the reader will say there simply is no alternative. *If* there is purpose in the world, there *must* be mind antecedent to the end. But let us see whether this is necessarily true. Possibly it is nothing but an inveterate habit that leads us to think always of efficient causality and no other kind, a habit much encouraged by our modern devotion to the physical sciences. Why must we always think that a thing is to be explained by what goes before? Why may it not be explained by the end for which it is *indispensable?* Ever since Kant in his striking *Critique of Judgment* taught us that an organism is something in which whole and part are reciprocally determined, philosophers have been puzzling over this strange problem and wondering whether we have a new kind of teleology here. In these concluding paragraphs let us consider this new way of regarding purposiveness in nature, and if the view seems strange and hard to understand, let us consider it merely as an in-

[1] L. T. Hobhouse, *Mind in Evolution*, 2d ed., p. ix.

teresting path of promise to be neither hastily rejected nor accepted.
Windelband has formulated this new teleology very clearly:

In the provinces of physics and chemistry we naturally express ourselves in mechanical terms: in the province of biology in teleological
language. When oxygen and hydrogen combine in the proportion
1:2, we get water; but we may just as well say, if there is to be water,
oxygen and hydrogen must, etc. On the other hand, we say that if
an organism is to have differentiated sensations of light, it must have
a peripheral structure like the eye; and in this case a converse mechanistic expression would not suit our purpose, at least unless we express
the invertibility of the causal relation by adding the word "only."
Thus we may say: Only at a moderate temperature are organisms
produced, and therefore, if organisms are to be produced, a moderate
temperature is needed.   This form of expression is most frequently
found in connection with the complex isolated events of history.   Only
where we have a spiritual atmosphere like that of Germany in the
eighteenth century and a genius like Goethe is a *Faust* possible; in
order to have a *Faust* we need, etc.

When we inquire into the correctness of these expressions, we must
first make their meaning quite clear. Let us take the classical illustration of the organism. Its vital activity and its development are made
possible only by these definite organs and their no less definite functions. But these definite organs and functions are, in turn, only
possible in this organism. Hence the whole, which causes the effect,
determines the parts which are required for it. They are only in it;
and it is possible only through them. In this reciprocal dependence
of the whole and the parts Kant has given us the classic definition of
an organism. A watch is a whole that may be put together out of
pre-existing wheels, etc. But the organism must itself produce the
parts of which it is to consist. From this we get two fundamental
types of the construction of a whole: the mechanical and the organic.
In the one the parts precede the whole and produce it by being put
together. In the organic whole, on the other hand, the parts themselves are conditioned by the whole and are only possible in it. In
the organic whole, therefore, the end, which is to come out of it,
determines the beginning.

This latter formulation is at first sight too much for ordinary views
of causation. The determination of the beginning by the end seems
paradoxical and impossible. That the pre-existing should determine
the present seems natural enough, though it is not quite so self-evident,
as it seems at first sight; but how can the future, which does not yet
exist, do anything? How can it itself determine the process of an event
to which alone it will owe its existence? It seems to be, not merely

incomprehensible, but impossible. We may, however, at once weaken the force of these objections by a few general considerations. In the first place, it has already been shown that causal determination by something pre-existing is, though a very common idea, yet one that proves logically incomprehensible when it is closely studied. Then there is another thing. If we, for instance, regard the time-relation as phenomenal, we see that pre-existence or post-existence is merely a thought-form of our restricted intellect, which ought not to make so much of the paradox of teleological dependence; the less so, as this way of looking at things is found to be impossible for certain groups in the phenomenal world. Both Aristotle and Schelling laid stress on this principle of indispensability, and Fichte, when he so clearly grasped that what ought to be is the reason of all being, pointed out the source of the prejudice against teleology: it is based upon the concept of substance and the assumption, connected therewith, that something must exist if anything is to come into being. The opposite conception, which regards *original action* as directed toward its achievement and therefore determined by it, is the true, genuine, and pure teleology of the organic view of the world.[1]

This "true" or "genuine teleology" must not be confused with the other teleology of the designing mind. In this latter we still adhere dutifully to the old causal relationship; only we put the *idea* of the end into the series as an efficient cause. It is not, we say, the coming reunion with my friends at the Christmas fireside that causes me to get the money from the bank and buy my ticket for the train, but the *idea* of the reunion. Certainly this is one way of looking at it, this analysis of the elements of the situation into the temporal relation of cause and effect, a way of looking at it highly useful in the physical sciences and the practical arts.

But is there not another way of regarding the whole question, pointing to a deeper understanding of the course of nature? Let us make the daring experiment of thinking that the end actually determines the means. This certainly seems to be the case in the organic world. It seems as if the parts of the eye come into existence in the process of evolution, not because of some material motions among atoms and molecules, but because they are *indispensable* to the act of seeing. No doubt, as Professor Windelband says, this

[1] Wilhelm Windelband, *An Introduction to Philosophy.* Translated by Joseph McCabe (Henry Holt and Company), pp. 144, 145, 146.

way of regarding nature is difficult for most of us, wedded as we are to the mechanical cause-and-effect way of thinking; but once grasped, this truer teleology may prove to be a kind of revelation.

From this new point of view, form and structure are the realities of the world; matter their mere potency. The world is a process of realization, an achievement. We have called it a kind of creative evolution. Such it is when viewed from any given stage in the evolutionary process; but now we see that its creations are the realization of patterns possessing final value in themselves. This was nearly the view of Aristotle and it is closely related to that of Plato. The world movement is a developmental process, in which matter is taking on form or structure. It is the form and structure, not matter, which are real. Form and structure are ideal realities — that is, values; and they are final causes. Plant and animal species are then final causes; life itself is a final cause; the human species, the mind of man, are final causes. Viewed all along the evolutionary line there is creative synthesis issuing in novelties and new and higher values; but the reason why the things which we have been accustomed to call efficient causes appear is because they are indispensable to the new realities. We may say that Nature is striving toward certain goals — life, individuality, mind, consciousness, social organization, freedom, morality — all of which are values or ends; we may say that it is all a struggle for existence, since these values *are* the realities of the Universe, the real existences. Such a view, of course, is wholly teleological — only now we are not thinking of nature or mind as envisaging these values, and then by a series of volitions bringing them into existence; we are thinking rather of these final values as wholes, of which the other things are parts; and we are thinking that the parts exist for and are determined by the whole.[1] Mind, therefore, does not plan the world, does not image it nor *will* it; and yet mind is the cause of the world, its final cause; for mind is one of the goals or ends toward which nature is tending.

Such a conception of the Universe as this is rather startling in our modern scientific age. It was common enough among the ancients.

[1] Compare the profound treatment of this subject in Bernard Bosanquet's *The Principle of Individuality and Value*, chaps. IV, V.

It reminds us vividly of Plato; but there are many signs of a return-ing Platonism. Says Paul Elmer More:

> In a general way it may be said that, with natural classes, such as men and animals, the difficulties of the nominalistic view are seemingly the more insuperable, and that, in the slow return of science and philosophy to a dependence on some sort of teleology in the process of evolution, we are forcing ourselves back into a belief in Ideas in something like the Platonic sense.
>
> The apex of our aesthetic experience which was attained by the as-cending steps of generalization is now conversely regarded as a creative energy reaching down into the world and imposing upon its fleeting substance the forms and order of stability. And this Cause of being, as contrasted with the not-being of chaos, will become to Plato, partic-ularly in his later years, when in the *Timœus* and the *Laws* he turns from the vexations of metaphysical inquiry back to the less inquisitive faith of youth, simply God.[1]

To put all this very bluntly, is it Push, or Pull, that drives or draws the world onward? It is the *vis a tergo*, the push from be-hind, that our habitual nineteenth-century mechanistic habit of thought has always emphasized. And yet in humility we realize that even the manner of this push, to say nothing of its *reason*, is unknown. So perhaps after all the world is pulled, not pushed. We are able from our own experience to get a glimpse, at least, of the manner of an *attractive* force. We know how we are drawn toward beauty and worth. Plato in his doctrine of love has elevated this into a world power. Royce called it the "homing instinct of the soul." Aristotle made a final suggestion that the great Prime Mover, God, moves the world by the power of attraction — as a picture draws us to it.

> Peer as deeply and as fixedly as you will into the abysses of your own being, you shall always find therein that it is all and only the Future that determines and in a way creates the Present. At every instant the Past crumbles into nothingness under our feet and we flee from it as from a levee sinking into the Mississippi, while the eternal Future, like the eternal Feminine, draws us upward and on. Not merely, mark you, the immediate Future; in higher and higher consciousness, yea, even in subconscious depths, the voice cries out from the wilder-ness of the far-beyond; the endless stretches of the ages-to-come catch

[1] *Platonism* (pp. 120, 169.) Princeton University Press.

up the call and plead with impassioned eloquence; the broad opening vistas of time-to-be resound with the hopes and fears, the aspirations and aversions, of the race of man, of the heart of existence itself, and these, yea, these alone it is that guide the bird of history through all her far-homing flight.[1]

In concluding we might add that the issue is not that simply of mechanism or teleology, because mechanism and teleology are not *necessarily* incompatible. A partial view of the world may make it appear to be governed by strict mechanical laws, adequate and true within their restricted limits of time and space; while "the spectator of all time and all existence" may see it under the aspect of intelligent plan and purpose.

In connection with this chapter read:

John E. Boodin, *A Realistic Universe.* Revised Edition (The Macmillan Company, 1931), chap. XVIII.

Sir J. Arthur Thomson, *Riddles of Science* (Liveright Publishing Corporation), chap. LII.

Gamertsfelder and Evans, *Fundamentals of Philosophy* (Prentice-Hall, Inc.), chap. XII.

Further references:

The Great Design, edited by Frances Mason (The Macmillan Company).

Jacques Loeb, *The Mechanistic Conception of Life* (University of Chicago Press), chap. I.

Edmund Noble, *Purposive Evolution* (Henry Holt and Company).

Edgar S. Brightman, *An Introduction to Philosophy* (Henry Holt and Company), chap. IX.

Has Science Discovered God? edited by Edward H. Cotton (Thomas Y. Crowell Company).

L. T. Hobhouse, *Development and Purpose* (The Macmillan Company).

Lawrence J. Henderson, *The Fitness of the Environment* (The Macmillan Company); *The Order of Nature* (Harvard University Press).

---

[1] William Benjamin Smith, "Push? or Pull?" *The Monist* (Open Court Publishing Company), **23**, p. 33.

PART III
THEORIES OF REALITY

CHAPTER XIII
THEORIES OF REALITY

The "stuff" of the world

FROM the earliest times philosophers have been interested, not merely in the *course of events*, in the study of growth and evolution and in the origin and destiny of the world, but also in the "stuff" out of which the world is made. This problem we must now study. What is the ultimate nature of that which undergoes growth and evolution? What is it that may or may not have originated and which has a destiny? This is the problem of Reality; the *ontological* problem as it is called.

It has been common in the history of philosophy and science to distinguish between appearance and reality. The stick in water appears to be bent but it is really straight. This man appears to be honest but in reality he is a rascal. This floor appears to be solid but, according to the physicist, in reality it is a cloud of dancing electrons. Thus are we ever distinguishing the apparent from the real.

The question of reality, the ontological problem, is, then, the one which has as its objective, the ultimate nature of the real. Is the whole course of nature in space and time but the appearance or cloak of a more ultimate reality? Is the world as it appears to me real or is it but the manifestation of a hidden reality which in itself is quite different from its appearance?

It was this problem of reality, as we have seen, that engaged the attention of the earliest Greek philosophers. Thales of Miletus, who lived in the sixth century before Christ and who is called the father of philosophy, said that all things come from *water*; but his successors in the Ionian school thought that they come from air or fire. Rapidly the early Greeks advanced beyond these crude conceptions and soon arrived at the theory that the world is made of atoms, or little material particles. Since then many theories as to the ultimate nature of reality have been advanced.

The three types of theory

It is obvious that if we are to speak of ultimate forms of reality at all, and if we are to believe that the world may be reduced to certain elementary substances or elementary forms of being, either there must be such elementary substance, or two, or more than two. So we have the three types of philosophical theories of reality, *Monism, Dualism,* and *Pluralism.* The tendency to seek for unity in plurality, to find the One in the Many, as Plato said, is persistent in the human mind, so that there has always been a strong hope among philosophers of finding some one elementary form of being — or, at any rate, two, the various manifestations of which will make up our world of experience. Consequently, monistic and dualistic systems of philosophy have been very popular. Just at present there seems to be less interest in trying to find out what the world is made of and more interest in discovering its meaning and value. Problems of life, problems of evolution, problems of experience, problems of value, have now somewhat eclipsed the older problem of "ontology."

But still these problems of reality are of perennial interest, and before we go on to the larger questions we must consider these. We must mention the different forms of Monism, and understand clearly what Dualism means, and examine the newer pluralistic views.

Dualism

Of these three theories of reality, perhaps the easiest one to understand is Dualism. Let us therefore begin with this. Probably the reason that this is most easily understood is because it is the popular belief, at any rate in America, where our philosophical traditions inherited from the Scottish school encourage this world view. Dualism is the theory that mind and matter are the two fundamental realities in the world and that they cannot be reduced the one to the other.[1] Among primitive people, as well as among moderns, it

[1] The word *dualism* is ambiguous, being used in philosophy in two senses. It has sometimes been used to designate the belief in a good and a bad principle, which lie at the root of all things. For instance, in the religion of Persia, Ahriman and Ahura-Mazda (Ormazd) stand for two eternal principles of evil and good. In this sense there is a dualism in Plato, for he taught that Being and Non-Being are two primordial principles, the latter being the source of imperfection.

seems very natural to distinguish mind from body in so sharp a manner as to make ultimate realities of each. Primitive man rarely failed to distinguish soul and body; the soul, though not perhaps immaterial, was a kind of duplicate of the body, or a shadowy image of it, and could leave it and might haunt the grave after death.

Even Thales and his fellow Ionians, although they seem to have been Monists, reducing reality to water or air or fire, still believed apparently that these material things were infused with life or with a divine and animate principle which made change and growth possible. Empedocles, in counting fire, water, earth, and air as the roots of all things, still thought he must add two others of a more mental or spiritual character, namely, love and hate, the latter serving as moving causes. And Anaxagoras postulated besides the world of atoms something which he called *Nous* (Noûs), or *Mind*, an eternal reality coexisting with the other elements. Medieval philosophy was likewise dualistic, following Saint Augustine, who considered man as the union of body and soul, the soul being an immaterial and immortal substance.

Metaphysical Dualism

The powerful dualistic current in modern thought, extending even to our firesides, took its rise in the philosophy of Descartes, who is called the founder of modern philosophy and whose *Meditations*, published in French and in Latin at the middle of the seventeenth century, have exerted an untold influence on our modern ways of thinking. Descartes' teaching was that there are in the world two wholly different kinds of reality, or "substances," as he called them, *thought* and *extension*, or, as we should say, *mind* and *matter*. The whole physical world, including the bodies of animals and men, is extended substance — matter, as we call it, or mass, governed absolutely by mechanical laws. Matter in motion constitutes the physical world. The lower animals are just mechanisms. An animal has no soul; he is only a material body. Not so man, for within his material extended body there is a thinking substance, the immortal soul, whose very being is to think.

This hard-and-fast metaphysical Dualism, as taught by Descartes, has at the present time few representatives in philosophy. We are not so fond of using the word "substance" now, either in referring to material or mental things. In the physical world we speak of energies and in the mental world of processes. And we are always searching for some principle of unity or of continuity or of evolution, so that the assumption of two elementary, wholly distinct, and mutually exclusive kinds of reality is less welcome. To modern philosophy it seems a little too dogmatic to make such wide generalizations, or to parcel out the Universe in this way into two exclusive regions. We are always trying to overcome this Dualism and find one rather than two ultimate forms of being; or else as is now still more congenial, to recognize at once an ultimate diversity in the world and a plurality of entities. Consequently, although Dualism is not without its able advocates at the present time, either monistic or pluralistic world views are more common.

In Chapter XX we shall see some of the wider implications of this type of Dualism and also some of the great difficulties which it raises. Many of the present problems in psychology and epistemology arise by virtue of this ultimate separation and differentiation of mind and matter.

Monism

Besides the dualistic theory which asserts that there are ultimately two kinds of reality, there are theories which insist that the ultimate stuff of the world is one. There are three types of monism which have appeared prominently in the history of philosophy: materialism, idealism and neutralism.

Materialism had its advocates among the Greek philosophers and has had many representatives in modern times. Such men as Democritus and Lucretius were as convinced that the world was reducible to material elements and their laws as was the nineteenth-century thinker, Haeckel. The doctrine of materialism asserts that there is finally one reality, matter. Mind, which Descartes held to be as ultimate as matter and independent of it, for the materialist is at best a function of matter, if indeed there is any such thing as mind at all. The world in the final analysis is matter operating under the laws which physical science reveals to us.

Idealism, too, asserts that reality is one, that *one* being mind or spirit. For the idealist matter is at best a representation or construct of mind. The world of "matter" is but the appearance of mind to itself. The world which the physical scientist talks about is, as Eddington says, in *The Nature of the Physical World*,[1] a "world of shadows." What really *is*, in the final analysis, is of the nature of mind. Thus the idealist would deny that the mechanical interpretation of the world is in any way final. The Universe is not a dead mechanical ruthless grinding of wheels, wherein values, religion and moral aspirations are but stupid delusions; it is, rather, a living dynamic reality which guarantees a cosmic worth to human striving and interprets the world in the light of spiritual values.

There is yet a third type of monism, which we have called neutralism, which holds that reality is neither mind nor matter but a single kind of stuff of which mind and matter are but appearances or aspects. Spinoza is the best classical representative of this type of monism. For Spinoza, there is one single reality which he called substance, and the world in its various aspects is but its attributes and modes. What Descartes called mind and matter are for Spinoza but two attributes of substance, two ways in which substance appears. What is called mind from one point of view is matter from another point of view. They are not really distinct but only apparently so.

Pluralism

This third type of metaphysical theory asserts that the world is not so simple. It cannot be reduced to one nor even two denominators. The reality of the world is manifold and it is a false analysis which reduces the welter of the Universe to two substances or one. This point of view was represented among the Ancient Greeks as well as among the moderns. Empedocles, for example, may be said to have been a pluralist when he asserted that ultimate reality is resolvable into earth, air, fire and water. Plato, again, was pluralistic in his point of view. With him many things were real — Ideas, forms, principles, and laws. Even non-being he considered to be real.[2]

[1] Page xv.
[2] William James, *The Will to Believe*, and *A Pluralistic Universe* (Longmans, Green and Company).

In modern times other forms of pluralism have been offered. William James is probably the most famous protagonist for the pluralistic philosophy. In the following chapters we shall study more carefully such typical theories of reality as pluralism, materialism and idealism.

In connection with this chapter read:

Gamertsfelder and Evans, *Fundamentals of Philosophy* (Prentice-Hall, Inc.), chap. XIII, pp. 450–63.

Further references:

William McDougall, *Body and Mind, a History and a Defence of Animism* (Methuen and Company), chaps. XIII, XIV, XXVI.

Joseph Alexander Leighton, *Man and the Cosmos* (D. Appleton and Company), chap. XXVII, "Mind and Body."

Friedrich Paulsen, *Introduction to Philosophy* (Henry Holt and Company).

R. W. Sellars, *The Essentials of Philosophy* (The Macmillan Company), chap. XVI.

William James, *The Will to Believe* (Longmans, Green and Company).

CHAPTER XIV
THE CONSTITUTION OF MATTER

IF WE are to judge the worth of the mechanistic theories of reality to be studied in the next chapter, we ought first to find out as much as we can about matter and its make-up. This is because, according to the older mechanistic or materialistic world-views, the whole of nature is the product of matter or mass particles in motion. Out of these alone is to come a world of order and beauty — and of mind which can appreciate this order and beauty and study it and speculate about it. It is highly important, therefore, to know as much as we can about the new theories of matter and their bearing on mechanistic philosophy. And this must be preceded by a brief historical study.

Strictly, matter is just an abstract term — a convenient name which we can apply to the substance of all possible physical things. All objects which we can touch, push about, or be pushed about by, are supposed to be made of matter. It is the permanent *stuff* of physical things. Popularly it is supposed to be more *real* than the objects which are composed of it.

There would seem to be two methods of studying the constitution of matter. The first is the method of physical and chemical analysis with the help of instruments of precision and magnification. While this method is of the utmost importance, it does not carry us far down toward the ultimate units, if ultimate units there be. The other is the method of mathematical and speculative construction and the making of hypotheses whose results meet necessary conditions. This method has been used with brilliant success.

The first scientific attempt to study the constitution of matter was made by the early Greek philosophers. Thales, who lived about 600 B.C., was the first to try his hand at it. He said that *water* was the first principle of all things. Anaximenes, another member of the Ionian school, suggested *air* or vapor as the primary substance. Heraclitus considered that all things are made of *fire*. Somewhat later Empedocles took a real step forward when he proposed the view that physical objects are mixtures or compounds of a certain number of primary elements, in this case, four — *fire, water, earth,* and *air*. He said also that since the primary elements are by nature inert, there must be a moving cause. To this end he proposed two other elements, love and hate, significantly choosing something mental to move the physical. Then came Anaxagoras, a celebrated astronomer and physicist, whom Pericles invited to Athens. Rejecting as child-like the four elements of Empedocles, he said that matter is composed of an infinite number of minute particles or *germs*, all different in quality but eternal and immutable essences. There were just as many classes of germs as there are qualities of things in nature. This has been called *qualitative atomism*. He too thought that there must be a moving cause, which he affirmed to be Nous (Noûs), or Mind.

Later came the atomists, Leucippus and Democritus. Democritus was a contemporary of Plato, but the two schools held views so completely opposed that they ignored each other. Leucippus proposed and Democritus perfected the celebrated Greek atomism, anticipating in many ways modern scientific views. Matter, they said — and indeed everything in the Universe — is composed of an infinite number of infinitely small particles, which for the first time, were called *atoms*, from two Greek words meaning that which cannot be cut. These atoms are all qualitatively alike, differing only in size, shape and motion. They are homogeneous, invisible, and indivisible.

All things in the Universe, whether physical or mental, are combinations or constellations of these simple atoms. They are not centers of force or mathematical points; they are minute bodies, having extension, size and shape. They are eternally in motion through the *void*, or empty space, and it is their unions and combinations which make up our objects of experience.

Crude as this theory appears when compared with the modern science of atoms, it was still one of the brilliant generalizations of the Greeks. To be sure, since the atoms were just little bits of matter, being solid, homogeneous, and of spatial dimensions, the real problem of the constitution of matter was not solved nor even understood, and the theory of mind as being composed of smooth, round, atoms was naïve to say the least.

The Epicureans adopted the atomism of Democritus; and Lucretius, the Roman poet, wrote a long and wonderful poem in hexameters developing this view. One significant modification of the theory was made by Lucretius, since he thought it necessary to assign to the atoms a kind of spontaneity, resembling, he said, the freedom of the will — else how would the world get started.

Plato's view of matter, gained from the standpoint of the idealist, was totally different. Only the Ideas are real; matter has no comparative reality. It is the dark and formless substratum of the physical world, having no qualities and equivalent thus to non-being. This was a subject of little interest to Plato. In the philosophy of Aristotle, Plato's disciple, matter seems still more vague. Aristotle thought of the world not as something *made out of* something, but as a great *process*, a process of change or development. Matter was just a relative term — the potency of something more real.

Plato, Aristotle, and Saint Augustine dominated the Middle Ages — and the scientific study of matter was to wait till later days. In the seventeenth century, Descartes taught that there are two and only two ultimate realities in the world — thought and extension, or mind and matter, the latter being an "extended substance," while mind is a thinking substance. Matter, having no other qualities than extension, would seem to be identical with space.

A little later Leibniz, an intellectual giant comparable to Aristotle or Democritus, made a great advance in proposing a *dynamic* theory of matter. The world consists of ultimate units or atoms, which he called *Monads*. The Monads are not material things. They are centers of force or energy. He calls them little perceptions, being thus mental rather than physical. The Monads of material bodies are sleeping or undeveloped Monads, while those we call minds have developed to complete consciousness.

It was the science of chemistry which ushered in the modern period in the search for the ultimate units of matter. Observation and experiment, rather than speculation, now became the method of study — and yet in all the wonderful advances which now began, speculation as before had an important part; but it now took the form of reflective thought and hypothesis, always controlled by observation and experiment. Chemistry followed the obvious rule that the best way to find out about the constitution of matter is to analyze it; and presently it made the important discovery that when we begin to analyze physical objects, minerals, plants, animal bodies, water, air and gases, we find that a certain number of so-called elementary substances constantly appear and reappear — such for instance as carbon, oxygen, nitrogen, hydrogen, calcium, phosphorus, lead, iron, mercury. Ninety-two of these comprised the complete list of elements; and these were believed to be simple substances, of which all matter is composed or compounded. The spectroscope reveals these same elements in the sun and heavenly bodies. It was concluded therefore that the elements of matter had been revealed; that there was a definite and final number of them; that they could not be destroyed or created, or transmuted into other elements, despite the hope of the alchemists that the transmutation of the baser metals into gold might be effected.

Accordingly it was something of a shock when the element, radium, was discovered by Professor Madame Curie in 1898, and radium was found to be disintegrating right before their eyes. Later it was known that other of the heavier elements are disintegrating, the product being simpler elements. Vague theories have been proposed since then concerning the ultimate transmutation after aeons of time of all the elements into simpler ones — to be followed, perhaps, by the reverse process. Such theories are, however, highly speculative.

The story of the atom

Returning to the progress of science in its search for the ultimate units of matter, it was early learned that the chemical elements combine in certain definite proportions, which could be explained only on the supposition that they are composed of discrete particles. The chemist, Dalton, early in the nineteenth century, revived the atomic theory of the ancient Greeks and showed that matter must be granular — not continuous. Since Dalton's time the atomic theory of matter has been universally accepted and perfected.

The atoms are not visible in any microscope, there being about 54,000,000,000,000,000,000 of them in a cubic centimeter of hydrogen gas, but the theory is indispensable in chemistry and has long since been verified in chemistry and physics.

It is, however, through the magic of modern physics that the marvelous story of the atom has been unfolded. Of all the brilliant triumphs of nineteenth and twentieth century science, these researches into the electric nature of the atom are most startling.[1]

The atoms exist — but what are they like? What are they made of? The individual atoms of iron or silver surely do not have the properties we associate with the familiar metals, iron and silver. There are, it is believed, ninety-two elements and ninety-two chemically different kinds of atoms. Of these, ninety are now known. The atoms of gold are different from the atoms of silver or mercury, and the atom of oxygen is different from the atom of hydrogen — but in what does the difference consist? The difference is now known. The atom is a complex structure made up of smaller units, and the difference lies not in the quality of the units but in their number, arrangement and motions. The units themselves are identical in all the atoms.

What are these units and how many kinds of them are there? Notwithstanding the brilliant contributions of recent research into the constitution of the atom, no final answer to this question can yet be given — perhaps no final answer will ever be given. The deeper the inquiry goes the more complex and even mysterious does the structure of the atom become. Previous to the discovery of the *neutron* by Chadwick in 1932, and the later discovery of the *positron*, or the positive electron in 1933, and previous to the further discovery that the construction of the atom has become a problem in the mathematically complex subject of wave-mechanics, physicists thought that they had really arrived almost at the solution of the structure and constitution of the atom. The result is sometimes called the Bohr atom, because of the important contributions made by Niels Bohr, the physicist. Although later discoveries have

[1] Among the distinguished names engaged in this research are those of Sir William Crookes, Röntgen, Becquerel, Sir J. J. Thomson, Sir Ernest Rutherford, Planck, Bohr, Sommerfeld, Born, de Broglie, Schroedinger, Heisenberg, and Millikan.

greatly modified this theory of the atom, it will be necessary to describe it here, since it has become the widely accepted view.

The Bohr atom involves both a theory of its constitution and an actual model of it. It was the beauty and simplicity of the model which contributed so much to the acceptance of this theory. But physicists now are becoming very cautious about atomic models; it is suspected that the structure of the atom can be elucidated only mathematically.

According to this theory, then, the ultimate elements of an atom are electrical charges, a positive charge called the proton and a negative called the electron. Each atom has a positive nucleus, encircled by one or more negative electrons. The atom of hydrogen has one proton encircled by one electron. Helium has two planetary electrons, and lithium three. Uranium, the heaviest element, has ninety-two planetary electrons. The nucleus in nearly all is composed of protons and electrons, with definite numerical relations corresponding to the number of the element in the table of atomic weights. In the heavier elements the electrons revolve around the nucleus with a speed comparable with the velocity of light, while the electron of a hydrogen atom has a velocity of only about one thousand and three hundred miles a second.

As regards the model of the atom, it was represented as a kind of planetary system, somewhat on the plan of our solar system, the nucleus corresponding to the sun, and the electrons to our planets, the distances, relative to the particles themselves, being comparable to the relative distances of the heavenly bodies. So again we are impressed with the amazing emptiness of the world, whether it be the emptiness of cosmic space or the emptiness of the atom.

But the student of philosophy is not satisfied with this description of the atom. He is searching for the actual, ultimate stuff of which the physical Universe consists. Thus far it appears that the final elements of the atomic world are the positive and negative charges of electricity. But what *are* these things? Science cannot as yet answer this question. Do they have a "structure" and hence are they capable of divisions into even smaller parts? Science believes not. As we learned in a previous chapter it is the *whole*, the structure, the organism that is real, each structure or organism having its own new properties. Even if we could isolate the ultimate parts of an organic whole and learn all about them as units, we should not know how they would behave when in relation to other units or parts of a given whole.

Perhaps this is a digression from our study of the progress of science in microphysics — but it is a digression forced upon us. It would almost seem that the inquiry as to what matter *is* is useless, for the term always refers to some ultimate stuff out of which things are made; and however far down we go in our attempted analysis of things, we always find wholes or organisms at work — and these organisms and their achievements are the entities of the physical world.

If, however, anyone should choose to halt his search for the ultimate stuff of the physical world at the stage which scientists call electricity, he may repair, if he wishes, to the physicist and ask him what electricity is. The answer will be that the question is useless. We do not know what it *is*, but only what it *does*. It is a name that we give to certain peculiar forms of energy; and if we ask what energy is, we are told that it is the potentiality of doing, the capacity for *doing* something, for doing work. We see work done and we can measure it — and these measurements are our data for the construction of our science. It is not *being*, but *process*, to which we are always led. Things *are* what they *do*. We cannot know what energy is; we can only know what mathematical ratios prevail in its various manifestations.

Such is the picture of the atom made familiar to us during recent years previous to the new discoveries beginning about the year 1930. From these it appears that the atom has other elementary constituents besides the protons and electrons, and that possibly the protons themselves are composed of these other units. The neutron is described as a particle having neither a positive nor a negative charge; and the positron as an electron having not a negative but a positive charge. We seem to be dealing with particles, and although the nature of these particles is not known, some further knowledge may be gained when we consider presently "the universe of light." For the moment, however, it would appear that the constituents of

the atom are four, namely, protons, electrons, neutrons and positrons, though recently even a fifth has been suggested.

Incidentally here we might notice that materialism would seem
to have no further meaning for philosophy; for the ultimate reality,
if there be any such thing, is nothing to which we could give the
name "matter," at least with the ordinary meaning.   If it had
turned out, or should turn out, that energy is the ultimate "stuff"
of which the atom is made, then *dynamism* would seem to be the
better name.   But such terms bring us little satisfaction.   Perhaps
there is no such science as ontology.

The universe of light

In our quest for ultimate things, as the physicist sees them, we
have omitted something.   We started from the standpoint of
the chemist; and our search for ultimate things led us to elements,
then to atoms, then to protons, electrons, neutrons and positrons.
This may be the story of the material world; but it is not the whole
story to the physicist.   There is still the "universe of light" — the
world of radiation.   We may be eating, drinking and treading upon
a world of material things; but we are bathed in a world of ethereal
things — or rather, we are bombarded by rays of many kinds.   The
light rays are the best known of these.   Through certain nerve
centers and certain highly specialized nerve endings of the eye we
become sensitive to these as light.   Then there are the heat rays and
the long wireless rays, and the short X-rays and the new and interesting cosmic rays.   All these forms of radiant energy differ from
protons and electrons in that they are travelers; they travel through
space all at the same rate, namely 186,000 miles a second.   They
differ in their wave lengths.

What are these *rays*?   Previous to the nineteenth century and
since Newton's time the corpuscular theory of light had been
generally accepted.   Light comes from the sun to the earth in
eight minutes and from the nearest fixed star in a little more than
four years.   What is it that travels in space from star to star?
Little corpuscles or particles, said the older theory.

In the nineteenth century this theory was discarded and during
the whole of that century the undulatory theory of light was ac-

cepted. It seemed to explain satisfactorily all the phenomena of light transmission, as the other theory did not. Light is a form of wave-motion. It travels through space as the waves of water travel across the sea. What is true of light is true also of all the other kinds of rays. But if they are waves, there must be some medium in which the undulations or ripples take place. Hence nineteenth-century science assumed the existence of a universal medium filling all space. It was the carrier of electro-magnetic waves. They named it the ether.

But strangely enough — incredibly, it might seem — the twentieth century is coming back to the eighteenth century view. Something like the corpuscular theory of light is now held. Light rays behave like waves — and yet in other respects they behave like actual particles. These are simply the facts and the theory of radiant energy must be made to fit the facts. The unification has not yet been made — but surely will be. Light has wave properties and these wave properties seem to be just the tools the mathematician needs to tell him where the light particle will be.

The quantum theory

Hence light has both particle and wave properties. It behaves like a stream of particles, quanta, droplets, bullets, darts, or wave-packets, and has an atomic character as well as a wave character. Light energy travels through space in the form of bundles. These light units are called *photons* — and this word applies also to other forms of radiant energy. Energy is therefore atomic, as are also matter and electricity. A photon encircles the earth seven times in a second.[1]

But this is not yet the whole of the story. It was found that light rays behave like particles — but now it is also found that particles, for instance, electrons, behave like waves. *"In other words, not only may waves be made to show all the properties of particles but particles may also be made to show all the properties of waves.* This is one of the most amazing situations ever encountered by any science."[2]

[1] Compare C. G. Darwin, *The New Conceptions of Matter*, p. 23.
[2] Robert A. Millikan, *Time, Matter, and Values* (The University of North Carolina Press, 1932), pp. 61, 62.

"The ultimate *elementary processes* which constitute light cannot be both waves and corpuscles," says Millikan. "Which are they really? and what kind of legerdemain has Nature played upon us to make them seem otherwise? How did the rabbit actually get into the hat?" Apparently the only way out of the seeming contradiction is to assume that all elementary processes, whether they are processes involving matter, light, or energy, are at bottom discrete-particle-processes. Of these processes the governing laws are those imposed by the wave-like character of their representation.

The principle of uncertainty

In connection with the experiments on the behavior of electrons as waves and as particles, a new and very interesting principle was discovered, called the Principle of Uncertainty. It is called also the Heisenberg Principle of Indeterminacy. Its striking repercussions in the field of ethics in its relation to the freedom of the will remain to be mentioned in a later chapter.

The strange character of this new principle is shown by the fact that it has been held to destroy definitely the universal validity of the determinism in nature upon which science itself is supposed to depend. It seems to contradict the law of causality, according to which every event in nature is fully determined by preceding events, the present being strictly the product of the past. According to the Principle of Uncertainty this does not hold true in the world of the atom. Physicists have means of measuring the velocity and position of an electron as it moves in one of its orbits within the atom. If the laws of mechanics, upon which during the centuries science has been able to rely absolutely, hold good in the microphysical world, the experimenter should be able to determine where the electron will be at any given instant. To his astonishment, the electron is not there. It is found to jump about in an erratic and bewildering manner. It seems indeed to jump from one orbit to another without traversing the intermediate space. All this gives us a dizzy feeling — as though the foundations of science were cracking up. Hence it was said that it might be necessary to develop new laws of mechanics to apply to the ultra microscopic world.

But statements like the above, although constantly made in recent years, somewhat overstate the difficulties. What really happens is this: The conditions of measurement are such that it is impossible to determine at a given time both the position and velocity of a particle. The very means which we use to determine the one disturbs the other. "The measure of one quantity disturbs the determination of a complementary quantity." There is a definite limit to the accuracy with which both the position and velocity can be simultaneously determined.[1]

The orthodox mechanist might put it in this way: "I see nothing in the Principle of Uncertainty which proves that the old laws of mechanics do not apply in the infinitesimal world of the atom. I see only that we cannot institute an experiment showing that this is true." But to this again it might be retorted that the mechanist himself cannot institute an experiment showing that they do so apply.[2]

The final interpretation of the Principle of Uncertainty seems to depend upon the particular philosophy which one holds. If we believe that there is a real external world independent of our sense perceptions and our measurements — a world in which the principle of causality and determinism reign supreme and universal, then we shall see that the Principle of Uncertainty arises merely from the limitations of our experiments in the microscopic world of the atom. If on the other hand we believe that our perceptions and scientific measurements are the only and ultimate data for the construction of the order of nature, or if we hold with the positivists that science is not concerned with anything beyond our perceptions and our measurements, then we cannot escape the conclusion that the Principle of

---

[1] Compare V. F. Lenzen, "Indeterminism and the Concept of Physical Reality," *Jour. Phil.*, May 25, 1933. Compare also C. G. Darwin, *The New Conceptions of Matter*, chap. IV.

[2] This subject is discussed by Max Planck in his book *Where Is Science Going?* "The concept of causality," he says, "is something transcendental, which is quite independent of the nature of the researcher, and it would be valid even if there were no perceiving subject at all" (pp. 156, 157). This is clearly stated by James Murphy in his Introduction to the above book. He says, "We cannot estimate simultaneously both the velocity and position in time-space of a particle and say where it will be a moment hence. But this does not mean that the causal sequence is not actually verified objectively. It means that we cannot detect its operation; because, as things stand today, our research instruments and our mental equipment are not adequate to the task. The Principle of Indeterminacy is in reality an alternative working hypothesis which takes the place of the strictly causal method in quantum physics. But Heisenberg himself would be one of the first to protest against the idea of interpreting his Principle of Indeterminacy as tantamount to a denial of the principle of causation" (pp. 31, 32).

Uncertainty reveals a kind of indeterminism or spontaneity or contingency in the inner world of the atom.

Sir James Jeans and many other writers take this more subjective view. The existence of matter except for a pragmatist is a pure hypothesis and the mechanical principles which have come down to us from Newton do not apply in the "inconceivably small," as we have learned that they do not apply to the "inconceivably great," either to the cosmic Universe as a whole or to the infinitesimal world studied in microphysics.

Another interesting result of these new studies is to increase the emphasis upon the statistical character of the laws of nature. We may not know how the individual electron will behave but we can establish reliable statistical laws regulating its average behavior; so that even in the world of the microscope the foundations of science are not likely to be disturbed. Other laws of nature are largely statistical, relating to average behavior. Social science knows about how many suicides will take place in a given group during a given time, although it is wholly uncertain whether any individual may so decide. In a larger way the new principle seems to attribute to the individual a measure of freedom.

Conclusion

The student of philosophy will perhaps be disappointed by the lack of finality in the scientific researches into the constitution of matter — and possibly confused. But he will find these studies of the profoundest interest and he will await eagerly those to follow. He will be impressed by the fact that the word *energy*, rather than the word *matter*, appears now to be the more appropriate name for that which manifests itself to our human senses; but he will probably import into that word more than it means to the physicist, and he will be puzzled to learn that energy exists in droplets and that mass is associated with every form of it.

It is indeed a strange world into which the new studies in physics and mathematics give us a partial glimpse. It does not seem to be a material world, nor yet a mechanistic one, since the old laws of mechanics are rudely violated. Is it a mental world, as Jeans and Eddington are fond of suggesting? Is it just a world of pure mathematics, in which equations in wave mechanics form the basis of all things physical? However this question may be answered, it would seem that our search for *reality* will lead us not into the depths explored by physical science, but up to the heights where things are *realized* through a process of creative evolution. Form will interest us more than matter, and organisms more than elements.

In connection with this chapter read:

Gamertsfelder and Evans, *Fundamentals of Philosophy* (Prentice-Hall, Inc.), chap. IX.

Further references:

C. G. Darwin, *The New Conception of Matter* (The Macmillan Company).

Robert A. Millikan, *Time, Matter, and Values* (The University of North Carolina Press).

Bertrand Russell, *The A B C of Atoms* (E. P. Dutton and Company).

A. S. Eddington, *The Nature of the Physical World* (The Macmillan Company).

W. F. G. Swann, *The Architecture of the Universe* (The Macmillan Company, 1934), chap. IV.

Sir James Jeans, *The New Background of Science*. Revised Edition (The Macmillan Company, 1934), chaps. V, VI.

Alfred Berthoud, *New Theories of Matter and the Atom*. Translated by Eden and Cedar Paul (The Macmillan Company, 1934).

Paul R. Heyl, "What is Electricity?" The Scientific Monthly, July, 1935.

CHAPTER XV

MECHANISTIC WORLD VIEWS

"There's machinery in the butterfly,
There's a mainspring to the bee.
There's hydraulics to a daisy
And contraptions to a tree.

"If we could see the birdie
That makes the chirping sound
With psycho-analytic eyes,
With X-ray, scientific eyes,
We could see the wheels go round."

And I hope all men
Who think like this
Will soon lie underground.

VACHEL LINDSAY

IN AN earlier chapter we studied the theory of mechanism as it applies to the explanation of living matter, and to animal and human life, leaving until later the consideration of mechanism as a world view. We are now in position to study the mechanistic philosophy as a theory of reality. This will be made easier by the knowledge we have gained in the preceding chapter concerning the constitution of matter. In its earliest and simplest form this philosophy is called Materialism, or Materialistic Monism.

Materialism

Materialism is the theory that matter is the one and only kind of being — the primary substance. The Universe is a material world, and all objects of experience are composed of matter. Mind is a form or function of matter.

As first taught by Democritus, the Greek philosopher, the Universe is made of material atoms. All objects of sense perception and all things whatsoever in the world are combinations or constellations of atoms and nothing more. There is no separate realm of mind or spirit. Nothing happens by chance, but all according to the laws of nature; the reign of law is absolute and universal. There was no creation, since the atoms are eternal; they are in motion through empty space. Ends or purposes do not exist in nature — nor freedom. Matter in motion under the operation of natural laws will explain the world and all that it contains. Democritus emphasized the method of analysis, philosophy being the search for the ultimate units of being; his followers, the Epicureans emphasized, however, the peace of mind which is the outcome of a materialistic world view. The term *Atomism* has usually been applied to the kind of materialism held by Democritus and his followers.

Thus we see that the older materialism, including the earlier forms of the modern theory, was very dogmatic. It felt quite sure that the whole world, including life and mind and human society and art and literature and human history, could be explained as the result of the redistribution of matter and motion, or of atoms moving in empty space — granting only sufficient time and the law of evolution and adaptation. It was particularly averse to assuming any creative force exterior to the movement of matter, any directive agency in the process, any vital principle or life force differing from mechanical forces, any entity such as mind — or any purpose, end, or value except in human affairs.

Materialism is usually described as a form of monism, reducing all reality to one single kind of being, namely, matter. Historically, however, materialism has never succeeded in realizing this ideal of oneness. Even the Greek atomists assumed two first principles, atoms and motion, besides empty space. Eternal motion in space was ascribed to the atoms, thus providing the primary cause of the present ordered world. Lucretius, the Roman poet, who adopted the atomistic philosophy of Democritus and Epicurus, departed still further from monism by ascribing to the atoms a characteristic "freedom," causing them to swerve from their downward movement, thus forming nuclei of evolving bodies. The German materialist, Ernst Haeckel, whose work will be referred to presently, although he called his system Monism, departed still further from the monistic standpoint by endowing his atoms with a richness of psychic qualities. "The two fundamental forms of substance, ponderable matter and ether," he says, "are not dead and only moved by extrinsic force, but they are endowed with sensation and will (though naturally of the lowest grade); they experience an inclination for condensation, a dislike of strain, they strive after the one and struggle against the other." [1] He seems to give to the psychic qualities a sort of creative function, saying that feeling and inclination are "the active causes" of the original primary division of substance into mass and ether. His system is thus a kind of Hylozoism, or the theory that matter is alive, somewhat similar to the view held by Thales and his fellow Ionians.

Naturalism

In recent times the term *Naturalism* has come into more general use, replacing the term *Materialism*. This is due partly to the rather naïve and dogmatic character of the older materialism and partly to the indefiniteness of the word "matter" and our changing views of it. Naturalism stresses the use of other words, such as energy, motion, natural law, causal determination. In general, Naturalism places emphasis upon the physical sciences, especially upon physics and chemistry; and it is inclined to think that the laws of these sciences are sufficient to explain the world even in its most evolved forms, such as organic life and mind and human history and human institutions. It places great emphasis upon the law of conservation of energy, and regards the world as a redistribution of energy, or of matter, or of both, and it relies profoundly upon the principle of evolution and adaptation as explaining the survival of structures and functions fitted to survive.

Thus, in its extreme form Naturalism differs little from Materialism, only stressing the concept of matter less and that of energy more. Recently, however, the term *Naturalism* has been used in a new and liberal sense to denote an explanation of the world based, not on physics and chemistry alone, but on *all* the sciences, thus recognizing that the biological and mental sciences have certain distinctive characteristics due to novelties in their subject-matter, and recognizing also the validity of the theory of levels in evolution. [2]

---

[1] Ernst Haeckel, *The Riddle of the Universe*, 220.

[2] Compare R. W. Sellars, *Evolutionary Naturalism*, and especially his more recent work, *The Philosophy of Physical Realism* (The Macmillan Company, 1932).

Mechanism

Since the beginning of the present century, the terms *Mechanism* and the *mechanistic conception of nature* have come into general use. They represent a physico-chemical interpretation of the world. This appeals deeply to many minds, owing to its simplicity and owing to its apparently close connection with the physical sciences, whose exact character has won for them our almost reverent respect. The picture of the world which it gives us is simple and attractive. One has only to think of mass particles in motion. It is just the possible groupings or constellations of these mass particles or atoms which constitute the objects of our experience — rocks and sea and air and animal bodies. The cooling surface of the once fiery Earth made possible finally those very complex carbon compounds called *colloids*, from which it was but a step to the colloids which we find in plants and animal bodies and to the simple cell, the unit of all life. Evolution shows us the method by which the simplest living cell may develop through chance variation and natural selection into the more and more complex bodies of plants and animals, until man himself appears with a highly differentiated nervous system capable of thought, feeling, and volition.

If the ancient Greeks found an atomistic and mechanistic picture of the world attractive, we can understand the powerful appeal which it makes in modern times when strengthened by Darwin's remarkable discoveries relating to the origin of species. The view commends itself by its simplicity, by the relatively small number of concepts which it must assume, and by the absence of troublesome problems of creation, of ends and purposes and final causes, and of vital and spiritual forces. In studying mechanism, naturalism, or materialism we should also avoid any prejudice against these theories of reality because of imputations of "baseness," which we have come to associate with the adjective "materialistic."

It must be pointed out that to be a materialist in the ontological sense carries with it no disgrace. It does not mean that the materialist is subject to baser moral interests than those which concern the idealist.[1]

---

[1] Gamertsfelder and Evans, *Fundamentals of Philosophy*, p. 463 f.

Historical

Historically the early mechanistic theories took the form of materialism. Leucippus, the Greek philosopher, and his more illustrious disciple, Democritus, were its first representatives. Democritus was a contemporary of Plato — but the two schools held diametrically opposed views and had nothing to do with each other. A little later, Epicurus and the Epicurean school accepted the Atomism of Democritus as the basis of their philosophy. Lucretius, the Roman poet, carried on the tradition in the first century before Christ. His great poem, *De Rerum Natura*, pictures in glowing hexameters the terrors of religion and the freedom and emancipation from fear gained in the knowledge that the whole Universe is nothing more than a grouping of harmless atoms, which were at first falling through infinite space.

In modern times, a materialistic world view was advocated by the English philosopher, Thomas Hobbes, in the seventeenth century. In the following century, preceding the Revolution in France, materialism was vigorously advocated by a school of writers of whom Diderot, Lamettrie, and d'Holbach were representatives. In Germany in the nineteenth century, after the downfall of the Hegelian philosophy, there was a vigorous school of materialists, of whom the better known are Moleschott, Vogt, and Ernst Haeckel.

Haeckel's little book, *The Riddle of the Universe*, presented in popular form, under the name of *Monism*, the philosophy of materialism, strengthened by the Darwinian theory of evolution, at that time new in Germany. Although this widely read book contained a good deal of pseudo-science and introduced into philosophy what we may call a false simplicity, it purported to be *the* solution of the world problem which the science of the nineteenth century sponsored. Science speaks and the world problem is solved. Haeckel wrote oracularly of a "law of substance," which is the conservation of matter and of energy; of infinite time and of infinite space, filled with the imponderable "ether" and the ponderable atoms; of the spontaneous generation of life from inorganic matter; of a certain kind of protoplasm called *psychoplasm*, which is the seat of conscious mind. The latter he considered to be only a function of the brain. All of this, coupled with the Darwinian theory of evolution, impressed a wide circle of readers and popularized the materialistic philosophy in Germany in the nineteenth century.

In the present century materialism in the older sense has few representatives. It has given way to the theory of mechanism, or to that of naturalism in the narrower sense as defined above. A mechanistic world theory has many able advocates now, not so much indeed in the distinct field of philosophy as among men of science who accept it as a working basis for scientific investigation. Even here, however, the interest is not so much in the interpretation of the world in mechanistic terms, as in extending the application of physical and chemical concepts to the explanation of organic life — and less commonly to the human mind. The former tendency will be found prominent, for instance, in Jacques Loeb's *The Mechanistic Conception of Life*, and the latter in Dr. G. W. Crile's *Man — An Adaptive Mechanism*.

The psychologists, whether in Europe or America, who are more closely in touch with philosophy than are the scientists in other fields, are not generally favorable to a mechanistic conception extending to the whole of nature. In America, however, the group of radical behaviorists, represented by John B. Watson, and Max F. Meyer, are energetically mechanistic. They favor a wholly objective method for psychology, which they regard as the science of behavior — not the science of mind or soul or consciousness.[1]

Critical

During the latter part of the nineteenth century and the early years of this century, the mechanistic conception of nature prevailed increasingly in the physical sciences. It became folly to try to explain things by an appeal to final causes, rather than efficient causes. There could be in nature no such thing as a goal. In no sense is the present determined by the future; it is determined only by the past and wholly in a mechanical way. Whatever happens is due only to the interaction of material particles, moving in space according to mechanical laws. What is true in the sphere of physics and chemistry applies also to biology and psychology. The fact that man

[1] The reader may consult John B. Watson's *Behaviorism* and the radically mechanistic philosophy exhibited in A. P. Weiss's book, *A Theoretical Basis of Human Behavior*.

possesses something called mind or consciousness does not exclude him from the mechanistic chain.

This philosophy seemed to be justified by its practical results — its fruits. Knowing nature's laws, we were able to control its forces, and the limits of our prediction of the future were only the extent and exactness of our knowledge. Gradually the other sciences, biology, psychology and sociology, began to follow the lead of the sciences of physics and chemistry. In biology it began to be "good form" to assume a mechanistic basis for all vital phenomena. Even in psychology, a vigorous school of writers began to explain all mental phenomena on mechanistic principles.

It was not until well along in the present century that the situation changed — and the change came from the science of physics itself, where the universal validity of the old mechanistic theory began to be doubted. The first discovery was that it does not apply to the infinitely large or the infinitely small. Troubles arose in astrophysics and microphysics. The planet Mercury was found to move in a path unexplained by the Newtonian laws. The infinitesimal particles of the atom violated these laws in a shameless manner. Next it was discovered that the theory itself was based on anthropomorphic conceptions, as shown through logical analysis. We are amused when we recall how the ancients introduced gods and goddesses to explain the movements of the heavenly bodies; but now we were told that our mechanical scheme of nature differs only in degree. It conceived that every object in the universe is pushed or pulled about by other objects, just as we push or pull them about in our daily life. We introduce the word "force" to denote something which one body exerts upon another to correspond to something which we experience as effort.

Carrying this conception down to the study of the constitution of matter, we explain material bodies as consisting of minute particles or atoms, which push or pull one another about, or exercise "force" upon one another, until they finally get into groups or aggregates called molecules, and ultimately into those peculiar constellations which we call living cells. Then evolution and natural selection do the rest.

Later when the atom is found to be not a minute solid "body," but a system of particles having electric charges — these particles being very far apart relatively to their size — electro-magnetic "forces" are introduced as the causes of the pushing and pulling which the particles are observed to do. But since the particles are so far apart, the problem of "action at a distance" comes to trouble us. So we again introduce some intervening mechanical medium — let us say an "ether."

A similar difficulty in the Newtonian mechanical conception of nature arose in connection with gravitation. Some "force," called "gravitational force," was invoked to explain the fall of an apple to the earth, and the paths of the moon and the planets. All physical bodies were supposed to "attract" one another inversely as the square of the distance. But what do we mean by attraction and how does it act across ninety million miles of empty space? Certainly the sun and the earth do not push each other about. So again a mysterious ether was invoked in an attempt to explain gravitation. But no evidence of an ether exists, and numerous experiments seem to show that it does not exist. Evidently the mechanistic picture of nature was having difficulties.

Mechanism and the new physics

Then came Einstein, Heisenberg, and a group of other brilliant physicists and mathematicians, from whose labors came nothing less than a scientific revolution. In previous chapters we have studied certain aspects of this revolution; here it is necessary only to refer briefly to its bearing on the problems of this chapter. The new universe of the space-time continuum and quantum mechanics escapes the difficulties of the older mechanical views. The new physics, as Jeans says, is neither mechanistic nor deterministic. It is definitely non-mechanistic — and perhaps non-deterministic. Action at a distance has "fallen out of the picture." The apple does not fall to the ground, nor the moon circle in its course because of any "attractive force." It was easy for us to think that we had explained these movements by a "pull" of the earth or the sun, because we ourselves move things by pulling them about; but *how* the earth and the sun exercised this pull no one ever knew.

The new view of nature dispenses with anthropomorphic terms

and for that very reason is hard to understand, and seems strange at first — and perhaps forbidding. Gravity is not due to any pull upon one body by another, but to the nature and structure of space itself. Space is curved — and its curvature is greater and of a different kind in the vicinity of physical bodies. Objects both celestial and terrestrial, keeping as best they can a straight course, are drawn out of this course by the curvature of space and approach other bodies because of the peculiar character of the curvature near them. The new theories have been able to explain a large number of phenomena which the mechanistic Newtonian theories could not explain, and have thus far met with no reverses.[1]

It is too soon to appraise fully the permanent results of the new physics as affecting the older mechanistic philosophy. It would appear that the mechanical theory of nature was just a stage in scientific progress, successful within a certain range of phenomena in explaining nature's happenings. It is a fruitful and workable generalization in physics so long as we are dealing with the familiar objects in our daily lives. In the fields of biology and psychology its adequacy was never shown. Recently it has been found to fail in the sphere of microphysics and of astrophysics. It fails when we have to do with the very small and the very large.

In the field of living beings, where human interests center, other theories are found to be more fruitful. If we are to understand the world in which we live, we succeed best when we give up our search for elements as the key to reality, and begin our study of organisms. The processes of evolution are more instructive than the quest of elementary forms of being. That there is some organizing agency at work throughout nature — not explained by any mechanistic theory — has become for many a clarifying and helpful hypothesis. It would seem that atoms and molecules do not arrange themselves by chance into living organisms. But living organisms do come into being and they exhibit capacities for the production or creation of new and significant forms of activity which themselves become effective in determining the further direction of evolution.

Some things there are that are very dear to the soul of man.

---

[1] Compare Sir James Jeans, *The New Background of Science.* Revised Edition (The Macmillan Company, 1934), p. 44 ff.

Among these is the belief in the significance of the human mind itself as something more than a chance by-product of mechanical processes. Another is the persistent feeling or conviction of some kind of freedom. Still another is the belief in inherent and abiding values as goals to be realized.

Now the truth of a world theory is not to be judged by its ministering or not ministering to our comfortable beliefs — but by its success in explaining actual facts of experience. These beliefs do indeed seem to be more consistent with an organic theory of nature than with a mechanistic theory. William Morton Wheeler, distinguished in many fields of biological research, believes that the organic theory of nature is not only vastly more fruitful in biology than is the mechanical view, but, when extended into other fields, is able to solve many of the antinomies hitherto resisting all solution.

> With extension of the concepts of emergence and organicism also to the physical, chemical, psychological and social domain, there arises the strong probability that the old "nothing but" attitudes of naturalism *versus* supernaturalism, materialism *versus* spiritualism, mechanism *versus* vitalism, determinism *versus* freedom, and pluralism *versus* monism, etc., may be abandoned and the way opened for a more consistent and more satisfying view of universal reality.[1]

The term *Naturalism*, as used in recent philosophical discussion, softens somewhat the rigors of mechanism with its insistence upon uniformity and predictability, since Naturalism permits the recognition of "levels" in nature and the emergence through evolution of new forms of reality, and perhaps of new values, such as life and mind, without assigning to these any metaphysical significance as lying outside the realm of natural laws and natural processes. It gives us a workable theory of the origin of life, mind, and moral values in accordance with the accepted laws of the physical sciences. Surely, says the disciple of Naturalism, nothing more than this could be asked of any philosophy. But the human soul still dreams of "eternal" values; of freedom, of cosmic patterns — even of Platonic Ideas. It welcomes this liberal Naturalism — but questions its somewhat dogmatic denial of anything lying beyond the orbit of the natural sciences.

[1] William Morton Wheeler, *Emergent Evolution and the Development of Societies* (W. W. Norton and Company, Inc., New York), p. 74.

In connection with this chapter read:

Ralph Barton Perry, *Present Philosophical Tendencies*, part III (Longmans, Green and Company).

Further references:

F. A. Lange, *History of Materialism* (Treubner and Company).

Sir James Jeans, *The New Background of Science*. Revised edition (The Macmillan Company), 1934, chap. IV.

Roy Wood Sellars, *The Principles and Problems of Philosophy* (The Macmillan Company), chap. XXIII; *The Philosophy of Physical Realism* (The Macmillan Company, 1932).

Hans Driesch, "The Breakdown of Materialism," in *The Great Design*, edited by Frances Mason (The Macmillan Company, 1934).

James Ward, *Naturalism and Agnosticism*, vol. I (The Macmillan Company).

J. S. Haldane, *Materialism* (Harper, 1932).

John Herman Randall, Jr., *The Making of the Modern Mind* (Houghton Mifflin Company), chap. XXI.

L. P. Jacks, *The Revolt Against Mechanism* (The Macmillan Company, 1934).

Rudolph Otto, *Naturalism and Religion* (G. P. Putnam's Sons).

William Ernest Hocking, *Types of Philosophy* (Charles Scribner's Sons), chaps. III-V.

CHAPTER XVI

IDEALISM

Definition

JUST as Materialism considers the Universe as grounded and rooted in matter, or in physical energy, so Idealism considers it as grounded in mind. In interpreting the world, Materialism puts the emphasis upon mechanical and efficient causes, upon the conservation of energy, upon the movements of mass particles in space. It makes mind an incident in the process of evolution, contingent upon a highly developed nervous system in the higher animals. Idealism, on the other hand, puts the emphasis upon mind, as in some way prior to matter. It says, in effect, if you seek for elemental things, you will not find them in matter and motion and force, but in experience, in thought, in reason, in intelligence, in personality, in values, in religious and ethical ideals. These are the world's realities and they have a cosmic rather than a mere human significance, while matter, physical bodies, and physical forces are in some way secondary, being perhaps a kind of externalization of mind or else a phenomenon or appearance to mind. Materialism says that matter is real and mind an incident or accompaniment. Idealism says that mind is real and matter just an appearance.

The two views seem thus to be radically and irreconcilably opposed. If either one is true, the other must be false; and philosophers generally have inclined to think that one of the alternatives is true. But the opposition has become much softened of late. Recent studies in physics have changed our notions about matter. Recent studies in psychology have changed our notions about mind. Perhaps what we call matter is not so primordial as we used to think. It may be reduced to the electric charge, to pure energy, to singularities in the space-time manifold, or, as Mr. Whitehead so wisely tells us, to the "passage of events," thus becoming a mere halting-place in the cosmic process. There seems to be something back of the physical, logically prior to it, conditioning it. And evolution itself may be creative.   Creative synthesis may be the condition of any advance in evolution, and creative synthesis seems to lie quite outside the system of physical concepts which used to be invoked so confidently in the older Materialism and Naturalism.

And our notions of mind have changed.   It is no longer that simple substance, whose nature is to think.   Mind is a highly complex affair, including profound impulsive cravings, adaptive behavior, selective choice, and finally consciousness and meaning and personality.   If in its most highly perfected form, as in human personality, it is found only in connection with a highly integrated nervous system, it will by no means follow from this that it is an incident in the evolutionary process or less real than matter.   Quite the contrary, it may be something which is the perfect realization of the whole evolutionary movement, the most real thing, in a sense the only real thing — itself creative, as we know that it is, of newer values, such as art, philosophy, literature, science, history, and appreciative of older values, such as beauty, righteousness, truth.

If Materialism means simply that matter and physical forces are structural stages which condition the full efflorescence of mind, a kind of ladder up which Nature climbs to mind, few could object to it.   But if it means that mind is a useless and otiose appendage to a world process essentially physical, it is doomed to be superseded by a more idealistic world view.   And if it means that something called matter was either the beginning or is to be the end of the evolutionary movement, or was indeed at any time an exclusive reality, it will be a philosophy difficult to defend.

Idealistic theories

But now we must examine more in detail that view of the world which is most opposed to Materialism.   This view has usually been called Idealism, but since the latter word is ambiguous, at times referring merely to a theory of knowledge, the idealistic world view is sometimes called Spiritualism.   But this is also an ambiguous word, referring in popular language to a certain religious belief which hinges upon the possibility of communication with an alleged spirit world.   Spiritualism in philosophy, however, means nothing more than that the world is grounded in spirit or mind.   If the word "spiritualism" is more exact, the word "idealism" is more attractive and in more common use.

To write the history of Idealism would be almost to write the history of philosophy, so many of the world's great thinkers have been Idealists. But they have represented many different kinds of Idealism, sure to be confusing at first to the reader.

Platonic Idealism

The oldest system of Idealism in European philosophy is that of Plato. Nothing more wonderful than this has been projected by the creative power of human thought, perhaps nothing more elevated, possibly nothing more true. No real account of it can be given here. Controversy still rages over the correct interpretation of Plato and scholars are not yet finally agreed on the chronology of his writings, nor have the many philological questions met with generally accepted solutions. It is best to read Plato himself.

Plato was not an Idealist in the extreme sense that there is nothing in the Universe except mind. His teaching was rather that the significant things in the world — that is the *real* things — are Ideas, and by "Ideas" he did not mean any kind of merely mental states. He meant real objective things or "forms" which are not material. They are eternal essences, forms, types — or archetypes, serving as patterns, ideals, standards, for the things of sense. These are the cosmic realities, while what we call matter he named Non-Being, not intending to say that it does not exist in a way, but that it is without significance except as a kind of crude stuff or material; and as such, a source of disorder and evil and imperfection. The world of sense has only a derivative "being" at best, in so far as it adumbrates the real world of Ideas. The Ideas are known by the reason or intelligence of man, whereas the world of matter appears to man through his senses. The Ideas are unchanging, they always *are*, whereas the world of sense is in a constant flux and never in fact *is*.

A simple example from modern science will serve to illustrate Plato's meaning. When Newton observed the apple fall from the tree to the ground, he not only saw that fact with his senses, but it was revelatory of a principle which he cognized through his intelligence, the principle of gravitation, known in mechanics as the law of the inverse square.   Now this law of the inverse square can be stated in mathematical form and as such is intelligible to the mind and is as unchanging and eternal as the principle that $2 + 2 = 4$.   Just as the falling apple adumbrates an intelligible principle which is constant throughout all time, so the universe as a whole is a "copy" of this intelligible world of forms.   The important, significant, and real things are not, then, events in space and time which are forever coming into being and then passing away into the oblivion of the past; they are rather the principles or forms of all coming into being and passing away, which themselves are eternal and the preconditions of there being anything at all.

Plato's Idealism is more than an affirmation that the real things are these forms or archetypes which are known not by the senses but by the reason of man; it is also profoundly rooted in a sense of value. Plato had little interest in things of the body, but an absorbing devotion to things of the spirit — to justice and beauty and social ideals, as well as to mathematical relations.   Such a philosophical system as that of Plato could hardly be called Spiritualism, and if it is to be called Idealism, it is of an objective, metaphysical type.   It is a philosophy of ideals as well as of ideas.   In some ways, thus, the Platonic Idealism is more like the modern popular conception of Idealism, as a kind of moral striving after ideals or higher values, than it is like strict philosophical Idealism, which is the doctrine that only mind is real.

Subjective idealism

Let us contrast the Idealism of Plato with a modern type, very different and perhaps harder to understand.   George Berkeley, a brilliant Irish philosopher of the eighteenth century, thought that the sin and evil of his time came from a wrong philosophy, from Materialism; and he essayed to show that there is no such thing as matter in the sense of an inert substance existing independently. The things which we call material are objects of experience, and these objects of experience, such as trees and houses and clouds, are not material things; they are just perceptions.   When we say that anything exists — for instance, a tree — we mean that it is perceived. It exists, of course, but it has no existence independent of a mind that perceives it. As we should say, an object like a tree is merely a bundle of sensations, and these are wholly subjective. The world, therefore, is a mental world.

What, then, *is* Reality? asks Berkeley. Only minds or spirits or souls are real, he replies. God exists, and you and I exist; in other words, God, the infinite Spirit, and a realm of finite spirits. That which we call nature, with its regular laws and sequences, is simply the action of the divine mind upon our finite minds. We must not suppose, however, that Berkeley taught that objects of sense are illusions or that God deceives us. Objects *are* real, only they are not independent of a perceiving mind. In fact, there is, said Berkeley, nothing in the Universe except the infinite Spirit and a realm of finite spirits.

This Berkeleian Idealism has sometimes been called "Subjective Idealism," and will be studied further in our chapter on Theories of Knowledge; for evidently it springs from an attempt to define the limits of our knowledge. It does not seem to give us a very satisfactory theory of reality, for the first thing one asks is, What was the world before human minds existed? Were not the mountains and the seas and the stars existing then as now? Of course, Berkeley can argue — and his reasoning is subtle and hard to refute — mountains and seas and stars are ideas in the last analysis. Surely, he would say, in those primeval days that you speak about, they were not *called* mountains nor seas nor stars, since there was no one to name them, nor were the mountains blue, nor the seas green, nor the stars red, for these colors are sensations depending upon the eye and there was no eye to see them. And so it is, said Berkeley, with all the qualities that make up these objects of perception. Try to imagine what you mean when you say that anything exists when not perceived. You will be sure to attribute to it some quality of sensation, just as if it were perceived.

This philosophy, so skillfully defended by the witty Irish bishop, certainly reduces the whole world to mind with a vengeance. Only minds exist. So-called external things are merely the perceptions of sentient spirits. This is Berkeley's celebrated subjectivism, subjective Idealism, psychism, or mentalism, as it has been called. Later we may inquire as to its validity. Science perhaps cannot prove the objective and external character of the things it studies, but it usually makes the postulate that they are real and independent of the perceiving mind.

The Idealism of Leibniz

Let us now consider another kind of Idealism quite different from that either of Plato or of Berkeley and more instructive than the latter, namely, that of the German philosopher, Leibniz. Leibniz believed, as we all instinctively do, that the physical things we see about us and study in the sciences have a real objective existence independent of the mind that perceives them; only when we come to examine into the real nature of these objective things, we discover that in their inner being they are mental or spiritual.

To understand this kind of Idealism, it is a good plan to go back to the theory of atoms. Consider that all objects of sense are made up of certain ultimate units commonly called atoms. But now think of these ultimate units, not as themselves physical or material things, having physical qualities such as size and shape, but as *psychical* units, little souls, having the power of perception and of development. They are centers of force rather than material things. Leibniz did not call them atoms, but Monads, and he thought that physical bodies are composed of groups of Monads; and that the human soul is a governing Monad. If it seems difficult to understand how physical bodies can be made of unextended centers of force, we may recall that our modern atoms according to the electron theory are nothing but energy systems, and we cannot understand how even molecules are made of them. That physical bodies may be made of centers of psychical energy need not present great difficulty to anyone who has attempted to master the structure of the modern physical atom. If, however, Leibniz's Idealism seems to anyone to be at a disadvantage here, it is, like other idealistic systems, at a great advantage when it comes to explaining mind, for the mind is as Leibniz shows, just a Monad, an immortal and spiritual being, differing from the Monads that make physical bodies only in its higher degree of development.

Panpsychism

Closely related to the last view, but more modern, is another kind of Idealism called *Panpsychism*. The word denotes the doctrine that all reality is psychic in nature. Panpsychism, as it is usually held, teaches that everything has mind. Mind is not something gained late in evolution when organisms acquire complex nervous centers or a brain. Mind is universal throughout nature. Every atom or particle in the Universe has life, mind, and memory. The whole world, organic and inorganic, is thus vitalized and mentalized.

But if we think of every atom and particle having something psychical in it, of course we ask the question, What is the relation of the psychical to the physical part? To this question Panpsychism answers that the *reality* of the particle is psychical, and its physical part is only its phenomenal or outer aspect. Reality is contrasted with appearance. The former is mental, the latter physical. The reality of the world is found in "mind-stuff," perhaps in consciousness.

This kind of Idealism is welcome to many modern psychologists who have upon their hands the problem of the connection of mind and body. Dualistic theories have their difficulties. Mind and brain seem to be in constant correlation. There is no psychosis without neurosis. And something like Panpsychism, or Psychical Monism, which affirms that the mind is the sole reality and the body its outer appearance as it is seen by others, seems to offer a solution of the problem.

Able and interesting expositions of this view may be found in Paulsen's *Introduction to Philosophy*, in the writings of W. K. Clifford,[1] in C. A. Strong's *Why the Mind Has a Body*, and in the writings of Samuel Butler. In James Ward's important book called *Naturalism and Agnosticism*, a somewhat similar theory is maintained, although the book is mainly critical, only the barest outline of a constructive view being presented. Ward points out that the concepts used in science and useful in the special work of science — such, for instance, as mechanism, causality, matter, and motion — do not have so profound and universal significance as is commonly supposed in these days of scientific progress. They do not apply to

[1] *Lectures and Essays*, vol. II.

the deeper spiritual realities which lie back of the phenomenal world, so that in the more real world of the spirit we can be assured of freedom, purpose, and God.

In the work of the remarkable German philosopher, Fechner (1801–87), a similar kind of Idealism appears. To Fechner the world is *ensouled*. The Universe is instinct with psychic life. Consciousness, as it appears in man, is only a part of a universal consciousness present in plants, in animals, in the Earth, and in the Universe. The world is a great organism, a psycho-physical organism, having, as has man, a body and a soul. This, however, is not interpreted dualistically, for the emphasis is all put upon the psychical side, which is the reality, while the body is the outer expression or appearance of the real inner soul life. Thus, plants and animals have souls, as well as man. Fechner speaks, too, of the Earth soul, and finally of the soul of the world, which is God. The physical world is but the outer expression of the inner life of God. The Material Universe is the body of God, "the living visible garment of God."

> ''Tis thus at the roaring Loom of Time I ply,
> And weave for God the Garment thou see'st Him by.' [1]

This Fechner calls the Day view, as contrasted with the Night view of Materialism.

We shall be interested in reading the spirited defense of Panpsychism by Paulsen. The following passage is worth quoting:

> Spontaneous activity everywhere! Your inert, rigid matter, movable only by impact, is a phantom that owes its existence, not to observation, but to conceptual speculation. It comes from the Aristotelian scholastic philosophy, which, after having completely separated all force or form from matter, left the latter behind as something absolutely passive. Descartes gets it from this source; it was a concept convenient to his purely mathematical conception of physics: Matter is without all inner determination, pure *res extensa*, whose only quality is extension. Modern natural science has utterly discarded the idea of such absolutely dead and rigid bodies. Its molecules and atoms are forms of the greatest inner complexity and mobility. Hundreds and thousands of atoms are united in the molecule into a system that preserves a more or less stable equilibrium by the mutual interaction of

[1] Read Carlyle's *Sartor Resartus*, book III, chap. IX, for this reference to Goethe's *Faust*.

its parts, and at the same time is quickened by other movements —
by such as are felt by us as light and heat, and others, which appear
in electrical processes.   And this system, in turn, is in constant interaction with its immediate surroundings as well as with the remotest
system of fixed stars.   Is it, then, absurd to ask whether we have, corresponding to this wonderful play of physical forces and movements, a
system of inner processes, analogous to that which accompanies the
working of the parts in the organic body?   May not attraction and
repulsion, of which physics and chemistry speak, be more than mere
words; is there not an element of truth in the speculation of old Empedocles that love and hate form the motive forces in all things?
Certainly not love and hatred as men and animals experience them,
but something at bottom similar to their feelings, an impulsive action
of some kind.[1]

Voluntaristic Idealism

When psychologists place great emphasis upon the *Will*, as representing the really essential and fundamental aspect of mind, we
speak of them as *voluntarists*.   So when philosophers say that *Will*,
or *Absolute Will*, or a society of individual Wills, is the really fundamental thing in the Universe objectively considered, we may call
this view Voluntaristic Idealism.   This world view in its modern
form goes back to Kant who affirmed the "primacy of the will."
Schopenhauer is, however, the best representative of this theory.
His great work is entitled *The World as Will and Idea*.   It begins
with the well-known statement, "The world is my idea."   Thus far
he agrees with Berkeley, but Berkeley's subjective Idealism he
changes into an objective Idealism.   If I examine my own mind, I
find that the essential thing in it is Will, rather than intellect.   The
soul is activity, striving, struggling, desiring.   My body is just the
outward expression of my Will.   So, Schopenhauer concludes, it is
with the outer world.   At heart it is Will, Absolute Will, and the
phenomenal world which I see and hear and feel is the outer expression of the universal Will.   Since, now, Will is something psychical,
spiritual, and since all reality is Will, this system of philosophy is
again to be classed as Idealism or Spiritualism.   And it is objective
or metaphysical Idealism, because the world is not merely my idea,
but has as its basis an objective reality, namely, the Absolute Will.

[1] Paulsen's *Introduction to Philosophy* (Henry Holt and Company), p. 101.

More recent forms of Voluntaristic Idealism have been advanced by Wundt and Münsterberg.

The Idealism of Kant

Schopenhauer's idealistic philosophy, like most of those of modern times, had its source in Kant. Kant's most famous work, *The Critique of Pure Reason*, was first published in 1781. In this great work Kant investigated the problems of theoretical knowledge. What is the nature of knowledge? What can man know? He showed that the mind has a structure of its own and that what we call knowledge is in a very large measure determined by this structure. There are certain forms of sense and categories of the understanding which precondition what we ordinarily call knowledge. Now these forms and categories apply only to things of sense, so that in the end the only knowledge man is capable of is confined to the region of actual or possible experience. Thus we can have no theoretical knowledge concerning the origins of the world, of the soul, of God, and the like, because these transcend all possible human experience. What knowledge we have is of the present world of experience which we study in the special sciences. This world is but a world of appearance, a phenomenal world, a world seen through these forms and categories of the mind, a mind-made world in a sense. This seems at first glance like the subjectivism of Berkeley, but Kant did not deny that there is some objective reality back of phenomena. True enough we know this world only as it is stamped with the mental structure of the knower; knowledge results from the mind's action upon sensations. But whence come sensations? Kant held that there must be some ground for these sensations and this ground he called the *Ding an sich* (thing-in-itself). This is objectively real, but we can have no theoretical knowledge of it because to know it means to know it under the conditions of knowing, namely, the forms of sense and categories of the understanding. We know the real as it *appears*, never as it *is*. For this reason Kant's philosophy is usually identified with *Phenomenalism*, which is a doctrine holding that knowledge is limited to appearances (or to phenomena).

But, after all, this is not quite the whole story for Kant. In his practical philosophy he undertakes an investigation of morality. Starting from the voice of duty, which speaks with an authority such as could not come from a merely phencmenal world, he arrives at a kind of noumenal or real world, a moral order, giving us as necessary postulates God, freedom, and immortality. Though we can have no theoretical knowledge of the world of reality, we get a strong hint as to its nature in the moral situation in which the autonomous will is challenged to decision. Here the real world is revealed to us as one in which moral values are profoundly rooted. It is an essentially "spiritual" reality, — something closely akin to our deepseated moral will.

Thus Kant's philosophy is thoroughly idealistic; it speaks of a world of ideas and ideals, yet is not that extreme Idealism which finds nothing real in the world except mind. We do not know in the last analysis what the real is; the moral situation does not provide us with theoretical knowledge of it, but intimates very strongly that in some way or other it is like our own innermost spiritual being.

Absolute Idealism

One of Kant's successors, J. G. Fichte, taught a still more outspoken system of Idealism, in which all reality is swallowed up in the Ego; but it is the Absolute Ego, which is the supreme reality, and so we have the beginning of the Absolute philosophy, which finds its most famous expression in the Absolute Idealism of Hegel.

What is the world? asks Hegel. What is reality? Reality, he answers, is thought, reason. The world is a great thought process. It is, as we might say, God thinking. We have only to find out the laws of thought to know the laws of reality. What we call nature is thought externalized; it is the Absolute Reason revealing itself in outward form. But nature is not its final goal. Returning, it expresses itself more fully in human self-consciousness and in the end finds its complete realization in art, religion, and philosophy.

Such a philosophy as this takes our breath away. It seems like Idealism gone wild. It is magnificent, divine, but is it true? It reminds us of Plato, who takes us to the heavens and makes us see that our home is there. Leaving out much of Hegel's forced and fanciful dialectic, there are aspects of his thought which are today

suggestive. There is something fascinating in Hegel's notion of the
world as a great process of development, a notion shared with him
by those two thinkers who have contributed so richly to the history
of thought, Aristotle and Darwin. But Hegel thinks of the world,
not only as a process of development, but as a thought process, and
adds finally that interesting suggestion that it has an ideal goal in
art, philosophy, and religion.

Modern English and American Idealism

Since Hegel's death, and drawing from him in greater or less degree as well as from Kant and Fichte, there have been many systems
of Objective Idealism. They represent a powerful stream of thought,
fed by many leading minds in Germany, Italy, England, and
America, ranging from Absolute Idealism through Theistic Idealism,
Voluntaristic Idealism, Personalism, and Panpsychism. Prominent
among English Idealists may be mentioned T. H. Green, Edward
Caird, F. H. Bradley, A. E. Taylor, J. M. E. McTaggart, Bernard
Bosanquet, H. H. Joachim, and R. F. A. Hoernlé; while in America
we have G. S. Morris, Josiah Royce, Mary Whiton Calkins, J. E.
Creighton, George P. Adams, G. H. Howison, Borden P. Bowne, and
many others. Books such as Royce's *Spirit of Modern Philosophy*,
Bosanquet's *Principle of Individuality and Value*, Green's *Prolegomena to Ethics*, Calkins's *The Persistent Problems of Philosophy*,
George P. Adams's *Idealism and the Modern Age*, Hoernlé's *Studies
in Contemporary Metaphysics*, Howison's *The Limits of Evolution*, and
Bowne's *Personalism*, represent the idealistic tradition in its modern
form. They should be carefully read by every student in philosophy. Their *wholesomeness* and their ethical Idealism insure their
lasting value.

No general summary can be made of all the forms of Objective
Idealism here mentioned without doing violence to some of them.
In general, however, these various forms of modern Idealism regard
the world as essentially spiritual, rational, intelligible, transparent to
our reason, having moral significance. More particularly the world
is some kind of organic unity, having internal relations such that the
whole is determined by the part and the part by the whole. Hence
results a final unity with harmony in diversity. As for man, he is

essentially a self, a person, and exists in organic relations to a society of selves and perhaps to an Absolute Self.

Nearly all of these systems of Objective Idealism are prone to speak of the Absolute, the Absolute Idea, or the Absolute Self, or Absolute Experience. And the Absolute, unlike the word *infinite* in philosophy, does not stand for a mere superlative of excellences. It means, rather, that final unity which has always been the quest of philosophy. It is the religious motive which gives us such joy in the shelter of the arms of the Absolute, and it is the intellectual motive which finds such comfort in the notion of a final unity or wholeness or perfection.

Personalism

Special mention should be made of an interesting form of modern Idealism known as *Personalism*.[1] This philosophy takes its stand firmly upon the incontestable fact of personality. The one thing which I cannot doubt is the existence of myself as a person and a member of a society of persons. This philosophy emphasizes personality, freedom, self-determination, moral responsibility, the existence of real evil in the world, and of a personal God, who struggles and strives with us for the overcoming of evil. The physical world is phenomenal, after the manner of Kant, so that this system of philosophy is decidedly idealistic or spiritualistic. But the monistic character of modern Idealism has disappeared and the uniqueness and decisive individuality of the self in the society of selves gives to this philosophy a decided pluralistic turn. Personalism seems in a high degree to satisfy our religious needs, as escaping the pantheistic tendency of many other kinds of modern Idealism and putting a much-needed emphasis upon freedom, moral responsibility, and the presence of real evil.

---

[1] Besides the writers mentioned, such as Borden P. Bowne, and G. H. Howison, attention should be directed to the journal called *The Personalist*, edited by Professor Flewelling at the University of Southern California. In England the personalistic emphasis is seen in the writings of H. Sturt, G. T. Stout, H. Rashdall, J. M. E. McTaggart, James Ward, and others. Most of these English Personalists emphasize the ethical quality of reality and the will in finite persons, while the American Personalists stick more closely to Kant and place more emphasis upon the idea of God and the religious motive.

Conclusion

What in conclusion are we to say in praise of Idealism or in criticism? To the student of philosophy so many different systems must seem confusing — as many systems, it would appear, as there are philosophers to make them. Perhaps they are all in error and no theories of ultimate reality are possible. But I think this attitude of discouragement is not at all justified. Perhaps there are common elements in all these systems. It may be that a careful analysis of them would show many points of agreement, or, what is better still, many converging tendencies.

Certainly the Idealists all have much in common. They refuse to believe that the world is a great machine. They deny the supreme importance of matter, mechanism, and the conservation of energy, as *explaining* our world. The Idealist can perfectly well accept the scientist's descriptions and analyses of experience, but he denies that the scientist is telling the final story.

The Idealists in general feel that somehow certain sciences, such as psychology, logic, ethics, aesthetics, have to do with things basal and intrinsic, that they are quite as much a key to nature's secrets as are physics and chemistry. They believe that the world has a *meaning*, a purpose, perhaps a goal; and that there is a kind of inner harmony between the heart of the Universe and the soul of man, such that human intelligence can pierce through the outer crust of nature and penetrate to its inner being, at least in some slight measure.

The Universe is a great organism and man is a vital function within it. Man's life is important, cosmically and eternally significant. His destiny is in a profound way the destiny of the world. Thus in Idealism we find a kind of responsiveness to our human longings in the whole of nature. There is not merely the idle longing for immortality, for beauty, for righteousness, for an ideal life — there is a *demand* for them. We should take care, however, not to impute delusive "wishful thinking" to the Idealist because he finds room in his philosophy for those values so cherished and sought by man. And yet Idealism answers to our ethical, aesthetic, religious, and romantic demands. It proposes an intelligent and an intelligible world, of which at least either the warp or the woof must be something akin to thought and feeling and will.

Perhaps nowhere has the spirit of Idealism been better expressed than by William James, the Realist, when he says that this world of wind and water is not the one divinely aimed at and established thing, but that we must believe in a spiritual order lying back of this material order and giving to the latter its value and significance.

The impatience that we feel toward idealistic theories of reality springs, no doubt, from several sources. Modern thought leans very heavily in the direction of the exact sciences, no system of philosophy being welcome which does not harmonize with the results of these sciences; and it has seemed to many that Idealism does not properly evaluate the concrete facts which are the objects of study in the natural sciences. We are irritated if we are told that these concrete facts are merely "phenomena" or appearances of some unknown thing-in-itself which "lies back of them," or that they are made of mind-stuff, or that they get either their form or their substance from the mind that perceives them.

But on the other hand, although perhaps in these days our prevailing moods are scientific, we are not always in such moods. Sometimes we are in quite different moods, such, for instance, as ethical, aesthetical, religious, or social, and then we can understand the great truths which are embraced in the idealistic philosophies. Indeed, later systems of Idealism, such as those of Royce and Bosanquet, are based directly upon such great truths as those of individuality and value — and their appeal to us rests upon a recognition of the fact that the world revealed to us by the physical sciences is a true world but not the whole world, nor even perhaps a fair sample of the whole world, and that neither in the study of the sciences nor in the experiences of our divided selves do we quite get down to what Bosanquet calls "the real thing." Hence in such idealistic philosophies we find a release from the fragmentariness and conflict and division which commonly hedge us about. We long for unity and wholeness and ideal value and we cannot help believing that in the whole of reality, if we could grasp it, there is such unity and wholeness and value, and that our thought processes and our ethical striving and our aesthetic pleasures are in some way revelations of the essential structure of the world.

And so I think we may be Idealists without reducing the Universe to mind-stuff, just as we may be scientists without reducing it to matter-stuff. It is possible that Idealists have emphasized too much the processes of thought and inference in our minds as revealing the structure of reality and not enough the equally fundamental — perhaps more fundamental — quality of *Striving*. If we could think of the world as a great movement in which "formative impulses are struggling up through chaos into ordered freedom" or as a developmental process in which values, mental, moral, aesthetic, and social, are being slowly but surely realized, perhaps even against real obstacles, then we could still be Idealists, but Idealists who would speak less of *ideas* and more of *ideals*.

In connection with this chapter read:

Josiah Royce, *The Spirit of Modern Philosophy* (Houghton Mifflin Company), chap. XI, "Reality and Idealism."

Ralph Barton Perry, *Present Philosophical Tendencies* (Longmans, Green and Company), part III.

Further references:

Arthur Kenyon Rogers, *English and American Philosophy Since 1800* (The Macmillan Company), chaps. V, VI.

George P. Adams, *Idealism and the Modern Age* (Yale University Press).

Josiah Royce, *The World and the Individual*, 2 vols. (The Macmillan Company).

Aliotta, *The Idealistic Reaction Against Science* translated by Agnes McCaskill (The Macmillan Company).

Clifford Barrett, editor, *Contemporary Idealism in America* (The Macmillan Company).

R. F. A. Hoernlé, *Idealism* (George H. Doran Company).

May Sinclair, *A Defence of Idealism* (The Macmillan Company) and *The New Idealism* (The Macmillan Company).

J. G. Fichte, "The Vocation of the Scholar," "The Nature of the Scholar," "The Vocation of Man," in his *Popular Works*, vol. I.

John Watson, *The Philosophy of Kant* (The Macmillan Company).

J. H. Muirhead, editor, *Contemporary British Philosophy* (The Macmillan Company). Contains personal statements by contemporary British philosophers.

CHAPTER XVII

PLURALISM

By PLURALISM is meant the abandonment of the attempt to reduce all reality to either one or two ultimate forms of being. The world cannot be reduced either to mind or to matter, nor to mind and matter. Reality is neither one nor two, but many.

The older Pluralism

Examples of Pluralism in this sense are abundant. Empedocles, the early Greek thinker, was a Pluralist when he said that the four ultimate elements of reality are fire, water, earth, and air. Plato was a Pluralist when he reduced reality to the eternal Ideas, such as the Good and the Beautiful, for there is a plurality of Ideas. Even Greek atomism, usually called the strictest materialistic Monism, was pluralistic in that the atoms have a kind of individuality depending on their size and shape. Modern Materialism — at any rate, previous to the advent of the electron theory — was a kind of Pluralism, since there are more than eighty different elementary substances.

Likewise Idealism, or spiritual Monism, often reduces to a kind of Pluralism, as in the case of Leibniz's system of Monads. Since the Monads are psychical in their ultimate nature, this system might be called spiritual Monism. Since they are all different from one another, each having a distinct individuality, we may call it Pluralism.

Obviously distinctions of this kind are of no great value in philosophy. The monistic impulse is satisfied when we find unity in variety, and when this unity is absent, it is better to speak of the system as pluralistic. Thus it is a question whether Leibniz's spiritual system of philosophy should be called Pluralism or Monism. It is pluralistic in so far as the Monads are held to be unique and independent self-enclosed entities. No two are alike and so we might say that Leibniz held to a theory of the world which reduces it to an infinitude of different ultimates. However, from another point of view Leibniz is monistic in thought. The Monads of the world do not present a chaos but rather a system — they are in a great harmony. They are dominated by rational principles and each reflects the total rational order of things from a certain point of view and at a certain level. As Leibniz would say, they are the same in essence. There is some difference of opinion with regard to Leibniz. Some hold that the unity and harmony among the Monads is insufficiently made out and thus his system is essentially pluralistic. Others would maintain that Leibniz has so analyzed the notion of the Monad that it is unintelligible apart from the rational order and unity which each Monad reflects. Obviously, if we hold to the first interpretation, Leibniz is a pluralist and the monistic element becomes insignificant; and if we hold to the latter interpretation, Leibniz is a Monist and the pluralistic element becomes insignificant.

No doubt most of the great historical philosophical systems present pluralistic tendencies and whether we are to call a system pluralistic depends very much on our concept of Pluralism as well as upon our interpretations of the philosophies in question. In recent times "Pluralism" indicates not so much an attempt to find out how many kinds of *stuff* the world is made of, and then to affirm that there are many kinds rather than one or two; nor even is it the attempt to construct the Universe of one kind of stuff moulded into many forms. It is rather an emphasis upon the many-sidedness and variety of the world; it is a protest against finding too much unity. This new Pluralism stresses the manifold character of the world, its variety and richness, its infinite diversities and novelties, even its discords and dissonances.

The monistic impulse

Possibly the monistic systems find their explanation simply in the infirmity of the human mind, which is helpless in the face of disorder and must find for itself some unity or system in things. It loves to reduce the manifold forms of experience to classes and the classes to larger classes, and in the end to reduce all things to some one final "substance" or being — to mind, to matter, or to God. Back of all minds it seeks the Absolute Mind; back of all spirit, the Absolute Spirit; back of all wills, the Absolute Will; back of all experience, Absolute Experience. The human mind in its eager effort to understand the world seeks always a guiding thread to find its way through the maze of details. It hopes to find a ruling purpose, which if it could be grasped would show that the whole thing is a plan — perhaps a wise and benevolent plan, having at its fountain head one absolute and omniscient ruler; and finally it hopes to discover one unitary substance, physical or mental, to which all reality can be reduced.

The pluralistic reaction

Now, Pluralism does not deny that there is a certain unity in the world; but in the face of the manifest diversities and inconsistencies and disharmonies which experience reveals, it hesitates to accept too easily the monistic solution.   Students of philosophy are beginning to feel that it is not quite so easy as at first appeared to find the guiding thread of life, and that it may be a trifle presumptuous to make too many affirmations about the *Absolute*.   There is, no doubt, a strong pluralistic tendency among philosophers at the present time. The new astronomy, the new physics, the new mechanics, the new logic, all emphasize the diversities, the immensities — not to say the strangeness or the wildness of the world.   In olden times it was very comforting and composing to believe that the Earth was made for man and rested securely in the center of the Universe, watched over by an omnipotent and friendly Being.   But now we learn that our Sun is only one of uncounted millions, and that there are stars whose light, traveling at the rate of 186,000 miles a second, requires millions of years to reach us.

If we wonder at the largeness of the world, we are amazed at the smallness of its parts, when we learn that the atom, which is so minute that a cubic centimeter of hydrogen may contain 54,000,000,-000,000,000,000 atoms, yet is itself a system of electric particles as far apart relatively to their size as the stars in the heavens.

Again, it was comforting to believe that space, though infinite, is subject to the geometry of Euclid, and that the Newtonian physics rules throughout the Universe, and that both time and space can be measured by fixed standards; but the theory of relativity has revealed here also a larger and a stranger world. Even the old Aristotelian logic, with its doctrine of substance, and of attributes inhering in the substance, and its classes of things additively grouped according to likeness and difference, is giving place to a new logic with its many kinds of relations and the relations themselves objective and real. Even evolution, which a few years ago seemed like a kind of magic key, destined to unlock the secrets of the Universe, is now found to be full of difficulties and at best to apply only to a part of what in the broader sense we may call nature.

So Hamlet, when he says —

> There are more things in Heaven and Earth, Horatio,
> Than are dreamt of in your philosophy —

sounds the note of the pluralistic movement. Although the mind craves unity, it loves variety, too, and the pluralistic world view is not without its compensations.

> The world is so full of a number of things,
> I am sure we should all be as happy as kings,

said Robert Louis Stevenson, and perhaps the adventurous spirit of the modern mind finds as much satisfaction in trying to solve the puzzle of a pluralistic world as the more fearsome spirit of the Middle Ages found in a wholly unified and comprehended system. Anyway, we have to face the fact of a world less unified, less integrated, and less harmonized than we used to think.

A pluralistic Universe

Not many years ago, William James wrote a little book called *A Pluralistic Universe*, which, together with his essay on *Radical Empiricism* and his *Will to Believe*, woke the philosophic world from its monistic slumber. It was James's mission in philosophy as well as in psychology to leave the old well-beaten paths of thought and strike out into new ones. A system of philosophy in the older sense he did not have, but both psychology and philosophy have been revitalized by the series of galvanic shocks which came from his pen.

James was weary of all the old absolutist philosophies, even as presented in their newest and most charming form by his colleague,

Josiah Royce. James was not interested in the One, but in the Many. It is the "each-form," rather than the "all-form" of things that impressed him — their discreteness, their separateness, their independence, their novelty, their freedom, their contingency, their spontaneity, their manifold, yes, even their chaotic character. He did not find any "block universe" with "a through-and-through unity." Reality, he said, is of "the strung-along type." "The word 'and' trails along after every sentence." Reality is distributive rather than collective. Freedom exists, and chance and novelty and progress. "New men and women, books, accidents, events, inventions, enterprises, burst unceasingly upon the world." Why seek for reality in such symbols as mind and matter and atoms and monads? "The perceptual flux is the authentic stuff" of the world. "There is no possible point of view," says James, "from which the world can appear an absolutely single fact. Real possibilities, real indeterminations, real beginnings, real ends, real evil, real crises, catastrophes, and escapes, a real God, and a real moral life, just as common sense conceives these things, may remain in empiricism as conceptions which that philosophy gives up the attempt either to 'overcome' or to reinterpret in monistic form." [1]

The universe, in a word, is tychistic. Chance is real in it. Destruction is as possible as salvation, and evil is as actual as good. What is central is the fact that evil and good are *relations*, and not substances, that each entity which struggles can of itself and in its own right contribute to the everlasting damnation or eternal salvation of the world. There is no eternal law; there is no overarching destiny, no all-compelling Providence. Law itself is no more than cosmic habit, a *modus vivendi*, which things that have come together by chance, and are staying together by choice, have worked out as men work out communal customs facilitating contacts. Whether gravitation or tobacco-smoking, there is a difference in scope, not in history! And the spontaneous individualities whose collective habits the "laws of nature" express are greater and more real than those laws. These individualities in their privacy and inwardness are reals in the completest sense of the term, and through them the axis of larger being runs. How otherwise should the history of the cosmos unfold itself? [2]

---

[1] *The Will to Believe* (Longmans, Green and Company), p. ix.

[2] Horace Meyer Kallen, *William James* and *Henri Bergson* (University of Chicago Press), pp. 182, 183.

Such a pluralistic world view as this does not in James's philosophy issue in any pessimism, skepticism, or fatalism. Quite the opposite. It gives us a real freedom, and it gives us a real God — not a mere all-embracing omnipotent world unity. And it solves the problem of evil, which in the absolutist systems seems so hard to explain. Monism, he says, really *creates the problem* of evil.

This pluralistic, pragmatic, radically empirical philosophy, as presented by James, has a spicy, stimulating flavor, whetting one's appetite for something more. But all we get is more of the same kind and in the end we feel that something is lacking. It is, perhaps, because of the mind's insistent demand for a unified world view that one feels a trifle impatient with the author of *The Pluralistic Universe* for not telling us something more definite about this Universe and the nature of the reality which lies beneath the perceptual flux. But perhaps James thought that we have already too many completely unified *systems* of philosophy.

Pluralism among the new Realists

If the "radical empiricism" of James issues in Pluralism, so also, it seems, does the quite different philosophy of the New Realism.[1]

In this case it is not the richness and variety of the perceptual flux which holds our attention, but the richness and variety of the world of reason, of thought, and of values. We are brought to the sudden realization that there are many things in the world besides physical and mental things. Physical and mental things, events and processes, are real in this realistic pluralistic system, but so also are principles of reason, logical principles, internal and external relations, numbers, space, time, series, and such ideal entities as justice and beauty. These latter non-physical and non-mental entities we may, if we choose, call *subsistents*, if we wish to limit the term *existent thing* to such as are conditioned by space and time.

There is something exhilarating and emancipating about this new pluralistic view of the world to those who have been led to believe that there is nothing in the Universe but the mental and the physical — and possibly nothing but the physical. Such things as atoms and

[1] A clear statement of this new Pluralism may be found in the book of Edward Gleason Spaulding, *The New Rationalism*, sec. IV.

electrons, which quite possibly really exist, get put now in their proper subordinate place. Physical things, events, and qualities exist, but so do mental processes and mental events and qualities, and thus we are freed from the old tyranny of the monism of substance and the problem of interaction in its older form.

Not only does this new Pluralism free us from the tyranny of matter, which has kept us so long enthralled, but also from the tyranny of evolution, a word which at the opening of the twentieth century had taken such complete possession of our thought. Pluralism reduces the significance and extent of evolution. The latter is a useful term in biology. With caution, perhaps, it may be extended to the inorganic world, but there are large fields of reality to which it does not apply. It does not apply, for instance, to the standards of truth and value by which evolution itself is judged. It does not apply to God, nor to truth, nor to logical principles, nor to the eternal values.

Again, even within the sphere of evolution the pluralistic view of reality gains striking support from the doctrine of creative synthesis and theory of levels. At each new level, as the result of organization, new realities emerge not found in the elements which make up the lower level. Life and mind are the most striking illustrations of such new realities emerging from the synthesis of simpler elements.

Spaulding goes even further here and discovers a still more remarkable fact, namely, that of freedom at each successive stage of organization. "At each level or stratum of reality formed by the non-additive organization of parts into a whole, qualities or phenomena are free to act in accordance with their own nature and their own causal connections with other qualities of this level." "No higher level *violates* the laws of those lower levels;... but also no *lower* level *causally* determines any *higher* level." Freedom subsists, therefore, at each level as we ascend from the inorganic to the chemical, and then to the living and then to the mental and then to the ethical. Thus, biology is not a branch of physics, nor psychology of biology, nor ethics of psychology. Each is a free and independent science correlated with the lower levels and not violating their laws, but introducing new entities and new laws and thus exhibiting its own peculiar freedom. So the time has gone by when physics and biology can dominate psychology and ethics, and Naturalism with its bonds of determinism, which it hoped to fasten on the world, has been superseded; for at each higher level something new appears which is free to follow its own laws. The world of life and mind cannot be reduced to matter and its laws. There are *different kinds* of things in the world which cannot truthfully be reduced to one kind.

Even here this realistic Pluralism does not stop. It throws light on the now much-discussed problem of *values*. It is no longer sufficient to say with Spinoza that things are good because we desire them, but now with Plato and the ancients generally we may say that we desire things because they are good. Justice and beauty and goodness are models, which we are ever approaching, but never realizing. They are limits, "but the limit is not a member of the series of which it is a limit," so that we may probably say with Plato, strange as it sounds in these empirical days, that justice and beauty and goodness and truth are all themselves subsistent entities, "eternal" values, not conditioned by space and time.

Again the pluralistic world view allows us to think of the Universe as purposive and creative of values, and it allows us to give real objectivity to such concepts as color and beauty and justice and truth. We can once more think of beauty as resident in the work of art and not merely as existing in the mind of the beholder, and we can think of justice as a real end to be gained and not as something relative merely to the subject, and we can think of truth, not in the pragmatic sense of that which affords maximum satisfaction, but in the realistic sense of conformity with reality. In the direction of simplicity, therefore, there seems to be a distinct gain in this realistic pluralistic philosophy.

Pluralism gives us finally a view of God, not as a mere object of faith, not as the hypothetical creator of the world, not as a pragmatic "working scheme," but as the "totality of values, both existent and subsistent, and of those agencies and efficiencies with which these values are identical." "God is Value, the active, 'living' principle of the conservation of values and of their efficiency." [1]

Both the pluralistic and realistic character of this world view

[1] Spaulding, *idem*, p. 517.

seem to be in harmony with many tendencies in present day philosophy. That strong desire which we have for unity and completeness is, to be sure, not satisfied in Pluralism; but there is compensation for this lack in its doctrine of freedom, of values, and of God.

Criticism

To most minds, however, this philosophy is in need of supplementing in two directions. First, a more satisfying conception of consciousness and of the mental life in general is desirable. Spaulding with certain other writers of the day speaks of consciousness as a dimension and a variable. But since a dimension is reduced to a linear series, and in the case of consciousness is about what we mean by a *process*, a more exact and significant description seems to be needed. The mere *serial organization* of such elements as are studied in neurology, physiology, physics, and chemistry, even though such organization results in a qualitatively distinct dimension of reality, which we call *awareness*, does not yield a satisfactory description of those forces in the world which we call mental or psychical.

The second thing which is lacking in this pluralistic system of philosophy is a more satisfactory determination of the source of the creative synthesis itself. We hear much of creative synthesis and organization, but the ground of them is not determined. This pluralistic Universe needs, after all, a *soul*, not a soul as a unitary principle, but a soul as a vitalizing agency. At any rate, some evolutionary urge in the existential world of time and space, some *élan vital*, some creative agency, some cosmic will is necessary, it would seem.

This pluralistic tendency in contemporary thought is a healthy check to the monistic impulse. Too often have philosophies, particularly those which have been dominated by the classical notion of substance, been over-hasty in reducing this bewilderingly complex world to an ultimate single "stuff." The early materialists of the Modern Era, for example, were probably too ready to reduce the facts of mind and life to the simple mechanical laws of physics. The present day pluralists with their notions of levels and their caution that analysis into elements is in danger of losing the uniqueness of synthesis remind us that simple reduction is in great danger of falsification.

In connection with this chapter read:

Edward Gleason Spaulding, *The New Rationalism* (Henry Holt and Company), pp. 432–37 and pp. 486–95.

Further references:

William James, *A Pluralistic Universe* (Longmans, Green and Company). *The Will to Believe* (Longmans, Green and Company), Preface.

C. A. Richardson, *Spiritual Pluralism and Recent Philosophy* (Cambridge University Press).

Mary Whiton Calkins, *The Persistent Problems of Philosophy* (The Macmillan Company), Introduction, chap. III; also pp. 71 ff., pp. 411 ff.

G. H. Howison, *The Limits of Evolution* (The Macmillan Company), Appendices A, B, C, and D.

Jean Wahl, *Pluralist Philosophies of England and America* (The Open Court Company, London).

Part IV

THE NATURE OF MIND AND OF KNOWLEDGE

CHAPTER XVIII

WHAT IS THE MIND?

HISTORICAL

ONE of the things which those who take up the study of philosophy hope to have speedily solved is the problem about the soul or the mind — and its destiny. It will probably be disappointing, therefore, to learn that this most vital of all questions is still far from solution. On the other hand, it will be encouraging to know that in the last twenty years remarkable progress has been made in unraveling the mysteries of this most intricate and yet most interesting of all the problems of philosophy. Although the search for the soul will really be our task, let us for the moment substitute the word *mind*, which in psychology has now generally taken the place of the richer word *soul*.

Can the mind understand itself?

But is it, after all, strange that the problem of the mind should be so baffling? Science proceeds from the simple to the complex. The stars, so remote from human interest, were the first objects of study in ancient Assyria and Egypt. How incompetent those early astronomers would have been to study the subtle processes of their own minds! Then after astronomy came mathematics and physics, and in modern times chemistry and biology; and finally the most difficult sciences of all, psychology and sociology. All the sciences are the creation of the human mind; but the mind itself can be known and understood last of all. *Can* the mind know and understand itself? That it should even conceive of such a thing, or attempt it, is a witness to its marvelous supremacy. It is worth something to live in a time when inquiries like these are in the focus of attention among scientists — and perhaps to have a share in their solution.

Initial perplexities

The attitude of the reader in approaching the problem of mind is probably something like this: I have studied psychology; everybody

takes a psychology course now. I have learned a lot about physical
and mental processes, neurones and synapses, reaction-arcs and conditioned reflexes, stimulus and response, impulse and instinct, sensations and memory images, feelings and emotions, conscious and
unconscious states, intelligence tests and I.Q.'s, complexes and inhibitions, conduct and behavior; and I understand that some of
these are described as physiological processes and some as mental
processes; but it has never been made clear to me just what the difference is between a physical and a mental process, nor how they are
related, nor how the mental processes are related to the mind, nor
what the mind is.

Furthermore, outside of psychological writings, I hear a great deal
about the *soul* — in poetry, in literature, and in religion. Having
found that the word *psychology* is derived from two Greek words
meaning *soul* and *science*, I supposed that this study would surely
enlighten me; but I discover that some of the latest textbooks in
psychology studiously avoid using the word *soul*, or even the word
mind. Worst of all, in sermons and religious meetings I have heard
so often about the human *spirit*, as if the spirit again were something
different from the mind. How I should like to have this whole
muddle cleared up! When I asked about these things, I was told
that these questions are metaphysical and that I should go to
philosophy. My very first invasion into philosophy did not, however, do much to remove my difficulties; for I learned that my beloved Professor James, whose psychology had been so helpful, when
he began to write as a philosopher, was the author of an article entitled "Does Consciousness Exist?" I had been told that souls were
no longer mentioned in psychology and that consciousness has taken
their place, and yet the very existence of consciousness was here
questioned; and I have learned that in some of the most recent textbooks in psychology the word *consciousness* is hardly used. And,
anyway, the meaning of the word *consciousness* was never clear to
me. Sometimes it seemed to be used as synonymous with our whole
mental life, while at other times it referred only to the present or
passing aspect of it.

Initial definitions

Later we shall distinguish between the words *mind* and *consciousness*, and we may find that the words *mind*, *soul*, and *spirit* have not quite the same meaning; but for the sake of simplicity we may take as a point of departure the fact of an inner life of experience, which we call our mental or perhaps our psychical life, and that when we use the substantive words, *mind, soul, consciousness, spirit, ego, self*, they are merely different names applied to this inner life. Of course, these words are not synonyms, for *mind* and *mental* suggest intellectual activities, while *soul* and *psychical* are apt to call up emotional and vital elements. And sometimes when we think of the mind as separable from the body, we use the word *spirit*, while the adjective *spiritual* suggests moral and religious values.

Plan of approach

How shall we approach this most difficult of all subjects? Probably the best way will be to devote one chapter to a brief historical review of theories of the mind. Then in the next chapter we may see whether it is possible to gain some reasonable view of what the mind is, basing our study on recent attainments in the science of psychology and in the philosophy of mind. In a third chapter we may consider the relation of mind and body. Incidentally we must distinguish our inquiry about the mind, which we call the *philosophy of mind*, from psychology, which is the *science* of the mind. Psychologists do, indeed, usually have some philosophy of mind — that is, some theory of what the mind is; but they may avoid this inquiry if they choose, confining themselves to a mere description and classification of mental phenomena and the formulation of the laws of mental behavior — that is, to strict psychology.

Historical [1]

Primitive man thought of the soul as a kind of shadowy image or replica of the body, perhaps like a vapor, or breath, capable of leaving the body during sleep and surviving it after death. Greek philosophy and Greek literature are permeated with the idea of the

---

[1] A luminous account of the history of theories of the mind may be found in William McDougall's book, *Body and Mind*, chaps. I to IX.

soul, the Greek word, *psyche*, carrying a rich connotation of life, soul, and consciousness. The earliest Greek thinkers believed in a "divine and animate essence," immanent in nature, appearing in man as the soul, the source of life and intelligence. This view found expression in the doctrine of Heraclitus, who taught that the soul is a fiery vapor, identical with the rational and vital fire-soul of the Universe. Greek science, however, culminated in Democritus, who proclaimed the fact that all physical things are composed of material atoms in mechanical interaction, and who believed that the soul also consists of smooth round atoms permeating the body.

Plato

But it is to Plato that we must look for the source of our popular modern ideas about the soul. To Plato the soul is a distinct immaterial essence or being, imprisoned, so to speak, in the body, its nature having little in common with the earthly, its home and destiny being the world of eternal Ideas. The personality and individuality and immortality of the soul all stand out clearly in Plato's teaching. Even its pre-existence is affirmed, the soul bringing with it a kind of reminiscence of its former exalted home, prior to its life in the body. It is, furthermore, the source of motion in the body, as well as the fountain of knowledge and aspiration. It is owing to its inner divine nature that the soul has intuitive knowledge of the world of Ideas and higher values.

In his famous *Republic* Plato distinguishes three parts, aspects or functions of the soul which correspond with what we now refer to as reason, will and feeling. The latter two are close to the physical body, and evidently are not immortal. The reason is the "divine" part of the soul and is in essence separate and independent from the body. Its terrestrial life is an imprisonment or enchainment to the body, but its ultimate destiny is life eternal in the intelligible world of Ideas. In speaking of the separateness, divinity and immortality of the soul, Plato probably had in mind this "divine" part which he called reason. Here, of course, we have a fairly clear distinction between soul and body.

It would be hard to exaggerate the influence of this pure and exalted immaterialism of Plato in the history of thought, particularly in the early doctrine of the Church. His sharp distinction between the body and the soul was the source of the dualistic theories which have come down to us through the centuries, and with them came the tendency to exalt the soul and its heavenly mission above the body with its earthly character. This Platonic doctrine of the soul permeates our literature, finds expression in much of our most inspiring poetry, and is embedded deeply in our ethics, our religion, and our daily life. The historical importance of this soul theory has lately led to successful attempts to trace it back of Plato to the Orphic Mysteries and the Pythagorean philosophy. Plato, to be sure, wavers in his account of the soul, ascribing an earthly origin to its lower parts and reserving its immortality to its pure, godlike, rational part. But posterity has seized upon the graphic picture of the unitary, individual, and immortal soul, which he presented in the beautiful dialogue, the *Phaedo*.

Aristotle

Aristotle, no less than Plato, emphasized the reality and essential character of the soul; but he brings it into much closer relation to the body. It is the very "form" and reality and perfection of the body. It is the "primary actuality of a natural body endowed with life." It has the same relation to the body that vision has to the eye; or the impression in the wax to the wax itself. At the same time, he considers the soul to be a sort of vital principle, almost identical with life — the source of movement and growth as well as of thought and reason. Finally, influenced by Plato, he ascribes to the soul an active or creative reason, which is of the very nature of the divine, and is immortal.

But the significant thing in Aristotle's psychology is his notion that the soul is the purpose and perfection of the body, that for which the body exists and in which it finds its realization. This keen observation of Aristotle that the soul is the entelechy — that is, the end or perfection or purpose of the body, as if it were something for which the body exists, something in which the body is *perfected* — has become the seed of a recent scientific movement of great interest in the attempt to establish a philosophy of mind.

The tendency toward the complete spiritualization of the soul and to a decided and uncompromising Dualism, already seen in Plato, culminated in the teaching of Saint Augustine and through him was handed on to the medieval Church and to modern thought. Plotinus, the Neo-Platonist, had already taught that the soul is an immortal *substance*, sharply distinguished from the body and separable from it. Thus there emerged the doctrine of the existence of two worlds, a mundane, material world and a divine spiritual world, the body belonging to the former and the soul to the latter.

Descartes

In the seventeenth century this dualistic conception was crystallized into a distinct philosophical system by Descartes. Despite the long tradition of the "two worlds," spirit and flesh, eternal and temporal, reason and faith, medieval science long remained dominated by a qualitative physics and a somewhat animistic view of nature. Descartes had early become profoundly impressed with the efforts which various thinkers of the modern era had made to interpret nature mechanically. If nature obeys the sort of laws which such men as Galileo and Copernicus had affirmed, then the qualitative physics of medieval science and the animistic view of nature must be wrong.

In his famous work, *Meditations*, Descartes attempts to show once and for all that mind and matter are two distinct, separate and independent substances. Matter, he concludes, is extensive, inert, subject to mechanical laws, having no desire, purpose, or power of spontaneous motion. It is on such a view as this that the impressive body of modern physics, from Newton to the middle of the nineteenth century, was built. The mind, on the other hand, was for Descartes a substance with no extension, whose essential nature is to think. By "thinking" Descartes meant all of those activities which we commonly associate with the mental, namely, desiring, feeling, judging, willing, and so on. The soul is unique, dynamic rather than inert, teleological rather than mechanical, and non-spatial. It is a simple, indivisible substance.

It is important to note that Descartes insisted on the "substantive" character of mind. His reason for doing so is simple enough, though possibly logically unsound. The mind, he says, is essentially active — its activity being to "think." Now it is impossible to think of activity as such apart from an agent or subject of such activity. There is no instance of running apart from someone or something which runs. There is no talking apart from someone who talks. In the same way, Descartes holds, there is no thinking apart from something which thinks. So the mind is that thing which thinks and that thing is a substance vastly different from and independent of the great space-time mechanical world of physics.

This extreme dualism of Descartes performed the great service of laying a solid foundation for the development of modern physical science and does no violence to the religious prepossessions concerning the soul. But, on the other hand, it brings up difficulties which have been the storm-centers of controversy for the last three centuries. What am I? Is there really a mental substance behind the activities of the mind? Again, just in proportion as the pure spiritual character of the soul and the rigid mechanical character of the body are insisted upon, so is the difficulty greater in accounting for their action upon each other; and that mind and body do interact, or at least are intimately connected in some way, seems evident at every moment of our experience. Thus the problem of the relation of mind and body, following from this strict Dualism, was bequeathed to Descartes' successors.

Hume

This appealing doctrine of an independent immaterial substance received its first rude shock from Hume, who bluntly said that we have no experience of any such thing as a soul at all, and no evidence for its existence. Experience gives us nothing but a lot of impressions or perceptions, and ideas or memory images, and we have no way of showing or reason for believing that the soul is anything more than the collection of these impressions and ideas.

There are some philosophers who imagine we are every moment intimately conscious of what we call our SELF; that we feel its existence and its continuance in existence; and are certain, beyond the evidence of a demonstration, both of its perfect identity and simplicity. ... For my part, when I enter most intimately into what I call *myself*, I always stumble on some particular perception or other, of heat or cold, light or shade, love or hatred, pain or pleasure. I never can catch *myself* at any time without a perception, and never can observe anything but the perception. When my perceptions are removed for any time, as by sound sleep, so long am I insensible of *myself*, and may truly be said not to exist. And were all my perceptions removed by death, and could I neither think, nor feel, nor see, nor love, nor hate after the dissolution of my body, I should be entirely annihilated, nor do I conceive what is farther requisite to make me a perfect nonentity. If any one, upon serious and unprejudiced reflection, thinks he has a different notion of *himself*, I must confess I can reason no longer with him. All I can allow him is, that he may be in the right as well as I, and that we are essentially different in this particular. He may, perhaps, perceive something simple and continued, which he calls *himself;* though I am certain there is no such principle in me.[1]

As has been pointed out by many critics of Hume, he uses in the above passage the pronouns *I*, *me*, and *mine*, very freely, implying a certain unity and concreteness of that which perceives and thinks, not very well characterized as a "bundle" of perceptions, or as a "theater" where impressions pass and repass in constant flux and movement.[2]

However, Hume would hold that the use of such words as *I*, *me*, and *mine* is due to the exigencies of language and that such words do not reveal a metaphysical "self." What is meant by *self*, according to Hume, is simply the totality of experiences and nothing more. These experiences are in large part conditioned and organized by principles of association, such as contiguity and resemblance. Thus the sound of thunder always has been associated with the sight of lightning, so that whenever I see lightning I at the same time anticipate the sound of thunder. Such principles account for the general organization of experience — and what I call *myself* is but such experiences dominated by certain principles of order.

Kant

Kant held that Hume was correct in saying that the self is never revealed in experience, but did not go far enough in his analysis of the situation. It lies in the very nature of the case that the self can never become the object of experience, because the self, whatever else it might be, is in the indefeasible situation of being the subject

---

[1] Hume, *Treatise on Human Nature* (The Clarendon Press), book I, part IV, p. 6.

[2] Compare the criticism in Mary Whiton Calkins's *The Persistent Problems of Philosophy*, chap. VI.

of experience. A knowledge of the self seems, then, in the very nature of the case fore-doomed. However, the "I think" is quite inescapable and it is not sufficiently accounted for in Hume's laws of association. The facts of memory and association in general point to a deeper function of unity than Hume has managed to clarify. In his *Critique of Pure Reason* Kant refers to this unifying function as the "transcendental unity of apperception." Without going into the subtleties and difficulties of Kant's position it is safe to say that Kant was in no doubt at all as to the fact of there being a self, but just what that self is is beyond the possibility of knowledge. In the end, however, Kant does emphasize the essential unitary spiritual character of the mind, of which nature is hardly more than the phenomenal product.[1]

The nineteenth century

During the last century the foundations were laid in experimental science and in empirical psychology for a philosophy of mind more in keeping with our inductive scientific methods. Before speaking of these later fruits, however, it will be well to review the principal theories of mind held by philosophers during the nineteenth century. They are still representative views, and by their several advocates are thought to harmonize with inductive and experimental studies.

We may then distinguish these four classes of theories:

1. Materialistic theories
2. Dualistic or animistic theories
3. Idealistic theories
4. Double-aspect theories

Materialistic theories of the mind

Materialism in its older form affirmed that there is no other reality than matter, or mass particles in motion; that mind is in no way a distinct or different form of being, but is itself either a form or function of matter. Man is an adaptive mechanism, wholly explicable in terms of the laws of physics and chemistry. Consciousness arises in the transformation of energy in the highly complex mechanism of the nervous system, but is not itself a distinct form of energy nor a distinct form of being of any kind.

[1] Cf. Paulsen's *Kant*, p. 185.

Democritus, the Greek materialist, considered the soul to be composed of atoms, like the body, only of a smoother, rounder kind. Some of the German materialists of the eighteenth century spoke of thought as being a secretion of the brain. Haeckel in his *Riddle of the Universe* believed that the mind is a function of the brain. Among writers of this school, psychology, not dealing with any forms of reality beyond those considered in physics and chemistry, becomes a branch of physiology or biology. In the Naturalism of the present day it is believed that the methods and presuppositions of the physical sciences are also those of psychology and that the latter requires no others.

Epiphenomenalism is a term sometimes given to one type of materialism. This word was first used by Huxley; it indicates that mind is not a factor in natural processes; mind is a name that we give to certain phenomena that merely *accompany* types of processes and changes in the nervous system. Mental states are like a kind of *aura*, hovering about cerebral processes without themselves having any function; they effect no changes and have themselves no significance in the world movement. The laws of physics, chemistry, and physiology cover the whole field, and if fully known would enable us to understand the world of man and society.

Dualistic or animistic theories

Here belongs the "soul" theory, coming down from Plato and Descartes and familiar to everyone. More specifically under this head we may mention, first, the everyday metaphysical Dualism taught by Descartes, accepted by Locke and popularized in America through the influence of the Scottish school. Mind and body are quite distinct, and represent the two universal realities.

Somewhat similar to this, if more cautious, is the psychological Dualism, brilliantly defended by William McDougall.[1] With much courage McDougall has revived the use of the word *Animism*[2] as a

---

[1] See his book *Body and Mind, A History and a Defence of Animism.* Fifth edition.

[2] The word *animism* has more commonly been used in anthropology to signify the tendency among primitive people to endow everything with mind, even things we regard as inanimate, such as sticks and stones. McDougall uses the term in its larger sense merely to indicate belief in mind (*anima*), as a reality.

name for his philosophy of mind, which is nothing else than the usual soul theory. The mind — or, if we choose to use the other terms, *soul*, *ego*, *self* — is a unitary and distinct psychic being, in nowise to be identified or confused with the body with which it interacts. It possesses, or is, the sum of certain enduring capacities for psychical activity, such as having sensations, reacting to them, and guiding the stream of nervous energy in such a way as to neutralize the tendency of physical energy to dissipation and degradation. This emphatic dualism of mind and body does not, however, in Mc-Dougall's opinion involve necessarily any Cartesian dualism of the world. It is content to affirm the distinction of mind and body in the human personality, and it is probably not this unequivocal distinction which contemporary schools are calling in question, but rather the more equivocal theory of interaction.

Among other representatives of Animism, or the soul theory, may be mentioned the German philosophers, Lotze, Stumpf, Külpe, and in America, George T. Ladd, and James (in some of his moods); while in France, Bergson has defended a somewhat closely related theory of mind.

Idealistic theories

In the third class we may include not only the strictly idealistic systems, but also the various panpsychic, personalistic, and mind-stuff theories. In this class we shall find the great majority of modern systems of thought; for Idealism has prevailed in all periods. And yet, perhaps, we shall get from none of them a perfectly clear notion of what the mind is; it is too all-inclusive to be clearly defined. Strictly they are theories of the world rather than of mind, interpreting the Universe in terms of consciousness, or will, or experience. So we hear much of experience, self, will, and ideas.

In the absolute or objective idealistic systems the whole Universe is rooted and grounded in mind or spirit; call it Absolute Ego, as did Fichte, or Absolute Idea with Hegel, or Absolute Will with Schopenhauer, or Absolute Experience with Bradley, or Absolute Self with Royce. The soul of man is thus intimate with, or participates in, or represents the very essence of reality. Mind is not something accompanying matter, or something generated in an evolutionary process, but something primordial and original; it is the very stuff of the Universe.

Still other forms of Idealism consider mind to be the essence of reality. In Leibniz's philosophy the units of things which we call *atoms* are called *Monads*. They are psychical, not material; they are little perceptions, but sometimes dim and confused. In the human soul we have a Monad which has developed to the stage of clear and conscious perception or representation.

Many of the modern panpsychic or mind-stuff theories go back to Leibniz. W. K. Clifford proposed the view that the whole Universe is made of mind-stuff, an ultimate cosmic reality, and that our human consciousness is built up from elementary feelings, and these from mind-stuff.[1]   James in one of his later writings [2] thought it might be necessary to assume the presence in the Universe of a kind of reservoir of soul-stuff, "a continuum of cosmic consciousness." James Ward in England, C. A. Strong in America, and Friedrich Paulsen in Germany have upheld various forms of Panpsychism, in which the very ground of the world is mind or feeling or consciousness, the body and the brain being appearances or phenomena of this essential psychical reality.

Double-aspect theories

According to this fourth view, mind and body are simply two aspects of the same underlying reality, itself possibly unknown. They are not different things at all, but identical in essence.   They are the same realities seen from different sides; two faces, as it were, of the same coin.   As stated in its original form by Spinoza, the one substance, which is called God, has two attributes, thought and extension.   In its modern form, as stated, for instance, by Warren, "conscious and neural phenomena constitute *one single series* of events," their different appearance being due to different ways of observing them.[3]

Fechner's theory, mentioned in a previous chapter, was quite similar.   But in Fechner it takes rather the form of ascribing to all matter a kind of elementary consciousness.   The whole world is en-

---

[1] *Lectures and Essays*, vol. II.   [2] *American Magazine*, 1909, p. 588.

[3] Howard C. Warren, *Human Psychology*, p. 415.   Titchener held a similar view.

souled. Everything has a soul—minute particles of matter, organic bodies, the planets, the whole Universe. This has been a favorite view with many modern thinkers. Even Haeckel said that the material atoms are not dead and inert, but are endowed with feeling and will.

Newer views

We have thus passed in briefest review the four principal classes of theories about the mind held during the nineteenth century. In one or another form they are still widely held. But now in recent years quite new views are appearing. The Freudians, the Pragmatists, the Behaviorists, the Neo-Realists, and the Gestaltists have taken up the problem with a freshness and enthusiasm that promise real contributions to the philosophy of mind, especially since these various movements have much in common. Before considering these new views on the problem of mind, we should notice certain general tendencies already apparent in the nineteenth century. Even then the foundations were laid in experimental and empirical psychology for a philosophy of mind which should be more in keeping with our inductive scientific methods. The critical work done by Hume could never be forgotten, in spite of the rather convincing answer of Immanuel Kant. It became, therefore, more and more the custom to speak of mental states rather than of the mind and its "faculties." Psychologists devoted themselves to the study of sensation, perception, memory, feeling, volition. What is given in experience is not a mind or soul, but a stream of thought. The use of the word *soul* was looked upon with suspicion; it disappeared finally from the language of psychologists. Even the word *mind* was distrusted, and when used often signified no more than the sum of our mental states. Psychology was defined sometimes as the science of mental states.

Still, however, the mind was often looked upon as a sort of receptacle in which all these mental states were held, or as a sort of stage upon which they appeared and disappeared. This notion of the mind was hardly more satisfactory than the old psychology of *ideas*, encouraged by Locke, based on the assumption that there are a lot of entities called *ideas*, which exist *in* the mind and may pass *out* of the mind and be again recalled as memories.

Gradually this structural psychology yielded to a functional view; mental activities took the place of mental states.   Mental activities could be subjected to experimental investigation — actually studied in the laboratory.   One thing, however, all these activities seemed to have in common; they were conscious.   Thus, the word *consciousness* came into general use to take the place of the word *soul* and *mind,* which were under suspicion because of their metaphysical associations; and psychology was sometimes defined as the science of consciousness.   I may not be a soul, or a mind, or even a body, but at any rate I am conscious; and *consciousness* seemed to be a safe term, which should take the place of the discarded *soul.*   But really it was a very unfortunate term, and its extensive use has introduced endless confusion into our modern philosophy of mind.   Finally, James himself called it in question and raised the inquiry whether consciousness exists at all.   In fact, he said that it does not exist as a real thing, being but the faint rumor of the disappearing soul.

The influence of the rising Freudian psychology, which makes so much of unconscious mental activity, tended also to discourage the use of the word *consciousness* as synonymous with *mind.*   So also did the new science of Behaviorism, which proceeded undismayed to construct the whole science of psychology without any reference to consciousness at all.   Whether either the Freudians or the Behaviorists are right in their attitude toward consciousness, we may learn later; here it is only necessary to take notice of the passing of that stage in the history of the philosophy of mind in which mind was identified with consciousness.   Very often consciousness was thought of as a kind of *stuff,* much as mind and soul had formerly been conceived.   McDougall speaks of the havoc wrought in psychology by the word *consciousness,* and says that it is a thoroughly bad word, and that it has been a great misfortune for psychology that the word has come into general use.[1]   In the next chapter we shall try to find out what the word *consciousness* really means.

Objective methods

Meanwhile actual reconstructive work was being done by the new schools mentioned above.   What is common to all these new

[1] *Outline of Psychology,* p. 16.

movements is that they begin by studying man as a member of the biological series, who acts or behaves in a certain way, and who has certain kinds of experience; and the question is to what kind of action or behavior we may give the name *mental*; and further what presuppositions are necessary to account for that particular kind of behavior which we call *mental*. Consequently the study of mind has become objective. The old method of introspection, while not wholly discarded, is held in abeyance, if not under suspicion. The method of general observation has largely taken its place; not because this method is certainly adequate in the study of mind, but because it is the method successfully pursued by the other sciences, and because, at any rate, *so far as it goes*, its results can be trusted. This objective method taken in connection with the verified results of all related sciences, such as biology, physiology, genetics, abnormal psychology, and anthropology, promises decided contributions to the philosophy of mind.

This new psychology begins with a study, not of minds, souls, consciousness, ideas, or sensations, but of mental processes in general. What kind of processes shall we call *mental*? We observe *mechanical processes* in the interaction of the parts of a machine. We observe *chemical processes* in atomic interchanges in gases, liquids, and solids. When we come to the simplest organism, we find other processes, which have to do with maintaining the integrity of the organism itself; for instance, growth and reproduction. These we call *vital processes*. But now we may distinguish processes of still another kind, when an organism begins to respond as a unit to an outer situation in such a way as to maintain its integrity. *Behavior* is a word which we apply to activities of this kind; it signifies the manner in which an organism functions with reference to its environment. We may then give the name *mental processes* to all those activities of an individual organism in which it adapts itself to a changing environment in such a way as to conserve or promote its well-being, its interests. In a simple reflex action there is stimulus and response. The response is purposive, conducive to the welfare of the organism; but it is relatively determined and invariable; there is no *specific* response, no selection or choice or control. It is not mental. Next come instincts, where reflex actions are further integrated, resulting in inherited tendencies to carry out a given set of responses under given circumstances. Such actions, only slightly adaptive, we hesitate to call mental, reserving the latter term for those specific responses by which on the basis of previous experience a new situation has been dealt with in such a way as to conserve or advance the interests of the organism. Responses like these are called *intelligent* or *mental*.

Now, something like this is the groundwork of the new philosophy of mind. We notice that it rests upon simple, direct observation of the behavior of individuals, and is fortified by a more or less complete knowledge not only of the brain and the neural mechanism, but of the whole body. Psychology, thus, is not the science of the soul or mind or consciousness, but the study of behavior, involving stimulus and response. In the case of man these reflexes become very highly organized and integrated and conditioned by previous reactions and accompanied by various checks and inhibitions; so we arrive at that kind of activity, behavior, or conduct, which we call *reflective, intelligent, mental*. Even what we call *thought* may be considered as a "motor setting," or "latent course of action." [1]

Behaviorism

The method we have just described is the general method of approach of the science of Behaviorism, which studies in a wholly objective way the conduct or behavior of living beings, and considers human psychology to have just this behavior of men as its subject-matter. [2]

As one method of advancing the science of psychology free from doubtful assumptions, Behaviorism must command our highest respect; but it can make no lawful claim to furnishing a philosophy of mind. If what we desire is a philosophy of mind, consciousness *cannot* be ignored, as the Behaviorist elects to do. The word *consciousness* is in daily use and means something; and it behooves us to find out what it means. Furthermore, since so much is made of organization and integration of reflexes, the source and secret of this

---

[1] See Edwin B. Holt, *The Freudian Wish and Its Place in Ethics*, p. 98. In the first two chapters of this little book the reader will find the clearest account of this way of regarding the mind.

[2] The behavioristic standpoint may best be understood by reading John B. Watson's *Psychology from the Standpoint of a Behaviorist*, or Max F. Meyer's *Psychology of the Other-One*.

organization must be studied. Behaviorism, of course, ignores all such questions. Still further, since organisms in specific response act in such a way as to conserve their well-being, or to bring themselves into a satisfied relation to the environment, psychology should inquire what these interests and satisfactions are; at any rate, they cannot be omitted in the philosophy of mind.

Neo-Realism

The movement known as Neo-Realism differs little in its psychological attitude from Behaviorism; only the Neo-Realists are philosophers rather than psychologists and are primarily interested in the problem of knowledge. Incidentally, they have worked out a philosophy of mind more complete than that attempted by the Behaviorists. The general approach to the study of mind which has been described as characteristic of the new schools is especially the attitude of the Neo-Realists; that is, the approach to the study of adaptive behavior through the objective study of organisms. Reflexes are progressively organized into more and more complex processes producing synthetic novelties, till finally adaptive behavior, or specific response, accompanied by *awareness*, signals the birth of mind.[1]

This philosophy of mind takes a slightly different form in an instructive chapter by Ralph Barton Perry in his *Present Philosophical Tendencies*. Perry distinguishes three parts of mind. First, the biological interests; second, a nervous system acting as instrument of the biological processes; third, those parts of the environment to which the nervous system specifically responds — the so-called *mental contents*.[2]

This seems confusing at first, but becomes clearer when we understand that it is nothing but Behaviorism (with a saving emphasis, however, upon the biological interests), considering the mind quite materialistically as the brain in its selective and controlling aspects. But Perry and Holt, following James, conceived the brilliant idea of regarding as actual parts of the mind those portions of the environment to which the organism specifically responds, the *mental con-*

---

[1] Compare Edwin B. Holt, *op. cit.*, pp. 51 ff.
[2] Chap. XII, "A Realistic Theory of Mind."

tents, as they are called. Then that other part of the environment to which there is no specific response by the organism may be called *physical*. So that it depends upon the context into which otherwise neutral entities get whether we shall regard them as physical or mental, the real world being neutral. Thus the doctrine of "Neutral Monism" appears on the scene. What would have been considered a decided Materialism at the time when James wrote is thus converted into an innocent Neutral Monism. But I would advise the confused reader to neglect this third division of the mind which the Neo-Realists offer and cling to the other two, namely, the biological interests and adaptive behavior. Whether this really does lead to any kind of Materialism we may consider later.

The most serious difficulty with the neo-realistic doctrine of mind is its failure to give us a clear notion of what consciousness is. Although Perry admits that "mind as observed introspectively differs characteristically from mind as observed in nature and society," nevertheless, one gets the impression that neither in Behaviorism nor in Neo-Realism does the subjective side of mentality get its proper recognition. Howard C. Warren, in his book entitled *Human Psychology*, outlines a philosophy of mind which seems to correct this deficiency, while giving full recognition to the objective method of study. Psychology, he says, is a science concerned, not *merely* with behavior — that is, with those complex processes by means of which an organism adjusts itself to the environment — but also with the *subjective* aspect of all these processes. They are not only adaptive processes as seen by another; they are also *conscious phenomena*, as seen by ourselves. By means of *self-observation* we get a new way of studying these adaptive processes. In addition to *mentality* there is also *consciousness*. Consciousness is the way all these mental processes appear to ourselves.

At first sight this seems to clear up the whole matter and give us a clear philosophy of mind. It uses the modern approach by studying in an objective manner that kind of activity in organic beings which we call *behavior*; but it also admits that all these adaptive — that is, mental — processes have a subjective or conscious aspect, a tremendously interesting and significant part of the life of man, thus supplementing the deficiencies of Behaviorism.

But still the question arises, What *is* this conscious subjective life? Is it anything that can find a place in the field of science? Is it a kind of by-product of the brain, an epiphenomenon? Or are we to fall back into some ancient Dualism after all? It was just to escape all such haziness that Behaviorism and Neo-Realism took their stand upon objective behavior.

To these questions Warren says that the experiences which we observe in ourselves *might* be considered as a *new set of occurrences.* That would lead to a theory of psychophysical parallelism with all its mysteries; or they might be considered as *another way of looking at the same set of facts.* This would lead to the double-aspect theory, which Warren adopts. Neural events, according to this view, are *observable* either as behavior in others or as our own experiences in ourselves. A merely objective study of mentality in others would furnish a very important and very true science of psychology; but it would, after all, be a partial view, for our inner life of conscious experience presents another side of the reality, supplementing that of outward behavior.[1]

The philosophy of mind thus clearly presented by Warren seems a distinct advance upon Behaviorism. Surely, the reader will say, there is something more than behavior, something more than mentality, if we are to call adaptive behavior mental. There is certainly an inner conscious life of experience — my own life of personal wishes, dreams, memories, volitions, and perceptions. This is true enough, but just what it means to say that neural events and brain events can be "viewed" in two ways is not so clear. It still remains to ask whether a better way of explaining consciousness than this double-aspect theory may be advanced.

Pragmatism

Another new and vital movement in the study of mind is Pragmatism. As a system of philosophy we shall consider this in another chapter; but what of the Pragmatist's philosophy of mind? The pragmatic approach to the mind problem is even more biological and evolutionary than the other new movements. We start with an organism, an animal or a man that has a practical problem to solve,

[1] *Op. cit.,* pp. 9. 1^ and 415.

perhaps to get food, perhaps to escape an enemy. Hence arises a situation, a problem to be dealt with; the environment is to be moulded to the needs of the subject. This involves experimentation; and what we have to do with, therefore, is the *experience* of the subject in this experimental moulding of the environment. Now, there is a certain stage in this experience, when it becomes reflective and intelligent, that we may describe as mental or conscious.

Pragmatists do not care to speak much of the mind, still less of the soul, and not so very much of consciousness. Consequently the pragmatic theory of mind is somewhat hard to formulate.[1] Perhaps we may put it in the following way. In the development of organisms there is a stage prior to that of reflection; it is characterized by mere liking or disliking, striving, endeavor, and is determined by definitely organized systems of neural discharge. In the next stage incompatible factors arise in some definite situation; conflicting stimuli indicate conflicting ways of response; there is trouble, tension, a perplexing situation. Hence arises the necessity for readjustment. The new situation has to be integrated; the response has to be adapted to the new situation. Experimentation follows, and selection; conduct is to be controlled by its consequences; future consequences become transformed into a stimulus for behavior. Now, such adaptive behavior is called *reflective, conscious, mental*. The mind, therefore, is *instrumental*, serving biological ends; and Pragmatism of this kind is sometimes called Instrumentalism.

In its initial emphasis upon adaptive behavior, therefore, we see that the pragmatic approach to the mind problem differs but little from the other modern movements; but the special emphasis is upon the moulding and remodeling of the environment through the creative activity of the individual. *Intelligence* is the name which the Pragmatists prefer for activity of this kind and they speak of "creative intelligence," and of "the courageously inventive individual as bearer of a creatively employed mind," and of the future as being determined by intelligence.

What we get in Pragmatism, therefore, is a stirring picture of free

[1] The clearest account will be found in the volume entitled *Creative Intelligence*, particularly in the chapter by John Dewey entitled "The Need for a Recovery of Philosophy," and a chapter by Boyd H. Bode entitled "Consciousness and Psychology." Compare also Dewey's book, *Essays in Experimental Logic*, pp. 8 ff.

dynamic personalities, striving, struggling, achieving. But since the Pragmatists make much of evolution and the biological approach, one is curious to know just how intelligence stands to the rest of the evolutionary process; whether we have a mechanistic or non-mechanistic philosophy of mind. The implications of Pragmatism are all quite non-mechanistic. The insistence upon experience, upon free dynamic personalities, upon creative intelligence, does not lead in a mechanistic direction.

On the other hand, there is expressly repudiated any belief in a distinctive psychic element in experience; that is, anything outside the sphere of physical and biological factors. Pragmatists have no use for minds or souls or consciousness in the old substantive sense. So the question arises, just what *is* this creative intelligence that is creative of values? In Pragmatism it seems just to appear on the scene, like a little cloud gathering in the clear sky, and we wonder what it is made of; we would like to see its credentials.

The same is true of the non-reflectional elements of experience, the esteem, aversion, suffering, endeavor, and revolt, of which Dewey speaks, as preceding reflection. Whence come they and what are they? Probably what the Pragmatists mean is that these non-reflectional elements of experience are what we commonly call the biological interests — impulse, craving, will-to-live, desire. Wherever there is life, these deep impulses are present; and intelligence is just a tool or instrument of these interests. But whence, then, come the freedom and creative power of intelligence? From the standpoint of biological evolution where do freedom and creative activity come in? [1]

However the Pragmatists may solve this difficulty, their wholesome insistence on the creative power, efficacy, and efficiency of intelligence is worthy of careful note.

That man is a real agent — and that the distinctive quality of his agency consists in the part played therein by the imaginative recovery and analysis of a physically non-existent past and the imaginative prevision of a physically non-existent future — these are the first articles of any consistently pragmatic creed. Such a creed is simply a

[1] The difficulties here referred to have been pointed out in a clear manner by Arthur O. Lovejoy in three articles in *Jour. of Phil., Psych., and Sci. Meth.*, vol. 17 (1920), pp. 589, 622, and vol. 19 (1921), p. 5.

return to sanity; for these two theses are the common and constant presuppositions of the entire business of life. Never, surely, did a sillier or more self-stultifying idea enter the human mind, than the idea that thinking as such — that is to say, remembering, planning, reasoning, forecasting — is a vast irrelevancy, having no part in the causation of man's behavior or in the shaping of his fortunes — a mysterious redundancy in a cosmos which would follow precisely the same course without it. Nobody at a moment of reflective action, it may be suspected, ever believed this to be true.[1]

The Gestalt theory

The Gestalt psychology has become a movement of such importance in the field of general psychology that it would be interesting to know just what philosophical theory of mind it involves. This is difficult to formulate, since the Gestaltists have for the most part limited themselves thus far to the theory of perception. Mr. W. M. Danner, Jr., of Stanford University, has offered a short summary, not of Gestalt psychology, but of the Gestalt theory of mind.

The *Gestalt* theory of mind is called (by many) isomorphism, defined as "the structural correspondence of excitatory fields in the brain with the experienced contents of consciousness." [2]

Gestalt psychology holds that explanation of conscious phenomena and organic behavior in terms of analytical units is unnecessary, even impossible. Gestalt theory revolts not only against the 'bundle hypothesis' of elementarism, but against the 'constancy hypothesis' of direct psychophysical relationship between stimulus and phenomenal perception. It also protests against associationism and against attention as being valueless concepts.

The Gestalt school of thought, dating from Wertheimer's revolutionary work in 1912, has freed itself from much of the incubus of the earlier mind-body views. It attempts to dispose of the mind-body problem by just accepting as 'givens' the facts ordinarily described separately as mental processes and physical structures. It reclassifies them all in terms of functioning patterns, dynamically organized wholes interacting toward equilibrium as their various

[1] Arthur O. Lovejoy, *loc. cit.*, p. 632. This doctrine of the Pragmatists Lovejoy endorses while pointing out its inconsistency with their metaphysics.

[2] Howard C. Warren, editor, *Dictionary of Psychology* (Houghton Mifflin Company, Boston), p. 145.

field-potentials shift. It postulates only one set of events in the world, but admits that abstracting from them in one way leads to description in terms of mental activities; abstracting in another way requires description in terms of physical and physiological structures.

Thus a dual monism is implied if not avowed in the Gestalt position.[1] Köhler[2] postulates a psychophysiological correspondence between experienced order in space and time and the underlying dynamical context of physiological processes.

Wheeler's various characterizations of mind[3] as 'the brain-in-action, a neutral dynamism, an objective functionalism, determinism, causation, energy functioning in an organismic sense' may not authoritatively represent the view of all Gestaltists. But Gestalt theory is without doubt anti-mechanistic and anti-vitalistic. It explains the fact that perception and thought are orderly simply by the parts-in-relation and their dynamical interplay as whole configurations or Gestalten which are greater than the additive sum of their parts.[4]

Historically the emphasis upon the whole being more than the sum of its parts is affiliated with the Gestalt-qualität theory of von Ehrenfels (1890). It bears some resemblance in that respect to theories of emergent evolution. The chief line of philosophical descent of Gestalt theory is closely akin to the phenomenology of Husserl and his followers, tracing back in part at least through the psychology of 'act' to Brentano.

The Freudians

What is the mind? With our question still unanswered, let us go to the Freudians. None of the new ways of looking at the mind is more vital and revolutionary than theirs. This school recognizes what should have been seen long ago, that philosophers and psychologists, being men in whom the rational and conscious part of the mind is highly developed, have a tendency to overemphasize these

[1] Edwin G. Boring, *The Physical Dimensions of Consciousness* (The Century Company, New York, 1933), pp. 75-77.

[2] Dr. Wolfgang Köhler, *Gestalt Psychology* (Horace Liveright, New York), pp. x + 403.

[3] Raymond Holder Wheeler, *The Laws of Human Nature* (D. Appleton Company, New York), pp. 4, 93.

[4] Oliver L. Reiser, "Gestalt Psychology and the Philosophy of Nature," *Philosophical Review*, 1930, vol. 39, pp. 556-72.

elements. Consequently it is a very one-sided philosophy of mind
that we find in the older traditions and the regular textbooks.
Really the irrational and unconscious mental elements are the more
important.

So the Freudians have discovered that the mind is not a collection
of sensations, perceptions, ideas, and rational processes, or a certain
spiritual substance *having* ideas, sensations, and the like; but rather
a deep and troubled sea, whose secrets are found, not in its placid
surface of consciousness and reason, but in its profound unconscious
and irrational depths.   They have laid hold of two great truths.
One is that mind is a much wider term than consciousness; the other
is that the most significant things in our mental life are impulses.
Night-dreams and day-dreams made in the old psychology quite an
insignificant chapter; here they are of prime importance, for they
reveal the deep springs of our mental life — those profound psychical
energies which are known as impulses, cravings, desires, wishes, appetites, and interests; such, for instance, as sex, hunger, self-preservation, gregariousness.   In our conventional, civilized life these
vital strivings are necessarily repressed.   Hence come unhappy
"complexes," systems of painful experiences lying below the thresh-
old of consciousness, upwelling into our conscious life under the influence of emotion.[1]

Now, all this is very interesting, very important, and probably
true.   It is a new psychology, but is it a philosophy of mind?   We
are introduced to a lot of new terms — the Unconscious, Psychical
Energy,[2] the Censor, Complexes, and others, and we are curious to
know what they are and how they are going to be built up into a real
philosophy of mind.   What is this Psychical Energy, and how is it
related to other well-authenticated forms of energy?   We shall turn
the pages of the Freudians and Psychoanalysts in vain for any clear
answer to this question.   The Unconscious, Psychical Energy, the
Censor are concepts, mental constructs, which serve the purpose of
all conceptual construction, as a framework on which to hang our
actual *facts*.   *If* such things exist — say a reservoir of unconscious

---

[1] An intelligible account of the Freudian philosophy of mind may be found in Tansley's
The New Psychology. Compare also Brill's *Fundamental Conceptions of Psychoanalysis*, and
Freud's *Psychopathology of Everyday Life*, and his *General Introduction to Psychoanalysis*.

[2] Jung, *Psychology of the Unconscious*, pp. 144 ff. Tansley, *op. cit.*, pp. 59 ff.

impressions — *then* the facts would be as they are. They have the same logical credentials as the soul had in former times. If the soul exists and has "faculties," then facts should follow as they do.

Tansley in his exposition of the Freudian psychology traces the evolution of mind, quite after the manner of the other new schools, through simple reflex action and instinctive behavior to the final stage of reflective thought and consciously purposive action. But when mind does arrive, it is something *sui generis*, something wholly distinct from the body and brain. "In short," he says, "we cannot dispense with the dualism involved in regarding mind as an entity with its own phenomena and laws." [1]

Summary

These, then, are some of the more important theories of mind familiar in the history of philosophy. These various theories might be summarized under the following five heads. First, the substantive theory of the sort that Descartes held, which asserts that the mind or soul is a separate, independent entity. Second, the epiphenomenalistic theory, which maintains that the mind is a sort of inefficacious by-product of the body. On this theory the soul would, of course, perish with the disintegration of the body and all so-called conscious or mental life is reducible to the physical. Third, the type of theory which denies a substantive mind and holds that what we mean by "mind" is nothing but a succession of experiences or mental states. This is the point of view of Hume. Fourth, there is what we might call the functional view, such as the Aristotelian theory and those in recent times which hold that mind is an adaptive instrument developed or emergent in the long course of evolution. Fifth, the extreme behavioristic type of theory which holds that mind at best is simply the behavior of certain organisms. This theory might be said to deny mind rather than account for it.

Whether out of these various theories any clear philosophy of mind will emerge we may inquire in the next chapter. Surely they are confusing at first; but the thoughtful reader will see that they do in some measure converge toward certain definite results. There are some things in this history of theories of the mind which seem

[1] A. G. Tansley, *The New Psychology*, pp. 20, 21.

like saving truths to be followed up and carefully weighed. One of these is the Freudian emphasis upon vital impulses, those deep biological interests which seem like psychical energies driving us on apparently with some unconscious purpose. Another is the view common to all the new movements, that the key to what we call mental activity is, objectively considered, that kind of behavior which we call *adaptive*. Another, pointed out by Warren, is the belief that adaptive behavior has a subjective side which we may call *consciousness* or *experience*. Still another, emphasized by Plato, is the peculiar unitary personal character of the self. Finally, there is that strange conception of Aristotle's that the mind is the perfection and fruition of the body. Aristotle's theory of the mind as an entelechy or dynamic entity intimately bound up with the organism is receiving more and more serious attention, as is evident in such a movement as the Gestalt theory. Would it be possible to forge all these elements into a consistent philosophy of mind?

In connection with this chapter read:

Gamertsfelder and Evans, *Fundamentals of Philosophy* (Prentice-Hall, Inc.), chap. xv.

William McDougall, *Body and Mind* (Methuen and Company), chaps. I to IX.

Further references:

Hume, "An Enquiry Concerning Human Understanding," as found in Rand's *Modern Philosophers*, pp. 307–46.

L. T. Hobhouse, *Mind in Evolution* (The Macmillan Company).

Henri Bergson, *Matter and Memory* (The Macmillan Company). *Creative Evolution* (Henry Holt and Company.)

J. S. Haldane, *Mechanism, Life and Personality* (J. Murray).

J. B. Pratt, *Matter and Spirit* (The Macmillan Company).

C. W. Morris, *Six Theories of Mind* (The University of Chicago Press, 1933).

D. S. Robinson, *Anthology of Recent Philosophy* (D. Appleton and Company, 1924), part 2, chap. VI; part 3, chap. V; part 4, chap. xxv.

Will Durant, *Mansions of Philosophy* (Simon and Schuster, 1929), chaps. IV, XXIV.

J. A. Leighton, *The Field of Philosophy* (D. Appleton and Company, 1923).

A. E. Avey, *Readings in Philosophy* (D. Appleton and Company, 1924), chap. xxv.

G. Watts Cunningham, *Problems of Philosophy. An Introductory Survey* (Henry Holt and Company), chap. xv.

Howard C. Warren, *Human Psychology* (Houghton Mifflin Company).

John B. Watson, *Psychology from the Standpoint of a Behaviorist* (J. B. Lippincott).

CHAPTER XIX
WHAT IS THE MIND?

RECONSTRUCTIVE

ONE of the causes of the confusion about the soul which is seen in the history of philosophy is found in the exceedingly complex character of the human organism and the many kinds of activities embraced under the term *mental* or *psychical*. We may as well recognize at once that the mind is a very complex thing, or group of things, or rather a group of tendencies, processes, and activities. We must distinguish three aspects of the mind and examine them separately.

I. The Conative Tendencies

Any true philosophy of mind must begin with the springs of conduct and behavior. In the recent literature of the subject it has been customary to speak of these as primary biological interests. Usually they have been treated descriptively in separate chapters under the head of *desires, instincts, will,* or *conative tendencies,* as if they were normal features of our conscious life to be described in passing, along with other mental processes.

But we must understand that they are in a wholly different category; they are tendencies and dispositions rather than activities and processes. Just in proportion as psychology now emphasizes activity, behavior, function, *doing,* so it is necessary to understand the springs or grounds of this doing. Deep down in the roots of our being there is a force at work which impels, and what we call *behavior* is the result of the operation of this force. We may call it conation, striving, wish, will, libido, appetite, hunger, sex, desire, craving, instinct, psychic energy, or just a kind of *drive.* In the last chapter, when we were studying the new movements in psychology, we noticed the prominence given to these profound conative elements, the non-reflectional elements of experience, as the Pragmatists call them. The Freudian psychology owes its vigor largely to the emphasis which it gives to these primary constitutive elements of the mind, the *wishes*. Plato and Aristotle were evidently impressed by the basal character of these elements, for they spoke of an appetitive *soul* and a vegetative *soul*. McDougall has shown at length that the instincts are the prime movers of all human activity and that human and animal behavior is a manifestation of this purposive or hormic energy.[1]

The conative tendencies as interests

It is doubtful whether the term *energy*, even when qualified as purposeful or "hormic," is the best name for these primary mental elements. What we have is something more than a *drive*, something more than a *drift* or a *tendency* or a *restlessness*, even something more than what one writer has called the "energy-influences seething and bubbling in the organism";[2] it is rather an *interest*. Wherever there are organisms there are interests. Life is purposive, looking toward self-maintenance and self-perpetuation. This, as we have seen, does not necessarily involve any general teleology, or any conscious purposiveness in the world. It is only that life itself is teleological. This is clear from the very notion of "interest" itself. Interest always involves an object and thus an end or goal. Life *tends* to self-maintenance in growth and assimilation, and to self-perpetuation in simple cell division. It exhibits what Patten calls a kind of egoism and altruism. This impulse of self-preservation and self-perpetuation is native to every organism; perhaps there is no better name for it than the *will-to-live*.

> Every clod feels a stir of might,
> An instinct within it that reaches and towers;
> And grasping blindly above it for light,
> Climbs to a soul in grass and flowers.

"The Greek naturalists saw (what it needs only sanity to see) that the infinite substance of things was instinct with a perpetual motion and rhythmic order which were its life, and that the spirit of man was a spark from that universal fire."[3]

---

[1] See his *Outlines of Psychology*, pp. 72, 213, *et passim*, and his *Introduction to Social Psychology*.

[2] Louis Berman, in his *Glands Regulating Personality*, p. 196.

[3] Santayana, *Soliloquies in England and Later Soliloquies*, p. 212.

Thus far we seem to be on solid empirical ground in our search for the soul. We have found at the roots of our mental life deep springs of action in the form of native impulses, instincts, or propensities. They *well up* in our conscious life, suffused with emotional tone, not merely as desires and appetites, but also as vague longings, aspirations, hopes, and ambitions; so that they become the springs of progress as well as the fountain of our love-life, our social life, our economic life. They are the power behind the throne in it all.

Before we go on to consider other elements of the mind, such as behavior, intelligence, memory, feeling, and perception, or to inquire about consciousness or personality, it may be well to delay a little longer upon these basal elements, to see what their connection is, forward and backward; that is, forward to their products in the complex self, and backward to their metaphysical sources. This, to be sure, would not be necessary, if our goal were simply to find out what the mind is; for it would be sufficient to point out the actual presence of these deep impulsive strivings in that total thing we call the mind. Then we could go on to discuss the other elements, such as adaptive behavior, intelligence, and personality — and we should perhaps be able to say what the mind *is*. But a philosophy of mind must try to do more than this; it must try if possible to find the significance of impulse and striving in the evolutionary process, in animal life, in the whole world. It must even inquire whether all the later mental processes may not be *instruments* of these vital strivings.

The conative tendencies as cosmic agencies

In previous chapters when we were studying the origin and nature of life, the philosophy of evolution, and the purposive world, we discovered the presence in nature of some sort of agency which makes evolution *creative*. To this agency many names have been given by various philosophers, such as the *élan vital, the evolutionary urge, the life-force, the organizing power, a common creative agency, an internal perfecting principle*. Sometimes these terms were applied only to the world of organic beings — sometimes, as in the case of Henderson, the *drift* or *tendency* was carried farther back to inorganic matter. Here, of course, we are on speculative ground and no such *cosmic principles* are necessary to establish a philosophy of mind; but certainly it is very tempting to think of the creative forces of the mind as a part of, or related to, the creative forces of the world, and perhaps the driving forces, not only in evolutionary change, but in social and moral progress.

Bergson has developed this thought in his own way. He calls it *mind-energy*, or vital impetus. In one striking passage he says, "It is to social life that evolution leads, as though the need of it was felt from the beginning, or rather as though there were some original and essential *aspiration of life*, which could find full satisfaction only in society." [1]

I wonder whether this driving force of mind-energy is looking forward not only to society and history, but to intellect, reason, personality, individuality, and freedom. We know that intelligence is creative; we see its creative power every day in art and literature, in science and invention, in commercial enterprise and business organization. Does it owe its creative power to the purposive energy which lies at the roots of all mental life? When we come to the study of intelligence and of adaptive behavior, we shall see that they depend upon the organization or integration of neural processes. If we are to explain these in this way, or explain attention and other higher mental processes as the "total integration of reaction-arcs," what is the integrating agency? In psychology now we do not speak primarily of mind; we speak of an organism which receives stimuli and reacts. Certain kinds of *activities* are now called mental. We think of the brain and the nervous system as instruments for more and more perfect adaptation to the environment. We know what they are instruments *for*, but what are they instruments *of*? Apparently of the biological interests, of "the energy-influences seething and bubbling in the organism."

Driving forces or aspirations

But now before we leave this part of the subject, a curious question comes up, a question that has confronted us in former chapters and will haunt us to the end, the question of *push* or *pull*. How

---

[1] *Mind-Energy.* Lectures and Essays. Translated by H. Wildon Carr, p. 33. The italics are mine.

shall we really interpret the biological interests? Shall we interpret
them as purposive energy, as driving force, or as cravings? The
phrase *driving force* is a telling phrase and fits in with the dynamic
philosophy of the day. It means the operation of a force working
from behind, and so we go back in a vain quest for the *initial* push,
and get no rest until we arbitrarily stop at some *original* creative
power, or God. The phrase *purposive energy* seems a little better.
It has the forward look — suggests the quest, the search, the striving; and yet I wonder whether the word *energy* is the word we want
here. If the world is an overflowing, outpouring, productive process
endlessly creative of new values in the pragmatic sense, then the
phrase is correctly descriptive of the reality in question.

But it is just possible that the word *craving*, or the word *interest*,
is the best of all. Is God the creative power back of us, or the ideal
which is drawing us on? Are the higher values the outcome of a
productive process, or are they ideal limits which we are ever
approaching — the "beauty-in-itself," the "good-in-itself," which
Plato never tired of telling us about? Possibly the simplest organism is *interested* in self-maintenance and self-perpetuation, just because life itself is good; possibly we are interested in thinking and
reasoning and in aesthetic production and in social justice, just because thought and reason and beauty and justice are good — are
values; possibly our biological interests are forms of *hunger* — but
that kind of hunger which Bergson calls *aspiration*, which we may
call *creative effort*. It is perhaps only because of the habits of
thought acquired in an age of mechanism that the phrase *driving
force* seems more apt than the words *aspiration* or *appreciation*. Perhaps the power behind the throne in our mental life is "a power that
makes for righteousness."

This all seems very metaphysical for a chapter on the philosophy
of mind — and too speculative. Let the reader who so thinks forget
these paragraphs and go back to the biological interests, which are
obvious facts, and without which any philosophy of mind would be
fatally lacking, and then let him meditate upon the word *interest* and
formulate an explanation of his own. Perhaps the slightly different
way this whole matter is put by Hobhouse will have a stronger
appeal to most of us. He considers the world to be a process of de-

velopment in which the principle of development is the principle of rational harmony or love. But the whole of reality is the entire process, in which the beginning is determined by the end as well as the end by the beginning.

A process thus determining and determined by its own outcome is of the nature of Effort, and the world development must therefore fall under this category....

This Effort is the creator of gods and men, of beautiful fictions and of what is noble in fact, of law and morals, of science and art, perhaps of what is beautiful in nature, certainly of the significance of that beauty to us. Its operation is intelligent and purposive and all-embracing. An effort involving, even one evolving into, purpose implies Mind, and Mind that makes for harmony must have some unity throughout, however rudimentary its achievement. Hence if the world-process is directed towards harmony we legitimately infer a Mind at its centre, but the form of unity which such a Mind possesses is less easily determined. It is possible that personality on the one hand and the social union of personalities on the other are rather its creations than adequate expressions of its substantive essence.[1]

If this be true, then that part of the mind which we call *impulse* is related, not only to that which we call the *biological interests* in the whole organic kingdom, but related also at the same time to a world-principle which Hobhouse calls *Effort*; and then possibly, as he suggests in the last sentence, personality and human society are creations of this universal cosmic Effort. Personality, then, might be a kind of world *goal*, for the attaining of which the human brain and the intelligence springing therefrom might be instruments.

II. Mental Processes

But now we are ready to take our next step in the philosophy of mind. Let us keep steadily in view, however, that the mind is a very complex thing, inclusive not only of what we commonly call mental or intellectual processes, but also fundamental proclivities, interests, or impulses. These latter we have been studying; now let us go on to the distinctively mental processes sometimes included under the general term *intelligence*.

Here we could follow the method of the new schools, whose illuminating work in the philosophy of mind we have studied in the

[1] L. T. Hobhouse, *The Rational Good* (Geo. Allen and Unwin), pp. 229, 230.

preceding chapter — the Pragmatists, the Behaviorists, and the Neo-Realists. We could begin with the study of the organism possessing the properties of stimulus and response; and we could trace the evolution of mind from the simple reaction-arc through tropisms and instincts to the first appearance of adaptive behavior; and we could then show that this adaptive behavior is what we call *mental*. We could point out that what we mean by mind is a certain kind of behavior, namely, that which involves selective control and specific response; that mind is a certain new capacity which an organism acquires as the result of higher and higher integration of vital processes, the capacity to respond as a unit to a new situation in such a way as to conserve and enhance its well-being. Thus far this would be the general behaviorist method of approach; and then we could supplement this objective and impersonal approach by going on to show that what we call *behavior* and *mentality* in others is, when *lived through* or *experienced* by ourselves, what we call *consciousness* or *experience*.

All this would be quite proper and, provided we did not leave out of account that very important part of the mind which we have just been studying, namely, the vital impulsive strivings or springs of behavior, would give us no doubt a sound and scientific philosophy of mind. Then, indeed, if we wished, we could limit the narrower word *mind* to the second of these stages in psychical evolution — that is, to intelligence or adaptive behavior — and apply the richer word *soul* to the whole group of impulses, activities, and relations which we differentiate as impulses, intelligence, and consciousness.

But I think there is a better method of approach than this. It would seem to the reader to be too cold and theoretical and abstract; it would be too biological. When fully completed he might say, "This is all a very fine philosophy of mind, but it is not sufficiently empirical. A philosophy of mind ought to start with facts of more immediate experience, not necessarily with my own subjective experience, but with well-recognized forms of mental activity. It should start with thinking, feeling, willing, perceiving, remembering, reasoning — not with physiological things like reaction-arcs and synapses and adaptive behavior. People don't behave — they think and reason and remember and forget and love and hate."

The empirical approach

Very well, then, suppose we begin more empirically with well-known mental facts, and then afterwards, perhaps, we can connect our results with the less known physiological facts. Suppose we address a question like this to anyone, a college student, a business man, a worker in the shops: "Are there such things as mental processes, and if so, mention some." He will answer, "Why, yes, of course there are; there are such things as thinking, feeling, remembering, forgetting, loving, hating, having pain or pleasure." Obviously such things as these exist and may be talked about, just as stocks and bonds, butter and cheese, roads and lanes exist and may be talked about. So thinking and reasoning, recollecting and planning, liking and disliking exist, and, indeed, for the moment, it does not make any difference whether they are things or processes or relations or faculties or brain states or even secretions of the endocrine glands; they just exist and are very interesting. Neither does it make any great difference at present how we come to know them, whether by introspection or intuition or immediate feeling, or by just watching the behavior of other people; they exist just the same. They are real, and there is no other kind of reality so very real as these mental things. In the actual daily experience of men, the ultra-real things, so to speak, are not butter and cheese, wood and steel, dinners and dollars, but pleasures and pains, love and hate, fear and jealousy, desires, ambitions, decisions, passions, longings, regrets, sorrows and sins. Dollars would have no meaning were it not for desires.

We have, then, made a good beginning in the study of the philosophy of mind; we have found that certain processes, such as we have named, have a very real existence and may be talked about and studied, that by common consent they are an interesting class of things, that they are usually called mental things, and are distinguished from physical things, such as houses and furniture and animal bodies.

But what is there common to all these things, all these processes which we call mental? Well, objectively they appear to be forms of behavior of an organism, say an animal or person. They are all modes of reference of some subject to some object. They are attitudes of a subject toward some object. Some subject, perhaps just an organism, is striving toward some object; some animal, perhaps, is pursuing or escaping from some other animal. Or possibly some subject is pleased at something, or pained at something, or holds a cognitive attitude toward something — that is, knows it or recognizes it. In all of these three kinds of reference there is this common element, namely, the behavior of some subject to some object.[1]

Objectively, therefore, these things or processes which we call mental are forms of behavior, attitudes of men or women or children, or perhaps of the higher animals; and let us for the present consider them only in this objective way, simply as a class of evident and undeniable facts in the drama of human history as it is played before us, or in the evolution of animal life. Of course, it will immediately occur to each of us to say that all this *display* of mental behavior in the world around has quite a different aspect as it unfolds itself in one's own inner consciousness, in one's inner conscious life of experience, as one gets it through *introspection*. This is no doubt true, but suppose, just as an experiment, we leave this side of mental life out of account for the present. Let us see if it is possible to construct a philosophy of mind on a strictly objective basis, as we would construct a philosophy of nature. The Behaviorist, who disregards consciousness and suspects the method of introspection, studies mental facts as objectively known; let us follow his method for a while. He too speaks of habits, instincts, emotions, illusions, dreams, thought, memory, fear, fatigue, imitation, and personality.[2]

But the reader may interrupt at this point. "May it not be," he asks, "that, after all, these mental facts or processes of mind, whose reality, interest, and importance I must admit, are nothing more than bodily attitudes, brain states, functions of the cortex or motor centers, or conditioned reflexes?"

Well, even if they had only an objective reference as bodily attitudes and no inner meaning as parts of my personal life, these processes would still be realities and they would still be *mental* realities. If you think of the consequences in the history of the world of

[1] Compare John Laird, *Problems of the Self*, chap. II.
[2] Compare Watson's *Psychology from the Standpoint of a Behaviorist*, Index.

such things as love and hate, ambition, avarice, remorse, thought, invention, reasoning, you will see that we are dealing with real things; if you were to try to express them in physical terms you would feel that you were not giving them their real names.

Neither shall we get any nearer to the reality of the mental processes if we try to analyze them into simpler elements, such as mind-stuff, or the movements of atoms, molecules, or cells. Butter and cheese are very useful and desirable things. They do not lose any of their reality when it is discovered that they are combinations of carbon, oxygen, and hydrogen. Butter and cheese do not need to hang their heads when they discover their composite nature and say, "We thought we were realities of intrinsic worth and now we find that we are nothing but a function of carbon, oxygen, and hydrogen." In a case like this, the "nothing but" contains a fallacy. The chemical elements are not the *realities* in butter and cheese; they are merely the *materials*. The reality is in the *form*, in the *organization*, and in the qualities which are the outcome of the organization.

If this fact is fully grasped, it will forever free us from the fear of any materialistic degradation of our mental life coming from the study of its material conditions. The things of our mental life are not material things or processes; they are spiritual, as we shall see later. What we have to remember is that, if we wish to speak of *reality*, there is nothing that is or can be more real than our mental life. The notion that it could be *reduced* to something more real, such as matter, motion, mind-stuff, electrical charges, arises from a misapprehension. It is also due to a misunderstanding when mental processes are "explained" as functions of the body or brain, or re-action-arcs, or synapses, or endocrine glands. These are, no doubt, all real, and are useful elements of the situation, but, having helped us to complete the whole structural picture, they have served their purpose. They can take a back seat and keep quiet. They have been transcended. We have passed into the sphere of higher reality and greater worth.

In mind we are in the very presence of reality. All such theories as are presented in materialism, naturalism, atomism, or even in psychism, which try to go back to some greater reality than that of the mental fact, or to penetrate by analysis down to the elements of reality, are misleading. Aristotle, with his notion of the mind as the form of the body, and of reality as attained through a process of development from the union of form and matter, the latter being merely potential reality, gives us a more faithful philosophy.

Thus far we have learned at least one useful lesson. We have learned that mental processes, thoughts, feelings, fears, aspirations, pains, pleasures, decisions, cognitive states, are real things, abating nothing from reality, however much we wish to stress the word. This is no small achievement; for suppose that with some psychologists we regard the mind merely as the sum of mental processes, a convenient term to express the totality of mental life, we have at any rate made some progress in attaining a philosophy of mind.

And, indeed, it would seem that we have thus far made no unlawful assumptions, any more than any scientist makes assumptions in collecting his facts and materials. The most confirmed Behaviorist, as has been seen, uses the same terms in describing the facts that he is studying. Thought does not cease to be a powerful factor in the world's history merely because it is described as highly integrated bodily activity. That it is only integrated bodily activity is, as the Behaviorist freely admits,[1] an assumption. But if it be that, what of it? There would be no "degradation" or materialization of thought in so describing it. In introducing such concepts as vital activity, organization, structure, a high degree of integration, the Behaviorist is speaking of a new and wonderful set of realities, quite as "lofty" and as dignified as thought or emotion. Only it happens to be thought and emotion that we are speaking of.

Personality

But now another illuminating fact appears in the situation. Still clinging persistently to our objective method of study, let us consider what we mean by personality, the Self, the Ego. Mental life is not merely a stream of thought, not just a bundle of sensations, not a mere series additively grouped; but a wonderful unity, taking the form of personality. Here again comes something new, something of infinite dignity and worth — namely, the self, the man, the ego,

[1] Watson, *op. cit.*, p. 326.

the personality, the *soul*, if I may be permitted to use this tabooed word, a word the richness of whose connotation will perhaps bring it back when psychology has progressed beyond its awkward stage.

The following quotation from John Laird brings this great fact of the unity of the mind into clear relief:

> It is a truism that no study is more perplexing and, at the same time, more interesting to a man than the study of mankind and, in the end, of himself. Even if the pressure of the day's business leaves the average man but little time for self-reflection, he is still intensely interested in the personality of others, and the most obstinate questionings which beset him concern his soul and theirs. Moreover, the great objects of human interest affect personality and are tinged with personality. It is unnecessary to prove this statement by referring to the drama, the novel, history, biography. The thing is too obvious to require comment, and it is enough to illustrate it by mentioning a curious fact. Even those who in general have no great fondness for the study of biography are more keenly interested in the personal history of the great writers in literature than in their works, or, at any rate, are interested in a degree out of all proportion to the intrinsic interest of the careers of those authors. How else is it possible to explain the mass of literature and the years of discussion devoted to the shadowy author of the *Odyssey*, or to the stray hints which are all that is known of the career of Shakespeare? Nor is the reason very far to seek. As Samuel Butler says, "Every man's work, whether it be literature, or music, or pictures, or architecture, or anything else, is always a portrait of himself, and the more he tries to conceal himself the more clearly will his character appear in spite of him."... It may be a rare thing for the artist to be more interesting than the whole body of his work, but his character and career usually excite more attention than those of any one of his creations, and thus it is that the self is central among the things which touch the spirit of man.[1]

In speaking here of *personality*, we are using the word in its objective sense — just as we use it in daily life when speaking of other people. In using also the word *self*, or *ego*, or even the word *soul*, we are not implying the existence of any mysterious core of reality such as was formerly meant by soul or spirit. We are speaking of personality as we meet it in our everyday experience. Call it, if you please, after the language of the Behaviorists, the totality of "inher-

---

[1] John Laird, *Problems of the Self* (copyrighted by The Macmillan Company, reprinted by permission), pp. 1, 2.

ited and acquired reactions and their integrations," an individual's total assets and liabilities on the reaction side, or "the total mass of organized habits, the socialized and regulated instincts, the socialized and tempered emotions, and the combinations and interrelations among these." Or call it, after the manner of Mr. Laird, the organization of our mental processes. Whatever we call it, we all know that there is nothing else quite so *real* or quite so potent as personality. It is personality that counts in our social life, in our commercial life, in our college and university life, in our homes.

It was this obvious fact of the peculiar dominating power of personality and the peculiar unity and uniqueness of the Self, which led all through the centuries to the notion that the human personality consists of, or is grounded in, a kind of entity or substance called the soul; a simple, indivisible, and indestructible being. It was a substance in the sense of "an unchanging being which persists throughout the changes of experience."

The soul was thought of as *having* the experiences, as if it could think, feel, endeavor, act. This came partly, no doubt, from the felt need of picturing the unity and persistency and identity of the Self in some concrete manner after the analogy of physical things, like an atom or grain of sand. Such a soul could be "located" in a particular part of the brain, as was done by Descartes; and of course it was immortal, leaving the body at death. No doubt, too, this way of regarding the soul came partly from the influence of Aristotelian logic and metaphysics which emphasized the doctrine of substance. Everything is either substance or an attribute of substance, according to this view, and since thinking, feeling, endeavoring and acting are not substances they must be attributes of an underlying substance. To point out the errors and difficulties in this point of view would lead us too far afield. Suffice it to say that as regards the general problem of mind our new evolutionary way of thinking has changed this. Complexity rather than simplicity may be the ground of reality. Perhaps personality represents the acme of complexity and yet the perfection of reality.

There results what we call the *Self* or the *Ego*, a personality possessing unity, continuity, personal identity. The reality of the Self is found in the *connectedness* of its parts, not in the parts themselves.

A thing, says Windelband, is "always the connectedness of its properties, a synthetic unity, in virtue of which they are not merely
found together, but are necessarily interwoven. Thus we define
chemical substances as the molecular unity of atoms which do not
casually co-exist, but belong to this unity." [1]

Mind is what it does

But now perhaps we can take a further step. We may be able to
find out something more about the mind than that it is an organization of mental processes taking the form of personality. To do this
we shall find it more profitable to study not what the mind *is*, but
what it *does*. The old notion that you will penetrate into the heart
of something by analyzing it, picking it to pieces, dividing it into its
elements, is not fruitful in studying the mind. If we take the other
way and inquire what the mind's powers are, its capacities, then we
get forward in a remarkable degree. When we adopt this method
of studying the mind, we instantly discover that it has certain wonderful powers differentiating it from any other form of reality. The
first and most characteristic of these powers is the one already noticed, that of adaptive behavior. Wherever we see among organisms
the ability to exercise selective response, "to adapt action to requirements on the basis of experience," "to make adjustments to
novel features in a situation, adjustments not provided for by familiar ways of response," wherever organic habits are reconstructed to
meet conditions which would otherwise bring the life activity to a
halt, there we have mind. Mind is self-assertive, self-maintaining.
What it is to have a mind is stated by Woodbridge as follows:

Today the idea that "to have a mind" means "to act in a certain
way" has become a commonplace in psychology. To think has become an adventure and a real instrument in adaptation. Knowledge

---

[1] Wilhelm Windelband, *Introduction to Philosophy*. Translated by Joseph McCabe, p. 71.
It should be kept in mind that personality is a fact — a reality, an existing thing, even an
entity, if you please. (Compare the discussion of these terms in Spaulding's *The New Rationalism*, chap. XLIV.) Furthermore, it would appear from the keen analysis in Laird's *Problems
of the Self*, chaps. XII and XIII, that the soul is a "substance" after all; not, to be sure, in the
old physical sense of an unchanging core or substratum of reality, but in the modern sense of
an organization of psychical experiences. Probably the whole controversy about the soul
substance came from taking the word *substance* too seriously. Lotze, for instance, calls the
self (soul) a simple and indivisible substance, but says he uses the word innocently to designate
its unity. (*Metaphysics*, English translation, vol. II, pp. 173–74.)

has ceased to be regarded as simply the mental counterpart or image of an objective order, and knowing has become an active participation in the order of events. In other words, to be conscious of objects does not mean to possess their psychical equivalents, or imply a possible consciousness which might possess the equivalents of all objects whatever, and so be the perfect and complete representative of the world. It means rather to operate with objects effectively, to seek and avoid, to work changes — in short, to organize experience. This newer conception of mind has spread beyond psychology and markedly affected anthropology and sociology.[1]

Mind is, therefore, an activity, a power, a capacity, and in evolution it is a new power and a new capacity, crowning the whole evolutionary movement. It seems that the creative synthesis present in successive stages of the earth's history, from the purely mechanical to the chemical, thence to the organic, thence to the psychic, increases in a kind of geometrical progression, the creative power of the human mind knowing scarcely any limits. In mind nature reaches a higher level, issues in a new reality, in the description of which a new set of terms is necessary. Not only has mind the power of envisaging the future and then of controlling the present to realize the future, but it is also at home in the field of values; it creates these values, then overcomes all obstacles to realize them; its field is the field of science, philosophy, art, literature, and criticism. It surveys and criticizes the whole world process, including its own self; it not only studies itself, but it has power over itself, self-control and self-direction lying within its scope. It not only knows and studies the world, but dominates and controls it; the most powerful of the lower animals cower before it and become obedient. The forces of nature are likewise subservient to mind. It changes the direction of energy, subverting to its own ends every form of energy, molar, molecular, chemic, thermic, and electric, and by means of these transforming the face of nature and modifying its own environment, conquering soil and sea and air. It institutes great commercial and industrial enterprises, revealing a resourcefulness and inventiveness almost uncanny.

Not only does the mind have the power of dominion; it has the

---

[1] F. J. E. Woodbridge, article on "Pluralism," in Hastings's *Encyclopedia of Religion and Ethics*.

finer faculty of appreciation. It discovers something in nature which we call beauty and is silent before it; a pure and peculiar joy is felt in its presence. Could there be any more signal evidence of the power of mind to transcend the forces of the physical world than the subtle gift of appreciation? Nothing except the power to transcend nature in the production of beauty; and this mind does in the field of art. In morals, again, it visions higher ideals of conduct than any known before and controls itself to realize these ideals. Finally, in human society it proposes a program of co-operation, love, peace, and sympathy to take the place of the older rivalry and war.

These are some of the things that mind *does*. We seem to be in the presence of a peculiar and distinctive form of activity which we may call *spiritual*, if we do not use the word spiritual in any ghostly or metaphysical sense, but merely to signify that kind of activity which includes not only the intelligent, the emotional, and the voluntary, but also conveys the notion of the power of appreciation and the creation of the things of highest value. Hoernlé describes the mind as follows:

> What seems required is a concept of mind, not so much merely as a "cross-section" of the universe, but as a *focus*, or *centre*, of experiences of the universe — a "subject" (in Hegel's sense of the term), not a substance; a new power, one might almost say, evolved in the world, endowed with the function of bringing past experience to bear on the interpretation of present data, of planning and guiding action in proportion to knowledge, of controlling desire and seeking new truth, of enjoying beauty, of loving and hating, of serving and fighting, of co-operating with its fellows and of persecuting them, of ascending, in short, to all the heights and falling to all the depths which men and women know to lie within the compass of human nature.[1]

We have seen, then, what the mind *does*, and from our modern point of view to know what it does is to know what it *is*. It is an activity, a power, a capacity, a process, or an organization of processes, *and it is real because we see in our daily experience these things done*. That the mind is a dynamic and effective factor in the world is the key to the new philosophy of mind of the present time. We are not to suppose that the mind is something different from the

---

[1] R. F. Alfred Hoernlé, *Studies in Contemporary Metaphysics* (Harcourt, Brace and Company), pp. 242, 243.

activity, as if some mysterious thing or substance called mind or soul or spirit were acting, or as if the world were divided into two realms, mind and matter. This dualistic notion does not follow from the facts before us and is passing away in philosophy.

But strangely enough at first sight, it is not necessarily replaced by a monistic conception, as if one should say, "Oh, I see. There is no separate kind of being called mind; it is only matter in a highly organized form in the human brain that does all these things." It is hard for us to escape from these old scholastic habits of thought, seeking reality in some metaphysical basis or substance called *matter* or *spirit*. What we call *matter*, as the term is used in physics, is the last thing on earth which could have these capacities, if we could speak of matter as having capacity. Or, if we wish to substitute atoms or electrons for the word *matter*, the situation is no better. Atoms and electrons, if we wish to think of them as substances which can do things rather than as symbols for certain forms of activity, cannot think or plan or fashion ideals or exhibit adaptive behavior; nor does it have any intelligible meaning to say that the atoms when organized in the form of a brain can *do* these things. Things are being done, but the atoms are not doing them.

Neither does an idealistic form of monism help us to a right understanding here, although it might be preferable to a monism of a materialistic kind. To say that there is an underlying unity or entity or substance in the world called *mind* or *spirit*, whose manifestations we behold in ourselves and the surrounding world or whose attributes are thought, feeling, memory and will, is likewise to fall back into outworn scholastic habits of thought. *In the study of the mind, the reality is before us; we are in its presence. Our mental life is not the manifestation of some hidden reality; it is the reality. There is a unity, but it is not an underlying unity, a world-ground, a presupposition of all things; it is rather a unity achieved, a unity of organization, a unity of real psychical experiences.*

But now the reader may say, "I do not quite get my bearings yet. That mental processes exist, that they are organized into a unity which we call *personality*, that mind in this sense is creative, and that it further has the power of imagination and appreciation — all this is evident fact. The creative and original power of the mind is daily seen in science, in the mechanical arts, in literature, and in the fine arts. I have only to recall the creative work of Humboldt, Darwin, Shakespeare, Beethoven, Edison, Burbank, and countless other great minds. But still, I do not yet quite see what this creative mind *is*. It is not the brain; it is not a mysterious spiritual substance called the soul."

Mind the fruition of the body

Perhaps it will help us to understand this if we think of the mind as a new power or capacity which has arisen as the outcome of the structure and organization of simpler elements. Atoms are real, body is real; but so also is mind. The world may be looked upon as a process of creative evolution, in which higher and higher realities are progressively realized. It is a process of *realization* — perhaps, we may say, of progressive achievement. Aristotle had the right idea when he thought of the mind as the "form," or the realization, or the fruition, or perfection of the body. The body and the brain are stepping-stones to the higher reality, the mind. Evolution displays a series of *levels*; and the secret of the successive stages is found in organization. The word *integration* might be used. The important thing to observe here is that the organization of vital or neural processes takes us into the realm of the psychical. Creative synthesis is at work all along the line in evolution, and *novelties* appear at each new level.

The theory of levels we have studied in a former chapter when we were examining the nature and origin of life. Just as we saw there that atoms are combined into molecules, not additively, but organically, giving rise to new properties which could not be inferred from the properties of atoms, and molecules again into living cells, in which emerge the new and wonderful properties of growth and reproduction, so now we find that *mind* emerges from the organization of vital processes.

Mind as spirit

Once again nature has risen to a new level, to the level of the psychical, to the realm of mind. Psychical processes are not neural processes; they are new processes, having their own distinctive subject-matter and their own laws. We are now up in the realm of the mental, of the psychical — we may even say, of the spiritual. By spirit we mean mind appraised from the standpoint of value; and since I believe that in the successive levels up which nature climbs in evolution there is a successive increase in value, it is proper to speak of the higher realm as the spiritual. It would be permissible for anyone who wishes to carry this thought further to speak of still higher levels in evolution, namely, the moral and the social.

Thus it appears that from the standpoint of evolution mind is an *achievement*, a fruition, perhaps a goal. We have learned that mental processes are real; that they take a form of unity which we call *personality*; that they appear as new and distinct powers and capacities, the power of adaptive behavior, of creative work, and of aesthetic appreciation; and, finally, that they represent a stage in the progress of evolution distinguished by the achievement of mind.

Of course, the question will be asked whether we really have a right to use the word *achievement*. Would it not be better — at any rate safer — to be satisfied with the ground we have gained and speak of structure and organization and the new qualities and capacities which structure brings? This alone would furnish an adequate philosophy of mind; why go farther and speak of the mind as an achievement? The word *achievement* seems to imply both a goal and an agency striving toward the goal. Have we any assurance of either?

I suppose in strictness that we cannot be sure that we have a right to use the word *goal* in speaking of the place of mind in the great world program. This will depend upon how far we may wish to carry our teleological view of nature. But our philosophy of mind may be reasonably complete without this belief. We may be content to speak of mind as something realized in the process of evolution.

Let it be remembered, finally, that in this second section of the chapter we have been studying the mind in its narrower sense, as *intelligence*, as adaptive behavior, including what we commonly call *mental processes*, such as thinking, perceiving, remembering, and judging; and we have learned that this intelligence is creative, and that it takes the form of personality.

Let it be remembered, further, that the word *mind* is often used in a broader sense (where the word *soul* would be preferable) to include also those conative tendencies, or biological interests, which we studied in the earlier section, as well as that peculiar thing which we call *consciousness*, to be examined in the section to follow.

III. *Consciousness*

It remains to speak of consciousness — a word having many meanings often confusing to the student. Owing to this confusion many psychologists have dropped the word from the vocabulary of their science. In particular the Behaviorists, while not denying that consciousness exists, have been very successful in constructing a science of mind without any reference to consciousness at all. In the two preceding sections of this chapter, we have made little reference to consciousness and yet have arrived at a philosophy of mind as a new power developed in the world, a sum of remarkable capacities organized into a personal unity or self, and actuated by deep underlying impulses and interests.

Consciousness and mind distinguished

Nevertheless, we must make the attempt to find out what the word consciousness means. A behavioristic psychology may, indeed, ignore it; but a philosophy of mind dare not do this. In the first place, we must not use the word *consciousness* as synonymous with *mind*, although this has often been done. We might, of course, say that something called consciousness *accompanies all* mental states and processes, but even this is very questionable. The Freudians have developed a vital and widely accepted theory of mind, in which unconscious mental elements play an important part. Or take this example: We may witness fear and anger in a child; they are fear and anger — not consciousness. If you say that you are conscious of the child's anger, you mean nothing more than that you perceive it or are aware of it. The child himself may be conscious of his own anger; but if he is, the two are certainly not the same; and, indeed, he may not be conscious of it. Very likely he is not; he is just angry. Many animals exhibit fear and anger when it would be gratuitous to think of consciousness entering into the situation at all. Clearly, then, mind and consciousness are not the same.[1]

Neither can we think any longer of consciousness as being a kind of substance or primordial *stuff*, out of which mind is made, or out of which the world is made, nor can we think of it as an entity, or quality of being in itself.[2] Nor can we any longer think of it as a kind of receptacle *in* which ideas and other mental things are or exist. Nor have we any "right to conclude that consciousness constitutes a series of existences parallel to other existences."[3]

Consciousness as inner experience

Eliminating these various misconceptions of consciousness, what remains as the real meaning of the word? One very simple solution of the problem and one which at first sight, at any rate, seems to be satisfactory, is the view set forth in the preceding chapter, when discussing historical theories of mind, the view held by Warren and by many other psychologists. Adaptive behavior when witnessed in others we call *mind*; when *experienced* in ourselves, it is called *consciousness*. Conscious phenomena are merely mental phenomena as they appear subjectively in our own experience. There are two ways of observing mental phenomena — in others and in ourselves; in the latter case they form a group of conscious phenomena. It is simply another way of looking at the same facts — this introspective way; but a very important and instructive way, giving us a new world of inner experience. Strictly, it is not a new world, but the same world regarded from a different point of view, namely, that of inner experience. Consciousness is thus a kind of privacy — an intimate, inner, serious aspect of mental life only half revealed to the observation of others. Consciousness is thus

[1] Witness the rather strong language used by Bertrand Russell in his book, *The Analysis of Mind*, p. 40: "It is therefore natural to suppose that, whatever may be the correct definition of 'consciousness,' consciousness is not the essence of life or mind. In the following lectures, accordingly, this term will disappear until we have dealt with words, when it will re-emerge as mainly a trivial and unimportant outcome of linguistic habits."

[2] See James, "Does Consciousness Exist?" *Jour. of Phil., Psych., and Sci. Meth.*, vol. I, pp. 447–91.

[3] See F. J. E. Woodbridge, "The Nature of Consciousness," *Jour. of Phil., Psych., and Sci. Meth.*, vol. II, pp. 119–25.

experience as it is *lived through* by the one who is having the experience, the one who is thinking, feeling, wondering, longing.[1]

There seems to be no objection to the recognition of this meaning of the word *consciousness*, provided it is not interpreted in a metaphysical way as a kind of double-aspect theory, as if reality had two sides, a mental and a material side. There is no reason why a person should not observe his own mental processes, and associated with such observation there would be a wealth of memories and of organic feelings not accessible to others.

Consciousness as a relation

But, after all, I believe that the truth in this theory of consciousness can be explained better by a slightly different approach. The very simplest and most natural meaning of the word *consciousness* is just *awareness*, involving nothing more than a peculiar *relation* between the perceiving individual and the object perceived, characterized by attention and interest. Suppose you are sitting alone reading in a room. Suddenly you become conscious of the presence of another person in the room. Evidently all that is meant is that you become aware of him; you hear a slight sound, your attention is arrested, you interpret the source of the sound as a person. It seems to be just a perceptual process, which arouses and holds the attention. The unique quality of the experience is found neither in the mental content, the sound, nor in the interpretation of the sound as a person; but rather in the *relation* between the object perceived and the percipient subject. It is not a matter of perceiving or of judging; but just of being aware.

Let us take a still simpler illustration. You are sitting in a room where a clock is ticking; you are engaged intently upon some interesting task; you are not conscious of the clock. Suddenly, however, you become conscious of the clock ticking, which means simply that you become aware of it, your attention is drawn to it. Evidently this is the very simplest case of consciousness, involving nothing more than awareness. Again, let us say, that a deer browsing in the woods suddenly becomes *aware* (conscious) of a

[1] Compare S. Alexander, *Space, Time, and Deity*, vol. I, Introduction; and Wendell T. Bush, "An Empirical Definition of Consciousness," *Jour. of Phil., Psych., and Sci. Meth.*, vol. II, p. 561.

hunter. The deer just hears him, or smells him, then attends, then perhaps reacts violently to the situation. Here there would seem to be nothing in addition to the cognitive and motor aspects of the experience except a certain kind of relationship characterized by attention and interest.

We see, thus, that while consciousness in its simplest form is just awareness, it gradually takes on the relation of interest and meaning. The sleeping violet receives the first warm rays of the sun in spring and responds. Shall we say that the violet is aware of the warmth of the sun and is conscious of it? We are hardly justified in saying either. The deer is aware of the hunter's approach; shall we say that the deer is conscious of the hunter? Evidently *aware* is the better word here. But the reader in the room is *conscious* of the other person's presence. There is evidently here a relation of *meaning* in addition to the mere awareness.

Consciousness appears, thus, to be a special kind of relation between the percipient subject and the thing perceived. If this be the primary sense of the word *consciousness*, much of the mystery and confusion about it is removed. It is not a name for the whole mind; it is not the same as mind or soul; it is not any special kind of stuff. We cannot any longer speak of *the priority of consciousness*, or *the stream of consciousness*; perhaps not even of *the field of consciousness*. In all of these expressions we are talking about something else, namely, the mind, or mental acts, or mental processes. And yet *consciousness*, as I have described it, is a distinct feature of that total thing which we call the *mind* or *soul*, and is different from all the other parts of it which we have been studying. When we speak of mind in the narrower sense, we are concerned with some kind of *doing*. There is a situation to be dealt with; a problem to be solved; resistant material to be controlled; a conflict to be adjusted. To all these "doings," to the whole system of actions, habits of actions, of plans and projects, of memory images and motor tendencies, we may give the name *intelligence, mentality,* or *mind* in its restricted sense; and to the organization of all these actions and habits and memories and names, we may apply the term *personality* or *self*.

But *consciousness* is different from all these. It is more like an evanescent something throwing light on the momentary situation. Perhaps this light is simply the *meaning* which things get by being grouped in certain relations.[1]

Self-consciousness

Sometimes, however, we use the word *consciousness* in a broader sense than that of the relation of meaning and interest which subsists between the perceiving organism and the thing perceived. Sometimes we distinguish what we call *self-consciousness*; but the principles involved are not different in kind. Self-consciousness is still a relation — a *togetherness*; only now there comes into the new grouping a wealth of subjective elements, memories, names, interests, and conative tendencies.

Perhaps the difference between consciousness and self-consciousness may be illustrated in this way. When we take ether, or any anesthetic, we say that we lose consciousness. One's experiences in regaining consciousness after the anesthetic are instructive. There is first a mere awareness, perhaps of certain noises, possibly of the nurses speaking, not brought into any clearly defined relation with oneself or the situation. Gradually the situation dawns; *I* am here and have been asleep. The voices, myself, the environment, are knit together into a connected story; I have regained my consciousness. Clearly we have here two uses of the word *conscious*. In a way I was conscious of those first voices; I was aware of them — that is, I merely sensed them. In the other meaning of the word, consciousness is the connecting together of a present experience with my past experiences into a kind of coherent story. In the latter sense it is more than mere awareness, or any kind of response or behavior or adaptive reaction. It is something new in the progress of evolution, something unique and

---

[1] On the relational theory of consciousness, consult

James, "Does Consciousness Exist?" *Jour. of Phil., Psych., and Sci. Meth.*, vol. I, pp. 477–91.

McGilvary, "Experience as Pure and Consciousness as Meaning," *Jour. of Phil., Psych., and Sci. Meth.*, vol. VIII, pp. 511–25.

Woodbridge, "The Problem of Consciousness," *Studies in Phil. and Psych.*, by former students of G. E. Garman. 1906.

Woodbridge, "The Nature of Consciousness," *Jour. of Phil., Psych., and Sci. Meth.*, vol. II, pp. 119–25.

Montague, "The Relational Theory of Consciousness and Its Realistic Implications," *Jour. of Phil., Psych., and Sci. Meth.*, vol. II, pp. 309–16.

distinctively human. And yet to understand this unique character, it is perhaps not necessary to call it, as some have done, a "new dimension of reality."[1] Call it, perhaps, a new and unique form of relationship, a grouping of the complex elements of the self and the environment.

Certainly the philosophy of mind will be greatly simplified if this view of consciousness should be accepted. If we find difficulty in accepting it, perhaps this will be because of our long cherished habit of identifying consciousness with mind. But I believe that something will be gained if we place the greater emphasis upon thought and creative intelligence as constituting the very essence of mind, and reserve the word *consciousness* for that peculiar and significant relation, or togetherness, which sheds a new light and meaning upon our whole psychical life.[2]

Conclusion

In conclusion it seems that the mind is a complex thing, including, first, a group of conative tendencies or biological interests; second, a system of adaptive processes which we may call behavior (mind in the narrower sense); and, third, consciousness. It would conduce to clearness if we could use the word *soul* for mind in the broader sense to include the totality of dispositions, processes, and

The Soul (Mind in the wider sense)	I. The Conative Tendencies	Impulse Desire Will Wish Libido		Personality *The Self* *Ego*
	II. Mental Processes Intelligence (Mind in the narrower sense)	Thinking Judging Reasoning Remembering Feeling	Adaptive Behavior	
	III. Consciousness	Simple Awareness Self-Consciousness		

[1] Compare the full discussion in Spaulding's *The New Rationalism*, pp. 470–86.

[2] Compare the full theory of consciousness given by Bertrand Russell in his *Analysis of Mind*, already referred to, pp. 288 ff.

Read also the account of consciousness in Boodin's *A Realistic Universe*, chaps. VII and VIII.

relations, and reserve the word *mind* for the narrower group of processes included in adaptive behavior, the corresponding adjectives, *psychical* and *mental*, falling into their appropriate places. The table on page 289 will show graphically this philosophy of mind.

Immortality

The view of the soul as a value realized through the long progress of time has a peculiar significance for the old problem of the immortality of the soul. It has always been felt that the doctrine of immortality ascribes to the soul a peculiar worth and dignity. The soul, since it is deathless, is a thing of priceless value, having something of divinity and a peculiar sacredness. Such a belief could not fail to have ethical implications of great importance, sanctifying conduct through the expectation of an endless life.

But all this lofty philosophy rested upon a faith in the survival of the soul after death, and this again depended sometimes upon certain religious tenets, which in times of religious doubt would lose their convincing power. Hence there would be danger that the loss of that particular tenet of religious faith — one having, perhaps, little relation to the essentials of religion — would issue in the loss of moral ideals. While the hope of heavenly rewards and the fear of future punishments for wrong-doing may have actually less effect upon conduct than is sometimes assumed, still the sudden loss of a long-established faith of this kind would undoubtedly have some effect upon conduct and morality, with possibly serious social consequences, at any rate for a time.

It would seem, therefore, that any philosophy of mind which should establish the absolute worth and dignity of the soul without reference to the doctrine of survival would have a high ethical worth. Plato, in his beautiful dialogue called the *Phaedo*, attempted to establish the truth of immortality upon philosophic grounds. In many passages in his writings the immortality of the soul is hardly to be distinguished from its divinity. The extremely exalted position which Plato ascribes to the soul, with its vision of the absolute, its kinship with God, its longing for immortality, is what glorifies his philosophy of mind, rather than his tales about the soul's pre-existence and its wanderings in a life hereafter.

It would seem that the soul of man is an achievement, crowning the development of life which extends through hundreds of millions of years. We may believe that there was a primeval "interest" in just this final product, a primordial "effort" to attain to this "one far-off divine event." We cannot, to be sure, hope for direct or positive evidence for this view of the evolution of the soul; it must take its place as a theory with other theories in philosophy and science, in which as our knowledge is perfected our belief may become stronger or less strong. If it should ever happen that we cannot think of the soul as Nature's greatest achievement, must we not at any rate think of it as Nature's most perfect work? If there are, indeed, higher values, such as truth, justice, beauty, love, yet the soul in a way is greater than these, since it recognizes them as values and strives for them.

Thus the word *immortal*, which means that which has a beginning and no end, is hardly the word to use in speaking of the soul; nor the word *everlasting*, which means that which has neither beginning nor end. We seem to need some word suggesting ideal worth and enduring value. Possibly the word *eternal* might without too great violence be used in this sense — so that we could say of the soul that it is eternal.

In connection with this chapter read:

Ralph Barton Perry, *Present Philosophical Tendencies* (Longmans, Green and Company), chap. xii, "A Realistic Theory of Mind."

David R. Major, *An Introduction to Philosophy* (Doubleday, Doran and Company), chap. x, "On Immortality."

Further references:

John Laird, *Problems of the Self* (The Macmillan Company).

Bertrand Russell, *The Analysis of Mind* (George Allen and Unwin, Ltd.). *Philosophy*, parts i, ii (W. W. Norton and Company, Inc., 1927).

DeWitt H. Parker, *The Self and Nature* (Harvard University Press).

G. Watts Cunningham, *Problems of Philosophy, An Introductory Survey* (Henry Holt and Company), chap. xvi.

Edwin B. Holt, *The Freudian Wish* (Henry Holt and Company), chaps. i, ii.

Durant Drake, *Mind and Its Place in Nature* (The Macmillan Company).

F. J. E. Woodbridge, *The Realm of the Mind* (Columbia University Press).

William James, *Essays in Radical Empiricism* (Longmans, Green and Company), chap. i, "Does Consciousness Exist?"

Bernard Bosanquet, *The Value and Destiny of the Individual* (The Macmillan Company).

Josiah Royce, *The World and the Individual*, second series (The Macmillan Company), lectures VI, VII.

Boyd H. Bode, "Consciousness and Psychology," in *Creative Intelligence* (Henry Holt and Company).

C. S. Sherrington, *The Integrative Action of the Nervous System* (Charles Scribner's Sons).

Joseph Alexander Leighton, *Man and the Cosmos* (D. Appleton and Company), book IV.

J. M. E. McTaggart, *Human Immortality and Pre-existence* (Longmans, Green and Company).

G. T. W. Patrick, *What Is the Mind?* (The Macmillan Company).

CHAPTER XX

MIND AND BODY

THE mind-body problem is almost as old as the history of philosophy, but it did not become critical until the time of Descartes in the seventeenth century. Since then it has caused great anguish among both philosophers and psychologists and is one of the "seven world-riddles," which have been said to be incapable of solution.[1] The problem is, indeed, vexatious, but possibly may be greatly simplified if the view of the mind which we have developed in the last chapter, namely, as a value achieved in the process of creative evolution, should turn out to be true.

Historical

But first we must review the history of the problem and the several classical solutions. It will be recalled that Descartes made a hard and fast distinction between thought and extension, or mind and body. This rigorous separation had the great virtue of establishing a metaphysical basis for the then young quantitative natural sciences but it bequeathed a most perplexing problem to Descartes' successors, namely, the problem as to the relation of mind and body.

Descartes himself maintained that mind and body interact. There is, he said, a causal relation between the two. That they do interact seems to be a fact of daily or even momentary experience. Constantly the mind acts upon the body, initiating movements of the limbs, regulating them, inhibiting them, stilling the rapid beating of the heart, controlling the expression of the eyes, modulating the tones of the voice; even diseases of many kinds may be either caused or cured by mental suggestion. Equally evident, as it appears, is the action of the body on the mind. Coffee stimulates, tobacco soothes, alcohol stupefies, drugs narcotize, labor fatigues, indigestible foods cause fantastic dreams, secretions

[1] Émil du Bois-Reymond, *Ueber die Grenzen des Naturerkennens* and *Die Sieben Welträtsel*.

of the endocrine glands or the lack of them may result in strange psychoses; while even the simplest sensation is caused by the stimulation of some sensory nerve. But how does all this happen?

Probably a better question to ask would be: If Descartes is right, how *could* all this happen. On the Cartesian theory there are two distinct substances, thought and extension, and these substantial realities are two "closed" systems. That is to say, what happens in one system happens according to the laws of that system and we do not need to go outside the system in order to explain such happening. It was for such a point of view that Descartes argued so strenuously. He was primarily interested in saving a mechanical interpretation of the physical world from the "souls" and "qualities" of the medieval point of view. The physical system (i.e., the body, matter, or extension) is through and through mechanical. Every physical event has a physical cause and no laws are obeyed in the physical system other than mechanical ones. Granting this, how can we consistently affirm that a non-spatial thinking thing is located at the pineal gland and exercises effective control over the mechanical system of the body? How can a non-spatial thing have spatial location? Again, every physical cause issues in a physical effect so invariably that the quantity of motion (we would today say "energy") is constant — not more or less constant but absolutely constant. Not even an infinitesimal amount of energy can escape the great mechanical physical order. How, then, can we say that physical events cause mental events and mental events cause physical events? There are other difficulties with Descartes' attempt to solve the problem by a simple theory of interactionism. It has been held, for example, that it is inconceivable that two such utterly different and independent substances could interact. Evidently, then, so absolute an independence of mind and body is not compatible with the most obvious solution of the mind-body problem.

The desperate character of the problem was felt keenly by Descartes' immediate successors. Nicholas Malebranche (1638–1715), for example, was persuaded of the truth of Descartes' general position, but realized at the same time that a simple theory of interactionism could not solve the problem. He propounded a

theory known as Occasionalism, which was widely held in his day.
According to this theory mind and body do not interact, but the
action of either one is the "occasion" of divine interference to effect
the corresponding change in the other. I *will* to raise my arm;
God raises it. This, of course, is a veritable *deus ex machina*.
Closely related to Occasionalism, and hardly less extravagant, was
Leibniz's solution of the problem, namely, that of pre-established
harmony. That Monad which we call the mind does not act upon
those Monads which compose the body, but the apparent harmony
between them is a harmony pre-established from the beginning
by the perfection of the divine creation.

With the shifts of the scientific stage since Descartes' time,
interactionism has come to be looked upon as a possible solution
of the mind-body relation, having advocates at the present time
fully able to defend it. The theory still boldly affirms the duality
of mind and body in the human personality and declares that they
act upon each other. The difficulty so often urged against this
view arising from the law of conservation of energy is false, or it
may be that the energy expended by body in producing mental
events is so slight as to leave the physical system unaffected so far
as empirical observation is concerned. Nor is the other objection
final that it is inconceivable that two wholly unlike things, such as
mind and body, could interact at all. This is no more inconceivable
than is the fact that two bodies attract each other according to
the law of the inverse square. The trouble arises, not in the possibility of interaction, but in the probability of there being two things
to interact. It is possible to think in a wholly different way about
mind than as a substance in the body or as a series of processes
"parallel" with bodily process. Today we think rather of an
organism that *acts*, and of mind as the organization of certain distinctive kinds of activities peculiar to man and the higher animals.
Certain types of "action-systems" we call mental. Hence at present we do not need to labor over the problem of interaction; what
we have to do is to ask whether there is any necessity for interaction of any kind.

Next, we recall the various *Double-aspect Theories*, originated
by Spinoza and held in one form or another by many modern psy-

chologists. These attempt to get rid of the mind-body problem by denying that there are two realities at all, affirming that mind and body are merely two aspects or phases of the same reality.

Sometimes this is called the *Identity Hypothesis*,[1] since it denies the metaphysical duality of mind and body and affirms their identity. Closely associated with this view is that of *Psychophysical Parallelism*. The latter, however, as commonly held in psychology, is not strictly a theory of the relation of mind and body, but the mere assertion of the apparent fact of their invariable association. It is said that there is no psychosis without neurosis; that there are certain brain processes accompanying all psychical processes; that the latter are just as real as the former and the former just as real as the latter; but no causal connection between the two is assumed, the relation being one of mere concomitance in time.[2]

Now, of course, such a *mere* parallelism could be only a working basis for a psychologist who sees in mental processes a series of facts and in brain processes another series of facts, and who, being unable to understand the relation between them, is content merely to describe and study each series by itself and to note the association in time between them. But it is evident that, if there be such a parallelism, no one could doubt that there must be *some* explanation of this relation; so that any psychologist in his philosophical moods must refer the observed parallelism back either to interaction, or to pre-established harmony, or to the identity hypothesis, or to some materialistic or idealistic theory. Psychophysical parallelism, therefore, although we may refer to it for convenience under the double-aspect view, is really no theory of the mind-body problem at all; it merely sidesteps the difficulty. Spinoza's double-aspect theory itself, when examined, turns out to be a solution in words only, not in fact; for the duality remains just the same after calling mind and body two "attributes" of one substance, since Spinoza defines attribute as that which intellect sees in substance as constituting its essence. So there seems to be an "essential" difference between the two after all.

[1] See the clear statement in Höffding's *Outlines of Psychology*, pp. 64 ff.
[2] See McDougall's *Body and Mind*, p. 131.

Then there is a third possible solution of the mind-body problem, namely, that of the materialistic schools, sometimes called *Epiphenomenalism*. This attempts to get rid of the whole mind-body problem by changing the dualism into a monism and affirming that the body is the only reality in the case; what we call mind being an epiphenomenon, a kind of functionless attendant upon certain forms of cerebral activity — a sort of shadow thrown by the body. Its weakness does not lie so much in its denial of psychophysical dualism as in its denial of the *efficacy* of mind and in its claim that *reality* is found in certain *elementary* things, such as material atoms and their motions, and in its insistence upon the prerogative character of the two sciences, physics and chemistry.

Finally, we recall a fourth standard solution of the mind-body problem, which goes by the general name of *Idealism*, or, specifically, in this case, *Psychical Monism*. Like materialistic Monism it gets rid of the dualism of mind and body by denying the reality of one of the factors, but here it is the body whose reality is brought into question. Mind, or consciousness, is evidently something very real — indeed, the only reality in the world. The body is the mind's manifestation to other observers, a kind of externalization or phenomenon of mind. In this case the mind is the reality, and the body, the shadow.

The strength of this important theory rests upon the felt priority of the mind over the body. But we should have to distinguish between an epistemological priority, a priority of value, and a mere priority in time. It would seem to be only the second which would admit of logical defense. Hence the theory of Psychical Monism often takes the form of Panpsychism. Go back in time as far as you please to the simplest organism or to the molecule or atom. The "essence," the real stuff of things, is mind-stuff; what we call its physical aspect, its outer form, is just phenomenon or appearance.

However, it seems to me that Idealism gets its strongest support, not in the denial of the independent reality of the physical world, nor in the claim that the latter is mere appearance, but in its insistence on the significance and reality and transcendental value of the mental life when it appears. In other words, this idealistic solution of the mind-body problem is purchased at too great a price.   The physical organism may be a stepping-stone to the "higher" reality of mind, or it may be a sort of "obstruction" to the upward striving of spiritual powers, but at all events it is something wholly real.

If, then, each of the four of the classical "solutions" of the mind-body problem presents almost insuperable difficulties, shall we just make our "ignoramus" or even our "ignorabimus" confession and resign the search, taking refuge in a kind of agnosticism?   Such resignation would not harmonize with the spirit of philosophy; we must continue the search.

The Emergent Theory

Lately a new view of the mind-body relation has been proposed, called the *Emergent Theory*, which is at least an interesting venture. It is closely associated with Aristotle's doctrine that mind is the realization or fruition of the body.   If we may accept this view, it is with a decided feeling of relief or even of emancipation that we discover that the new conception of mind sets us free from all the old so-called "solutions" of the mind-body problem, from Inter-actionism, from Parallelism, from Epiphenomenalism, from the Double-aspect Theory, from Subjectivism, and from Materialism; all these "isms" would be superseded.   So also would be the Ex-pression Theory and the Transmission Theory.[1]

Mind and body do not interact, as Interactionism and Dualism teach.   The mind is not a form of the mechanical interplay of atoms, as Materialism teaches.   The body is not a phenomenon

---

[1] James thought it might be possible that the whole world may be a "mere surface-veil of phenomena hiding and keeping back the world of genuine realities," and that this opaque veil might at certain times and places become thin and transparent, letting through gleams from the world of higher reality.   Then let it be assumed that the human brain is such a thin and half-transparent place in the veil.   In that case the life of souls might reveal itself through the human brain, which thus transmits messages, so to speak, from the world of spirit.   Some-thing like this was James' transmission theory, which I think he put forward only as a possi-bility worthy of further consideration.   See his *Human Immortality*, pp. 15 ff.

Bergson's theory is somewhat similar.   He regards mind or consciousness as a real inde-pendent form of being, the consciousness of each individual forming a part of a vast cosmic sea of consciousness, focused, as it were, in individual organisms and having its individuality determined by the form of the physical organization.   The brain is thus a mechanism trans-mitting something of this cosmic conscious stream and making it effective in the world of matter.

For the Expression Theory of the relation of mind and body, see DeWitt H. Parker, *The Self and Nature*, chap. IV, "The Relation between Mind and Body."

or appearance or externalization of mind, as Idealism teaches. Mind and body are not parallel, as Psychophysical Parallelism teaches. Neither are they two sides or aspects of the same reality, as the Double-aspect Theory teaches. You cannot represent the relation of mind and body by any system of parallel lines, whether merely parallel, interconnected, or correlated with a third line, nor by two lines one of which is the shadow of the other. Mind is something which the body achieves, or which nature achieves by means of the body. If you must have a diagram, the ladder will be better than the parallel bars. When nature achieves the molecule, the atom ceases to be the thing of primary importance, worth, or reality. When nature achieves the cell, the molecule is eclipsed. When the organism is achieved, the cell is eclipsed. When mind is achieved, the body is eclipsed. Mind is a new reality, gained, achieved, won; it is, in Aristotelian phrase, the form of the body.

Evidently, if we want a name for this new notion of the relation of mind to body, we may call it the *Emergent Theory*.[1] Mind emerges from the body. The theory of levels would take the place of Parallelism, Interactionism, and the Double-aspect view. It is hard to say which of these theories is the most unsatisfactory, and the escape from them would be wholesome. All the dualistic theories are unconvincing. There is no magic about the number two. Nature having achieved two, goes on to three and four. Pluralistic world views seem here to be more promising; mind is real, body is real, and so are many other things.

But, some reader will say, the mind-body problem cannot be disposed of so easily — in this high-handed manner. Mental processes seem to be correlated with bodily processes. With every mental image, every sensation or perception, some neural process is correlated. In answer to this it may be said that, according to the Emergent Theory, there *is* no correlation, there is no parallelism, there is no double-aspect. It is rather a case of different levels of reality. What we really have is a series of vital processes, which, when integrated or organized, exhibit capacities that we call *men-*

[1] S. Alexander, who has made the Emergent Theory familiar to us, says that Lloyd Morgan and George Henry Lewes had previously used the term. Compare his *Space, Time, and Deity*, vol. II, p. 14. Morgan, in his recent book, *Emergent Evolution*, has applied the principle of emergence to the whole evolutionary movement.

tal or *psychical*. When they reach the point of attaining to that kind of activity which we call *intelligent control*, we no longer speak of them as vital or neural processes, but as psychical; we are up on a new level, among new realities, in a new atmosphere, dealing with new things having their own laws and peculiarities. Mind has emerged from matter; the spiritual has emerged from the physical. After long centuries of misuse, the word *spirit* gains a definite and profitable meaning; it means the level of the psychical as viewed from the standpoint of value.

This solution of the mind-body problem seems too simple and easy to be true. There must be some hitch in it somewhere, else it would have been adopted long ago. It was, to be sure, accepted by Aristotle, but why was it ever given up?

There are at least two very powerful motives which could account for this. One is the religious motive and the other the scientific. The Church had always taught the doctrine of the immortality of the soul and, from the beginning, had been indoctrinated with Augustine's and Paul's separation of the spirit and the flesh. Except for the "active reason," Aristotle's doctrine of the soul as form or realization of the body involved its mortality and its disappearance with the disintegration of the body. Thus the influence of religious predilections was such as to disfavor Aristotle's doctrine of the soul. Again, the scientific motive, which operated so strongly in the case of Descartes, was one which attempted to free the "true" mechanical account of nature from teleology, animism, and qualities. It was Descartes' great mission to show the seventeenth-century man that matter is a substance real and complete, quite independently of all considerations of mind. On such a theory mind is not the "form" of body but something independent and apart.

Limitations of the Emergent Theory

In truth, however, the Emergent Theory does encounter some difficulties, and should not be accepted without careful inquiry. The first thing that we must notice is that the mind, as we have learned in the last chapter, is very complex, and includes more than that sum or organization of mental capacities which goes to make up either adaptive behavior or creative intelligence. If we

use the word *mind* in its narrower and simpler meaning as creative intelligence, I see no reason for refusing to adopt the Emergent Theory; it emancipates us from much mystery and confusion.
But what about that elusive thing we call *consciousness*, and what
about those primordial things which we call *conation, will, impulse,
instinct,* the springs of conduct and behavior?

I think all this goes to show that the old mind-body problem
was a kind of pseudo-problem. It considered the mind as a simple
spiritual essence or thing which had to be got into some kind of
definite relation to the body. Consciousness, for instance, is not an
entity standing over against the body which must find its relation
to the body; it is itself a relation between the perceiving organism
and the thing perceived, or in its higher form it is a complex relationship which makes a connected story of all the elements of our
mental life.

If, then, consciousness is to be kept distinct from thought, intelligence, and creative activity, and is to be defined in its simplest sense as *awareness,* and in its fuller sense as that peculiar
kind of relationship or *togetherness* among the various elements
of our experience which goes to make them a connected story,
then we see that it becomes rather meaningless to ask about the
connection between consciousness and the body. When we do
so, we are still thinking of consciousness in the old way as some
unitary or substantial thing which could interact with the body
or be parallel with it or be another aspect of it. This becomes
very clear when we take consciousness in its simplest form as *awareness.* Suppose we should say that the wild flower is in a rudimentary way "aware" of the sunshine toward which it bends? Would
it not then be a rather meaningless question to ask about the relation
of the awareness to the "body" of the flower? The awareness is
itself a relation of the flower to something else. Even the Emergent
Theory would not apply here, although we might say that consciousness, certainly in the higher sense of self-consciousness, is something
which *arises* in the course of evolution.

And then there is that third class of elements belonging to the
total thing which we call the mind, namely, the conative tendencies, or impulsive strivings, or biological interests — how are these

connected with the body? Here again we see how complicated, if not misleading, the mind-body problem is; and here again we see that it is better to look at it from the evolutionary point of view rather than from that of parallelism or interaction, or the double-aspect. The relationship here is evidently not the same as in the case of consciousness, nor is it the same as in the case of thought, behavior, and intelligence; for the conative tendencies are the profound springs of our mental life. Perhaps mind in the sense of intelligence is the *instrument* of these deep conative energies. The Pragmatists tell us that thought and intelligence are instrumental; they are instruments for environmental control; they enable an organism to deal with a new and perplexing situation. But who or what is it that is using intelligence as an instrument for control? Evidently it is the biological interests that are served in this way. It would be possible therefore to think of the brain, and indeed also the muscles and bones and many other parts of the body, as well as the peculiar mental powers which emerge from all this organization, as the instruments of the biological interests. In that case a new form of the instrumental theory would appear as the solution of that part of the mind-body problem relating to the conative tendencies or the biological interests.

To be sure, those who prefer a naturalistic or materialistic interpretation of everything would, no doubt, prefer to say that the vital strivings, the conative tendencies, emerge as a result of organization of simple physical and chemical elements. But our present state of knowledge does not permit us to hold that the conative tendencies emerge from the organization of material units. The reverse seems to be more probable, as we have seen in the fuller discussion in the preceding chapter. If there is anything that we *must* think of as original and primitive and primordial in the world, it would seem to be something which we may call *effort* or *impulse*, rather than *matter* or *body*. Bergson believes that inert matter represents the inversion or interruption of life, reality having its form in the original impetus, "the internal push that has carried life, by more and more complex forms, to higher and higher destinies." [1]

[1] *Creative Evolution*, p. 103.

In connection with this chapter read:

Durant Drake, *Invitation to Philosophy* (Houghton Mifflin Company), chap. XXI.

Friedrich Paulsen, *Introduction to Philosophy* (Henry Holt and Company), pp. 128-44.

Further references:

S. Alexander, *Space, Time, and Deity* (The Macmillan Company), vol. II, book III, chap. I.

E. G. Spaulding, *What Am I?* (Charles Scribner's Sons, 1928), lecture I.

William McDougall, *Body and Mind* (Methuen and Company).

Morton Prince, *The Nature of Mind and Human Automatism* (J. B. Lippincott Company).

J. B. Pratt, *Matter and Spirit* (The Macmillan Company).

C. D. Broad, *The Mind and Its Place in Nature* (Harcourt, Brace and Company).

G. Watts Cunningham, *Problems of Philosophy. An Introductory Survey* (Henry Holt and Company), chap. XVII.

R. W. Sellars, *Evolutionary Naturalism* (The Open Court Publishing Company), chap. XIV. *The Essentials of Philosophy* (The Macmillan Company), chap. XXII.

C. A. Strong, *Why the Mind Has a Body* (The Macmillan Company).

Descartes, *Meditations.* Especially I to IV.

Spinoza, *Ethics*, book I.

CHAPTER XXI

FREEDOM

A NEW and unique interest has now centered on the ancient controversy over the freedom of the will, owing to the discovery of the Principle of Uncertainty in the field of modern physics. This has led some to suppose that science itself, popularly believed to be the foe of any kind of indeterminism, has gone into reverse and acknowledged a certain kind of freedom even in the world of physical reality. Later in this chapter we shall inquire how far such an interpretation of the Principle of Uncertainty is justified. Furthermore, an unusual interest in this subject had already been aroused by the outspoken stand taken by Bergson and James as regards the freedom of the will. We shall reserve this also for later consideration, meanwhile trying to remove some of the obscurity which has unnecessarily attached to the problem. Is it a problem or a puzzle? Someone has said that the difference between a puzzle and a problem is that the latter yields to reflective thought. Will reflective thought unravel the difficulties of this old problem? Possibly a careful definition of terms would remove part of the trouble.

What is it to be free?

In its simplest meaning *freedom* refers to the absence of compulsion or restraint or constraint by any external power. The slave is not free because other men constrain him. A caged lion is not free because the bars restrain him. The lion released from his cage and back in his jungle is free to live out the life of his kind, and this is what freedom means for him. The emancipated slave, with the privilege of mingling on equal terms with other men, of working for himself, of cultivating his own land, and disposing of the products of his labor as he sees fit, is free.

Of freedom in this sense the man and the woman of the twentieth century have a large measure. Unenslaved, unfettered, and unrestrained, they are free to work out their desired ends. Our government is founded on the principle of individual freedom. Successively we have sought and gained emancipation of the individual from autocratic government, emancipation of the negro from slavery, emancipation of women from inequalities of sex, emancipation of men and women from foolish restrictive traditions and conventions, and are now demanding and getting emancipation of labor from capitalistic oppression and freedom for the unemployed to work. One wonders sometimes whether our mania for freedom may not blind us to the necessity for wholesome discipline. At any rate, we seem to have in these modern days all the freedom that we can safely use — perhaps more.

Determinism

But, you reply, in the free-will discussion this is not what we mean by freedom. The question is whether a person's actions are free in the sense that they are not necessitated, determined, made certain and predictable by antecedent factors in the total situation. Are not human actions, like everything else in nature, under the reign of natural law, which rigidly determines whatever happens in the world, including human behavior? Are we not all caught in the clutches of the law of cause and effect, so that every act of ours is caused by some preceding event or condition? Can the human will escape the chains of mechanism which prevail throughout nature?

This is the familiar argument of the determinist. Human acts like all other events in nature obey nature's laws. They are strictly deducible from other antecedent events. All transitions are *necessary* transitions. It would be impossible to conceive of an event, even a human act of choice, as being *uncaused*. Human volitions are strictly determined by preceding volitions, by acquired habits, traditions, customs, and education. An all-seeing eye could predict with absolute certainty the motives, actions, and behavior of an animal or man. A man's character is determined by his heredity, his social environment, his circumstances, and his education. The feeling of freedom is an illusion, arising from the fact that we are unconscious of the causes which determine our conduct. Statistics also show that human acts are quite uniform and to an outside observer have all the earmarks of determined quantities. Marriage, divorce, and suicides vary rather uniformly with economic, social, and moral conditions.

This line of reasoning seems very impressive. In the closing years of the nineteenth century it found general acceptance — especially among those who had grown accustomed to hold the physical sciences in a certain veneration. The advent of Darwinism greatly strengthened the position of the determinist. Man is not above nature, but a mere product of it. His humble origin has been discovered. He is only a highly developed form of the simplest animal life. There is no break in nature — no place where its laws cease to operate. The leaves of the tree unfold in accordance with these laws. In the same way the child eats, sleeps, grows, thinks, and chooses, all in conformity with natural law. Thus, the theory known as *Determinism* came to be widely accepted, not only among physical scientists, but among moralists, sociologists, and even theologians. It was said that there is nothing in determinism in any way repulsive either to morals or religion. It is consistent with good conduct, good citizenship, and human responsibility. Evil would still be evil and good would still be good, and we should be responsible for our conduct just the same. It would be useless for the offender to go before the judge and say: "Do not punish me. I am not responsible for my actions; they are fatally determined for me by the laws of nature. My acts of will are determined by my motives." The judge would reply: "Very well, we will give you some new motives for good behavior. Thirty days. Next case."

Jurisprudence and good government find nothing objectionable in determinism. Every man with average intelligence, who can understand the difference between right and wrong, who is capable of deliberation, and can weigh the worth to himself or to society of different courses of action, is held responsible for his deeds, and frankly recognizes his own responsibility. If his actions are determined by his former choices, by his appetites and passions, by his habits and traditions, these are all parts of himself, and so thus far his determination is self-determination; that is, it is freedom. Thus it has come about that determinism has been and still is accepted by many of the most careful, scholarly, and conservative

writers both in morals and in philosophy. A certain truth in the
position of the determinist, indeed, contains the only assurance
that education will be effective and character dependable.

For this is what we mean by dependability. We mean that a
man's education, his family and social traditions, his respect for
the laws of the state, and for the rules of honesty and integrity will
be powerful factors in the control of his conduct. We mean that
we can count on the man. We know what he will do. We can
trust him. Otherwise, character would count for nothing. If free-
will meant the absence of this kind of control, no one would wish
to have it; certainly no one would wish his child or his friend to have
it. In time of need your friend might or might not come to your
aid. Your trusted clerk might or might not turn over the proceeds
of a sale. Your mother might or might not minister to you in sickness. Commercial insurance of bank clerks would be at an end.
Chaos would rule in society and caprice in personal conduct.

Thus the theory of determinism seems to hold its ground against
all comers. There appears to be no escape from its rigid conclusions.
Of course, the free-willist, striving to retain his belief in freedom,
will reply: "It is true that a person is influenced in his choices by
his education, his traditions, and by social customs; but he is not
determined by them. He weighs and deliberates, of course; but
when he chooses, his choice is free. He is conscious of his own freedom. At the very least he can freely turn his *attention* to a given
course of action, and attention, as is known, is the precursor of
actual volition — and attention is free." But the determinist replies that attention, like any other mental process, flows inevitably
from its antecedent mental processes, being linked thereto with the
fatal linkage of causality.

Weaknesses in the logical basis of determinism

Nevertheless, the case for determinism is not so clear as might
appear from the usual popular statements of it. The argument
as set forth above is full of loose generalizations, which the careful student of science would hesitate to endorse. One should not
take *too* seriously such expressions as the *reign of law* and *causal
necessity*. The laws of nature do not "reign" and they do not

"determine" anything. They are not compelling forces, nor *forces* of any kind. They are simply formulae summarizing a certain amount of experience concerning uniformities in nature. Science knows nothing of *necessity*, or *absolute certainty*, in the behavior of phenomena — only uniformity. When certain sequences are uniformly observed in nature, there is a reasonable expectation that the given antecedents, when they occur again, will be followed by the given consequents, but there is no necessity in the case. There seems to be sufficient uniformity in nature to enable us to predict the future with a high degree of probability at the level of the mechanical sciences, with varying degrees of certainty in the organic sciences, and with some degree of certainty in human affairs.

A more careful analysis of the notion of cause — such, for instance, as that made by Bertrand Russell — shows that we must get rid of any element of *compulsion* in it, and that the uniformity found in nature is in nowise inconsistent with freedom.

> Freedom, in short, in any valuable sense, demands only that our volitions shall be, as they are, the result of our own desires, not of an outside force compelling us to will what we would rather not will. Everything else is confusion of thought, due to the feeling that knowledge *compels* the happening of what it knows when this is future, though it is at once obvious that knowledge has no such power in regard to the past. Free will, therefore, is true in the only form which is important; and the desire for other forms is a mere effect of insufficient analysis.[1]

Another method of approach

But now there is another way of approach to the whole subject of freedom, somewhat more biological and evolutionary. We have to ask the question whether there may not be in nature and in mind something which we may call *real spontaneity*. If so, it would not, of course, follow that every human volition is free; it would only follow that the possibility of real freedom exists. Evidences are accumulating which point to the presence of spontaneity rather than uniformity at certain stages of the evolutionary process. Nature seems to escape more and more from the mechanis-

[1] Bertrand Russell, *Scientific Method in Philosophy* (Open Court Publishing Company), p. 236.

tic treadmill and to blossom out into marvelous novelties, such as life and mind and morality and conscious co-operation. Organic life is characterized by a kind of behavior which the word *spontaneity* defines more accurately than the phrase *mechanical necessity*. At the organic level, factors enter upon the scene which we speak of as *interests*. The appetency, urgency, insurgency of life, its character of craving, desire, and striving, are no longer adequately described in the vocabulary of the physical sciences, where something like the mere impact of physical particles makes us think in terms of compulsion and necessity. Living organisms do not seem to be *driven* along, like the wings of a waterwheel by the blows of the water. They seem rather to be seeking something, needing something, desiring something. There is the forward, not the backward look. In organic nature the "conative bow is bent ever toward the future." The phraseology of determinism is drawn from the mechanical sciences and is only awkwardly adapted to a vital situation.

A recent writer calls attention to the fact that "at the autumnal climax of productivity in lakes, there may be to the square yard seven thousand millions of a well-known Diatom, *Melosira varians*, so that the water is like a living soup."

But in addition to the abundance of life — alike of individualities and of individuals — there is the quality of insurgence. Living creatures press up against all barriers; they fill every possible niche all the world over; they show that Nature abhors a vacuum. We find animals among the snow on Monte Rosa at a height of over ten thousand feet; we dredge them from the floor of the sea, from those great "deeps" of over six miles where Mount Everest would be much more than engulfed. It is hard to say what difficulties living creatures may not conquer or circumvent.... When we consider the filling of every niche, the finding of homes in extraordinary places, the mastery of difficult conditions, the plasticity that adjusts to out-of-the-way exigencies, the circumvention of space (as in migration), and the conquest of time (as in hibernation), we begin to get an impression of the insurgence of life. We see life persistent and intrusive — spreading everywhere, insinuating itself, adapting itself, resisting everything, defying everything, surviving everything! [1]

In fact, throughout the whole evolutionary movement Nature

[1] Quoted by permission from *The Outline of Science* (vol. III, p. 708), edited by J. Arthur Thomson (4 vols., New York: G. P. Putnam's Sons, 1922).

seems to be struggling to free itself from the mechanistic chains, trying like a growing child to acquire a will of its own. Evolution, as we have seen in a former chapter, has been described as a long struggle for freedom. When living organisms reach the stage represented by the human mind, vital interests become conscious. Behavior is deliberately adapted to the realization of definite ends. The human mind escapes from the control of circumstances — indeed, circumstances themselves are controlled in order to realize purposes. The value of different possible courses of conduct is *appraised*, and means are consciously *chosen* to gain the *higher* values. To a situation like this the old phraseology of determinism is still less adapted than to the situation represented by organic life in its lower stages. The language of freedom, while not wholly applicable, seems here more appropriate.

Indeed, it is just this spontaneity of nature which accounts for evolution itself. In organic evolution nature seems to get a new "thought" every little while, and syntheses take place from which new wonders emerge. Relations arise which do not seem to be well expressed by the phrase *cause and effect*; it seems more like a case of the emergence of new qualities. The new values do not seem to be "determined"; they seem to be "realized." The movements of a machine are determined. Supply oil and fuel, and mill-like the machine goes on until worn out. The language of determinism fits it perfectly; but such language is ill-adapted to describe the behavior of organisms, and is wholly inadequate to describe the conduct of intelligent beings. Here means and end take the place of cause and effect. In adaptive behavior the individual is engaged in controlling a hostile environment in order to meet a situation and attain a desired end. Incompatible factors in some perplexing situation issue in experimentation and successful adaptation. Future consequences are dynamic factors in the course of action. If we must choose between the words *free* and *determined* to describe such action, the word *free* is surely to be preferred.

It seems thus that the old dispute about freedom and determinism has become antiquated in this newer way of regarding the behavior of living organisms. Determinism is not disproved; it is simply transcended. Its language does not fit the situation. Neither are such words as *indeterminism* or *libertarianism* particularly happy. The word *freedom* is better, but it has been brought over from another realm of thought and is not just the word we want. Let the traditional Martian visitor come to earth and say to man: "Are you free?" "No!" would be the answer, "we are *hampered*." "Are all your movements controlled and determined?" "Nonsense, No! We are striving for certain ends and we are gaining them with difficulty, but on the whole we are successful."

Thus, in the end it comes about that as a simple description of the actual situation in respect to human conduct, while the language of freedom is inadequate, that of determinism is obsolete. We seem to need a new set of terms all around. It is probable that there would never have been any controversy over the freedom of the will had not confusion arisen about the question of moral responsibility. When theologians taught the doctrine of retributive rather than natural punishments (realizing as they did the heinousness of sin and its fearful consequences), they began to raise the question whether a person could be justly punished when his conduct is so intimately connected with circumstances of heredity, education, and environment. The answer to this should have been that punishments are not retributive, but natural or disciplinary. In this way, having discovered that people are in any case responsible for their conduct, the psychological problem of freedom could have been wholly disassociated from the moral problem; and then it would have been seen that terms such as *freedom* and *determinism* are not particularly happy ones in describing human conduct. What we have is a striving organism, subject to influences on every side, accepting or resisting them, threading its way through them, battling against them, pressing ever on.

The new philosophy of contingency

It was something of a shock to the complacent thought of the closing century, comfortably resigning itself to a philosophy of determinism, when James and Bergson came out bluntly in favor of freedom.[1] James startled his generation by his vigorous defense

---

[1] A clear account of these new studies may be found in Gertrude Carman Bussey's brief monograph entitled *Typical Recent Conceptions of Freedom*.

of freedom at a time when freedom seemed to conflict with every scientific canon. Why, he asks, should we stumble over a certain law of causality, if it contradicts an immediate fact of experience, such as our consciousness of freedom and the fact of regret for wrong-doing. The law of causality is "an altar to an unknown God." The world is not so closely and fatally articulated as determinism supposes. It is not a necessary presupposition "that those parts of the Universe already laid down absolutely appoint and decree what the other parts shall be." It is not certain that "the future has no ambiguous possibilities hidden in its womb." It may well be that possibilities are in excess of actualities and that the parts of the Universe have a certain amount of "loose play." There is room in the world, so James believes, for novelty, contingency, activity, and real freedom. There are discontinuities as well as continuities.

> Our sense of "freedom" supposes that some things at least are de-cided here and now, that the passing moment may contain some nov-elty, be an original starting-point of events, and not merely transmit a push from elsewhere. We imagine that in some respects at least the future may not be co-implicated with the past, but may be really adda-ble to it, and indeed addable in one shape *or* another, so that the next turn in events can at any given moment genuinely be ambiguous, i.e., possibly this, but also possibly that....
>
> To some extent the world *seems* genuinely additive: it may really be so. We cannot explain conceptually *how* genuine novelties can come; but if one did come we could experience *that* it came. We do, in fact, experience perceptual novelties all the while. Our perceptual experi-ence overlaps our conceptual reason: the *that* transcends the *why*. So the common-sense view of life, as something really dramatic, with work done, and things decided here and now, is acceptable to pluralism. "Free will" means nothing but real novelty; so pluralism accepts the notion of free will.[1]

The world is not quite so orderly, so continuous, so inert, so care-fully predetermined, so absolutely single, as we used to think. There is room in it even for irrelevances, and for real possibilities, real beginnings, real catastrophes, real decisions, and real regrets. It is, indeed, the fact of regret — genuine and lasting regret — which leads James unequivocally to espouse the cause of indeterminism.

[1] William James, *Some Problems of Philosophy* (Longmans, Green and Company), pp. 139–41.

What interest, zest, or excitement can there be in achieving the right way, unless we are enabled to feel that the wrong way is also a possible and a natural way — nay, more, a menacing and an imminent way? And what sense can there be in condemning ourselves for taking the wrong way, unless we need have done nothing of the sort, unless the right way was open to us as well? I cannot understand the willingness to act, no matter how we feel, without the belief that acts are really good and bad. I cannot understand the belief that an act is bad, without regret at its happening. I cannot understand regret without the admission of real, genuine possibilities in the world. Only *then* is it other than a mockery to feel, after we have failed to do our best, that an irreparable opportunity is gone from the universe, the loss of which it must forever after mourn.[1]

Even chance, if we insist on using the word, is preferable to destiny. The "frightful" associations connected with the word *chance* have prejudiced people against indeterminism as much as the eulogistic associations of the word *freedom* have prejudiced them in favor of it. James thus sounds the note of optimism and of possible victory. With his pluralistic and restless Universe, his real possibilities and real choices, his real good and real evil, he offers to many a gospel of hope and courage. To others, lovers of order and rationality and unity, his disorderly and chaotic Universe brings fear and dismay. As he frankly says, it is to some extent a matter of temperament. All that he wishes to show is that there is a place in the world for freedom, if for ethical or practical or purely empirical reasons one prefers this belief. James' pluralistic philosophy does not, of course, prove that human volitions are free, but only that the Universe is of such a kind that there is room in it for freedom,[2] so that if one believes in freedom he need not be frightened away by the too plausible arguments of the determinists.

James himself accepts freedom as a fact on ethical grounds and on the grounds of immediate experience. Hitherto we have been so zealous to show the logical coherence of the world that we have forgotten that it must also have moral coherence. The moral struggle must be a genuine one, not a sham; and it could not be genuine without the postulate of freedom. It was James' peculiar

---

[1] William James, *The Will to Believe* (Longmans, Green and Company), pp. 175 and 176.
[2] See good discussion in Perry's *Present Tendencies in Philosophy*, chap. XI, secs. 5, 6, and 7.

mission to try to do justice to facts of all kinds from all departments of life and experience.

His knowledge and appreciation of human nature were such as to make it impossible for him ever to assent to the view that all human experience is describable in terms of the motion of molecules. His moral vigor, moreover, led him to demand the recognition of the genuineness of human struggle. Again and again he insisted that life loses its dramatic quality and its significance if human activity has no part to play here and now in the destiny of the universe.[1]

Bergson's view

Bergson, like James, accepts unreservedly the freedom of the will, but now, in place of James' fearless and sometimes perhaps a little reckless affirmation of contingency in the world at large, we have a carefully reasoned philosophy of contingency. Freedom is involved in the very structure of reality from Bergson's point of view. The fundamental reality of the world is a "psychical life unfolding beneath the symbols which conceal it"; and *time* is the very stuff that this psychic life is made of. Time, therefore, in the sense of *duration*, is something very real to Bergson, in fact the reality of all realities; and "duration means invention, the creation of forms, the continual elaboration of the absolutely new." Freedom, therefore, is the very essence of the psychical life. Life itself *is* freedom, spontaneity, change, creation. The law of causality, which depends upon uniform sequences, can have no application here where there are no repetitions, where creative activity is ever at work, and where there can be no uniform sequences.

When we once come to understand the nature of life and mind, the old puzzle about freedom disappears; for we see that the future is not something to be *chosen*, but something to be created. What we have is not a choice of alternatives, but a changing, growing Self. The real world to Bergson is not the geometrized and spatialized world known to the intellect, but the world of duration, consciousness, mind-energy, growth, change, and primeval impulse seen in intuition. In these profound and original depths of reality there can be no question of compulsion — only of impulsion. Here is *free creative activity*. Matter, indeed, is a kind of *obstruction* to the

[1] Gertrude Carman Bussey, *Typical Recent Conceptions of Freedom* (Morey), p. 29.

original creative activity. But it does not seek to impose its laws upon this activity; it has no such power. "Consciousness appears as a force seeking to insert itself in matter in order to get possession of it and turn it to its profit."

> Consciousness and matter appear to us, then, as radically different forms of existence, even as antagonistic forms, which have to find a *modus vivendi*. Matter is necessity, consciousness is freedom; but though diametrically opposed to one another, life has found the way of reconciling them. This is precisely what life is — freedom inserting itself within necessity, turning it to its profit. Life would be an impossibility were the determinism of matter so absolute as to admit no relaxation.[1]...
> I see in the whole evolution of life on our planet a crossing of matter by a creative consciousness, an effort to set free, by force of ingenuity and invention, something which in the animal still remains imprisoned and is only finally released when we reach man.[1]

With such a philosophy as this the old problem of freedom and determination presents little difficulty; life and freedom are almost synonymous.

> When we put back our being into our will, and our will itself into the impulsion it prolongs, we understand, we feel, that reality is a perpetual growth, a creation pursued without end. Our will already performs this miracle. Every human work in which there is invention, every voluntary act in which there is freedom, every movement of an organism that manifests spontaneity, brings something new into the world.[2]

Hence we see again how the old discussions have confused the issue. It is not a question of freedom and determinism, but a question of freedom and *incumbrances*. The primeval impetus, the *élan vital*, may meet with defeat, but defeat is not determination. No one claims that life may not sometimes be enslaved, that even man may not sometimes be enslaved. Too often just this has happened. But the free spirit of man still lives and slowly overcomes its conquerors, emerges as a victor, and expresses itself in art, philosophy, and science, and in free political institutions. Bergson states it somewhat differently:

[1] Henri Bergson, *Mind-Energy, Lectures and Essays*. Translated by H. Wildon Carr (Henry Holt and Company), pp. 17–18, 23.

[2] *Creative Evolution* (Henry Holt and Company), p. 239.

Radical therefore, also, is the difference between animal conscious-ness, even the most intelligent, and human consciousness. For con-sciousness corresponds exactly to the living being's power of choice; it is co-extensive with the fringe of possible action that surrounds the real action: consciousness is synonymous with invention and with freedom. Now, in the animal, invention is never anything but a variation on the theme of routine. Shut up in the habits of the species, it succeeds, no doubt, in enlarging them by its individual initiative; but it escapes automatism only for an instant, for just the time to create a new autom-atism. The gates of its prison close as soon as they are opened; by pulling at its chain it succeeds only in stretching it. With man, con-sciousness breaks the chain. In man, and in man alone, it sets itself free....

Our brain, our society, and our language are only the external and various signs of one and the same internal superiority. They tell, each after its manner, the unique, exceptional success which life has won at a given moment of its evolution. They express the difference of kind, and not only of degree, which separates man from the rest of the animal world. They let us guess that, while at the end of the vast spring-board from which life has taken its leap, all the others have stepped down, finding the cord stretched too high, man alone has cleared the obstacle.[1]

Freedom, the secret of progress

It should not be inferred that James and Bergson are alone among modern thinkers in their affirmation of freedom. I have dwelt upon their views rather because of the prominence of these two men in the philosophy of the present, and because of the uniqueness of their positions.[2] In estimating the value of this new philosophy of contingency, it must be kept in mind that it relates to the theo-retical problem regarding the possibility of freedom, whether in organic evolution or in the conduct of men. It affirms just this possibility; it does not affirm that human actions are always or even usually lawless and capricious and unpredictable. The single instance of the influence of heredity on the behavior of individuals

[1] *Creative Evolution*, pp. 263–64 and 265. The reader will understand that Bergson is using the word *consciousness* in a different sense from that in which we have used it in the preceding chap-ters on the philosophy of mind. Bergson uses the word in its older and more popular meaning re-ferring to the impulsive, creative, and selective capacities of that total thing which we call the *mind*. It is more nearly what we should call the *will*.

[2] Innumerable modern writers have taken the position of freedom, while innumerable others have written on the side of determinism. One of the best presentations of the grounds for free-dom may be found in James Ward's *The Realm of Ends*, lectures XIII, XIV. Compare also the activistic philosophy of Eucken, Boyce Gibson, Boutroux, and F. C. S. Schiller.

would banish any such idea. The spirit of man certainly moves on earth ballasted with social customs and freighted with hereditary dispositions; but that it can with all this burden soar aloft is attested by the whole history of progress and even by the fact of evolution itself. Every advance in life, from the first bit of protoplasm all the long way up to human personality, seems to be a struggle to escape from mechanistic determinism and to blossom out at successive levels into new and marvelous forms and realities. In the Darwinian plan the new appears in the form of variations and mutations, and these furnish the materials for the advance of species. Even Darwin's "struggle for existence" implies freedom. Here the language of determinism seems almost grotesque. We can think of struggle as repressed or thwarted — but not "determined." Even Lucretius, after Democritus the extremist of ancient Materialists, gave to his primordial atoms a kind of spontaneity.

Terminology

In the whole discussion about the freedom of the will confusion sometimes arises because we do not understand just what is meant by the *will*. And with this comes a sense of irritation and a feeling that the whole question is one to be referred to the psychologist. But the psychologists have not helped us greatly here. Usually they ignore the subject. Often they dwell rightfully upon the direction given to our actions by our interests and desires and by our social customs and hereditary tendencies.[1]

But the psychologists make it clear, of course, that there is no special faculty or element which is called the *will*. It is merely a term which may be applied to all the "activities of control." The will is "the whole mind active." To avoid this confusion the worn-out expression *freedom of the will* should be replaced by some such expression as the *freedom of the self*, or of the person, or of the organism. Better still, would be the phrase *freedom of the soul* or *freedom of the mind*. Best of all, perhaps, as I have already hinted, would be the plan to drop the old terms and adopt a new language, as is done, for instance, in the following quotation from *one* psychologist:

[1] Compare, for instance, James Rowland Angell, *Psychology*, pp. 436–37.

That the human mind, in its highest flights, creates new things, thinks in ways that have never been thought before, seems undeniable in face of any of the great works of genius. Those who tell us that the mere shuffling of the letters of the alphabet in a dice-box will produce a great work of literary art, or even a single perfect verse, may be speaking literal truth, if we grant them the continuation of the process through unlimited time. But the striking peculiarity of the human race is that, in the last few thousand years, it has produced such things, created such novelties, over and over again.

If, then, the human mind is greatly creative in its highest forms and flights, how can we deny that it may be creative, in a small way, in the moral struggles of the common man? By a long series of such creative acts on the part of men both great and small, the moral tradition, the highest product of organic evolution, has been painfully and slowly evolved. Why should we doubt that organic evolution is a creative process and that Mind is the creative agency? We have no theory of organic evolution remotely adequate to the problem.[1]

In this brief chapter it has hardly seemed worth while to dwell on the controversial aspects of this old problem. Succinct statements of the various positions may be found in the books referred to at the end of the chapter and in the footnotes to the pages. The theory of determinism may be stated in such a way as to seem irrefutable. Those who love to dwell in a tidy, well-ordered, and unified world will prefer this philosophy — and they will be convinced that the law of causality applies to all material things, to all animal species, and to all human conduct; and they will define freedom as rational action or self-determination; and the feeling of freedom will be explained by our knowledge that some of the determining factors are within ourselves or products of our past decisions. Readers of this class will enjoy the scholarly treatment of the subject found in the writings of Bernard Bosanquet,[2] S. Alexander,[3] J. M. E. McTaggart,[4] and A. E. Taylor.[5]

Those, on the other hand, in whom the logical impulse is not quite so strong and the spirit of adventure stronger, those who love a wilder and more exhilarating world, a world offering hazards and

[1] William McDougall, *Outline of Psychology* (Charles Scribner's Sons), pp. 447-48.
[2] *The Principle of Individuality and Value*, lecture IX.
[3] *Space, Time, and Deity*, vol. II, chap. X.
[4] *Some Dogmas of Religion*, chap. V.
[5] *Elements of Metaphysics*, book IV, chap. IV.

opportunities for conquest and achievement, will prefer a philosophy with a more radical kind of freedom; such, for instance, as that proposed in the adventurous teachings of the Pragmatists, or in the ethical philosophy of the Personalists, or in the fearless doctrine of contingency presented by James and Bergson and Ward.

And yet philosophical problems are not to be settled by a question of temperament, as though determinism could be true for you and freedom for me. The goal of philosophy is objective truth, although in questions such as the one now before us this goal may be difficult to attain. And so I think that the problem of freedom is not a question of temperament but rather a question of securing a terminology fitted to the real character of the problem.

There is one suggestion made by Ward which seems fruitful. He also uses the terms *self-determination*, but the meaning he gives to it is something quite different from that which it usually bears. It is the kind of determination of a "determined" child, or a "determined" man. It is this which characterizes personality. It implies efficient causation, self-direction, and purpose. It considers the self to be a *personal agent* and the activity which proceeds from this self to be a kind of self-expression.[1] We have seen already some reasons for believing that the whole world movement, a part of which we speak of as evolution, is a kind of *self-expression*, as though the universal Self were trying to express itself and "determined" to do so.

The principle of indeterminacy

A remarkable new interest has lately been given to the ancient problem of the freedom of the will by the discovery of the principle of uncertainty, or the Heisenberg principle of indeterminacy, in the science of physics. As interpreted by some, this seems to show that science itself, whose deterministic theories of nature have always presented difficulty in accepting the freedom of the will, has gone into reverse and acknowledged a certain freedom in the realm of natural phenomena. But it is not so interpreted by all.

It is too early to say what the final effect of this new principle will be upon the free-will controversy. Eddington says that it is "a

[1] James Ward, *The Realm of Ends, or Pluralism and Theism*, pp. 277–78.

fundamental general principle which seems to rank in importance with the principle of relativity."[1] P. W. Bridgman says that he believes "it is fraught with the possibility of a greater change in mental attitude than was ever packed into an equal number of words."[2]

At first sight, this new principle seems to disturb the foundations of science itself, since from the beginning of scientific study of natural processes it has been assumed that nature is uniform, that the law of cause and effect is of universal validity, that the present is determined by the past, and that the future will be determined by the present.   Natural laws rule always and everywhere throughout the universe, so that predictability is always possible and reliable. If we know the position of a heavenly body and its velocity we can predict just where it will be at any time in the future.

But trouble has arisen respecting all these fundamental principles, and it has originated in the world of microphysics.   Notwithstanding the infinitesimal size of the atom, the physicist is quite at home in the study of its inner mechanism, which incidentally may turn out to be not a mechanism at all.   He finds the electron flashing with the speed of lightning around the nucleus.   He can measure its position, and, again, he can measure its velocity.   He sees no reason, therefore, why he should not determine its path and its position at any desired moment.   But he finds, after repeated experiments, that this cannot be done, and that the position of the particle cannot be determined in advance by any measurements which he can make.[3]

But the scientist is not disturbed by this failure.   He seeks and finds the explanation.   It is because the conditions under which either the position or velocity of these minute particles is determined are such that the measurements themselves exert a disturbing influence upon the particle.

Now the innocent bystander says, when this explanation is made, "I see nothing in this situation which indicates that the principle of determinism and the relation of cause and effect do not apply to the inner world of the atom.   I see only that the physicist cannot

---

[1] Sir Arthur Eddington, *The Nature of the Physical World* (The Macmillan Company), p. 220.
[2] P. W. Bridgman, "The New Vision of Science," *Harper's Magazine*, March, 1929.
[3] For a brief statement of the Principle of Uncertainty, see above, chapter XIV.

institute an experiment to show this. It is not the fault of the electron that the experimenter cannot measure simultaneously both its position and its velocity. There is nothing to show that the particle in its dizzy flight within the atom does not move in perfect obedience to the laws of nature as manifested by other bodies. There is no reason to think that the universality of the law of causality is violated in the sphere of the infinitely small.[1] And this, indeed, is the position taken by many physicists, notably by Max Planck himself, from whom I have quoted on this point in a previous chapter.

It turns out, however, that the matter cannot be so easily disposed of as this. While few scientists perhaps would go so far as to take a distinctly positivistic attitude, nevertheless, it is becoming more and more evident that human measurements are and must be the final data for our knowledge of the external world. Of an unobserved electron we know nothing. It does not exist for us and therefore, so it is said, it does not exist in any intelligible sense. This has been clearly stated by Professor Bridgman from whom I quote:

> The meaning of the fact that it is impossible to measure exactly both the position and velocity of the electron may be paradoxically stated to be that an electron cannot have both position and velocity. The justification of this is to be found in the logical analysis of the meaning of our physical concepts which has been stimulated by the relativity theory of Einstein. On careful examination the physicist finds that in the sense in which he uses language no meaning at all can be attached to a physical concept which cannot ultimately be described in terms of some sort of measurement. A body has position only so far as its position can be measured; if its position cannot in principle be measured the concept of position applied to the body is meaningless, or in other words, a position of the body does not exist. Hence if both the position and velocity of the electron cannot in principle be measured, the electron cannot have both position and velocity; position and velocity as expressions of properties which an electron can simultaneously have are meaningless. To carry the paradox one step further, by choosing whether I shall measure the position or velocity of the electron, I thereby determine whether the electron has position or velocity. The physical properties of the electron are not absolutely inherent in it, but involve also the choice of the observer.[2]

[1] Cf. Hillis Kaiser, *Physical Causality in the Light of Recent Developments in Physical Theory* (doctoral dissertation, Harvard, 1934), pp. 165, 166.

[2] P. W. Bridgman, "The New Vision of Science," *Harper's Magazine*, March, 1929.

Thus it appears that in the world of the atom, *as it is known to us,* indeterminism exists. Of a world of reality beyond the sphere of our perceptions, it is said, science knows nothing — and therefore makes no claim there either of determinism or indeterminism. In the world of our perceptions indeterminism exists — and beyond this world of our perceptions we do not know that it does not exist. If, with Kant, we could believe that the human will is not a part of the phenomenal world but belongs to a noumenal world of being having a certain kind of deeper reality, the argument against freedom would seem to have lost its force. Probably modern psychology would not receive with favor such a theory of the will.

We are driven therefore to the conclusion that the final interpretation of the Principle of Uncertainty depends, as Lenzen says, upon one's philosophical attitude.[1]

The tough-minded realist will insist on the universal reign of determinism and the absolute validity of the law of causality, while the more tender-minded idealist or neo-positivist will welcome the new studies in physics as a vindication of some kind of freedom even in the world of physical reality; but I suppose that science itself is tending now toward a greater degree of tender-mindedness than was formerly suspected. On the whole it is probable that the total results of the new physics indicate a world less bound by mechanistic and deterministic chains than was formerly believed possible.

If, however, many of us cannot accept indeterminism in any sphere of physical reality, nevertheless it may be permitted to us to think of freedom as something realized step by step in creative evolution. I have referred often in these chapters to my belief in "formative forces struggling up to freedom." No description of these forces in the usual terminology of scientific determinism would be adequate.

In connection with this chapter read:

Durant Drake, *Invitation to Philosophy* (Houghton Mifflin Company), chap. XXII.

---

[1] V. F. Lenzen, "Indeterminism and the Concept of Physical Reality," *Jour. Phil.*, May 25, 1933.

Further references:

A. S. Eddington, *The Nature of the Physical World* (The Macmillan Company), chap. xiv.

W. G. Everett, *Moral Values* (Henry Holt and Company), chap. xii.

Gertrude Carman Bussey, *Typical Recent Conceptions of Freedom* (Press of T. Morey & Son, Greenfield, Mass.). Résumé of the views of Haeckel, James, Bergson, Ward, and Bosanquet on Freedom.

Friedrich Paulsen, *A System of Ethics* (Charles Scribner's Sons), book ii, chap. ix.

W. K. Wright, *A Student's Philosophy of Religion* (The Macmillan Company), chap. xxi.

William James, *The Will to Believe* (Longmans, Green and Company), "The Dilemma of Determinism," pp. 145–83.

H. Bergson, *Time and Free Will* (The Macmillan Company). See also his *Creative Evolution* (Henry Holt and Company), Index.

Josiah Royce, *The Spirit of Modern Philosophy* (Houghton Mifflin Company), lectures x–xiii. An appreciation of the freedom discovered in the higher idealism.

Ralph Barton Perry, *The Present Conflict of Ideals* (Longmans, Green and Company). See Index.

David Hume, *Essay on Liberty and Necessity.*

Bertrand Russell, *Our Knowledge of the External World* (*Scientific Method in Philosophy*) (The Open Court Publishing Company), chap. viii.

Henry Sturt, "The Problem of Freedom in its Relation to Psychology," in *Personal Idealism*, edited by Henry Sturt (The Macmillan Company).

Sir James Jeans, *The New Background of Science* (The Macmillan Company), Revised edition, chap. vii.

Max Planck, *Where Is Science Going?* (W. W. Norton and Company), chaps. iv and v.

C. D. Broad, *Determinism, Indeterminism and Libertarianism* (The Macmillan Company, 1934).

CHAPTER XXII

WHAT CAN WE KNOW?

INTRODUCTORY

Up to this point in our treatment of the general problems of philosophy we have adopted, somewhat, the method of the special sciences, taking for granted the reality of an external world as reported by the senses, and assuming the ability of the mind to know it and to think and reason about it. But now we must ask ourselves whether or not the human mind is capable of dealing with the difficult problems of philosophy. Does the human mind possess some "faculty," such as reason or intuition, by means of which we can go beyond the facts of experience and learn of the great world of reality beyond our experience, if there be such a world? Are we not limited in our knowledge to what our senses reveal and do they reveal *reality* itself or just *phenomena* or appearances? Are we, indeed, certain that there *is* any external world? May not the appearances revealed through our senses be merely the projection of our own minds — our ideas? At the very best, is our knowledge of the world anything more than a relative knowledge, depending upon the peculiar structure of our minds and bodies?

Such questions we cannot avoid any longer, and must, therefore, finally make an inquiry as to the sources and validity of human knowledge. In the history of thought much has been said concerning the problems of knowledge and it would be impossible to give an adequate history of the subject within the compass of a single chapter. Rather than attempt anything more than the briefest historical survey we will, in this first short chapter, indicate and describe succinctly some of the more important types of positions which have been held, and then in the two chapters following make a systematic effort to determine at least the general direction in which we would have to go in order to answer the questions as to the source and validity of that which we call knowledge.

Theories of knowledge

In the history of thought, "Theory of Knowledge" has been construed as that branch of philosophy which deals with problems concerning the origin, nature, validity, limits, and conditions of knowledge. All of these problems and their various aspects are reducible to two — the problem as to the source of knowledge and the problem as to its validity.

J. F. Ferrier, in his *Institutes of Metaphysics* (1854), called this general inquiry "Epistemology," a term which has been widely adopted since that time. "Epistemology" comes from the Greek words *episteme* meaning knowledge and *logos* meaning discourse or science. We shall then use the terms "epistemology" and "theory of knowledge" interchangeably.

Historical remarks

Epistemology probably made its first appearance in Western philosophy when the critical reflection of the Greek sophists brought the speculations of their predecessors into question. Conflicts among the early philosophical systems naturally raised the question as to what may be accepted as true knowledge. This, in turn, suggests the problem, what is knowledge? Socrates, Plato, and Aristotle dealt extensively with epistemological problems. Probably the finest ancient document on the subject is Plato's *Theaetetus*.

The general problems of the theory of knowledge were further entrenched in the tradition of Western philosophy through the criticisms of the sceptics, the most extreme of whom brought serious indictments against everything which had been or might be accepted as knowledge.

In the modern world John Locke, a most influential post-renaissance philosopher, makes epistemology the starting-point and center of philosophical discussion. In the *Epistle to the Reader*, in his famous *Essay Concerning Human Understanding*, Locke relates that when he was a young man he was discussing with five or six friends gathered in his chamber certain problems of philosophy. He says, "It came into my thoughts that we took a wrong course, and that, before we set ourselves upon inquiries of that nature, it was necessary to examine our own abilities, and see what objects our understandings were or were not fitted to deal with." In short, Locke felt that epistemological problems are prior to all others. This point of view profoundly influenced the course of European thought. The British thinkers following Locke, particularly Berkeley and Hume, subscribed to Locke's opinion on this point. Immanuel Kant, who stands as a sentinel between the eighteenth and nineteenth centuries, devoted his best philosophical efforts to the theory of knowledge and in this field exercised his greatest influence.

The continental thinkers of the seventeenth and eighteenth centuries did not treat epistemology as a prior subject to all further inquiry. These thinkers (particularly Descartes, Spinoza, Leibniz, and Wolff) were preoccupied with metaphysics and developed an epistemological doctrine incidentally. Their theory of knowledge is generally known as rationalism, which we shall discuss later.

In Kant the main currents of the empirical British tradition and continental rationalism converge and, as we have already pointed out, he again emphasizes the very fundamental character of epistemology. He felt as Locke did that it is wiser to find out what knowledge the human mind is capable of before attempting to solve such riddles as those concerning the soul, God, the origins of the world, and the like. To attempt a solution of such problems without first dealing with the questions raised by epistemology is like attempting to navigate on a wide ocean without a compass and without a knowledge of the stars and directions.

Theory of knowledge was variously treated by the many schools of philosophy which followed Kant. The German idealists held that epistemology was included in logic and metaphysics and was thus not a separate and prior discipline. On the other hand the many so-called "neo-Kantian" thinkers maintained the point of view that a critical examination of knowing should form the basis for all speculation. At the present time the problems of epistemology are looming large and many thinkers find that at the present stage of science we cannot well ignore them. In the new physics, for instance, scientists find themselves seriously involved in questions of epistemology.

Before proceeding to a systematic inquiry into the theory of knowledge we will mention and briefly characterize some of the more important types of positions which have been advanced in the history of thought. It is important that we have at least a bowing acquaintance with these points of view.

Authoritarianism

Authoritarianism is an unsatisfactory epistemological doctrine which we shall quickly dispose of. It is important for two reasons. First, it has been used in many periods of history, particularly those in which religious authority has been dominant. Second, we invoke this standard or doctrine quite frequently in the course of our everyday practical living.

Briefly, authoritarianism asserts that knowledge is guaranteed or validated by authority. Since man is naturally suggestible and is not in a position to verify all of his so-called "knowledge," it is not surprising that such a doctrine has been propounded.

It is held that there are certain criteria for determining sound authority. The ubiquity of an opinion, for example, is held to be such a criterion. If a great number of people hold to a doctrine, that doctrine is true. For example, our ordinary standards of morality often rest on such a notion, as do our nationalistic prejudices. Obviously this is essentially worthless. The *vox populi*, if it is the voice of God, is often the voice of a false God, as a most cursory observation of history readily reveals. At almost every turn of the tide in history there are evident the tragic errors into which majority opinion can fall. The fact that it was universally accepted in ancient times that the earth is flat is a simple illustration of the worthlessness of this criterion.

Another criterion which has been advanced is that of temporal duration. Opinions which have been held over great lengths of time are held to rest on good authority and thus to constitute knowledge. This criterion is of course open to the same objections as the one above.

A third criterion is that of prestige. This we are constantly using. We accept a diagnosis of a disease on the authority of the most successful, experienced, and learned of doctors; most of our "scientific knowledge" rests on the prestige of our author or teacher, or favorite saint. We even transfer prestige from one field to another as is common today when we build our religious and philosophical beliefs on the prestige of the scientist who might, as a matter of fact, be a child in such subjects. It would seem unnecessary to dwell upon the fallibility of such a criterion.

Authoritarianism, though we mention it as a type of epistemological theory, should rather be construed as a doctrine concerning the psychology of belief. It is decidedly weak as a rigorous treatment of the theory of knowledge and is completely helpless in adjudicating between conflicts of authority which are prevalent in all fields, such as science, philosophy, art, politics, and religion. We often commit ourselves on the basis of authority and it is well to realize that such commitments are likely to rest on sand.

Scepticism

Scepticism is a doctrine which denies that there is any genuine knowledge. Such a position would, then, "solve" the problems of epistemology by denying the problems themselves. The history of scepticism is long and its literature is rich. So significant historically and so prevalent is scepticism even at the present time that it is well to examine briefly the major arguments for the doctrine. These arguments can be treated conveniently under the heads of: (1) the historical argument, (2) the dialectical argument, (3) the physiological argument, and (4) the psychological argument.

In the historical argument the sceptic points out the hopeless disagreements among the experts in the various fields of knowledge. In almost every field of knowledge there are to be found divergences of opinion, and the experts seem incapable of settling the disputes. Such a situation would indicate that certainty is beyond our reach. This argument is, of course, lacking in cogency. It points out that up to the present we have not succeeded in attaining the type of knowledge we seek, but it does not show that such knowledge is unattainable. All that can be concluded from such contentions is that so far man has not attained certainty.

The so-called dialectical argument which the sceptic often employs is probably more persuasive than the historical argument because it tends to show that in the very nature of the case reason finds itself frustrated in attempting to deal with ultimate issues. The sceptic argues that in the process of knowing we are beset with contradictions or antinomies which defy solution.

As an instance of the dialectical argument let us take such a simple example as that of motion. The ancient Eleatic philosopher Zeno was not a sceptic but he propounded some famous paradoxes to support his own position, which were later used extensively by sceptics and continue to the present day. One such paradox of motion is that of Achilles crossing a race-track. Achilles cannot cross the race-track because in order to do so he must first traverse half of the distance, then half of the remaining distance, half of that, and so on *ad infinitum*. It is as impossible for Achilles to get across the race-track as it is for us to reach zero by carrying out the progression $1/2$, $1/4$, $1/8$, $1/16$, $1/32$, $1/64$.... This same argument would hold for any movement no matter how small. Thus our senses testify to the fact of motion but we are doomed to remain in darkness so far as knowledge of it is concerned because it involves an absurdity. We might think that motion is the displacement of objects in space through time; but, since any motion whatsoever would require infinite time, what we ordinarily designate as motion is really an absurdity. In the very nature of the case there can be no knowledge here.

This particular argument could, of course, be enlarged. Our scientific "knowledge" of the world is a knowledge of laws of motion, but since motion is self-contradictory, how can we talk intelligently about the physical world which we assume to manifest motion? To talk of such sciences as constituting knowledge is to descend to the ridiculous.

There are many more paradoxes and antinomies which have been developed in the history of thought and which have been skillfully employed by the sceptic in his blanket indictment of knowledge.

The physiological argument of the sceptic is probably the most forceful of all the sceptical arguments against knowledge. It asserts that we cannot have true knowledge of the real world and even if we happened to have such knowledge, which would be very unlikely, we could not know that it is true. Why does the sceptic make such assertions as these? Because, he says, the nature of experiencing is such that the real world, which we ordinarily think is truly represented in our perceptions and the like, is distorted in knowing. The sounds we hear, the colors we see, the shapes and hardnesses we feel, the odors we smell, the tastes we experience, are all modifications of ourselves and they are no more in the outer world of reality than is the pain of a pin-prick in the pin itself. Our physiological make-up, in a word, the conditions of knowing, are such that any claim to veridical knowledge is no better than any irresponsible claim we might choose to make. There is no reason to believe that we have true knowledge of the real world and every reason to believe the opposite. Thus, the sceptic at a single blow brings into serious question all of our so-called empirical knowledge.

The psychological argument of the sceptic is simple and can be disposed of briefly. This argument asserts that we live in an eternal *now*, that the future is our present anticipation, and the past our present memory. Memory is a most uncertain basis for knowledge and the future is in the highest degree speculative. Knowledge, then, that would derive from the past and predict the future is but an empty name.

Scepticism in general is not a defensible position but it is an excellent corrective for satisfied dogmatism. The sceptic denies knowledge and our capacity to obtain true propositions; yet he affirms his own position as true and at every point of his argument appeals to knowledge in his attempt to discredit it.

At this point we cannot answer the sceptic's more basic arguments, namely, the dialectical and physiological. Suffice it to say here that the paradoxes and antinomies are not as challenging as they seem at first glance. Clarification of the problems involved and rigorous treatment of them frequently lead to a satisfactory solution. Zeno's paradox of motion, for example, is easily solved if we realize that time is continuous, and thus any span of time has the requisite character of infinity which Zeno's statement of the problem of motion requires. Later we shall deal somewhat more extensively with the physiological argument. The psychological argument of a solipsism of the present is not very devastating, the argument resting primarily on a notion of a mathematical present with no temporal extensity. We do not live in such a present.

Mysticism

The doctrine of mysticism as a theory of knowledge is one which either denies or relegates to a position of relative insignificance the ordinary sources and avenues of knowledge, namely, sensation and discursive thought. True knowledge, true insight, is to be found in a unique experience which has been called mystical. To really understand the nature of a mystical experience one must actually have had one. It is inadequately described as an ineffable experience of unity with God or the universe and thus differs greatly from the ordinary communicable experiences of life.

The doctrine of mysticism as it has appeared in varying forms in history has usually rested on certain metaphysical and religious notions which would deny that the world of sense is ultimately real. Knowledge in the true sense of the word is not acquaintance with the world of space and time or with the world of concepts; but rather is it insight into the self, mind, God, substance, or entity which transcends the phenomenal world. This insight is gained through a kind of identification of the knower with this transcendental being. This insight is the mystical experience.

Without debating whether mysticism is a true or false doctrine, we may at least say that it leaves untouched the more pressing problems of knowledge. Whether this world is illusion or not, science seeks a knowledge of it and philosophy seeks an analysis and interpretation of such knowledge which shall be articulate. It is primarily with problems raised outside of mysticism that epistemology is concerned.

Intuitionism

Often closely associated with mysticism is the doctrine of intuitionism. It is perhaps a mistake to speak as if this were a separate epistemological doctrine, because intuition certainly plays a most important rôle in all knowing of whatever kind, and elements of intuitionism are present in all theories of knowledge. However, what we here refer to as intuitionism is primarily the sort of position which the famous present-day French philosopher, Henri Bergson, has made so popular.

In this view it is contended that knowledge which is conceptual is essentially inaccurate and unsound.   What we ordinarily take to be knowledge is discursive, abstract, and false.   The chief instruments of such knowing are concepts which in the very nature of the case falsify reality.   The only way to know reality is through intuition, which reveals a living dynamic world of constant change and novelty.   The essentially creative nature of the world is altogether lost in conceptual knowledge and only the intuitional experience gives a true report of it.

It is held that intellectual knowledge uses dead, static concepts and thus falsely reports the character of the world, which is in constant process and never dead nor inert.   Again, intellectual knowledge reports at best only the external, the outward semblances of things, whereas through intuition we gain an insight into the inner reality of the world.   Conceptual knowledge also has the defect of being relative.   The intellect picks and chooses in relation to its interests, experience, and capacity and thus what knowledge accrues is always relative to these factors.   In intuition we experience and know the world as it is — not only as it is in relation to an arbitrary set of concepts but as it is in itself.   It is also contended that concepts are abstract and thus can give only incomplete and partial accounts of reality.   Our intuitive grasp of reality, on the other hand, is definitely concrete and thus not subject to the defects of concepts.   A last objection to intellectual knowledge is that it is fundamentally analytical in character.   The real world is not to be correctly understood by analysis into parts and fragments, because it is essentially a process everywhere manifesting unique wholeness which cannot be understood in terms of parts.

Thus the intellect is a necessary evil in the knowing situation. Without it we could not communicate our thoughts and insights; but what it does communicate is at best only approximately correct and is unreliable as a source of knowledge.   It is an instrument developed by the life-force which contributes to man's survival.   It is highly useful but not true, whereas intuition is true but not very useful in itself.

We may conclude then that intellectual knowledge which depends on concepts is secondary and instrumental to life.   Through intuition, on the other hand, we get a true insight into the nature of the world. This intuition is a non-intellectual cognition which is a direct and immediate *rapport* with objects in which their real nature is revealed. This alone is true knowledge.

No doubt much conceptual knowledge might justly be criticized on the grounds Bergson urges, and his criticisms are good correctives against procedure which we might call over-intellectualized. On the other hand, granting the fundamental importance of intuition, it might well be asked whether Bergson is not a little too severe on conceptual procedure. The intellect does not necessarily falsify reality. If we do not separate concepts from an intuition of their meanings, it would seem that Bergson's criticisms are overstated. Intuitionism does not necessarily have to lead to irrationalism, although it is this type of intuitionism which is so distinctive as an epistemological doctrine.

Rationalism

Rationalism is a very broad doctrine. In theory of knowledge, however, the word is usually used to designate the type of epistemological position of the so-called "rationalists" of the seventeenth and eighteenth centuries. Descartes, Leibniz, Spinoza, and Wolff are probably the best representatives of this standpoint.

It is maintained that the most perfect form of knowing is the sort which is found in mathematical demonstration. Such demonstration consists in starting with premises which are self-evident, intuitively certain, or are said to be clear and distinct, and deducing the consequences of these axioms or truths. By this method we can assure ourselves certainty in knowledge. The source of our first premises is the "natural light" of reason and our developed knowledge would have the validity characteristic of strict logical deduction. Just as this is true of mathematical knowledge, so can it be true of our knowledge of the world.

It was held that there are certain basic principles of the world which are recognized as true by the reason of men and from these we can acquire a rigorous deductive knowledge of the world. These first principles have their source somehow in the reason of man and are not derived from empirical experience. In fact, precisely the reverse is the case, our empirical experience depends upon these principles.

Classical rationalism is well illustrated by Christian Wolff (1679–1754). He conceived the field of knowledge to be divided into three great segments, which he called rational cosmology, rational psychology, and rational theology.   In rational cosmology Wolff starts with certain principles which are "clear and distinct" to reason and proceeds to deduce the consequences of such principles.   Examples of his premises are the following: The world is limited in space, is made up of ultimate indivisible units, had a beginning in time.   In his rational psychology he carried on the same procedure starting with such notions as the following: The soul is a substance, indivisible, spiritual, simple, and so on.   From these he deduces the further principles of its nature, its faculties, and its immortality. In his rational theology he starts with the clear and distinct notion of God as the most real, the most perfect being, and deduces his necessary existence, his relation to the world, and the like.   A very good example of the procedure of rationalism is to be found in the famous ontological proof for the existence of God.   It is self-evident that God is an absolutely perfect being and therefore must exist, because a lack of existence would be a lack of a perfection which would render God in a degree imperfect; he would not then be absolutely perfect.   But God is truly known to be absolutely perfect and therefore must exist, since his lack of existence would involve a contradiction.

Wolff represents, of course, a most extreme form of rationalism which has turned into an absurd dogmatism.   In principle, however, he represents the rationalist's epistemology and exhibits the rationalist's rejection of the empirical source of knowledge as well as his conviction that the reason of man by its own autonomy can solve the problems of the universe.

Empiricisn.

Empiricism is not in itself a theory of knowledge but there are many epistemologies which are empirical in character and it is this general type that we wish to describe without dealing with the many forms of it.

In general, empiricism affirms that the source and validity of knowledge are to be found in the empirical aspects of experience.   The rationalist is wrong in trying to start with rational principles, because these rational principles, so-called, are really derived from experience. In fact all knowledge whatsoever comes from experience and whatever validity and truth it may have is again its validity and truth for and within experience.

The reason of man is not provided with innate or *a priori* knowledge. In fact the mind of man is a *tabula rasa* upon which experience writes. Thus, whatever knowledge man attains is finally rooted in and dependent upon experience. Sensation is the beginning of all knowledge and all our ideas are ultimately reducible to sensory experience. Thus, the empiricist would hold that knowledge rather than being deductive is essentially inductive in its procedure. Sound knowledge is to be obtained only by generalizations from experience.

Experience consists of two types or manifolds of sensation — the inner and the outer. The former are "sensations" of a subjective character, such as desire, feeling, and thinking. The latter are our sensations of the external world, such as those of sight, smell, and taste.

We have dealt with empiricism and rationalism more as tendencies in epistemology or types of it. They are generally characteristic of many specific theories and are important for us here because most of the basic issues in theory of knowledge, particularly those of the source and validity of what we ordinarily call knowledge, are brought into striking relief by them.

There are other theories of knowledge, some of which are definitely empirical, such as the current logical positivism and pragmatism, and still other theories which are midway between rationalism and empiricism, such as some forms of current realism which combine elements of both. We shall not deal with these various positions here, but the issues involved will be brought up in our later inquiry into the sources and validity of knowledge.

The two problems

As was pointed out in the beginning of the chapter, the theory of knowledge is essentially concerned with the source and with the validity of knowledge. The first problem of course raises the great issue between rationalism and empiricism, and the second introduces us to the famous dispute between the Realists and the Idealists. In the chapters which follow we shall study these two phases of epistemology.

In connection with this chapter read:

Gamertsfelder and Evans, *Fundamentals of Philosophy* (Prentice-Hall, Inc.), chap. v.

Further references:

W. P. Montague, *The Ways of Knowing* (The Macmillan Company), chaps. II, IV.

Roy Wood Sellars, *The Principles and Problems of Philosophy*, chap. X; *The Philosophy of Physical Realism* (The Macmillan Company), chap. IV.

John Locke, *An Essay Concerning Human Understanding*.

A. N. Whitehead, *The Principles of Natural Knowledge* (Cambridge University Press).

F. S. C. Northrop, *Science and First Principles* (The Macmillan Company), chap. VI, "The Foundations of Experience and Knowledge."

Durant Drake, *Invitation to Philosophy* (Houghton Mifflin Company), chaps. I, II.

W. T. Stace, *The Theory of Knowledge and Existence* (Clarendon Press, Oxford).

CHAPTER XXIII
WHAT CAN WE KNOW?

THE SOURCES OF KNOWLEDGE

The genetic approach

ONE of the oldest of the epistemological problems relates to the *sources* of knowledge. Each of us has a certain "store" or "body" of knowledge, such, for instance, as of the world around us, of our own minds, of mathematical principles, of right and wrong, of goodness and beauty. Hence the question arises, Where did we get this knowledge? Its truth and value may depend upon its source. We want each bit of knowledge to show its credentials.

In the history of philosophy it has been customary to say that all of our knowledge has come to us in one of three or four ways. In the traditional language of epistemology, knowledge must either be inborn; or it must come from reason; or it must come through the special senses, namely, sight, hearing, pressure, taste, smell, temperature, and strain; or finally, it must come from direct insight or intuition. A more accurate psychology and a more modern logic, however, have resulted in a shifting of the points of interest as regards the "sources" of knowledge. Knowledge is not something which comes in packages to be traced to authentic sources; ideas are not entities which can be built up into knowledge; there is no faculty of reason which guarantees a kind of divine sanctity to its utterances; and since Locke's time few people, if any, believe in innate ideas. Innate dispositions, tendencies, interests, ways of reacting, we have in plenty; but no ready-made knowledge.

The way to a better understanding of the theory of knowledge is through a genetic study of the subject, beginning with the attitude of the simplest living organism toward its environment. The first thing that happens is a response of some kind to a stimulus, accompanied by a simple awareness. Indeed, this is not the first thing that happens either. The first thing is the organism itself with certain new-found powers belonging only to living organisms and certain inborn interests which serve as driving forces. So at the very beginning we see how meaningless a theory of sensationalism or pure empiricism would be, affirming that all knowledge comes from sensation or experience, as if in Locke's phrase the mind at birth were a blank tablet, upon which sense impressions make their record; as meaningless as the rival theory which would derive knowledge from a faculty of reason.

Thus the very simplest form of knowledge would be mere awareness, such as an organism has of an object affecting it. Very soon, however, when an organism begins to respond to a stimulus and then presently to respond specifically to a situation, the situation begins to have a meaning; it is interesting, promising, threatening, to be avoided. Thus a relation arises which may be called *acquaintance*. Then language comes with names of things and events, and abstract terms, and classes, and judgment, and reasoning.

Pursuing the subject psychologically in this way, we see that there is no faculty called reason that oracularly hands down something called knowledge, as Rationalism used to teach; nor any transcendental *a priori* laws of thought which experience presupposes, as apriorism used to teach; nor, on the other hand, are there any such things as simple sensations considered as units of knowledge, which could be combined or built up into a body of knowledge. What we have rather is an organism with profound interests and propensities exploring a hostile and a friendly world and interacting with its environment. The result is experience; and this experience may be funded, drawn upon in specific new situations, and these situations may be intelligently dealt with, controlled, mastered. Evidently it is this *funded experience* which we call knowledge, later classified, expressed in language, codified into the shorthand of scientific terms. Knowledge, therefore, is experience rationalized; that is, organized. Empiricism and Rationalism thus lay aside their historic rivalry and join friendly hands.

John Dewey and his associates have enlightened us not a little about the real nature of knowledge by studying it in its genetic stages. This is what Dewey says:

> The interaction of organism and environment, resulting in some adaptation which secures utilization of the latter, is the primary fact,

the basic category. Knowledge is relegated to a derived position, secondary in origin, even if its importance, when once it is established, is overshadowing. Knowledge is not something separate and self-sufficing, but is involved in the process by which life is sustained and evolved. The senses lose their place as gateways of knowing to take their rightful place as stimuli to action. To an animal an affection of the eye or ear is not an idle piece of information about something indifferently going on in the world. It is an invitation and inducement to act in a needed way. It is a clue in behavior, a directive factor in adaptation of life in its surroundings. It is urgent not cognitive in quality. The whole controversy between empiricism and rationalism as to the intellectual worth of sensations is rendered strangely obsolete. The discussion of sensations belongs under the head of immediate stimulus and response, not under the head of knowledge....

The rationalist was thus right in denying that sensations as such are true elements of knowledge. But the reasons he gave for this conclusion and the consequences he drew from it were all wrong. Sensations are not parts of *any* knowledge, good or bad, superior or inferior, imperfect or complete. They are rather provocations, incitements, challenges to an act of inquiry which is to *terminate* in knowledge. They are not ways of knowing things inferior in value to reflective ways, to the ways that require thought and inference, because they are not ways of knowing at all. They are stimuli to reflection and inference. As interruptions they raise the questions: What does this shock mean? What is happening? What is the matter? How is my relation to the environment disturbed? What should be done about it? How shall I alter my course of action to meet the change that has taken place in the surroundings? How shall I readjust my behavior in response? Sensation is thus, as the sensationalist claimed, the beginning of knowledge, but only in the sense that the experienced shock of change is the necessary stimulus to the investigating and comparing which eventually produce knowledge.[1]

This statement shows very clearly how knowledge arises, and we see that it is better to inquire as to the *conditions* of knowledge than its *sources*. Its conditions are a self with certain innate interests, an environment with which the self enters into relations, an intelligence that can fund, capitalize, and organize this experience and deal effectively with new and complicated situations. Knowledge is funded experience, but in the funding process mental powers and activities are the significant things — memory, thought, conceptual analysis, reflection, selective organization, creative synthesis.

[1] John Dewey, *Reconstruction in Philosophy* (Henry Holt and Company), pp. 87, 89, 90.

Knowledge is therefore not something which *drifts in* from a ready-made world in the form of impressions, as the old Sensationalism taught; nor is it the distilled product of certain *a priori* universal principles of thought, as the older Rationalism taught. It is a product of the interaction of the self and the environment, in which the remarkable powers of the self are the most significant factors. Hence it is not necessary to assume any *a priori*, super-empirical "categories" or principles of knowledge. Previous to the experience of the individual there are, to be sure, certain innate tendencies learned in the process of evolution through actual contact with the environment and actual success in dealing with it. If *a priori* be taken to mean racial habits of dealing with experience and organizing it, then indeed we may believe in *a priori* elements in knowledge.

But knowledge is also contemplative

This genetic account of knowledge is of the greatest value in giving us an insight into its real nature; but it is a little one-sided because it overemphasizes the instrumental character of the mind. The intelligence that is described is primarily that of the animal which has a practical problem to solve, probably that of getting food or outwitting an enemy. But even the animal has an instinct of curiosity, and in man the desire for knowledge for its own sake is very strong.

There is, then, another kind of knowledge than the experimental. Granting that sensations are primarily stimuli to action, they may also serve other ends — they may be revelations. They may serve our scientific interests, our desire merely to know. Sensations need not be always "urgent." They may be suggestive of external reality, leading to thought and scientific hypothesis, which in the end may result in discoveries concerning the actual structure of the world. They may, indeed, be revelatory of external reality itself. The world is intelligible as well as plastic; and present in intuition as well as intelligible. What Dewey calls knowledge may indeed change and mould and modify its objects, but there is a knowledge which is merely *contemplative*. The stars in the heavens are not changed by being known, except in the puerile sense of entering into a new external relation. As Leighton so well says:

The functions of consciousness and reason are not exhausted in meeting novel situations and controlling behavior by a reference to the future. When I am engaged in aesthetic contemplation of nature or art, when I am enjoying the companionship of a friend, when I am contemplating the logical symmetry, beauty and impersonal grandeur of some scientific or mathematical construction, when I am living in some significant period of the past, for example Elizabethan England or the Athens of Pericles, when I am following the career and feeling myself into the life of some one of the race's worldly or spiritual heroes, my consciousness, keen, vivid and expanding, may have no reference to my own future behavior or that of anyone else. The human spirit lives not by deeds of adjustment to external and future situations alone. It lives deeply in pure contemplation and free imagination. The instrumentalist errs by taking one important function of conscious intelligence and making it the sole function. Disinterested contemplation and enjoyment of the beauty, grandeur, meaning and order of things for their own sakes are for some human beings inherently worthful functions of consciousness.[1]

If this view seems quite opposed to the pragmatic account given by Dewey, perhaps the reconciliation may be found just in this, that, while thinking was at first instrumental, it has finally become an end or value in itself. As bluntly stated by Montague, "Man began to think in order that he might eat, he has evolved to the point where he eats in order that he may think." [2]

Thus the ancient dispute between the Empiricists and the Rationalists seems much softened and need not detain us longer here; nor need we dwell further on the theory called *Sensationalism*. Knowledge is organized experience, and experience includes both stimulus and response, and in the process of organization, memory, thought, and reasoning are all involved. It may be well, however, for us to linger a little on that theory of knowledge called *Rationalism*.

The new Rationalism

Philosophy of the present time, so far as it is rationalistic — and it is so to a considerable extent — follows none of the older forms. The mind is a product of nature, has grown up with it, is at home in it, partakes of its rationality, but understands and appreciates only

[1] Joseph Alexander Leighton, *The Field of Philosophy* (D. Appleton and Company), p. 360.
[2] *Journal of Philosophy and Scientific Method*, vol. IV, p. 489.

a part of its limitless riches. Knowledge is a selective process, choosing those aspects of reality which it can make use of, appreciate, or understand. It gets, perhaps, only glimpses of the whole of reality, but its vision so far as it extends is not illusory. Mathematical and logical truths are not drawn down from a heavenly kingdom where they have reigned in majestic isolation from eternity; they are involved in the very structure of the Universe. The order in the world and the rationality are objective, are there to be seen, felt, and enjoyed. The real world is logical and mathematical, and the mind is just a part of this real world, has grown up with it, and lays hold of every aspect of it which it can use and appreciate. Yes, and it lays hold not only of the logical and mathematical realities of the world but also of its moral and aesthetic realities — its goodness and its beauty, its "objective significant structures." [1]

So, then, knowledge comes neither from the senses nor from reason. We may say that it comes from experience, but experience means, in Mr. Santayana's well-chosen words, "so much of knowledge and readiness as is fetched from contact with events by a teachable and intelligent creature; it is a fund of wisdom gathered by living in familiar intercourse with things."

The new Rationalism emphasizes not merely the objective reality of logical relations, but also the importance of the constructive and creative power of the mind in the acquisition of knowledge. It is very far from returning to any theory of Sensationalism. Consider, for instance, the case of the scientist at work in his laboratory. It is indeed a *labor*atory rather than an *observ*atory. The fruitful contributions to knowledge that come from it are the results of intelligent labor rather than of passive sense perception. The very building in which the apparatus is housed is planned for its special purpose. The discovery of the best method, the formation of an hypothesis from which to work, the planning of the experiment, the designing and setting up of the apparatus, the computation of the

---

[1] I refer again to George P. Adams's book, *Idealism and the Modern Age,* which should be read as a corrective of a certain onesidedness in the pragmatic theory of knowledge. Read especially Chapter VI in connection with Chapter V. Professor Adams seems to think that this view is inconsistent with an emergent theory of mind, evidently fearing that whatever emerges from the body must be very "bodily." But what if some original interest or desire for righteousness and beauty is achieving the vision of them by means of the body, as life is achieved by means of carbon, oxygen, and nitrogen?

results — all these are the significant things, and they are the work of the mind. And yet it is just as true that none of this *labor* would avail unless in the end *observation* of the event, of the objective fact, were accurately and impartially made and truly recorded.

So in conclusion we see how our modern conception of the mind simplifies the whole subject of knowledge. We can forget all about a faculty of reason, and in place of it substitute the power of creative thinking. Of the latter James Harvey Robinson says:

> It is this kind of thought that has raised man from his pristine, sub-savage ignorance and squalor to the degree of knowledge and comfort which he now possesses. On his capacity to continue and greatly extend this kind of thinking depends his chance of groping his way out of the plight in which the most highly civilized peoples of the world now find themselves. In the past this type of thinking has been called Reason. But so many misapprehensions have grown up around the word that some of us have become very suspicious of it. I suggest, therefore, that we substitute a recent name and speak of "creative thought" rather than of Reason. *For this kind of meditation begets knowledge, and knowledge is really creative inasmuch as it makes things look different from what they seemed before and may indeed work for their reconstruction.*[1]

It is rational thinking which has marked every advance in the history of mankind, not merely in science and invention, but especially in morals and manners and civilization.

In connection with this chapter read:

William James, *Essays in Radical Empiricism* (Longmans, Green and Company), chaps. II–IV.

Durant Drake, *Invitation to Philosophy* (Houghton Mifflin Company), part II.

Further references:

Edward G. Spaulding, *The New Rationalism* (Henry Holt and Company), part 2.

C. D. Broad, *Scientific Thought* (Harcourt, Brace and Company), part 2.

R. F. A. Hoernlé, *Studies in Contemporary Metaphysics* (Harcourt, Brace and Company), chaps. IV, V.

Bertrand Russell, *The Problems of Philosophy* (Henry Holt and Company), chaps. I–III.

R. W. Sellars, *Essentials of Philosophy* (Houghton Mifflin Company), chap. V.

John Dewey, *Essays in Experimental Logic* (University of Chicago Press).

[1] James Harvey Robinson, *The Mind in the Making* (Harper and Brothers), p. 49.

CHAPTER XXIV
WHAT CAN WE KNOW?

THE TRUTH AND VALIDITY OF KNOWLEDGE

THIS is the second problem in the Theory of Knowledge and is quite distinct from the one we have been discussing. It is not a question of where our knowledge comes from, but whether it is valid when we get it. In its general form it is the problem of the relation of our ideas to the world of reality. It introduces us to the famous dispute between the Realist and the Idealist. The alternative theories of *Realism* and *Idealism* now confront us and in this epistemological discussion these two words are used in different senses from those in which they were used in theories of ontology. The problem which we have now to discuss is simply the question whether the world is in itself a distinct independent reality, or whether it is just a reflection of our own minds, an idea, a perception, a mental construction. To the former belief the word *Realism*[1] is applied; to the latter, the term *Idealism*.

Subjectivism

Idealism of this kind is sometimes called *Subjective Idealism* or *Subjectivism*, to distinguish it from Objective or Metaphysical Idealism, which is a theory of ontology, not of epistemology. The latter, we remember, is the theory that, although the objective world is real and independent of the perceiving mind, nevertheless, in its inner nature it is psychical, mental, or spiritual. It is very important to keep this distinction carefully in mind and not confuse this Subjectivism or epistemological Idealism, which we are now to study, with the various forms of objective Idealism. Any impatience which we may perhaps feel with Subjectivism should not be carried over to the more helpful and dignified forms of Idealism, teaching that in the objective world which we all believe exists

---

[1] The word *Realism* as well as the word *Idealism* is ambiguous, having quite another meaning than the present one. In this other meaning it is often called *Platonic Realism*, and refers to the belief that concepts, general notions, universals are real entities, not just names. In this sense Realism is opposed to Nominalism.

around us and above us, the essential and abiding things are mind or spirit or eternal values. Whether the latter view be true or false, its truth is not dependent upon any form of subjective Idealism.

It is only since the time of Berkeley that the difficulty has arisen about the independent reality of what is called *the external world*. The naïve belief of mankind is that the world of objects around us, such as trees, mountains, and rivers, really exists very much as we see it, quite independent of the perceiving mind. Bishop Berkeley's "strange" philosophy taught that there is no such reality as inert matter existing apart from our perception. This seems so absurd to most of us that we can hardly appreciate the strength of Berkeley's position until we have read his own arguments in his own charming and persuasive style. Fortunately these are readily accessible in his *Principles of Human Knowledge*, published in 1710, and in a more popular form in his *Three Dialogues between Hylas and Philonous*.

> It is indeed an opinion strangely prevailing amongst men, that houses, mountains, rivers, and in a word all sensible objects, have an existence, natural or real, distinct from their being perceived by the understanding. But, with how great an assurance and acquiescence soever this principle may be entertained in the world, yet whoever shall find in his heart to call it in question may, if I mistake not, perceive it to involve a manifest contradiction. For, what are the forementioned objects but the things we perceive by sense? and what do we perceive besides our own ideas or sensations? and is it not plainly repugnant that any one of these, or any combination of them, should exist unperceived?[1]

But they have no such distinct existence, being merely our own ideas. In Berkeley's celebrated phrase, *esse est percipi*, to be is to be perceived.

> Some truths there are so near and obvious to the mind that a man need only open his eyes to see them. Such I take this important one to be, viz., that all the choir of heaven and furniture of the earth, in a word all those bodies which compose the mighty frame of the world, have not any subsistence without a mind, that their *being* is to be perceived or known; that consequently so long as they are not actually perceived by me, or do not exist in my mind or that of any other created spirit, they must either have no existence at all, or else subsist in the mind of some Eternal Spirit — it being perfectly unintelligible, and involving all the

---

[1] George Berkeley, *Of the Principles of Human Knowledge* (Open Court Publishing Company), part I, sec. 4.

absurdity of abstraction, to attribute to any single part of them an existence independent of a spirit. [To be convinced of which, the reader need only reflect, and try to separate in his own thoughts the *being* of a sensible thing from its *being perceived*.] [1]

It is probable that this controversy between the Realist and the Idealist has received more attention in the history of modern philosophy than it deserved.   There is at the present time a strong realistic reaction against all forms of Subjectivism and a tendency to return to a "common-sense" view.   Berkeley's Idealism is not, however, refuted by an appeal to common sense, any more than it was by the argument of Dr. Samuel Johnson, who in Berkeley's own day struck his foot with mighty force against a stone till he rebounded, saying, "I refute it thus!" [2]   For all that was given in Dr. Johnson's own experience was a group of visual and muscular sensations and possibly a pain, which he located in his toe.   Whether the controversy is fruitless or not, a short outline of the argument must here be given.   It is a kind of initiation, which every aspirant to a knowledge of philosophy must go through.

The ego-centric predicament

The difficulty which arises between the Realist and the Idealist has sometimes been called the *ego-centric predicament*.[3]   What we mean when we say that a thing exists, say a tree, is that it is perceived.   So said Berkeley.   For, just as soon as you try to think of it as not perceived, you are still *thinking* of it; it is a *thought* object. Try to think of the tree as an existence in itself, unperceived by any mind.   You still think of it as having certain sense qualities; it is green, or hard, or rough.   It is an object of ideal perception.   Hence we can never know what objects are in themselves — only what they are as perceived; perhaps they are nothing *but* perceptions. Possibly there are no objects independent of the perceiving mind; possibly they are merely projections of the mind, like the forms I see and the voices I hear in my sleep.   But *if* I think of them as independent objects, I am still *thinking* of them as they would be perceived.   I think of them, for instance, as colored, and yet color

[1] George Berkeley, *op. cit.*, part I, sec. 6.

[2] Boswell's *Life of Johnson*, edited by Glover, London, 1901, vol. I, p. 313.

[3] The phrase is to be credited to Ralph Barton Perry.

depends upon an eye. I think of them as making noise or sound, and yet sound and noise depend upon the ear. Roses would not be red apart from the seeing eye, nor fragrant apart from the sensing nose, nor beautiful apart from the appreciating mind.

Hence the ego-centric predicament. An object in order to be known is an object known; it is in a cognitive relation to the knowing subject. What it would be *out* of this relation there is no telling, for just as soon as you approach it to find out what it is, it enters into a cognitive relation to you. It is always an object known, not an independent thing in itself.

The effect of this argument upon anyone hearing it for the first time is to cause first incredulity and then exasperation. One tries to answer Berkeley by saying that it is nonsense to affirm that the rose does not exist unless perceived. Suppose the rose lies upon the table and we all go out of the room. Does it not then continue to exist? To which Berkeley patiently replies — What do you mean by existence in this case? Name some quality that such an existing rose would have. When you do so, you mention some sense quality, such as red, white, large, small, or fragrant. All the qualities of the rose are simply sense data.

But the reader is unconvinced by this reasoning and proposes to offer a proof for the reality of the external object in this way: A given thing, say a rose, is seen, not by one person, but by many. It might, to be sure, be a phantasm of my own, so far as I am concerned; but if I can call in another person to testify that he, too, sees the rose, then it must be there. But this argument fails, because you have no more evidence that the other person exists than you have that the rose exists. The other person is known to you only through sense perception; you can see him and hear him and touch him, but in the end he is nothing more than the sum of certain sensations. Some sensory nerve is stimulated, some brain center is excited, some perception results.[1]

---

[1] Berkeley attempted to show that our knowledge of other minds, other persons, is not quite the same as our knowledge of bodies and material objects. He said that we *perceive* the physical object, but have a *notion* of other minds. This was a forlorn endeavor, and the distinction has little worth. More recent writers have tried to show in other ways that we have a more direct or a different kind of knowledge of other minds than we have of physical objects. For instance, it is said that I feel the power of your will or personality controlling me or coming into conflict with my will. Apart from mystical or telepathic influences the argument seems to have little weight.

The situation begins to get desperate. How do I know that there is any world at all? How do I know that there is anything in the Universe except myself and my impressions or ideas? To this extreme form of Subjective Idealism, which affirms that I alone exist, the name *Solipsism* has been given, from the Latin *solus* and *ipse*, meaning myself alone. Berkeley did not hold this view. It is the *reductio ad absurdum* of this kind of Idealism.

Objections and answers

At this point the reader may say, "Wait, I am not convinced of Berkeley's position; I am not even convinced that his argument is sound. I see two weaknesses in it. In the first place, physical science tells us about the external world. If there were no material world around us, what is it that science studies? No scientist would listen to Berkeley's claim that there is no such thing as matter." But this objection, again, has little weight. Berkeley did not deny that the objects which science studies exist, but that they exist independent of the perceiving mind. We must not forget what is meant by the word *exist*. The rose and the tree and the human body and all the things studied by science are perceptions, objects of experience. As such, they are objects of scientific study, and the scientist does not need to trouble himself with any metaphysical questions as to the relation of these objects of experience to some reality beyond perception. Indeed, very distinguished scientists have expressly taught that the objects of science are merely phenomena, just objects of perception, bundles of sensations, or "complexes of sense data." [1]

The second weakness in Berkeley's position, continues the doubter, is this: "Suppose we grant that objects of experience, such as roses, trees, houses, are just complexes of sense data, or perceptions, nevertheless, the perceptions must have a cause. Objects come and go quite against my will or expectation. They break in most unpleasantly sometimes upon my train of thought. How could they do this if they were merely subjective, just phantasms of

[1] Compare Karl Pearson, *The Grammar of Science*; Ernst Mach, *The Analysis of Sensations*; and Bertrand Russell, "Our Knowledge of the External World," chap. III in his *Scientific Method in Philosophy*. Compare also Huxley's appreciation of Berkeley's position in Huxley's book entitled *Hume*.

the mind? There must therefore be some objective cause or source of these perceptions; and, furthermore, if we may be allowed to accept the existence of other minds, as Berkeley does, the objective source of the perceptions must be something abiding and persisting, affecting all minds alike."

This difficulty is more serious than the others and must be carefully considered. Objectivity of some kind is certainly revealed by this demand for a cause of our perceptions. Berkeley, Kant, and all the Subjectivists recognize this demand and provide for it. We shall be interested to learn how they do this. Kant's solution is the easiest to grasp, if not the most convincing — and may be examined first.

It is true, said Kant, that our sensations must have a cause and that this cause must be outside the mind. We will, therefore, recognize the existence of such a cause as absolutely necessary. It is the unknown *Thing in Itself (Ding an sich)*. It is not even in time or space, because, as we recall, time and space are subjective. Science can tell us nothing about this ultimate reality, for science deals with phenomena, things as they appear to us, conditioned by the nature of our sense organs and the constitution of the mind.

The world, then, according to Kant, the world of science as well as of familiar everyday perception, is a mental construct or creation. The understanding makes nature. It does not, to be sure, make it out of nothing. The raw material is given in sensation, but the whole form and structure of it, its whole texture, even its temporal and spatial character, are all contributed by the mind. What is given to us in sensation is a chaotic manifold only; all that makes the world orderly, coherent, having form, meaning, structure, comes from the peculiar constitution of the mind. Since all objects of knowledge are phenomena, we may call Kant's theory *Phenomenalism* rather than complete Subjective Idealism.

Berkeley's own solution of the difficulty is quite different and seems very strange to one who hears it for the first time. There is, we remember, no such thing as matter in the sense of an objective inert substance. Things are just perceptions; but some objective *cause* of my perceptions there must of course be. Matter being inert could not, even if it existed, be the cause of my perceptions.

Perceptions being mental states could only proceed from a spiritual source, an active will, a divine will. What we call the world of natural objects is, therefore, the regular and systematic operation of God, the infinite spirit, upon a society of finite spirits; that is, upon human minds.

At first sight this introduction of God as the cause of our ideas, instead of an external material reality, seems a lame and forced explanation. It seems a fitting climax to an absurd system. But Berkeley had an exasperating ability in defending his position, and this last hypothesis may be less unreasonable than it sounds. If Berkeley were here to defend his philosophy, and if he were acquainted with the results of recent science in its investigation of the nature of matter, he might reason as follows: "You say that something called matter is the cause of your sensations. Well, what is matter? It has been reduced to units of energy, dancing and vibrating electrons, as far from one another relatively to their size as the planets. What do you know about this energy as regards its quality? Nothing; it is the capacity for doing work. You assume, then, that something, almost an x, which you call matter, exists, and that it is perhaps nothing more than a form of energy, and that this energy working upon your organs of sense gives rise to those various sensations which you call heat or light or sound or impact, making up your world."

"Very well," continues Berkeley, "now tell me whether your theory is any better than mine or, indeed, very different. You say that the only reality outside the perceiving mind is a world of energy, the nature of which is unknown, operating upon the mind. I say that the only reality outside the mind is God, who causes the perceptions. If this view seems absurd to you, it is because you do not think of God in the right way. God is an omnipresent, all-encompassing, divine energy, revealing himself to us in those multiform impressions which make up our world of objects. The only difference in our two positions is that you call this encompassing energy *material*, while I call it *spiritual*; but since you admittedly do not know anything about your material energy except that it is the capacity for effecting changes, the advantage is all in favor of calling it, as I do, spiritual energy, or God, for then we can understand how its operation is rational, orderly, and progressive. Try, for instance, to explain in your way the beauties of nature or the wonders of evolution."

Certainly Berkeley's philosophy works out in a strange way. He seems to have found some objective world after all, only he calls it God, while others call it matter. One cannot but wonder whether Berkeley's view is so far wrong. The beauty of the sunset, mountain, cloud, and sea, the exquisite perfection of the microscopic world, the almost miraculous order of nature as shown in animal instinct, in the marvels of evolution, in variation, in heredity, in the mystery of life itself — all these make it reasonable, indeed, to say that the living energy, which surrounds us on every side, acting as stimulus to our sense organs, is God. If anyone were to urge as a further objection to this philosophy that it is Pantheism, since it reduces the world to God, Berkeley could reply that it is not Pantheism since he expressly affirms the reality, independence, freedom, and responsibility of finite minds or human souls. Perhaps the greater error in Berkeley's philosophy is to be found, not in this ontological part, but in his theory of knowledge.

Criticism of Subjectivism

Such, then, is the famous epistemological Idealism which teaches that the world is my idea. It seems to resist all ordinary methods of attack, but, as carried out to its final conclusions by Berkeley himself, leads to nothing very startling nor very strange. But the question arises whether it really is so impregnable a philosophy as it seems — whether there may not be some initial assumptions in it which are unnecessary or even false.

There is a "catch" about the ego-centric predicament, which has been pointed out again and again by recent writers. It does not follow that, because the things which I know exist in a cognitive relation to me, they cannot exist also without this relation. You say that the rose or the tree is my idea, and that anything at all which I approach with a view of knowing it becomes something known, or an idea. Well, if that be true, it does not follow that the rose or the tree might not exist in *other* relations. If it be true that I cannot know anything about things not experienced, it does not follow that there are no unexperienced things. Let us make the supposition that there is a world of reality quite independent of human experience, say a material world, a world of nature objects, a world, if you please, of green trees and brown mountains and blue sky. The postulate is permissible. Then let us suppose that sensitive organisms should arrive, perceptive minds, reasoning men. They could surely prove to their own delight that all the trees and mountains and other objects were just bundles of sensations, 'complexes of sense data.' But by hypothesis this conclusion would be false. So we can, at any rate, make the postulate that there is a real objective world independent of our perceptions. Science usually makes this postulate, and when made it is found to yield satisfactory results. Incidentally it conforms to common sense.

But there is a more serious error underlying the whole subjectivist theory, an error so fundamental as to cause a feeling of indignation that it could have been imposed upon so many generations of students of philosophy. It goes back to John Locke, who said that knowledge is the perception of the agreement or disagreement of two ideas. For instance, the knowledge that the rose is red is the recognition of the agreement between the ideas "rose" and "red." Locke's notion seemed to be that there are certain things or entities *in* the mind, which he called ideas, and that then this entity, called the mind, surveys these ideas and recognizes their agreement or disagreement, such recognition being knowledge. It is this false psychology which has done so much mischief in epistemology. In modern psychology this error has been perpetuated through the misunderstanding that arises in the use of such terms as *sensations, states of mind*, and *states of consciousness*, in which these things of subjective interest only have been confused with the sense qualities of objects. Then the red of the rose, the blue of the sky, and the brown of the mountains have been called sensations or mental or conscious states, instead of being called, as they should be, qualities of objects.

The account of knowledge already given in this chapter, when we were discussing the sources of knowledge, removes many of these difficulties and leads to a kind of common-sense Realism. Knowledge is not the recognition of the agreement or disagreement of ideas, but the direct experience of things. It arises in the interaction between a percipient organism and a thing perceived. In its simplest form it is a mere awareness of an object. An amoeba, for instance, comes in contact with something which may or may not be available for food. It becomes aware of it. After repeated contacts an elementary memory leads to recognition. The object is appropriated or avoided. The amoeba has had experience, knowledge. Surely there is nothing very mysterious about knowledge when we consider it in this way — and it certainly involves, not only a perceiving subject, but an object perceived. It presupposes a world external to the perceiving organism; that is, a real world, having real qualities, existing with its qualities before it is known, and when known coming into a new relation — a relation with a knowing mind.

Now, in the case of human knowledge we have a complex environment in interaction with a complex organism and the character of the knowledge is determined by the nature of both. Since the perceptive organism is itself a very complex affair, having a certain limited number of sense organs receptive to only certain kinds of stimuli; using these stimuli primarily, not as gateways to knowledge, but as incentives to action; having the power of memory adding associative elements to what is given in sense perception; and having peculiar needs with likes and dislikes, the question is, of course, always coming up whether the knowledge which such an organism has of its environment is an "accurate" knowledge. Hence arise all the discussions with which the literature of epistemology has been burdened; for example, about illusory experience, truth and error, and the distinction between primary and secondary qualities. We hear much about the straight stick appearing bent in the water, and the converging parallel rails, and about secondary qualities belonging not to things, but only to minds.[1] But the laws of light will explain why the straight stick appears bent in the water and why the parallel rails appear to converge; and there are many now who do not think it necessary to regard as subjective such qualities as color and

---

[1] It was said by Locke, and before Locke by Galileo, and even by Democritus in ancient Greece, that while certain qualities, such as solidity, motion, and extension (the so-called primary qualities), belong really to the object, certain other qualities, such as color, sound, taste, and smell (the so-called secondary qualities), do not belong to objects really, but are subjective, existing only in the mind.

sound, but only to remember that different qualities of objects are revealed under different conditions.[1] Perhaps the simplest solution of this ancient problem is the best. We may still believe that the world which we know — a world of objects existing in space and time, a world of causal relations, a world of color and sound, a world of proportion and beauty — is not a world which we create in knowing, or which is changed by being known, but a world which has existed all the time and which has created us, the knowers. The objective world, then, is real, and our knowledge of it is true even if partial; and this true knowledge of the world is constantly being enlarged by the application of scientific methods of investigation.

Types of Realism

This discussion of Realism and Idealism should not be concluded without some reference to recent realistic schools. This may be prefaced by a notice of some older forms of Realism. A realistic world view is the natural one, and the plain man takes it for granted. Unless, however, he has some knowledge of physiology and psychology, he is apt to hold it in too naïve a form.

Naïve Realism is the name given to the view carelessly held by the unthinking man, who may believe, perhaps, that the eyes are windows through which some inner eye gazes at the real world and sees it just as it is; or, again, that the mind is a kind of tablet upon which is impressed through sense perception a *copy* or *picture* of the world without. When we study the structure of the brain and the organs of sense and the pathways of the sensory nerves, we begin to understand the naïveté of these first views and so proceed to examine more critically the way that knowledge arises. This leads to some form of *Critical Realism,* which in its broader meaning is the attempt to reconstruct a scientific Realism based on a more accurate physiology and psychology.

An early attempt of this kind was made by Locke, whose view is called *Representative Realism.* This holds that the real external world consists merely of material particles in motion and that our ideas of the qualities of matter merely *represent* these qualities, and, indeed, even then represent only such *primary* qualities as motion

[1] Compare A. N. Whitehead, *The Concept of Nature,* chaps. I and II.

and figure, while such *secondary* qualities as color and sound exist only in the mind, their objective source being some form of matter in motion. Such a Realism tends, as we have seen, toward some kind of Phenomenalism or Subjective Idealism. Herbert Spencer, again, proposed a form of Realism which he called *Transfigured Realism*. The external world is a world of matter, motion, and force; but as revealed to us through perception it is transfigured, as the image of a cube is transfigured in a mirror.

The New Realism

Lately a new form of Realism has appeared in America and in England called *The New Realism*, or *Neo-Realism*, heralded by a school of vigorous writers.[1] It represents a return to the common-sense doctrine of a real objective world directly known in perception. Knowledge is not mediated by any mental state, idea, or sensation. Real objects are directly presented in knowledge. In the act of knowing, the object of knowledge is not an idea or sensation which is considered as a copy or representation of an outer object, but the outer object itself is present to us as an actual outer independent reality. When we are aware of an object, say a tree, it is the tree itself which we are aware of, not our visual, auditory, or touch sensations. The New Realism, therefore, rejects Subjectivism in all its forms. It denies that things are either created or modified by a knowing mind, and thus represents the emancipation of philosophy from epistemology, which, indeed, has too long tyrannized over it. Beginning as a protest against the domination of Subjectivism, the New Realism has developed into a unique and rather vigorous school of philosophy opposing both Subjectivism and Absolutism. It does not believe that the world is an organic whole or unity of such a nature that analysis will destroy its reality, but encourages the vigorous use of the analytic method known to the special sciences, and believes that reality is revealed in such analysis. Hence the New Realism is intellectualistic, renouncing all mystical philosophies and

---

[1] This movement first became generally known in 1912 through the publication of a book entitled *The New Realism*, by Edwin B. Holt, Walter T. Marvin, William Pepperell Montague, Ralph Barton Perry, Walter B. Pitkin, and Edward Gleason Spaulding. In England the movement is represented by G. E. Moore (see his *Philosophical Essays*) and S. Alexander (see his *Space, Time, and Deity*).

all modern forms of anti-intellectualism which rely upon intuition or ineffable insight.   It rejects the doctrine that all relations are internal, and holds to the externality of relations, such that the nature of the thing is not necessarily determined by the relations in which it stands; it may get into all kinds of relations with other things without changing these other things or being changed by them.   It may even happen to be *known*, if some knowing mind comes along, and it remains unchanged by this cognitive relation.

Again, according to the New Realists, relations are not only external, but they are objective.   Things are not related by the mind which grasps them, but the relations in which they stand are real, just as real and just as objective as the things themselves.   If John is taller than James, not only is John real and James real, but the relation expressed by the words *taller than* is also real.   Hence a pluralistic world view is favored over monistic and dualistic systems.   Reality is diverse and rich in its manifoldness.   We cannot lightly affirm that the Universe is one great systematic unity, nor, on the other hand, can we say that there is nothing but mind and matter; for there may be many other real things — space and time relations, logical principles, perhaps even ethical ideals.   Thus this rigid analytical Realism approaches in the end to a kind of Platonic Realism, in which the world of merely physical or mental reality is enlarged by a realm of subsistent entities.   Even such ideal concepts as justice and beauty may, according to some members of this school, find their place again as real entities.[1]   The New Realism is thus inconsistent with both Materialism and Dualism and with that extreme form of Spiritualism which affirms that nothing exists except mind.[2]

[1] Not all New Realists would be willing to include ethical and social ideals among real entities. Their status is not quite the same as that of logical and mathematical forms, yet their reality within the sphere of conduct and society might equally well be affirmed.   Certainly there would seem to be nothing inconsistent with the New Realism in this part of Plato's philosophy. See the discussion of this subject in Spaulding's *The New Rationalism*, pp. 344–521.

[2] For a brief statement of the principles of the New Realism, see:
   The New Realism, esp. Introduction, pp. 2–42.
   Perry, *Present Philosophical Tendencies*, chap. XIII.
   Rogers, *English and American Philosophy Since 1800*, chap. VIII.
   S. Alexander, *Space, Time, and Deity*, vol. II, chap. IV.
   G. E. Moore, *Philosophical Studies*, chaps. I, II, V.

The New Critical Realism

The powerful realistic tendencies of the present time are seen in the rise of another recent school called *Critical Realism*. We may name this the *New Critical Realism* to distinguish it from the older form already mentioned.[1] The representatives of this movement have analyzed the knowing situation with great keenness and found difficulties not merely with the old idealistic theories, but also with the results of the New Realism. Perception of objects is not so immediate as the New Realists think. Except by inference we cannot go beyond the *sense data*. If we carefully note what is actually given in perception when we see a coin lying on the table, or a wheel three feet in diameter rolling away from us, we shall at once recognize the fact that the circularity of the coin or the wheel is not immediately perceived, nor are many others of the features which we attribute to the real coin or wheel. Surely the heat of the fire is not directly perceived, for the heat differs with our distance from the fire. Illusions and hallucinations of all kinds offer difficulties, too, which no naïve Realism can solve.

Nevertheless, the Critical Realist is also a *real* Realist, for he rejects with emphasis the position of the Subjectivist and of the absolute Idealist. He accepts the objective existence of things because the view is plausible and conforms to common sense and works in practice. He accepts this, however, by "faith," rather than by knowledge, differing in this respect from the New Realist, who accepts the reality of the physical object because knowledge is merely the relation between such an object and the knowing mind.

The Critical Realist is, indeed, very much exercised over the question, which has perhaps too long lent itself to controversy, just what it is that is given in perception. He is no longer content, with the Subjectivist, to speak of such things as color and sound as sensations belonging only to a mind, nor yet is he willing to go to the extent of the New Realist and consider them as qualities of real objects. He does not believe that the outer object is actually and immediately apprehended. The outer object in its bare, brute

[1] The doctrines of this school may best be reviewed in a book entitled *Essays in Critical Realism*, also of composite authorship. The several chapters are written by Durant Drake, Arthur O. Lovejoy, James Bissett Pratt, Arthur K. Rogers, George Santayana, Roy Wood Sellars, and C. A. Strong.

reality is not given in experience. Only the *sense data* are present in experience, and they are complexes which, indeed, reveal the character of the object, but contain many other elements; that is, they reflect the nature of the perceiving mind as well as that of the perceived object.[1]

The outer object really exists quite independent of the perceiving mind, but it is something very different from the "datum of perception," the "character-complex apprehended," which has traits not belonging to the outer object. It is the outer object *as* the object appears to the perceiving mind, reflecting, indeed, some of the qualities of the real object, the primary qualities, but containing many secondary qualities, which reflect the character of the perceiving organism. The Critical Realist is, therefore, disposed to consider the sense data, or *sensa*, as something intermediate between the perceiving mind and the physically existent thing. So we hear a great deal about the *datum*, or *character-complex*, or *essence*. The mind cannot reach out to the object itself; it reaches out to the *essence*, the *datum*.

Thus it seems that in the knowing situation there are three kinds of entities: first, the perceiving mind or the conscious organism; second, the outer object, the ultimate brute reality, having only the primary qualities, not immediately apprehended in knowledge; third, the datum of perception, that which is immediately given to sense, named also the *character-complex* or *essence*. The latter is not mental, nor any part of the perceiving mind, nor is it a part or aspect of the outer object; it is an intermediate "logical entity."

This particular part of the knowledge problem is, to be sure, filled with difficulties, and, no doubt, any final Realism must be of the "critical" kind; but the difficulties will probably ultimately be solved by a somewhat "less critical" and more naïve Realism than that of this school; but if so, the researches made by the Critical Realists will contribute to the final results.

Mr. Santayana, for example, in his books called *Skepticism and Animal Faith* and *The Realm of Essence*, has written in his engaging manner much of "essences"; but the plain, blunt man finds difficulty in understanding what they are. One would fain believe that

[1] Compare Durant Drake, "The Approach to Critical Realism," in *Essays in Critical Realism.*

Santayana means that the perceiving organism grasps so much of
the physically existing thing as is significant to it — its essence for
him, the interested observer. But "essences" have a scholastic
flavor, and one can but wonder whether we need them. If physical
objects are real, it would seem hardly necessary to regard the way
they appear, their appearances, as "logical entities," floating between the organism and the object. It would seem quite natural
that they, the real objects, should call forth different reactions under
different circumstances. The "essences" of the Critical Realists
remind one of the "neutral entities" of the New Realists — things
that perhaps we can get along without.

It is, of course, true that the heat of the fire is sensed in a different
way according as the observer is near or far; but no mysterious essence, as object of intuition, is here necessary, for the real outer
object is heat-modified-by-distance. A patch of brown leaves may
be seen as a bear. But the sensing organism does not intuit an
"essence." It intuits a patch of brown leaves, and, owing to its own
mechanism, its past frights and subjective interests, it reacts as it
would react to a bear.

Possibly in some such way as this the problem could be worked
out. But we must remember that it is only in later stages of culture that sensitive organisms become interested in questions of
reality in the cognitive sense. For the most part the organism's
only interest is in the appropriate reaction to a given stimulus.
"How," it asks, "does this experience affect me and my welfare?
What is its meaning?" But when, in the case of human beings,
animal curiosity develops into scientific interest, then the observing mind begins to inquire about objective "reality"; and then the
observer desires to know what the objective world is *really* like —
that is, what it would be as intuited by an observer with no subjective interests — and he rebels against being told that no approach to the living reality is possible except through "faith," or
that he is hopelessly limited in his knowledge to phenomena, or to
"essences," or to his own sensations. He feels that he has a direct
contact with things, or at least with certain sides or faces of things,
and that sense perception reveals in part what things *are*, not merely
what they mean. The realistic movement of our day would seem

to lose much of its zest if we are to find in sense perception no direct approach after all to the outer existent thing. The latter seems to have receded again to a kind of mysterious Kantian *Ding an sich,* eluding every attempt to grasp it. If the logical position of the Critical Realist is better than that of the New Realist, he gains his advantage at great sacrifice, finding himself well on the way back to the camp of the Idealist.[1]

Conclusion

In our treatment of the general problem of the truth and validity of knowledge we have carried out a more or less dialectical argument of the case of Realism *vs.* Idealism. It is here, of course, that our epistemological viewpoint leads us into metaphysics, but in this discussion our primary interest has been that of the source and validity of knowledge. There are several prominent and highly significant points of view which we have omitted. The work of Ernst Cassirer,[2] for example, is a notable omission. In his epistemology he carries on the Kantian tradition and might be described as maintaining a position in many respects like that of critical Realism. An exposition of his doctrine would lead us too far afield in an introductory book on philosophy, but it should be said in passing that his comprehensive work in epistemology and philosophy of science, as well as in other fields, is unsurpassed. The interested student could well afford to consult his writings. Another omission is that of the work of the so-called *Wiener Kreis,* generally known as *logical positivism.* Probably the most outstanding representative of this school is Rudolf Carnap,[3] who holds that the province of knowledge lies within experience and that significant meaningful questions are those which permit of verifiable answers in the realm of possible experience. This of course challenges the traditional metaphysics. A further epistemological doctrine of great importance is the thesis that all scientific questions are co-terminus and thus a philosophical analysis of language will enable us to reduce all knowledge to a single logical order. A full account of this

---

[1] Compare Bosanquet's criticism in his *Contemporary Philosophy,* chap. VII.
[2] See his *Substance and Function* and his *Philosophie der symbolischen Formen.*
[3] See his little book *The Unity of Science.*

position here is beyond our present scope, but the student might well read "Logical Analysis of the Psycho-physical Problem," [1] by Herbert Feigl, which illustrates the method and some of the presuppositions of this standpoint. It is difficult to ascertain whether logical positivism is really an epistemological position. It seems to be more of a *method* in philosophy which emphasizes the strict analysis of concepts than either an epistemology or a metaphysics.

There remains a most important position in epistemology, namely, Pragmatism, which we will discuss in the next chapter.

In connection with this chapter read:

Gamertsfelder and Evans, *Fundamentals of Philosophy* (Prentice-Hall, Inc.), chap. vii.

Ralph Barton Perry, *Present Philosophical Tendencies* (Longmans, Green and Company), chap. xiii, "A Realistic Theory of Knowledge."

Further references:

G. P. Conger, *A Course in Philosophy* (Harcourt, Brace and Company), part 3.

J. A. Leighton, *The Field of Philosophy* (D. Appleton and Company), chaps. xii, xxi.

Bertrand Russell, *Our Knowledge of the External World* (*Scientific Method in Philosophy*) (Open Court Publishing Company), chap. iii.

G. E. Moore, *Philosophical Studies* (Harcourt, Brace and Company), chap. i, "The Refutation of Idealism"; also chaps. ii, v, vi, vii.

Durant Drake and others, *Essays in Critical Realism* (The Macmillan Company).

Edwin B. Holt and others, *The New Realism* (The Macmillan Company).

Sir James Jeans, *The New Background of Science* (The Macmillan Company), Revised edition, chap. i.

Durant Drake, *Mind and Its Place in Nature* (The Macmillan Company), chaps. i, ii.

Roy Wood Sellars, *The Philosophy of Physical Realism* (The Macmillan Company), chap. vii.

C. I. Lewis, *Mind and the World Order* (Charles Scribner's Sons).

[1] Article in *Philosophy of Science*, vol. i, no. 4, October, 1934.

CHAPTER XXV
PRAGMATISM

A philosophy of real life

PRAGMATISM is a new philosophy, having its rise within the twentieth century It is not so much a new philosophy as a new attitude, a new method of approach to philosophical problems. The word is from the Greek, having almost the meaning of our word *active*, or *efficient*. We may thus understand at once the spirit of Pragmatism, if we keep in mind that it always puts the emphasis upon what is practical, efficient, useful, fruitful, or satisfying.

So when the reader comes to this chapter on Pragmatism, he will perhaps say, "This is the philosophy for me! There is one fault I have to find with philosophy, namely, that it is too theoretical, too far removed from our practical concerns, too metaphysical and scholastic. What I want is a philosophy of life — of real life."

Well, this is what Pragmatism is. It is distinctly a philosophy of life. Life is real and the real is life. It is decidedly a human philosophy and has sometimes been called *Humanism*. When, therefore, philosophy becomes the science of human interests and the things which are vital to men become the subject of philosophical study, then, many will say, has come that regeneration of philosophy which has long been needed.

Pragmatism is distinctly a philosophy with a modern outlook. The ancient Greeks, with their aesthetic contemplative habits, with their mathematical and astronomical interests, with their curiosity to understand a ready-made perfected world, would have cared little for Pragmatism, which is a philosophy of action, doing, experimenting, achieving, overcoming. The Pragmatist does not think of the world as ready-made, perfect, beautiful, something to be enjoyed, contemplated, or worshiped; he thinks of it as a world to be made, or made over — remodeled to his desires and wishes. Consequently, it is not the astronomical Universe, the Cosmos, the world which the physical sciences try to penetrate, that the Pragmatist is interested in; it is the human world, the social world, the industrial world, the world of human affairs, which holds his attention. The world is in the making, and he wants to know how to make it better, that it may subserve his interests and his welfare.

Ideas as instruments

Consequently, the Pragmatist has a new and original notion of the mind, of ideas, of intelligence. He thinks of them as *instruments* for attaining certain ends, or removing difficulties and perplexities. So Pragmatism is often called *Instrumentalism.* The modern man is very much interested in instruments or tools. This peculiar interest has been growing ever since Archimedes invented the lever, with which he boasted he could move the world, if he had a place to stand. Archimedes, to be sure, was a Greek, but the Greeks of the classical period would not have understood him. They did not wish to move the world; they wished to study it, to contemplate and enjoy it.

But ever since the Industrial Revolution we have been trying to move the world, and inventing new tools for moving it, and for moving ourselves faster and faster around it. The modern man is the instrument-maker, and, taking his cue from this, the Pragmatist conceives of Nature as the instrument-maker and evolution itself as a process of experimentation, leading to the discovery of new instruments by which living organisms may attain their ends. Intelligence itself is such an instrument or tool, the result of Nature's experiments in evolution. Even philosophy is considered no longer as an end in itself, something of intrinsic worth and dignity, but as an instrument of social welfare.[1]

A difficulty

Now, all this seems quite exhilarating. It is certainly a new and fresh view of philosophy with wonderful practical possibilities. But our first acclaim may be attended with a little shadow of doubt. It is all just a bit confusing, for the reason that we had come to look upon philosophy in quite a different way from this. We had looked upon it as the search for knowledge and truth, as an attempt to

[1] Compare Dewey, *Reconstruction in Philosophy*, p. 124.

understand the world. We had thought of it as more like science, a wholly dispassionate and critical investigation of things, and their interpretation; and by their interpretation we had not meant their evaluation for any *end*, but their relation to one another and to the whole. Hence this sudden intrusion of "interests" and "cash values" and "satisfactions" and "fruits" is confusing. To be sure, the study of human interests, values, and satisfactions is a fascinating theme; just as *applied science*, which is the application of theoretical science to practical human problems, is a fascinating study, engrossing the attention of a vast army of seekers after wealth, power, comforts, and conveniences. But we had never thought of philosophy in this way.

If there is really any difficulty here, let us overlook it for the present and see if we can catch the real spirit of this new movement. It has certainly become a very famous philosophy, and we hear on every hand about James and Dewey and their numerous disciples. Whether Pragmatism be a true philosophy or not, it is certainly a vital one; and to the Pragmatist its vitality is evidence of its truth. Whatever we may conclude in the end about its value, we must recognize the fact that it has had a very wholesome effect upon philosophy in general, purifying it from many wordy subtleties and misty abstractions, and forcing it into the narrow path of hard fact and common sense.

Way of approach

It would be well for the reader to begin with James' little book, entitled *Pragmatism*. The rapid rise of the whole movement was largely due to James' brilliant defense of it.[1] He spoke directly to real men in real language which they could understand. This, they said, is not metaphysics; this is plain blunt truth about both pleasant and unpleasant facts. It seems like a good democratic philosophy.

If the successful launching of Pragmatism was due to James' spicy and pungent lectures and essays with his instinct for facts

---

[1] The credit for the original principle upon which Pragmatism is based is usually given to Charles Peirce, who in 1878 wrote an article for the *Popular Science Monthly*, entitled "How to Make Our Ideas Clear."

and the outcropping of his religious and mystical interests, the continued strength of the movement in America is to be attributed to Dewey's dialectic skill, connected with his widely known interest in educational reform and social welfare. With Dewey Pragmatism takes the form of *Studies in Logical Theory*, leading to an instrumental theory of knowledge and of truth, and is called *Instrumentalism*. In England, it has been ably defended by F. C. S. Schiller, with whom it takes the form of *Humanism*.

A book bearing the suggestive title *Creative Intelligence*, published in 1917, and co-operatively written by Dewey, Moore, Brown, Mead, Bode, Stuart, Tufts, and Kallen, sets forth the principles of Pragmatism in their various applications to philosophy, logic, mathematics, physical science, psychology, ethics, economics, art, and religion.

Pragmatism and religion

Although the interests of religion have usually been associated with "tender-minded" Rationalism rather than with that "tough-minded" Empiricism which is the father of Pragmatism, nevertheless, the latter has been found to have close affinities with religion and has been somewhat widely accepted by religious workers and thinkers. This is because of its emphasis upon the adventurous and strenuous character of life, upon the venture of faith and the will to believe, and because of its share in the prevailing interest in the psychology of religion. Hitherto the theoretical truth of religious beliefs has too much engrossed our attention. In practice religion *works*, and what works is in so far forth true, says Pragmatism. Even science, as Schiller points out, makes the venture of faith, setting out with strange hypotheses and theories, which await experimental verification.[1] "Our passional need for taking the world religiously," says James, "justifies the venture. It is better to yield to the hope that religion may be true than to yield to the fear that it may be false, since yield we must to one or the other." [2]

Pragmatism, then, is pluralistic and voluntaristic. It leans

[1] See F. C. S. Schiller, *Studies in Humanism*, p. 361.
[2] *The Will to Believe*, especially chap. 1.

toward Indeterminism, Nominalism, and Utilitarianism.   It is
evolutionary and naturalistic.   It has close affinities with Positivism
and with Empiricism.   It is anti-rationalistic and energetically
anti-intellectualistic, being therefore radically empirical and, in
James' picturesque phrase, "tough-minded."   Finally, it har-
monizes easily with the attitude of religion.

Pragmatism as a method

Pragmatism is a tendency and a movement rather than a philosophy.   In fact it holds philosophical systems in profound suspicion.   It is more like a "corridor" through which one may enter
upon philosophical studies.   It is an attitude and a habit of thought
— a habit of looking forward to results rather than backward to
first principles.   Everything is to be judged by its fruits, by its
consequences.   Thus it follows that any idea, theory, or dispute
which does not *make a difference* in its practical consequences
for us ceases at once to have any significance.   All these are simply
dropped; they cannot be tested.   Hence a great number of ancient
philosophical controversies, theories, hypotheses, systems just collapse; they fade away under this rigid pragmatic test.   *They do
not make any difference.*

> A pragmatist turns his back resolutely and once for all upon a lot of
> inveterate habits dear to professional philosophers.   He turns away
> from abstractions and insufficiency, from verbal solutions, from bad
> *a priori* reasons, from fixed principles, closed systems, and pretended
> absolutes and origins.   He turns towards concreteness and adequacy,
> towards facts, towards action and towards power.   That means the
> empiricist temper regnant and the rationalist temper sincerely given
> up.   It means the open air and possibilities of nature, as against dogma,
> artificiality, and a pretense of finality in truth.[1]

Everything moves and changes

In the older philosophy there was much talk about certain ideas,
such as God, Matter, Reason, the Absolute, the Soul.   These ideas
were ultimate, and we felt that we could rest in them.   But the
Pragmatist does not take this attitude toward them.   He does not
want to rest.   He inquires as to their cash value.   He will put them

---

[1] William James, *Pragmatism* (Longmans, Green and Company), p. 51.

to work and see what consequences they may yield. If they will not work, they are not true. "Pragmatism unstiffens all our theories, limbers them up and sets each one at work." In actual life we have always to deal with definite concrete situations, and these situations are to be met and solved on their own merits — not on abstract traditional principles. Life is a maze through which we are threading our way as best we can, finding the path as we go along. Answers which solved former situations will not solve this one. Everything changes, grows, develops; nothing is fixed, static, final.

Even moral laws change; they grow and become perfected. There are no fixed or final moral laws and no eternal principles either of conduct or knowledge. Reality is in the making; you and I are making it. The road to the future is an open road, obstructed by no overruling providence or limiting fates, and determined by no *a priori* principles of thought. Reality is found in the flow of experience. The world is moving toward no predetermined end; each hill is surmounted as it comes into view. What happens next is not determined, but is contingent upon what has happened. Life is a series of problems to be solved — a succession of real struggles with real difficulties. *To think* is to deal effectively with these problems — and ideas are tools to help in the solution.

Reality is fluid, changing, evolving. Pictures of a God-made, perfect world, governed by eternal principles of justice or by eternal mathematical laws, are just fancies. Leibniz' theory of the world as the best of all possible worlds is false. The only real world is the world of real experience. James mentions the case of a man with a wife and six children to support. The man was out of work and tramped for days through the snow searching for work in vain and then returned to find his family starving and a notice of dispossession on the door. He committed suicide by drinking carbolic acid. This is a piece of reality, but it does not mean that reality is bad. Reality is just experience, and this is a part of experience.

The spirit of Pragmatism is the spirit of youth, adventure, and experimentation; it has no patience with idle vaporings about fate and destiny. No philosophical ideas are true which cannot be put to some practical use. Take such words as *God, free-will*, or *design*.

Other than practical significance, says James, they have none. "Yet dark though they be in themselves, or intellectualistically taken, when we bear them into life's thicket with us, the darkness *there* grows light about us. If you stop in dealing with such words with their definitions, thinking that to be an intellectual finality, where are you? Stupidly staring at a pretentious sham. Pragmatism alone can give a rich meaning to them. God's in his heaven, all's right with the world."

Pragmatism is thus the forward-looking philosophy of hope and promise. Take, for instance, says James again, that ancient controversy between Materialism and Idealism. In themselves the two rival theories have no significance. Suppose the world to be now ending, having no future. What possible difference would it then make whether it is the product of blind mechanical energies or of living divine spirit? None whatever; the old controversy is dead. But now, with the Pragmatist, suppose the world to have an undetermined future. Then, indeed, it *will* make a difference whether we are Materialists or Idealists. For according to Materialism the blind forces which have built up the world will certainly destroy it. We must look forward sometime to a dead world, from which all hope is gone, and in which all ideals have perished. But if Idealism is true, if there is a God in the heaven, somehow the *good* will survive; we are assured of an ideal order that shall be permanently preserved.

Thus far Pragmatism seems tremendously stimulating. It gives to philosophy a life and movement which other systems lack. It is refreshing when philosophy is brought down to earth in this way and put to work. It is comforting to learn that all our experiences are integral parts of reality. But all this is only a manner of *approach* to philosophy, just a method. We are impatient to learn what the Pragmatist actually believes about the things usually studied in philosophy, about reality, about God, the soul, purpose, causality, knowledge, evolution, conduct.

I am afraid we shall be somewhat disappointed in the answers which the Pragmatist gives to these questions. His very purpose is to shift the interest away from some of these problems to those of practical importance. We must keep in mind that Pragmatism is a doctrine of method — not a theory of the Universe; and the Pragmatists, so far as they have ventured out into the field of metaphysics, have usually done so in order merely that they might find examples to illustrate their method. In demanding of them a philosophy of the world in general, we are asking more than they have promised to give. It seems, however, at least at first sight, that in their theory of radical empiricism they have ventured into metaphysics, trying to tell us what reality is. This we must now notice.

Radical empiricism

The view that philosophy is limited to actual experience brings us to one of the cardinal doctrines of Pragmatism, taking the form of *radical empiricism* with James and *immediate empiricism* with Dewey. If philosophy is to divest itself of all the excrescences that have accumulated through the ages, if it is to be concrete, vital, and real, it must start with something *actual*; and immediate experience is the only actual reality. Matter and spirit, body and soul, subject and object, *a priori* rules of thought or conduct — all these are too far away, too abstract, too unreal. Philosophy cannot begin with them — can perhaps have nothing to do with them. It has to do only with experience; the world is a world of pure experience. Expressions such as these have of course led to the charge that the Pragmatists have after all entered the field of metaphysics and proclaimed a theory of reality. Although the charge of subjective Idealism has repeatedly been laid at their door, and although numerous passages in their writings seem to admit of no other interpretation, nevertheless, they repudiate vigorously any subjectivism of the Berkeleian type, and constantly speak in a very realistic and common-sense way of the reality of the world beyond human experience.[1]

As for James, I think he did not mean that all reality is experi-

[1] There has been a long and not very profitable discussion in philosophical journals as to whether Pragmatism is idealistic and subjectivistic, the outcome of which seems to be that there is nothing in *essential* Pragmatism inconsistent with a realistic view of the world. A clear summary of the reasons may be found in four articles by W. P. Montague in volume VI of the *Journal of Philosophy, Psychology, and Scientific Method,* but Montague does not think that the Pragmatic *theory of truth* is consistent with Realism.

ence, but that "the only things that shall be debatable among philosophers shall be things definable in terms drawn from experience." He was concerned with the problem of analyzing experience to show that it does not imply any *a priori* categories, or substantial soul, or consciousness as an entity. He was desperately anxious to escape from all the old puzzles of subject and object, and the old dualism of mind and body. All these oppositions are not to be solved by calling in any higher unifying agent from some spiritual realm or some sphere of pure reason. The difficulties disappear if we regard these various oppositions as just different kinds of actual relationships, which really exist between the terms of experience. From this radically empirical standpoint even the old opposition between the mental and the physical disappears, for it depends upon the context into which the neutral stuff of pure experience gets, whether we call it mental or physical.

On the whole, it seems unfortunate that the Pragmatists should have insisted that all reality is experience. It has led to much misunderstanding. Their problem is psychological and epistemological rather than metaphysical. They want to show by the analysis of pure experience what knowledge does and does not imply. But one might be interested in fields of reality quite outside these provinces and be wholly unwilling to admit that all reality is experience in any sense of the term.

Instrumentalism

A further glance at that kind of Pragmatism called *Instrumentalism* will help us to understand why there is so much emphasis upon experience. The Instrumentalist is a biologist and an evolutionist. He is interested in showing how knowledge has arisen in the evolutionary movement, and in pointing out the function of intelligence. He therefore assumes outright the presence of the organism with its vital interests — its will-to-live, as you or I might say — and he assumes the presence of a real environment consisting of natural energies. Experience, then, is the intercourse of the living organism with its physical and social environment.[1] The questions why organisms exist, what they are made of, why they come to be organisms, why

[1] See *Creative Intelligence*, pp. 7 ff.

they strive and wish to live and propagate their kind, seem to many students of philosophy exceedingly interesting problems belonging properly to their field; and hence, since the Pragmatists in their theory of knowledge put so much stress on biological needs, one is apt to feel impatient with them for not *grounding* these biological needs more deeply.

The Instrumentalist, then, taking for granted the organism and its needs, goes on to show by the analysis of experience how such things as thought, reflection, intelligence, ideas, and concepts may be explained. He shows that the environmental energies are sometimes friendly and sometimes hostile to the good of the individual. The latter, therefore, is confronted with the task of controlling and moulding the environment to his own welfare; he must achieve the good and avert the evil. In such an enterprise, memory, imagination, reflection, and thought will be of priceless advantage in the struggle for existence, and by Darwinian laws will be encouraged and preserved. Thought is not a process of reduplication or copying of a determinate objective world, but a process of experimenting with it, changing it, moulding it to suit one's vital demands.

We are not to think of experience as the expression of any psychical entity or subject, such as a soul or spirit or consciousness. It is rather the interaction of organism with environment. Ideas are not psychical entities or subjective representations of an objective reality; they are plans of action, taking into account future consequences with reference to the weal or woe of the organism. By intelligence is meant just this ability to organize responses with constant reference to future consequences.

The process of intelligence is something that goes on, not in our minds, but in things; it is not photographic, but creative. From the simplest perception to the most ideal aspiration or the wildest hallucination, our human experience is reality engaged in the guidance or control of behavior. Things undergo a change in becoming experienced, but the change consists in a doing, in the assumption of a certain task or duty. The experiential object hence varies with the response; the situation and the motor activity fit together like the sections of a broken bowl.

The bearing of this standpoint on the interpretation of psychology is readily apparent. If it be granted that consciousness is just a name for behavior that is guided by the results of acts not yet performed but reflected beforehand in the objects of experience, it follows that this behavior is the peculiar subject-matter of psychology.[1]

Purpose and conflict

Two things stand out prominently in the pragmatic psychology; first, the purposive character of thought, and, second, the importance of conflict. All thinking is purposive. Pragmatism itself is defined by Schiller as "the thorough recognition that the purposive character of mental life generally must influence and pervade also our most remotely cognitive activities." Pragmatism is thus thoroughly teleological, not in the wider sense of a cosmic purposiveness, but in the sphere of mental life. It is what we may call a teleological voluntarism.[2]

The notion of conflict is equally important. Our whole conscious life arises in conflict, where a difficult situation has to be surmounted, where a problem of readjustment has to be solved. We may conceive that consciousness itself arose when some animal awoke to the discovery that the old habitual responses were not adequate to the new difficult situation. A sudden interruption of the even flow of vital functions made it necessary for the animal for the first time in his life, or the life of his kind, to do some thinking, to awake to consciousness — to sit up and take notice. So Pragmatism reverses the old belief that first comes the soul, and then the soul thinks. Quite the contrary, the soul is born in thought and thought is born in struggle and in tension. But the significant and joyful fact remains that the difficulty *is* overcome, the problem *is* solved. Pragmatism is thus the forward-looking philosophy of promise and fulfillment.

Hence it comes about that intelligence is creative. It is constantly moulding and making reality. But this creative force is always a process of experimentation. It is different from the creative work of the artist, who is striving to approach to some pattern or ideal.

[1] Bode, "Consciousness and Psychology," in *Creative Intelligence* (Henry Holt and Company), p. 255.
[2] Compare F. C. S. Schiller, *Humanism*, p. 8.

What is truth?

We have left till the last the mention of one of the most distinctive of the pragmatic doctrines, the theory of truth. It is this which made Pragmatism famous — some would say, infamous. It is the striking and paradoxical character of the theory which has brought it into such prominence.

In order to understand this doctrine of truth, it would be a good plan for the reader to lay down this book and ask himself the question, What *is* truth? What does the word *truth* mean? What do we mean by saying that a proposition is true or false? The statement that the shores of New England are bathed by the waters of the Pacific Ocean is said to be false. Why? That they are bathed by the waters of the Atlantic is true. Why?

The correspondence theory

Probably the answer would be something like this: Truth is that which *conforms* to fact, which *agrees* with reality, which *corresponds* to the actual situation. This is called the *correspondence theory of truth*. It is the view of the so-called plain man, who distinguishes the fact from the statement of the fact, and when the statement corresponds with the fact, then it is true. The reason, then, that the statement is true that the shores of New England are bathed by the waters of the Atlantic, is that this statement corresponds with the facts. Before anyone ever made this *judgment*, the waters of the Atlantic did actually bathe the shores of New England.

Now, all sorts of objections may be made to this definition of truth. The difficulties in defining truth were known long before Pragmatism exploited them. It is said, for instance, that it is impossible to compare a judgment or statement with external reality. You can lay your yardstick alongside a board and observe whether they correspond, but you cannot lay a judgment beside a fact to see if they correspond. Does it mean anything to say that a judgment "corresponds to" a fact, or that it "copies" external reality?

Furthermore, it is complained, it is mere tautology to say that a judgment, such as the rose is red, corresponds to the fact, for facts themselves are merely cases of knowledge. The fact and the truth are the same thing, so that it is useless to say that truth is correspondence to fact.

Now, in recent years, as a result of the pragmatic theory, a whole new literature has sprung up relating to the meaning of the word *truth*, a discussion altogether too technical to be of interest to us in this brief chapter.   It will be possible here only to state the other theories of truth, particularly the pragmatic theory, intimating to the wise reader that a whole course of study would be necessary before he could decide between the rival views.   Meanwhile, if one wishes to *tell* the truth, there is not much difficulty in knowing what it is.

Concerning the correspondence theory of truth, however, it may do no harm to say that, in spite of its difficulties, it is probably more widely held by philosophers and scientists who have given thought to the subject than any other theory.   Possibly the word *fidelity* may be preferable to the word *correspondence*.   Truth, then, would be defined as fidelity to objective reality, and I do not see that any serious difficulties need arise with this definition.

Let us make the postulate, harmless as such, that there are real independent things, such as oceans and shores, suns and planets, roses and qualities of roses.   Let us suppose that these things with their relations and their qualities really existed before there were any sentient beings to observe them, or reasoning men or quarreling philosophers to make judgments about them.   Then suppose such reasoning beings should come and observe these things and invent language to designate them and their relations and qualities, and should then say, for instance, that the sun is larger than the earth. Such a judgment would be a faithful one, and such fidelity might be called truth.   It should be observed also of the fidelity theory of truth that this or something like this is what the word *truth* means in common usage; so that if anyone uses the word *truth* in a wholly different sense, this fact should be made perfectly clear.

The coherence theory of truth

Owing to the difficulties in the correspondence theory, another view has been propounded to the effect that truth is *consistency*. What do we mean when we say that a theorem in geometry is true? Here we do not mean primarily that it corresponds to objective reality, but that it fits perfectly into a certain system of other theorems, propositions, axioms, and definitions.   There is perfect coherence, and this coherence with other certain and accepted things is called truth.

Undoubtedly the word *truth* is used in this narrower sense. If we start with premises that are true in some other sense of the word *truth*, and if our conclusions are logically drawn, we call our conclusions true. In geometry we start with a few axioms and definitions, and proceeding logically, the whole system will be true, or as true as the initial assumptions. But this is evidently not what we mean by *truth* in common usage as it is applied to judgments of matters of fact. Indeed, it would seem to be possible to have a whole consistent system of falsehoods. For instance, Johnny's mother tells him not to go in swimming; but he goes and then tells her that he did not go, and then, buttressing his statement with that of his pals, builds up a chain of evidence to support his lie that makes it seem to his mother to be a coherent and consistent system, his own statement fitting in perfectly with all the other elements in the situation. All the parts of this system are coherent, and yet we could not say that the various statements are true. If we say that the several parts are not coherent with the original act, then we are going back to the correspondence theory. Certainly, however, consistency is an element in some kinds of truth. A group of propositions is not up to the ideal of truth, if the propositions are not internally consistent. The consistency theory and the correspondence theory supplement rather than contradict each other. Perhaps the simplest and best view is just this, that truth is fidelity to reality; but since in innumerable cases we cannot compare our ideas and judgments with reality, the best we can do is to see if they are *consistent* with other ideas and judgments which we have accepted as true.

The pragmatic theory of truth

According to the Pragmatist, who starts with the mere flux of experience and finds reality in this flux, the two older theories of truth seem to have no application. Possibly, also, the Pragmatist, in working out his new theory of truth, has been influenced by the Idealist's belief in something called *absolute truth*, the notion that there is somewhere laid up a body of truth that is sacred and unchanging. Now, the Pragmatist is not friendly to the notion of the absolute in any form. At this point it does not occur to him to drop the word *truth*, since his system has no place for it in any sense in which it has commonly been used; but he proposes to redefine *truth*, giving it quite a new and unexpected meaning.[1]

To make clear the pragmatic theory of truth, let us begin by inquiring, first, not about the *nature* of truth, but about its criterion. This is not the question of what truth is, but how we are to know it, how it is to be tested. The world is full of theories, hypotheses, general opinions, and guesses, where direct verification by an appeal to observed facts is not possible. Various criteria of truth have been proposed in ancient and modern times, such as "irresistible conviction," "inconceivability of the opposite," "presenting itself to the mind with such clearness and distinctness that it cannot be doubted." Now, the Pragmatist proposes another criterion, and a very practical one, to the effect that any theory or hypothesis or idea is true, *if it leads to satisfactory consequences*, if it works out in practice, if it has practical value. Truth is revealed by its usefulness, by its fruits, by its practical consequences. Value becomes the measure of truth. Truth works in the long run, and if any idea or theory works, we may suppose it to be true. Satisfactory working, fulfillment of function, successful leading, are the marks of truth.

Now there seems to be nothing very revolutionary or strange about this. It is reasonable to suppose that truth in the long run will lead to good and satisfactory results; and usefulness, while it may not be the sole criterion of truth, or an infallible one, still is a good practical test.

But, unfortunately, the Pragmatist does not stop with this wholesome doctrine. He goes on to say that workableness is not merely the *test* of truth, it is the *nature* of truth. You and I, perhaps, took for granted that the nature of truth is its agreement with reality and anything which agrees with reality will probably lead to satisfactory results in practice; so that, if it leads to such results, it is probably true. But the Pragmatist — that is, the extreme Pragmatist — says that the usefulness of truth is all there is to it. Truth *is* that which works. "True ideas," says James, "are those that we can assimilate, validate, corroborate and verify. False ideas are

---

[1] James, harassed by his critics, did finally propose to leave the adjective *true* for the older notion and adopt the word *truthful* for the pragmatic one. (See *The Meaning of Truth.* p. 225.)

those that we cannot." "The truth of an idea is not a stagnant property inherent in it. Truth *happens* to an idea. It *becomes* true, is *made* true by events. Its verity *is* in fact an event, a process; the process namely of its verifying itself, its veri-*fication*. Its validity is the process of its valid-*ation*." [1] Hence it follows that ideas and judgments are not true until they are verified, and their verification consists in their leading to satisfactory consequences. If the statement is made that there is another planet within the orbit of Mercury, the statement is neither true nor false, but becomes so in the process of verification or non-verification.

This theory, propounded by the Pragmatist, that truth is what works well in practice, that it is a kind of expediency, met with a storm of criticism and disapproval. It was only the eminent character of its proponents that gave it a wide hearing. Hitherto truth had been regarded as something cherished and, in a way, sacred, as something definite and stable, at least as stable as the things about which the truth was asserted. The statement that there is another planet within the orbit of Mercury is, it was supposed, either true or false when it was made, depending upon the actual constitution of the solar system. Hence the pragmatic notion of truth as something that happens to a judgment in the course of its verification came as a kind of shock to students of philosophy. This extreme form of the theory has been difficult to defend, and it has been modified in many ways by later writers of the school.[2] It seems possible to maintain it only on the basis of a subjectivist philosophy. When it is still maintained, it is evident that the word *truth* is used in a sense different from its generally accepted meaning.

Pragmatists are very fond of speaking of the truth of ideas, rather than of judgments, and, since ideas in pragmatic philosophy are merely "plans of action," just what do they mean when they say that they are true? A plan of action might be a good plan or a bad plan, but we should hardly speak of it as true or false. If a town

[1] William James, *Pragmatism*, p. 201.

[2] A useful summary and criticism of the pragmatic theory of truth may be found in D. C. Macintosh's *The Problem of Knowledge*, pp. 401–37. No one interested in this discussion should fail to read the book, *What Is Pragmatism?* by James Bissett Pratt, especially lectures II and III. Compare also the keen criticism of James' theory of truth by G. E. Moore in his book, *Philosophical Studies*, chap. III.

were threatened by a flood and someone proposed a plan of action, his fellow townsmen would not ask whether the plan is a *true* one, but whether it is a *good* one or a *feasible* one.

So it all seems to come to this: If the Pragmatists mean that satisfactory working is a test or criterion of truth, the view is as wholesome as it is old and innocent.[1] If they mean that ideas or judgments as plans of action are true because of leading to satisfactory consequences — that is, find their truth in the satisfactory consequences — they are using the word *true* where other people would use the word *good*; and a lot of trouble and misunderstanding would have been avoided if the Pragmatist had used the word *good* or invented some other word expressing value. The *test* of truth is one thing; the *structure* or *nature* of truth is quite another.

The whole controversy is coming now to have only an historical significance, since later pragmatic writers seem to recognize, though perhaps guardedly, the validity of the correspondence theory, at least within limits.[2] What the Pragmatists were alarmed at was the absolutist doctrine of a body of unchanging truth laid up, so to speak, in the heavens. Possibly now Pragmatists and others could agree that individual perceptions and judgments are true when they are adapted to the facts of the environment,[3] emphasizing as Schiller does that the reality which philosophy seeks is a *selected* reality. God, matter, purpose, and such concepts are the selected portions of reality which philosophy considers best worth knowing.[4]

[1] Of course, satisfactory working is not even an infallible test. Take again the case of Johnny and his mother. Johnny goes in swimming and derives great *satisfaction* from the adventure. On returning home Johnny's mother asks him if he has been in swimming, and he says "No," and offers a wholly plausible and *satisfactory* explanation of his absence. Johnny's mother unreservedly accepts this explanation and gets great *satisfaction* from the supposed veracity of her offspring. Johnny's companions in the adventure, who know the whole situation, derive much *satisfaction* from it all. Johnny's bath resulted in very *satisfactory* hygienic conditions, and on Saturday night Johnny's mother, after an examination of Johnny's arms and legs, derives an increased *satisfaction* from Johnny's increasingly cleanly habits. Hence, if truth is that which leads to satisfactory results, Johnny's statement that he did not go in swimming must have been true. And if, to escape this difficulty, the Pragmatist adds that the statement is true "in so far forth," then the whole thing reduces to the truistic result that satisfactory working is a help in the discovery of truth.

An illustration of this kind is of course a parody on the pragmatic doctrine of truth and is only justified in silencing those who have attempted to make *emotional* satisfaction rather than logical satisfaction the test of truth.

[2] Compare Murray's *Pragmatism*, pp. 45, 46.

[3] Compare the clear article by Montague in *Jour. of Phil., Psych., and Sci. Meth.*, vol. VI, pp. 233–38.

[4] Compare F. C. S. Schiller, *Humanism*, chap. III.

The permanent contributions of Pragmatism

It is a little difficult as yet to estimate the actual contributions to philosophy of this new movement. It has certainly done good service in again calling philosophy down from the heavens to the hearths and homes of men. Philosophy hitherto had been very much an avocation of a few select "highbrows," who frequented college and university classrooms, distant from the practical interests of common men. The recent widespread revival of interest in philosophy has been partly due to the work of the Pragmatists. People who shivered at the very name of philosophy, confusing it with the Hegelian dialectic or the Roycean Absolute, now began to study Pragmatism, and entering through this gate, found philosophy interesting and helpful. If we are shocked at the extravagances and paradoxes of the Pragmatists, it is well to remember that nothing but a jolt like this would have brought philosophy down to earth.

Particularly was the theory of knowledge a dark and forbidding field for any but the elect. The very word *epistemology* suggested something quite awful. Dewey, by showing that all those different and difficult things like concepts, ideas, syllogisms, thought, and imagination, are merely practical instruments for solving the problems and perplexities of life, and are quite naturally evolved as new powers which animal organisms develop when new conditions arise, has brought the whole subject within the comprehension of practical-minded men. The genetic treatment of knowledge has thrown much light upon this difficult chapter in philosophy. Much of the mystery has been removed from a long list of psychological terms, such as thought, intellect, reflection, imagination, mind, and consciousness, fitting them into the general evolutionary scheme. Pragmatism has become a live branch of philosophy because it emphasizes the things which everybody is interested in now — evolution, growth, will, purpose, initiative, practical results, human hopes and desires, human progress. It was fully time for a reaction against the excessive intellectualism of preceding systems, and Pragmatism represents this reaction in its extreme form.

Another fine thing which the Pragmatists have done is to call our attention to the creative power of the human mind, or creative intelligence. It has been a revelation to many that a philosophical system which is at once strongly evolutionary and naturalistic may still speak of the creative mind, of new ethical and social ideals, of moral and social progress. People had thought of naturalism and evolution as associated with materialism, determinism, and fatalism, as though man were helpless in the face of mechanical forces, as though he were a puppet awaiting his fate at the hands of the physical forces of the Universe. Pragmatism teaches that the world is in the making and you and I are making it, and that there is no limit to our effective agency. Even moral laws change and may be much improved.

What has been called *Essential Pragmatism* seems to me to be a genuine philosophy of life. In its early enthusiasms, however, it was beguiled into extreme positions,[1] and so plunged us into hair-splitting dialectic which would put the old Schoolmen to shame. As examples of such positions may be mentioned, first, the extreme pragmatic doctrine of truth, with the unhappy dialectical entanglements which followed; and, second, the identification of experience with reality.

But something is lacking

What seems to be lacking in Pragmatism is a high idealism. There is too great an emphasis upon the striving and not enough upon the goal. The pragmatic world view seems confined to that particular part of reality which begins with the organism already in possession of certain unexplained interests and desires, and is concerned only with the means of satisfying these desires. Thought becomes a mere tool for satisfying our vital demands without a sufficient examination of the demands themselves. The Pragmatists have frequently resented, and perhaps with much justice, the imputation that they hold a narrow utilitarian view of life; and Dewey speaks of the "intrinsic, aesthetic, and immediate value of thought and of science," and of the joy and dignity of life which intelligence adds.[2] But intelligence is never really considered as a goal, but only as a guide. What it is a guide to, no Pragmatist seems

---

[1] James, himself, to whom Pragmatism owes almost its very life, was one of the worst offenders in this respect.

[2] See his article on the "Development of American Pragmatism," in the *Revue de Métaphysique et de Morale*, October, 1922. Manuscript translation by Herbert W. Schneider.

to know. We are exhorted to have faith in intelligence as the savior of men; but what we are to be saved from, or what we are to be saved for, is not made clear.

Is the empiricism of Pragmatism, after all, deep enough? Do not men instinctively strive toward a goal rather than search for some instrument for increasing their satisfactions? Pragmatism boasts of being fundamentally teleological, of always turning toward the future, and yet the end is never clearly defined.

The Pragmatists in reacting from the old intellectualism, which looked upon the intellect as an oracle, have come to regard it as a mere tool or contrivance, in which the will is nothing but a will-to-live, not actuated by any lofty purpose or pursuing any sublime ideal, but tinkering with its environment in order to find *some* way through, endlessly trying experiments to see if *some satisfaction might happen,* and always retreating if vital needs are not enhanced. This may all be true, but *it certainly is not the way it feels to be a man,* and it certainly is not the notion of the human spirit that has been handed down to us by our fathers — even in this utilitarian America. Dewey, to be sure, speaks about social welfare as the end and aim of philosophy, but somewhat vaguely and obscurely. One gets the impression that it is just the satisfaction of biological needs which constitutes social welfare. And, indeed, it does not seem to me that philosophy exists for the sake of social welfare. Philosophy and science, religion and art, are themselves ends to be attained in any perfect society.

There is certainly some justification for Windelband's severe criticism of Pragmatism, when he says that it is "a grotesque confusion of means and ends." "It represents a victory of noetic individualism which, in the decay of our intellectual culture, would release the elementary force of the will and let it pour itself over the realm of pure thought. It calls into question one of the greatest achievements of civilization, the purity of the will to truth." [1]

The great things of the world have been done by men who were inspired by great ideals, ideals of justice, righteousness, beauty, and truth. These lofty ideals are not something to be made and then

[1] Wilhelm Windelband. *An Introduction to Philosophy.* Translated by Joseph McCabe (T. Fisher Unwin), p. 175.

tested by their satisfactoriness; they are something to be attained. Beauty which exists just to be *appreciated*, truth which exists just to be *contemplated*, laws of nature which just have to be *discovered* and *wondered at*, ideals which just have to be *aspired to* — all these great things would seem to have no place in pragmatic philosophy, which is too subjective. *Something eternal must draw us on.*

In connection with this chapter read:

William James, *Pragmatism* (Longmans, Green and Company).
Arthur Kenyon Rogers, *English and American Philosophy Since 1800* (The Macmillan Company), chap. vii, "Pragmatism."

Further references:

James Bissett Pratt, *What Is Pragmatism?* (The Macmillan Company).
A. W. Moore, *Pragmatism and Its Critics* (The University of Chicago Press).
John Dewey and others, *Creative Intelligence* (Henry Holt and Company).
F. C. S. Schiller, *Studies in Humanism* (The Macmillan Company).
David Leslie Murray, *Pragmatism* (Constable and Company).
A. O. Lovejoy, "The Thirteen Pragmatisms," *Jour. of Phil., Psych., and Sci. Meth.*, vol. v, p. 5.
John Dewey, *The Influence of Darwin on Philosophy* (Henry Holt and Company); *Essays in Experimental Logic* (The University of Chicago Press); *Human Nature and Conduct* (Henry Holt and Company).
Josiah Royce, "The Problem of Truth in the Light of Recent Discussion," in *William James and Other Essays* (The Macmillan Company).
Bertrand Russell, *The Analysis of Mind* (George Allen and Unwin, Limited), lecture xiii, "Truth and Falsehood."
Eric Temple Bell, *The Search for Truth* (Williams and Wilkin Company).
C. W. Morris, "Pragmatism and Metaphysics," *Phil. Rev.*, vol. xliii, p. 6.

Part V

THE HIGHER VALUES OF LIFE

CHAPTER XXVI

THE IDEA OF GOD

No DOUBT every writer upon the God problem approaches the subject with diffidence and hesitation. Apart from the purely philosophical difficulties of the problem there is so much divergence of opinion and such great confusion as to the meaning of the word *God* that the diffidence and hesitation can well be appreciated. In dealing with this problem we shall endeavor to avoid dogmatism or reliance upon authorities in our effort to determine what we can reasonably understand God to be and to ascertain what reasons there are for faith in his existence. Philosophy being an intellectual enterprise, we cannot surrender ourselves to emotional or wishful thinking, even though we deal with such a time-honored and lofty theme as the one in hand.

There has been a slow and gradual evolution of the idea of God from the very crudest notions of primitive man to the larger and truer conceptions of the present. One thing which makes this subject very difficult for us is that somewhat the same evolution of the God idea takes place in the mind of the individual that has taken place in the history of mankind. As we outgrow our childish notions, a period of readjustment is necessary, which is often the occasion of perplexity and even of scepticism. Notwithstanding all these difficulties, there are certain things to be said in this chapter which should bring to the student of philosophy some assurance and comfort. We recall Francis Bacon's saying that it is a *little* philosophy which leads to atheism.

Methods of approach

There are several methods of approach to the God problem, many of them quite beyond the compass of an introductory book on philosophy. The subject may be approached from the standpoint of one's own individual religious experience. It may be approached from the standpoint of religious faith in the teachings of the church or religious authority. It may be approached from the standpoint of profound philosophical reflection.

In a short introductory chapter such as this the God problem cannot be studied in any of these ambitious ways; but it may be stated, the terms may be defined, and some of the older and some of the more recent views may be given. Oftentimes we are more interested to know what the great men of the world, the philosophers and the poets and the scientists, have thought and said about God than we are in tracing through a subtle argument to prove or disprove his existence. And we are all anxious to know whether the methods and results of science, in which we have such unbounded trust, have any bearing on the subject, and if so what this bearing is. Perhaps the most important thing of all is to find out just what we mean, or ought to mean, by the word *God*.

Authority has been so much abused in the history of religion that we have come to rebel against this method of instruction; yet after all for most of us authority counts more than argument, especially if it is the authority of our own particular saints, be they religious teachers, philosophers, poets, scientists, or men of affairs. For instance, it is to many interesting and perhaps convincing to know that Lord Arthur J. Balfour, formerly English Premier, among his other philosophical works wrote a book called *Theism and Humanism* in which he based the necessity for God upon three spheres of human thought and action, namely, ethics, aesthetics, and the principles of knowledge. Others find their faith in God strengthened when they recall that Browning, in his earliest long poem written at the age of twenty-one, exclaimed, "Sun-treader, I believe in God and truth and love," and that then, after a long life rich in human experience, he wrote in his "Francis Furini":

> Though Master keep aloof,
> Signs of his presence multiply from roof
> To basement of the building!

Others, again, like to trace the God idea through the history of races from the earliest primitive tribes to our present civilized peoples, or to follow it in the history of philosophy from Plato and Aristotle to Josiah Royce or William James. This insurgence of the God idea in almost every philosophy, ancient or modern, and this saturation, so to speak, of popular as well as religious thought with God stimulate our interest and curiosity in this problem. We long to have it made clearer, and to learn of the attitude toward it of our modern scientific and philosophical thinkers.

Definition of terms

The prominence of the idea of God in the history of thought is shown by the richness of the vocabulary. We should become acquainted with the exact meaning of some of the most important terms. *Theism*, from the Greek word for God, is the term applied to the common belief in God as a personal, spiritual being, with whom it is possible to come into intimate relations. *Deism*, from the Latin *deus*, is a term applied to the beliefs of a school of eighteenth-century thinkers who accepted the existence of God as creator and lawgiver, but who distrusted the personal relationship and who denied the possibility of miracles. *Pantheism*, from two Greek words meaning all and God, is the doctrine that God is all and all is God; God is identical with Nature or with the world. *Polytheism* means any system of religion or doctrine that recognizes a number of gods or many gods; *Monotheism* is a system insisting that there is only one God. *Atheism* is the name applied to a consistent attempt to deny or disprove the existence of God. Atheism in modern thought has largely given place to the more modest doctrine of agnosticism. *Agnosticism* teaches that human knowledge by its very nature is limited, and attempts to describe the kind of limitation it finds characteristic of our knowledge. In any case it finds knowledge of ultimate reality impossible, and there-fore, of course, knowledge of God impossible.

Philosophy, however, although it may not be able to penetrate very far into the mystery of God, must not shrink from the attempt. It can at least investigate the meaning of God in human experience, and it can ask whether the belief in such a being is consistent with the science and philosophy of the present day, and whether it answers to any actual need in our experience.

In his famous *Critique of Pure Reason*, Kant reduced the many proofs for the existence of God to three — the cosmological, the teleological, and the ontological. The cosmological proof rests on the notion that there must have been a first cause; there is a final ground for the existence of this world. The argument is useless, however, because the same problem then attaches to the "first" cause. What brought this into being? If nothing brought it into being, it always was; but this hypothesis helps little because we could equally well assume that the world itself always was, and thus would not have to assume a first cause or God to account for it. The teleological argument is very similar to the cosmological. The world seems everywhere to reveal a rational ordering and a benevolent design, which certainly points to the fact that there must be a divine architect or designer of the world. This argument is often challenged on the basis that the Universe is not benevolent, and if this argument is sound, God is an evil king. But both of these arguments rest on the ontological argument, which asserts simply that God is a being whose very nature implies existence. God is said to be most perfect, most real, and thus must exist, otherwise he would be neither of these. There are many objections to this argument, the most obvious of which is the fact that by calling God most real or most perfect we have merely declared his existence and not proven it. The teleological and cosmological arguments rest on the assumption that there is a being which exists through its own necessity or nature, but Kant holds that this assumption is fraught with difficulties which render a rational demonstration of God's existence impossible. While Kant thus rejects the validity of these "rational" proofs of God's existence, in his Practical Reason he establishes it again on moral grounds.

This mode of procedure, however, is somewhat antiquated. The more hopeful task is that of determining the meaning of the God idea and inquiring whether in the outer world of science or the inner world of experience there is anything which calls for or answers to this meaning. This is our task in the present chapter.

God in human experience

What, then, does the word *God* mean to us. At the very first, when we begin to reflect carefully about this subject, we see that we must distinguish between the way we image or visualize God or think about him in our everyday thought, and the meaning which we attach to the word, when we reflect seriously about him. Influenced by paintings which we have seen in childhood, or by the vivid imagery of Milton's *Paradise Lost*, we think of God in human form, magnified, perhaps, and glorified, but having human attributes both of body and mind. *Anthropomorphism* is the technical term which describes this common tendency to give to God the form of man. Xenophanes, an early Greek philosopher-poet, bitterly complained that human beings think of the gods in human form. Modern critics have also ridiculed the anthropomorphic habit, not, perhaps, always realizing that those who practice it do not take it too seriously; for when asked, first, what they mean by the word *God*, and, second, how they think of him, the results in the two cases are found to be quite different. The criticism also has been made that in referring to God we use the pronouns *He* and *Him*, with the implication that God is masculine. Evidently this, too, should not be taken too seriously. We have no pronoun which can be applied to a *person* who is neither masculine nor feminine, and he and him are of course used generically in this case. The Christian Scientists speak graciously of the Father-Mother God.

What most people *mean* when they use the word *God* is a supernatural being, spoken of as a Spirit, who is righteous and supremely powerful, who has a certain control over our destiny, and with whom we may come into friendly relations, if our own character and attitude are right. They regard him, perhaps, also as the creator of the world, and as moral lawgiver and judge, and believe that he is everywhere present in the world as an indwelling presence.

An analysis of this or any current conception shows that the God idea resolves itself into the idealization of certain fundamental and characteristic values which have ranked high in human experience, particularly *power, righteousness, love, justice,* and *personality.* These are the things which appeal to us as of supreme worth, and God is the embodiment or personification of these ideals. In our own lives, which have from the beginning been social, we have experienced the joy of power when we ourselves exercise it, and the fear of it when exercised by others. As for righteousness, it has been the very condition of all social life; only by its practice can men live together in social groups. Love is equally fundamental in human intercourse, not only in the family, but in the form of co-operation in the community; while justice, which is the adequate adjustment of rewards and punishments to conduct, answers to a deep inner demand of the heart.

But we live not only in a social world; we live in the presence of objective nature. We are its product, its children, perhaps its puppets. God, then, is that mysterious and unknown Power, fearful yet friendly, which manifests itself in the productive power of nature, in life and death, in the raging storm, in the vast ocean, in the deadly flash of lightning, in the beneficent life-giving sunshine, in the timely rain. God is fearful, yet friendly. He made the world and made us. He demands righteousness and justice; yet ultimately he has a kindly attitude toward man, responding to his prayers. It is no doubt due to our efforts to give expression to these ideal excellences that it has been customary to give God such attributes as Absolute, Eternal, Infinite, Omnipotent, Omniscient, and Omnipresent. These terms, formerly much used, may be regarded as so many superlatives by means of which we attribute to God power, knowledge, and presence *very* great.

But while these two ideas of God, as the personification of all ideal excellences and the embodiment of natural forces, have predominated in religious thought, they do not quite express the whole meaning. God, to many, perhaps to finer souls like that of Emerson, is the Over-Soul, "the wise silence, the universal beauty, the Eternal One," while to Wordsworth he is "a presence that disturbs me with the joy of elevated thoughts; a sense sublime of something far more deeply interfused, whose dwelling is the light of setting suns, and the round ocean and the living air, and the blue sky, and in the mind of man; a motion and a spirit that impels all thinking things, all objects of all thought, and rolls through all things." Wordsworth, therefore, needs no proofs of God, for he is *felt*, and felt as a *presence*, a presence disturbing, yet disturbing with the joy of elevated thoughts.

The Mystics of all ages have in a similar way felt and experienced God rather than thought or reasoned about him, and felt him as *life* or *love* or *infinitude*.

William James and the divine MORE

Thus far, then, in this chapter we have learned nothing definite at all as to whether God exists or not. We have merely noticed something of the importance of the problem in the history of human thought, and we have seen in general what the meaning of the God idea is to common people, to the poet and to the mystic. Let us now try to learn something of the attitude of science toward the subject and the attitude of philosophers of the present day. James' method of approach to the problem may be our first concern. It is in the concluding chapter of his remarkable book, *The Varieties of Religious Experience*, and in his essays, "Is Life Worth Living?" and "Reflex Action and Theism," the last two found in his book, *The Will to Believe*, that James gives us his most significant thoughts about God and ultimate spiritual reality.

James does not proceed by the old method of displaying grounds for one's belief. Rather he reminds each of us of our own experience of God. Dr. Cabot in his book, *What Men Live By*, says the four things we live by are work and play and love and worship. So James shows us by the pragmatic method that God is what we live by. In many of our experiences, we seem to touch another dimension of existence than the sensible and merely "understandable" world. Call it the mystical or the supernatural or the unseen world, as we may, or merely some kind of extension of our subconscious mind, nevertheless we feel a real connection with it, we get real power from it, and in it find the source of our ideal impulses. This strong feeling, or even conviction, which so many of us have that this natural world, this world of wind and water, is not the whole of reality; but that it is, so to speak, soaking in or is bathed in another order or another kind of reality to which we may give the name *spiritual* or *ideal*, seems, so James thinks, to be pragmatically verified by its results.

The notion that this physical world of wind and water, where the sun rises and the moon sets, is absolutely and ultimately the divinely aimed-at and established thing, is one which we find only in very early religions, such as that of the most primitive Jews. It is this natural religion (primitive still, in spite of the fact that poets and men of science whose good-will exceeds their perspicacity keep publishing it in new editions tuned to our contemporary ears) that, as I said a while ago, has suffered definitive bankruptcy in the opinion of a circle of persons, among whom I must count myself, and who are growing more numerous every day. For such persons the physical order of nature, taken simply as science knows it, cannot be held to reveal any one harmonious spiritual intent. It is mere *weather*, as Chauncey Wright called it, doing and undoing without end.

Whatever else be certain, this at least is certain — that the world of our present natural knowledge is enveloped in a larger world of some sort of whose residual properties we at present can form no positive idea.

That the world of physics is probably not absolute, all the converging multitude of arguments that make in favor of idealism tend to prove; and that our whole physical life may lie soaking in a spiritual atmosphere, a dimension of being that we at present have no organ for apprehending, is vividly suggested to us by the analogy of the life of our domestic animals.[1]

Call it, if you please, just "a stream of ideal tendency," but unless there is such a stream, it is difficult to account for the sources of all those ideals which make life worth living. That we live by these ideals is strictly true. In our experiences we distinguish a lower and a higher part of ourselves and we feel that this higher part is in some way continuous with *more* of the same quality. This divine MORE is exterior to us, and yet we are in some way connected with it, in some kind of harmony with it, and upon this harmony our peace and security rest. "The visible world is part of a more spiritual universe from which it draws its chief significance," and to the spiritual world we give the name God.

If, now, it be replied that all this is mystical and points only to subjective and abnormal experiences of individuals and will not stand the test of science, James proposes this remarkable test: "So long as we deal with the cosmic and general, we deal only with the symbols of reality, but as soon as we deal with private and personal phenomena as such, we deal with realities in the completest sense of the terms." If this strikes any of us as reversing the true order, we must remember that the concepts which science uses and which

---

[1] William James, *The Will to Believe* (Longmans, Green and Company), pp. 52, 54, 57, in the essay "Is Life Worth Living?"

seem so real to us — such, for instance, as matter, energy, ether, atom — are only symbols of reality which are useful in explaining the facts of experience.

God in the science and philosophy of the present

Now, this picture which James gives us of a world of spiritual reality beneath or beyond this physical order, a world which, indeed, gives to the physical world its significance and value, no doubt seems to us very beautiful and perhaps true. But to many of us it will seem rather poetic and perhaps too religious, lacking scientific support, and we shall probably demand a firmer and more definite basis for our belief in God. We would like to know the attitude of present-day science toward the God idea, and the attitude of our modern hard-headed and "tough-minded" realistic philosophers. We know, of course, that the idealistic philosophers and the ethical philosophers and the theologians have less difficulty with the problem of God. We know that Plato with his *Idea of the Good*; Aristotle with his *Prime Mover*; the Stoics with their *Providence*; the neo-Platonists with their *Ineffable One*; the Hebrews with their *Jahveh, the righteous lawgiver*; the Christians with their *Christ, the beloved Redeemer*; the Churchmen with their *God, the Creator*; Spinoza with his *one Substance, God, and two attributes, mind and matter*; Berkeley with his *Father of Spirits*; Kant with his *Moral law and God its sanction*; Hegel with his *Absolute Idea*; Eucken with his *Spiritual Life*; Herbert Spencer with his *Infinite and Eternal Energy*;[1] Bradley and Royce with their *Absolute Experience* — that all these find God as the very ground or substance of the world. But we are not quite sure how far we can trust all these men. Our faith in them is great, but it weakens if we mistrust that their views are not found in agreement with the science of the present day, for our faith in this is still greater.

A few pages above we spoke of what God means in human experience — the personification of all our superlative excellences, the

---

[1] "But one truth must grow ever clearer — the truth that there is an Inscrutable Existence everywhere manifested, to which he [the man of science] can neither find nor conceive either beginning or end. Amid the mysteries which become the more mysterious the more they are thought about, there will remain the one absolute certainty, that he is ever in presence of an Infinite and Eternal Energy, from which all things proceed." — Herbert Spencer, *Principles of Sociology* (D. Appleton and Company), vol. III, p. 175.

embodiment of the primeval powers of Nature, the not-ourselves which makes for righteousness, the Over-Soul, and the divine MORE. Here we are on solid ground; this is what God does really mean to us, but what we want to know is whether this God exists.

Well, anyway, we have discovered one ground for believing in God's existence in James' striking test, when he shows that in physical science when we deal with matter, motion, and energy, we are dealing with certain symbols which are useful in interpreting the facts of outer experience, while in the case of our private and personal phenomena as such we are dealing with realities in the strictest sense.

Would it be possible, however, to formulate some conception of God which would be in complete harmony with present-day science and philosophy and at the same time express what God actually means in human experience? President Eliot attempted such a formulation as follows: God is an "omnipresent eternal energy, informing and inspiring the whole creation at every instant of time and throughout the infinite space." The word "energy" fulfills our desire to ascribe *power* to God, the word "informing" expresses his moulding and creating activity, while the word "inspiring" suggests that God is the source of *values*.

Could these ideas be expanded and made explicit in the following formula?

God is the soul of the world, an indwelling spiritual presence, a creative, organizing and perfecting power, the source of our moral, religious, and aesthetic ideals.

This, perhaps, is nearly what God means to us — a spiritual presence, a creative power, an exponent of righteousness, beauty, and love. Do science and philosophy confirm us in the hope that such a being really exists?

In the preceding chapters, as we have been studying the nature of life and its evolution, we have seen that it is necessary to assume some creative agency at every stage of the evolutionary movement, not only in the original organization of atoms into molecules and of molecules into living cells, but also of living cells into higher and higher forms of life — all the way up to man. Evolution is a creative process and implies some organizing, integrating, and perfecting agency. It has even been suggested that there is a present-day creation of matter from simpler elements, and the constant creation of life at the organic level.

It would seem, if we would speak of elemental things, that the direction and co-ordination of energies is as elemental as the energies themselves. In the scientific thought of the day the energy concept is very fundamental. Matter itself may be reducible to energy. But the energy concept itself is full of difficulties and uncertainties. It is a symbol, useful in science, standing for whatever it is that effects changes and does work. Its expressions are quantitative rather than qualitative, and if we ask what energy really *is*, physical science cannot tell us. The hypothesis that that mysterious thing which we call energy is something psychical, something like mind, has, as we have learned in a previous chapter, been a favorite one in philosophy and has often been proposed by physicists themselves. Such an hypothesis as this would give us an idealistic view of the world, reducing the whole "physical" Universe to "mind-energy" — and this mind-energy would be God. This view seems to harmonize science and religion, and has, of course, been held in many of our great systems of philosophy.

Lofty and inspiring as this world view is, the tendency is somewhat away from it now. This is not what God *means* to us in actual human discourse. "'God,'" says James, "in the religious life of ordinary men, is the name not of the whole of things, heaven forbid, but only of the ideal tendency in things, believed in as a superhuman person who calls us to co-operate in his purposes, and who furthers ours if they are worthy." [1] However fundamental the energy concept may seem to us, there are other concepts which are equally profound. There is something in the Universe perhaps more elemental than either energy or matter, namely, the *direction* of energy. Just as in psychology we have learned that there is something more elemental than sensation, perception, and thought — namely, impulse, the conative tendencies, hunger, and craving; and just as in biology we have suspected that deeper than organic life itself there is some elemental struggle for life, so in the whole world there may be some original impulse which is making for order

[1] William James, *A Pluralistic Universe* (Longmans, Green and Company), p. 124.

and structure and life and mind — perhaps for righteousness. These are the eternal values. God, therefore, is not energy, but *creative activity*; and not merely creative activity, but "ideal tendency."

The human mind is so constituted that it must believe in progress. Progress of some kind there must be, if it signifies only those orderly changes toward greater complexity and higher organization which go by the name of evolution. But there is evidence that evolution in the broader sense means more than this. It means, according to Edwin Grant Conklin,[1] not merely orderly and progressive change, but progression toward increased co-operation and specialization. It means, according to William Patten,[2] that there is a common creative agency, a progressive, creative, constructive process, looking always toward co-operation and mutual service. Deeper down in the roots of the evolutionary movement than the ruthless struggle for existence, there is another power at work, whose aim is constructive, altruistic, and benevolent.

We seem justified, therefore, in saying that there is in the world some fundamental agency, whose work is that of an integrating, organizing, perfecting power — a power that works for wholeness, for unity, for individuality, perhaps for co-operation and righteousness. Underneath all our over-beliefs "rests the basic fact that God exists — that there is an Ideal working itself out in the historic process, a great Power irresistibly drawing us on to some far-off and unknown goal, and demanding our entire allegiance."[3]

God as the source of ideals

Finally, have we any grounds for believing that God is the source of our moral, religious, and aesthetic ideals? Well, these ideals exist in man, and man is a part of the world. Some source of these ideals there must be. History seems to be a process of the realization of ideals. Although present social, political, and economic conditions are probably better than they ever were in the past, they seem very imperfect to us, and we are dissatisfied with them. Our ideals are always above our practice. We complain about the social injustice

[1] See his book, *The Direction of Human Evolution*.
[2] See his book, *The Grand Strategy of Evolution*.
[3] Durant Drake, *Problems of Religion*, p. 147.

of our present social order and are making great and successful efforts to correct it. Yet, as we look back, we see no age so advanced in this respect as our own. In the days of slavery, we envisaged freedom and won it. In the days of economic slavery, we envisaged economic freedom and are winning it. Through this vision of ideals and the struggle to realize them, we have gained the emancipation of our women from an absurd position of inequality; we have asserted the right of our children to be freed from labor and to have the privilege of education. We have protested against autocracy and affirmed the principles of democracy; and now we are hoping to abolish war and devise some system of international cooperation. Any reader can multiply at will illustrations of the progress of humanity in the realization of ideals.

But whence come these ideals? Do we create them as we go along? If so, evolution is again creative, and creative of values, moral and aesthetic, than which we can conceive of nothing higher. If science permits such an interpretation of the world process, surely religion should be satisfied, for a creative energy such as this meets our conception of the divine.

But are the values, on the other hand, not created as we go along, but eternal types, patterns, verities, realities, essences? Is there a system of *ideal values*, in which our ideals "subsist," using the language of recent writers? There is a perennial appeal in the ancient Platonic teaching. We may think of these ideal values as not only real, but as possessing agency or efficiency, "an efficiency which would seem to be confirmed by the fact that human beings are *actuated by ideals that have never yet received concrete existential form.* For who would be so rash as to maintain, e.g., that any society of men has ever yet attained the ideal of an organization in which perfect justice is rendered to all? Yet who among thinking men denies that this ideal is something to struggle and to strive for? And upon whom does the efficiency of this ideal not fall with compelling force?" [1]

It would seem, therefore, that the conception of God as the soul of the world, an immanent spiritual power, a creative and perfecting agency, the source of our ideal values, may give us a helpful notion

[1] E. G. Spaulding, *The New Rationalism* (Henry Holt and Company), pp. 516–17.

of God, which shall be consistent both with science and philosophy and with the meaning of the word *God* in common speech.

"If we believe in something, in anything, which gives great worth to human life, something bigger than our personal ambitions and passions, something that can lift us out of ourselves and give our little lives a deeper meaning and value, then, in the widest sense, we may be said to have a God."[1]

The spirit that denies

Our modern world has placed great emphasis upon the energy concept. We are living just now in the biological age, and the ideas of activity, growth, struggle, development, achievement, have become almost an obsession. We want to control everything and to govern. We want forever to create something new, and we judge of the value of anything by what it can *accomplish*. Efficiency is the idol of the age, and the God we believe in is an efficient God. The ancient Greeks looked at all this differently. They thought that the world of higher realities was not one to be made or achieved, but one to be contemplated, appropriated, and enjoyed. They looked up to the things that be, not forward to the things that are to be made, and they looked up with wonder, admiration, and even worship, desiring not to conquer, but to understand and enjoy.[2] There is something about this older Greek notion of limits which commends itself to us. Our modern gospel of efficiency has been quite disappointing in its results. The twentieth century sees threatening clouds of doubt rising to trouble us. Our doctrine of an efficient God does not now seem quite adequate. We feel more like emphasizing other divine attributes — not God's infinity, omniscience, and omnipotence as in former times, but rather the ideal values which after all constitute God's chief meaning to us; and we are beginning to see that the ideal values are not energy of the efficient type, but power of the integrating type, and harmony and balance and unity and proportion. God is righteousness and God is love. Yes, possibly God is even "the spirit that denies."

[1] Durant Drake, *Invitation to Philosophy* (Houghton Mifflin Company), p. 511.

[2] This thought has been developed in a forceful manner by George P. Adams in his admirable book entitled *Idealism and the Modern Age.*

For the last fifty years, under the influence of Darwin and his doctrine of variation, struggle, and survival of the fittest, we have come to over-emphasize the affirmative, self-assertive, and self-expressive virtues and to prize too little the virtues of restraint and self-control and balance and sacrifice. It was in the form of a reaction against an over-repressive age that William Blake a hundred and fifty years ago launched his new gospel of vitality and affirmation. It is the devil, he taught, not God, who says, "Thou shalt not." Since then a host of writers have held aloft the flag of revolt against law and convention and authority and tradition and the repression of our deepest instincts and longings. The absolute which they worship is "the absolute affirmation of energy," which until the close of the Great War dominated the world. Rousseau and Nietzsche and Ibsen and Bernard Shaw and Bergson and Browning have been the leaders in the philosophy of energy and affirmation. In Nietzsche, the "Yes-sayer," it appears in its extreme form. Let us say "Yes" to our desires, to our instincts, to our natural passions, to our inner needs. Let us say "Yes" to our longings for empire, to our *Kultur*. Let us say "Yes" to our political, economic, and commercial ambitions. Let us say "Yes" to our individual traits, to our budding genius, to our personality, to our need of self-expression.

> And the sin I impute to each frustrate ghost
> Is — the unlit lamp and the ungirt loin.

But the philosophy of expansion and affirmation has not turned out so well in practice as we had hoped. The Great War was its fruit, and the events since the war have still further shown its defects. And so we are coming to emphasize somewhat less the notion of efficiency and energy and somewhat more that of measure and reason; and I think we are beginning to understand that God is not a mere creator in the sense of a moving cause or an evolutionary urge, but rather the creator in the sense of a constructive, integrating, and perfecting power, the power which makes for wholeness and beauty and truth and righteousness — yes, also, for restraint and harmony and obedience and love and co-operation. The presence of such a power in the world helps us to understand not only the ideal tendency in things, not only the vision of ideals in the soul of man, but it clarifies immensely the coming and the progress of life in nature and its evolution to higher and higher forms. *How* this agency becomes effective in nature perhaps we cannot yet determine, but at least some difficulties might be met if we should think of it not as a driving force but as a drawing power.

In connection with this chapter read:

Irwin Edman, *Human Traits and Their Social Significance* (Houghton Mifflin Company), chap. XII.

James B. Pratt, *The Religious Consciousness* (The Macmillan Company), chap. X.

Further references:

Has Science Discovered God? A Symposium of Modern Scientific Opinion. Edward H. Cotton, Editor (Thomas Y. Crowell Company).

William E. Hocking, *The Meaning of God in Human Experience* (Yale University Press).

W. K. Wright, *A Student's Philosophy of Religion* (The Macmillan Company), chaps. XIX, XX.

John Elof Boodin, *God* (The Macmillan Company).

Joseph Fort Newton, Editor, *My Idea of God* (Little, Brown and Company, Boston).

Josiah Royce, *The Conception of God* (The Macmillan Company).

Francis J. McConnell, *The Diviner Immanence* (Eaton and Maine).

Grant Allen, *The Evolution of the Idea of God* (Henry Holt and Company).

G. A. Coe, *Religion of a Mature Mind* (Revell, Chicago), chap. XIII.

Richard La Rue Swain, *What and Where Is God?* (The Macmillan Company).

E. Westermarck, *Early Beliefs and Their Social Influence* (The Macmillan Company).

Fries and Schneider, *Religion in Various Cultures* (Henry Holt and Company).

George Santayana, *Some Turns of Thought in Modern Philosophy* (University Press, Cambridge, England), chap. V.

Robert A. Millikan, *Time Matter and Values* (University of North Carolina Press, 1932), chap. III.

CHAPTER XXVII

GOOD AND EVIL

The new pessimism

THE ancient problem concerning the origin of evil, and the old controversy between the pessimist and the optimist have in our day taken on a new and different form. There are plenty of troubles now and evils enough; but for these we no longer arraign God or Nature, but men and institutions. Our evils now take the form of economic depressions, political corruption, social injustice, excessive nationalism, war and international rivalries, and social and individual insecurity. To find the cause of these troubles it is only necessary to scan the front page of any newspaper. They are, for the most part, such things as human greed, injustice, ignorance, folly, suspicion, fear, indifference, betrayal of trust, and so on through the long list of human weaknesses.

In current discussion, we trouble ourselves much less about metaphysical questions regarding good and evil and about the place of evil in a theological framework. Our interests have turned to specific kinds of evil, mostly social, political, and economic. We no longer ask why God created a world so full of evil, but why "the times" are not getting better. Economic depressions, political corruption, social decadence, are the things that bother us. The fault we find is not with God, who made the world, but with economic systems, social conditions, political institutions, and human folly and incapacity. We usually admit that these systems and conditions are infinitely better than they used to be — but immeasurably worse than they ought to be.

The difference between the old and the new pessimism may be shown by the following illustration: When America was discovered by white men, it offered the possibility of a kind of human paradise, fertile soil, vast forests of timber, rich deposits of coal, oil, gold, silver, iron, copper, and other metals, great navigable lakes and rivers, rich fisheries, convenient harbors, a varied and equable climate, beautiful scenery, and protection from foreign invasion by wide oceans. Our founders provided a democratic form of government, offering both freedom and opportunity such as had not before been conceived. To the profusion of the gifts of nature, modern science has added its almost miraculous technique in preparing natural products for human use, surrounding us with comforts and conveniences of every kind, rapid and luxurious transportation, instantaneous communication, pure running water, gas and electricity, sanitary disposal of waste, manifolding of books and newspapers, and so on through the long list of potential benefits.

In such an environment human happiness would seem to be assured. It has not, however, been realized, and pessimism today abounds perhaps more than ever before, while the number of suicides yearly is greater relatively to our numbers than in the lands from which our fathers came seeking freedom and opportunity. This is because man's happiness depends only in part upon his physical environment and largely upon himself and his behavior. It is possible for him to denude his forests, permit erosion of his soil, waste his coal and oil, squander his biological inheritance by the violation of eugenic laws, fail to preserve the integrity of his government by neglecting his privileges of franchise, amass great wealth through nature's rich gifts and fail to provide for its just distribution.

But our distrust of man may go as much too far as in former times did our distrust of God. Possibly what we need is an appreciation of the good we have and a consciousness of our own power to right the wrongs that exist. But a discussion of the social evils of the day does not belong in a book on philosophy. We must turn to the philosophical and psychological problems involved.

The problem of evil

Anyone who writes upon the philosophy of good and evil encounters a peculiar difficulty. It is because the sympathy of the reader is almost always with the one who speaks of the sorrows of the world rather than of the joys. The optimist, or even the meliorist, has at the very start a handicap. No one likes to be told what a good world this is. A pessimist has been defined as a man who has to live with an optimist. This powerful *conviction* in the minds of so many that there is something essentially wrong with the world is *one* fact that must be reckoned with whether we will or not. I shall, therefore, in the pages to follow, point out some of the grounds for believing that the presence of evil in the world — even a good deal of it — does not justify any arraignment of Nature or of God. But I hope that I may present these reasons without dogmatism, reserving to a later paragraph a recognition of unsolved factors and of the presence of certain unanswered psychological problems. Perhaps the pessimist will go thus far with me that he will see the force of certain arguments for a brighter world view. Meanwhile the query may abide with us whether our conviction of the essential evil of the world does not arise from the fact of the very large *demands* that we make upon life. For instance, when our ever mounting demands upon Government do not harmonize with our utter dislike of increased taxation, we think that our Government is bad.

The existence of evil is one of the older difficulties which has caused perplexity to students of philosophy through all the centuries from the earliest times. The author of that ancient dramatic masterpiece called the Book of Job was perhaps the first to labor with the problem. Sophocles — he who "saw life steadily and saw it whole" — still wondered how the gods could look down complacently upon so much suffering and sorrow; and later, in Persia, Omar gave up the riddle of explaining human sorrows and proposed the easier method of drowning them in the 'juice of the vine.'

This is the way the difficulty is usually stated: If God created the world, or if he sustains, manages, or supervises it, and if God is infinitely good, how shall we explain all the pain and evil, all the sin and sorrow and suffering, and all the thwarted plans and disappointed hopes which are evident everywhere? If he could not prevent them, he is not God; if he could and does not, he is not good.

The whole argument rests upon an anthropomorphic view, as if God in heaven, contemplating the creation of a world, sits down to meditate on what kind of a world to make, and then foreseeing all the sin and evil and pain and suffering and sorrow, nevertheless with malice aforethought issues the creative fiat.

But the world did not come into being in any such way. Just as soon as we cease to think of it as a "plan" and begin to think of it as a growth, a development, *a realization of values,* our difficulties begin to disappear.   It all seems different when we think of God no longer as a monarch, but as the power which makes for righteousness, perhaps working with us to overcome every obstacle to good.   As higher and higher levels of good are successively realized, the lower levels become evils.   In geological time, when only simple forms of animal life were found upon the earth, the evils of which we so bitterly complain did not exist.   When man arrived with his power of rational thought, God did not create the evils, nor did man create them, nor even discover them.   He discovered a better way of doing things, whereupon the older way became an "evil."   Social organization and co-operation, for instance, represent a better way, a new value; whereupon egoism and narrow individualism become evils. With our widening social and economic interests, internationalism represents a new value, so that a selfish nationalism becomes an evil.   In early times war served a purpose in making social groups strong and sturdy; now conditions have changed, and war is under judgment and will have to go.   Sympathy and love are values of the highest order, as are personality, rational and voluntary choice, and conscience.   It seems as though Nature has labored to bring them forth; when they were born, the older ways became evils.

As we advance, the virtues of one age become the vices of the next.   We get very sensitive, critical, conscientious, as new ideals disclose themselves.   Some years ago Professor Ross wrote a book called *Sin and Society,* describing a brand-new set of sins which changing social conditions had brought forth, many of them hitherto being merely customary practices.

This does not mean that good and evil are just relative terms.   It seems rather that there are certain ideals to be attained, and in struggling to attain them obstacles are encountered.   These obstacles are real, and offer real resistance to the good; they must be overcome.

The modern point of view is different from the ancient.   The ancients, with their contemplative attitude toward nature, simply *saw* the evil, *wondered* at it, and tried to *explain* it; we, with our more pragmatic minds, granting that there are still evils a plenty all about us, propose the task, not of explaining them, but of overcoming them.   As one writer says:

Modern thought takes evil, not as a given fact, but as something which is capable of being transformed, and made to be that which we choose to have it be. It does not find the world good or bad. It sets out to *make* the world good, and it is able to do this because it has the source of good within a self who can master events.[1]

Moral evil

It has sometimes been the fashion to catalogue the evils of the world under three classes: first, metaphysical evils or imperfections in nature, such as earthquakes, cyclones, drought, and flood; second, physical and mental evils, such as pain and suffering and death; and third, moral evils, such as sin and wickedness. By enumerating and parading these, a pretty severe indictment may be drawn against Nature, or against God as creator.[2]

Of these three classes, moral evil is clearly the worst. We are amazed sometimes at the revelations of wickedness in every part of the world: injustice and cruelty, greed and hate, vice and crime, domestic tangles and divorce, exploitation of labor and oppression of the weak, murder and theft, smuggling and bootlegging, intemperance and drunkenness, gambling and prostitution, bribery and adulteration, avarice and profligate spending, and unashamed and unrestrained revelry and frivolity. Talk about such a world being the best possible one, or even a good one, or even a decent one!

Probably no philosopher now would be interested to show that this is the best possible world, but the mere enumeration of a list of sins such as these is no proof that this is not a good world, or even the best one possible. It would be still easier to enumerate a list of virtues; they are so obvious that they would not be interesting. A list of crimes always makes better reading, because they are the striking exceptions to the daily life of a given time. "Sins" appear at that stage of evolution when man emerges as a moral being. Had the evolutionary process been stopped at that level, there would have been no moral evil in the world, but such a world would not have been as "good" as this one. There would have been no sin,

---

[1] Arthur Kenyon Rogers, *The Religious Conception of the World*, p. 256.

[2] Such an indictment may be found, for instance, in John Stuart Mill's *Three Essays on Religion*, pp. 28 ff., or in A. J. Balfour's *Foundations of Belief*, pp. 33, 34. In Bertrand Russell's "A Free Man's Worship," in his *Mysticism and Logic*, chap. III, may be found a more recent plaint over a "pitiless" and "hostile" world.

to be sure; but there would have been no moral conduct of any kind, only animal behavior and instinctive action. A moral order involving conscience, freedom, rational choice and growth, seems better.

If you or I had the task of planning a world, we should hesitate, after thinking it over, to plan one without pain or evil. It might prove to be "weary, stale, flat, and unprofitable." It all seems very different from our modern energetic, dynamic, and biological point of view. We are not so sure whether it would be well for us to be eternally happy. We assign higher value now to growth through conflict. If there were no evil and no temptation, there would be no victory over evil and no *character*. We place more emphasis now upon character than upon happiness. A race of sinless beings would not be perfect beings — they would be a race of innocents; and while we prize innocence in children, we prize force of character in men — the ability to stand firmly against temptation, to overcome and conquer evil. With the passing of the hedonistic ethics, which emphasized pleasure or happiness as the end of life, the problem of evil has changed. What the man of today wants is to achieve rather than to enjoy. He likes something of adventure and of risk, and perhaps even of pain, if great things may perchance be won. Even death may be looked upon in this way. It is reported of Charles Frohman, the theatrical manager, who went down with the Lusitania, that he said, as the ship was struck by the torpedo, "Why should we fear death? It is the most beautiful adventure in life"; a sentiment anticipated by Browning:

> And I shall thereupon
> Take rest, ere I be gone
> Once more on my adventure brave and new.

Lucretius, at the opening of the second book of the *De Rerum Natura*, says:

> It is sweet, when on the great sea the winds trouble its waters, to behold from land another's deep distress; not that it is a pleasure and delight that any should be afflicted, but because it is sweet to see from what evils you are yourself exempt. It is sweet also to look upon the mighty struggles of war arrayed along the plains without sharing yourself in the danger.[1]

[1] Munro's translation.

This "safety first" motto might do for an Epicurean poet or serve as a prudent caution at a busy metropolitan street crossing, but as a rule of life it does not appeal to us. We sympathize more with the mood of James, at the close of his lecture entitled *Is Life Worth Living?*

> But the faithful fighters of this hour, or the beings that then and there will represent them, may then turn to the faint-hearted, who here declined to go on, with words like those with which Henry IV greeted the tardy Crillon after a great victory had been gained: "Hang yourself, brave Crillon! We fought at Arques, and you were not there."

Man is a striving animal. Happiness is not found in rest or in freedom from pain, but in the activity of his powers, especially in the creative activity of his highest powers, of reason, thought, invention, artistic creation, and humanitarian effort. We are not impressed by the attitude of the man in the story who had partially recovered from a stroke of some kind and said to his physician: "I sleep better than ever before, I have a better appetite than ever before, and in general am happier than ever before. To be sure, I have lost my mind, but I don't miss it." The retired farmer is seldom as happy as he thought he was going to be in his new house in town with its bathroom and library and modern conveniences. That long-dreamed-of *leisure* is not so desirable as it had seemed in prospect. The old days on the farm, with their problems to be solved and their recurrent joys of fields ploughed and harvests gathered, have no compensations in the life of rest. There is a good homely philosophy in the saying that if you get done all that you set out to do, you didn't set out to do enough.

So, finally, although we can formulate the phrase "a world without evil," the words can have no distinct meaning. In that perfect and happy world in which there is no evil, pain, or sorrow, I think there are some things we should miss. We should miss our Browning with his "jagged phraseology of struggle and strife"; our Dante with his Hell and Purgatory and redeeming love; our Goethe with his gospel of salvation through rich human experience; our Lincoln with his knit brow and sad sympathetic face; our Raphael with his Sistine Madonna; our Shakespeare with his stories of Macbeth and Lear; our Æschylus with his dramas of tempestuous fate, and our Jesus with his gospel of redemption.

Pessimism

Pessimism in philosophy is the doctrine that life is essentially evil, that there is more pain in the world than pleasure, more evil than good. It is not difficult to make many of us believe this, because pain and evil, being the exception rather than the rule, attract our attention. Pain indicates *abnormal* function, and is therefore exceptional in normal life. Moral evil indicates a departure from those rules of conduct which experience has shown to be necessary for social welfare. Since social groups usually survive and prosper, moral evil must be the exception rather than the rule.

Arthur Schopenhauer, a talented German philosopher of the nineteenth century, has been called the prince of pessimists. He attempted a logical proof that this is the worst possible world. The Will is the fundamental reality. The "will-to-live" is forever urging us on, blindly seeking satisfaction which is never attained, or, if attained, is succeeded by new desire. Life is eternal striving, a desire for the unrealized. Hence life is full of unsatisfied longing, full of misery and suffering. This is the worst possible world, for if the evil forces which prey upon us were any worse than they are, we could not survive.[1]

The fallacies in Schopenhauer's reasoning are not difficult to detect. He says that all life is suffering, because it is all striving, and striving is suffering. Life is by no means *all* striving, though striving accompanies it. But that striving is suffering is not true; it may be and usually is quite the opposite. Successful striving may be counted as life's greatest joy; striving that is not successful is still a pleasure. Great is the joy of the vision of a coveted goal; greater still the joy of trying to attain it; and great is the satisfaction of having attained it. Even if we fail, there is joy in trying, and what right have we to assume that failure is normal? More often we succeed than fail. We expect to succeed, and so are more impressed by the failures. This whole matter of the pessimistic or optimistic attitude depends much upon the emotional reaction of the individual, and it is easy to confirm either the philosophy of despair or the

---

[1] Arthur Schopenhauer was born in 1788 and died in 1860. His principal work is called *The World as Will and Idea*. It is a work of high literary and philosophical merit, and has become a classic in philosophy. For Schopenhauer's pessimism, the student should read vol. III, chap. XLVI, "On the Vanity and Suffering of Life."

philosophy of joy by seizing upon, emphasizing, and exaggerating either the sorrows or the joys of life. Schopenhauer himself was a genius, and genius is often associated with psychopathic traits. Such traits, indeed, abound in his family history, sometimes in extreme forms.

Schopenhauer's other argument — designed to prove that this is the worst possible world from the fact that, if the evils in it were any worse than they are, we could not survive — is also misleading. Theoretically it is true that if the environment in which any animal species lives were different from what it is, that species would be different. Each species is adjusted to its environment. Hence in a way it is true that if the world were either worse or better than it is, we should not survive; we should be modified to meet the new conditions. Practically, of course, our human environment might be much worse or better than it is without leading to our destruction.

The causes of pessimism

Pessimism may be considered as a disease, its causes diagnosed and its cure prescribed. It was formerly said to be due to a defective liver, but is now attributed to a failure of the endocrine glands to function. It becomes chronic and the cure is difficult. Perhaps something of this kind ailed Carlyle. It is related that he was once walking with Leigh Hunt, who called his attention to the beauty of the stars and the grandeur of the heavens; but Carlyle said, "Eh, it's a sad sight!"

Melancholia represents an extreme form of the complaint, when, owing to pathological nervous conditions, *everything*, even the singing of the birds in the spring, is tinged with an unspeakable sadness. Often it takes lesser forms, and is then sometimes due to a lack of proper balance between the sensory and motor functions of the nervous system. Man is naturally and physiologically an *actor*, a *doer*. Stimulus is followed normally by response; and if for any reason no adequate motor outlet is possible, a pathological condition follows, leading perhaps to some degree of melancholy.

College and university students sometimes pass through such a period of forced inaction, spending four years in *taking in* and assimilating material, but being forced to bide their time for action and achievement. Athletics and extra-curricular activities of all kinds then act as a kind of *catharsis*, purifying the mind from its disorders, but sometimes at too great a cost, since valuable opportunities for study may be lost, or health impaired. Students who *must* have a lot of extra-curricular activities in order to keep from getting pessimistic no doubt suffer a certain handicap in future life. Those who *can* keep the cobwebs out of their brains while they lay in a stock of useful knowledge and disciplinary thinking will perhaps be the ones who forge ahead in the end, provided only physical health is not sacrificed.

There are other causes why young people are often pessimistic. The vast enthusiasms and idealisms of adolescent years are often quenched and dimmed when the first real contact comes with life. Disillusionment and disappointment follow, sometimes with thoughts of suicide.

David Starr Jordan puts it in this way:

> The joys of life have been a thousand times felt before they come to us. We are but following part of a cut-and-dried program, "performing actions and reciting speeches made up for us centuries before we were born." The new power of manhood and womanhood which seemed so wonderful find their close limitations. As our own part in the Universe seems to shrink as we take our place in it, so does the Universe itself seem to grow small, hard and unsympathetic. Very few young men or young women of strength and feeling fail to pass through a period of pessimism. With some it is merely an affectation caught from the cheap literature of decadence. It then may find expression in imitation, as a few years ago the sad-hearted youth turned down his collar in sympathy with the "conspicuous loneliness" that took the starch out of the collar of Byron. "The youth," says Zangwill, "says bitter things about life which Life would have winced to hear had it been alive." With others Pessimism has deeper roots and finds its expression in the poetry or philosophy of real despair! [1]

Probably the most confirmed optimist would not undertake to show that in the half-million years of human history which have elapsed thus far there might not be periods when the human species has gone astray in its manner of living. Whether we have gone astray in our manner of living since the discovery of coal, iron, and

[1] David Starr Jordan, *The Philosophy of Despair*, pp. 13, 14.

oil has revolutionized society, whether our present industrial
system is a boon or a curse, whether this system might be modified
so that creative labor could be substituted for drudgery, or whether
the hours of labor might be so reduced that all men could find a real
joy of life in the eight or ten hours of leisure which might then be
provided, are questions not belonging here.

But I would suggest that even this problem might be solved if
only a part of that amazing inventive power of thought which has
produced the airplane and the wireless telephone could be turned
in the direction of social and industrial betterment. If a mere
fraction of the tremendous intellectual power exhibited in scientific
research and invention could be turned toward the solving of our industrial and social troubles and our problems of unemployment and
of unprofitable and uninteresting labor, there is no reason why
happiness commensurate with the wealth and promise of our rich
land could not be realized.

Optimism

Almost as bad as pessimism is a superficial and careless optimism.
Browning's optimism has been criticized on this ground. His
Pippa goes singing through her brief holiday, saying, "God's in his
heaven — all's right with the world." But all's not right with the
world, as everyone knows. Browning's optimism, however, should
not be judged by this one line. In general it is wholesome and
sound, based on his belief in God and Truth and Love, and on his
philosophy of endeavor and progress. Another famous optimist
was Leibniz, who in his *Theodicy* proved by rational arguments that
this is the best possible world. Sir John Lubbock in his book, *The
Pleasures of Life*, proceeds by the opposite inductive method to an
optimistic view of life.

Our idealism

But, after all, there is little meaning in either optimism or pessimism. These superlatives are misleading. Looking forward and
measuring the world by our ideals, we find it bad; looking backward
and measuring the present by the past, we find it good. So, then,
the really significant thing is not the goodness or the badness of the

world, but the progress of it; and still more significant than this is the idealism in the human mind which makes every present good seem imperfect in the light of the higher good that we conceive. In the philosophy of the present neither optimism nor pessimism is in good standing. Meliorism has taken its place, and it teaches that the world is neither the worst possible nor the best possible, but that it is getting better, and that the task before each one of us is to lend a hand in making it better.

"'Evil, O Glaucon,' says Socrates in Plato's *Dialogue*, 'will not vanish from the earth.' How should it, if it is the name of the imperfection through whose defeat the perfect types acquire their value?"[1]

The lure of pessimism

The curious appeal which the literature of pessimism always makes is a 'problem' in itself, a psychological one. People seem to love to write and love to read about the woes of life. If the latter is partly explained by the superior literary character of the pessimistic writings, this superiority itself presents a problem. The beautiful but somber utterances of the Book of Ecclesiastes seem to be in little harmony with the other literature of the Hebrew Bible, yet fascinated readers for more than twenty centuries have sympathized with the author's gloomy sentiments.

> Vanity of vanities, vanity of vanities, all is vanity. What profit hath man of all his labour wherein he laboureth under the sun?
> All things are full of weariness, man cannot utter it, the eye is not satisfied with seeing nor the ear filled with hearing.

Buddhism offers a particularly pessimistic faith, yet uncounted millions have been its devotees. Edwin Arnold thus renders some lines from the Devas' song:

> We are the voices of the wandering wind,
> Which moan for rest, and rest can never find,
> Lo, as the wind is, so is mortal life —
> A moan, a sigh, a sob, a storm, a strife.

As translated by FitzGerald, Omar Khayyám's *Rubáiyat* is a perennial best-seller. How much of the powerful appeal of these

[1] S. Alexander, *Space, Time, and Deity*, vol. II, p. 420.

quatrains is due to the somber philosophy and how much to the
exquisite rendering of the translator?

> Myself when young did eagerly frequent
> Doctor and Saint, and heard great argument
> About it and about: but evermore
> Came out by the same door where in I went.
>
> With them the seed of wisdom did I sow,
> And with my own hand wrought to make it grow;
> And this was all the harvest that I reaped —
> "I came like water and like wind I go."

Or Byron:

> Count o'er the joys thine hours have seen,
> Count o'er thy days from anguish free,
> And know, whatever thou hast been,
> 'Tis something better not to be.

Or James Thomson in *The City of Dreadful Night*:

> Speak not of comfort where no comfort is,
> Speak not at all: can words make foul things fair?
> Our life's a cheat, our death, a black abyss.
> Hush and be mute envisaging despair.

Or Matthew Arnold:

> Wandering between two worlds, one dead,
> The other powerless to be born,
> With nowhere yet to rest my head,
> Like these on earth I wait forlorn.

I do not know why we like to read these disconsolate things, but
they seem to strike a responsive chord.   Perhaps it is because there
are woes enough in the world to make the subject interesting and not
enough to make it flat.   Every life has its dark shadows, and usually
we have to keep silent about them.   When we find some poet, philosopher, or writer of fiction who speaks out about them, we feel as if
we had found a sympathetic friend.   For the most part we have to
keep smiling, whether we feel like smiling or not.   So occasionally
we slip away to dear old sympathetic Thomas Hardy, who does not
even pretend that the world is all good and honest and right, and
just let ourselves go.   It is a kind of relaxation and purification.   I
wonder, by the way, whether the realism in fiction of the present day
is truly realism, or whether it simply means that the evils of life,
formerly not much mentioned, are now truthfully and vividly de-

scribed, while the good things, being too common to be interesting, are omitted.

But perhaps there is some deeper reason for the appeal which the poetry of despair makes to so many of us. It is easy to point out the grounds for a hopeful philosophy of life. But I have little doubt that many readers will say, "Your arguments perhaps are unanswerable but the facts are against you. The things that stand out most clearly in our lives are disillusionment, defeat, thwarted ambitions, disappointed hopes. Life's promises have not been fulfilled, justice has not been gained, the glaring inequalities of fortune cannot be pardoned in this facile fashion. It is easy for the well-fed theorist, sitting in his study, to show that the world is good and getting better — but life's grim realities lend little support to this philosophy of hope." One who writes in this way has not looked into the despairing faces of the great army of the unemployed, nor into the hearts of those who are receiving necessary but unwelcome doles from the funds of public relief. If there is abundant pessimism among our people, much of it is due to a consciousness of the injustice arising from inequalities of wealth, of social position, and of political power. Lives otherwise not embittered may become so by the knowledge of supposed joys possessed by others but denied to them. But perhaps these inequalities will soon be lessened. Economics may soon become a science as perfect as our physics and chemistry. This at any rate is certain, that the people of the Earth have now to learn a new lesson, the lesson of co-operation and peace. We do not know yet whether they can learn this lesson in time to save our present civilization; but sooner or later it will be learned, and then we hope for a new civilization finer and better than any we have known. It is possible, though I do not think probable, that an interval of social chaos may separate our time from that. The vision of the better way is clearly seen in so many minds that we cannot doubt the coming of a new social order, in which co-operation shall take the place of rivalry and distrust.

Perhaps, though, the present crisis has its roots deeper than the alternatives of peace and war. When God creates a masterpiece like man with freedom to go his own way, there is always danger that he will go wrong — for a while. There are some indications that he is going wrong now. There are those who think that human progress has reached a peak, and that we are riding for a fall.

Just as the violation of the laws of health in the case of the individual may lead to disease and sorrow and pain, so the violation by a social group of the laws of social welfare may lead to decadence. Though it is very doubtful whether our present society is decadent or even approaching a period of decadence, there is immediate and imperative need that certain evils be summarily ended. Organized intelligence can end them.

In a catalogue of evils such as I have mentioned, as well as in the pictures of misery in our crowded cities and industrial centers, it is difficult to get a correct perspective. As regards the amount of evil in the world, there is certainly enough of it; but we are often misled by the fact that as our ethical ideals advance we are more impressed by the evil that we see. Railroad and automobile travel have become so safe that accidents are paraded in headlines. So great advance has been made in morals and manners that wrong-doing has become "news," and furnishes rich material for the front page of our daily paper. Crime makes a 'sensation,' and our sensational journals exploit it for that reason. Diogenes is said to have gone through the world with a lantern looking for a *man*. Our news gatherers of today go through the world with a hundred-candle-power electric torch looking for crime, disaster, accident, or suicide, and keep the wires centering in our great cities hot with their stories. As I am writing these words a daily paper lies at my side. The first page contains two single and three double columns, all of them with violent headlines heralding crime or disaster. We lay down such a paper with a sigh, saying, "The world is full of crime and misery." But really the whole world, telegraphically in touch with our daily paper, is combed for news with a fine-tooth comb, and things are not so bad as they seem. To emphasize this, it is only necessary to turn from that sensational first page and think of our neighbors and friends. They are for the most part honest and decent folk, whom you could trust with your gun or your daughter.

When all is said, there has been for some centuries a rather steady growth in the things which we have come to prize — freedom, oppor-

tunity, security, physical comforts, medical, surgical, and dental service, control of contagious diseases, household conveniences, conveniences of travel and communication, a world-wide news service, the
passing of fear and superstition, educational facilities for our children,
constantly increasing rights and privileges of women, and so on through
the long list. We should not care again to face hunger and cold and
constant fear, nor should we be willing to sacrifice the security which
law and order during the longer and longer intervals of peace have
gained for our women and children and for our lives and property.
When radical social reformers clamor for the overthrow of our present
social system and arraign it as a system of slavery and poverty and
cruel injustice, it is evident that they use these terms relatively, having
in mind some ideal social order in which all our present freedom and
security and our comforts and conveniences are to be retained and the
glaring imperfections removed! [1]

Mr. H. G. Wells, in his *New Worlds for Old*, paints in strong
colors the sins and evils of the day; yet in the same book he does
not hesitate to say:

In spite of all the confusions and thwartings of life, the halts and
resiliencies and the counter-strokes of fate, it is manifest that in the
long run, human life becomes broader than it was, gentler than it was,
finer and deeper. On the whole — and nowadays almost steadily —
things *get better*. There is a secular amelioration of life, and it is brought
about by Good Will working through the efforts of men....

The world is now a better place for a common man than ever it was
before, the spectacle wider and richer and deeper and more charged
with hope and promise. Think of the universal things it is so easy to
ignore; of the great and growing multitude, for example, of those who
may travel freely about the world, who may read freely, think freely,
speak freely! Think of the quite unprecedented numbers of well-
ordered homes and cared-for, wholesome, questioning children! And
it is not simply that we have this increasing sea of mediocre well-being
in which the realities of the future are engendering, but in the matter
of sheer achievement I believe in my own time. It has been the cry of
the irresponsive man since criticism began, that his own generation
produced nothing; it's a cry that I hate and deny. When the dross has
been cleared away and comparison becomes possible, I am convinced
it will be admitted that in the aggregate, in philosophy, and significant
literature, in architecture, painting and scientific research, in engineer-
ing and industrial invention, in state-craft, humanity and valiant deeds,

[1] From the author's book, *The Psychology of Social Reconstruction* (Houghton Mifflin Company).

the last thirty years of man's endeavors will bear comparison with any other period of thirty years whatever in history.

And this is the result of effort; things get better because men mean them to get better and try to bring betterment about; this progress goes on because man, in spite of evil temper, blundering and vanity, in spite of indolence and base desire, does also respond to Good Will and display Good Will. You may declare that all the good things in life are the result of causes over which man has no control, that in pursuit of an "enlightened self-interest" he makes things better inadvertently. But think of any good thing you know! Was it thus it came? [1]

Now this "improvement" which Mr. Wells speaks of has been going on — have you ever thought of it? — for five hundred thousand years. When the first man stood upright, sharpened a flint, pointed a stick for a spear, invented the bow and arrow, or discovered the use of fire, he *improved* his condition. There were better implements, new power, happier conditions of living, as well as creative work and the joy of discovery. Carry this on down through the ages to our last labor-saving devices, the latest discoveries in the hygiene of food, dress, or house construction, or the latest perfected implements of agriculture or means of transportation. There has been constant *improvement*. Now, we cannot suppose that the first man was *unhappy*. His condition was certainly 'better' than that of the apes which preceded him, and we cannot consider them as unhappy, nor any of the animals still lower down in the scale; they are all eager to live, and no doubt happy in living. Looking at the matter in this way, there does not seem to be much ground for a philosophy of pessimism.

There is a little book entitled *A Modern Symposium*, by G. Lowes Dickinson. Thirteen speakers representing different points of view

[1] H. G. Wells, *New Worlds for Old* (copyrighted by The Macmillan Company, reprinted by permission), pp. 5, 10, 11. This was written before the Great War. For an equally striking account of social progress *since* the war, see Robert Briffault's *The Making of Humanity*. Chronicles of "the good world" since the Depression may be found in countless magazine articles and editorials.

The fallacy of the good old times deceives few of us now. In the Museum at Constantinople the writer was shown an ancient tablet dating from 3800 B.C. Translated, it read: "We have fallen upon evil times and the world has waxed very old and wicked. Politics are very corrupt. Children are no longer respectful to their parents." In an article entitled "An Answer to Pessimists" by David F. Houston in *Harper's Magazine* for June, 1924, one finds a severe arraignment of Congress, where the business of the Nation is left undone or is badly done, and of the demagogues in public office whose principles hang laxly upon them. After the reader has duly read and approved of this, the author quietly informs him that it was written by Mr. Justice Story of Massachusetts in the year 1818.

make speeches after the manner of Plato's *Symposium*. Two of them discuss the problem of evil. This is what Aubrey Coryat, a poet, says in part:

> Whereat Coryat rather comically remarked, "Oh, well! Yes! Perhaps then my poetry isn't quite good enough. But there's Shakespere and Milton, and — I don't care who it is, so long as it has the essential of all great poetry, and that is to make you feel the worth of things. I don't mean by that the happiness, but just the extraordinary value, of which all these unsolved questions about Good and Evil are themselves part. No one, I am sure, ever laid down a great tragedy — take the most terrible of all, take 'Lear' — without an overwhelming sense of the value of life; life as it is, life at its most pitiless and cruel, with all its iniquities, suffering, perplexity; without feeling he would far rather have lived and had all that than not have lived at all. But tragedy is an extreme case. In every simpler and more common case the poet does the same thing for us. He shows us that the lives he touches have worth, worth of pleasure, of humour, of patience, of wisdom painfully acquired, of endurance, of hope, even I will say of failure and despair. He doesn't blink anything, he looks straight at it all, but he sees it in the true perspective, under a white light, and seeing all the Evil says nevertheless with God, 'Behold, it is very good.'" [1]

But we dare not let this evident meliorism blind us to the dangers of the present world situation. Hope as we may, we cannot hide from ourselves the menace of a possible decline of our civilization; due, first, to the danger of a declining birth-rate of our more intelligent and gifted people; second, to a bungling economic system which concentrates our vast wealth among the few; third, to a political system in America which refuses to select for positions of responsibility highly educated men having special qualifications for their work; fourth, the waning power of the home as a source of social stability; and fifth, a serious decline in the permanence of marriage and in the morality of sex, threatening the biological integrity of the race; — all of which, of course, giving encouragement to pessimists of the Spengler type.[2] There is, however, nothing in the situation which the people of Europe and America have not the power to remedy, *if they will*. If they fail, the new social order

---

[1] From *A Modern Symposium* by G. Lowes Dickinson, copyright, 1905, by Doubleday, Doran and Company, Inc.

[2] See Oswald Spengler, *The Hour of Decision*. Translated by C. F. Atkinson (Knopf).

of which so many have the vision and in which peace, good-will, and co-operation shall prevail, will be delayed — perhaps even for half a thousand years — but it will come.

In connection with this chapter read:

Josiah Royce, *The Spirit of Modern Philosophy* (Houghton Mifflin Company), lecture XIII.

Arthur Schopenhauer, "The Assertion and Denial of the Will," selection from *The World as Will and Idea in Rand's Modern Philosophers* (Houghton Mifflin Company), pp. 658–71.

William James, "Is Life Worth Living?" in *The Will to Believe* (Longmans, Green and Company).

Further references:

John Stuart Mill, *Three Essays on Religion* (Henry Holt and Company), pp. 3–69.

James Ward, *The Realm of Ends* (G. P. Putnam's Sons), lectures XV, XVI, XVII.

W. K. Wright, *A Student's Philosophy of Religion* (The Macmillan Company), chap. XX.

R. M. Wenley, *Aspects of Pessimism* (William Blackwood and Sons).

Josiah Royce, *Fugitive Essays* (Harvard University Press), "The Practical Significance of Pessimism," p. 133; "Pessimism and Modern Thought," p. 155.

Friedrich Paulsen, *A System of Ethics*. Translated by Frank Thilly (Charles Scribner's Sons), book II, chaps. III, IV.

J. Arthur Thomson, *The System of Animate Nature* (Henry Holt and Company), vol. II, lecture XVIII, "Disharmonies and Other Shadows."

James Sully, *Pessimism, a History and a Criticism* (D. Appleton and Company).

H. Rashdall, *The Theory of Good and Evil* (Oxford University Press), vol. II.

Arthur Schopenhauer, *The World as Will and Idea* (Ticknor and Company), vol. III, chap. XLVI, "On the Vanity and Suffering of Life."

Oswald Spengler, *The Hour of Decision*. Translated by C. F. Atkinson (Knopf).

CHAPTER XXVIII
WHAT OUGHT WE TO DO?

THE THEORY OF MORALS

ONE of the very oldest of philosophical problems is that of the Highest Good. As applied to life and conduct, it becomes the problem of the Good Life. It is closely related to the Theory of Value. Are values objective or subjective? Do they exist beyond the sphere of human action? Do we desire things because they are valuable, or are they valuable because we desire them? Thus we are introduced to the science of Ethics, with its perplexing questions about right and wrong, about duty, conscience, and moral laws.

We see at once that we have here a different kind of problem from those we have been considering. Hitherto we have been wondering about reality, about the constitution of the world and of the mind. We have been prying into the nature of things, into the texture of reality. Now, when we take up the Theory of Morals, we seem to be engaged in the study of a practical question, a question of values — the higher values of life. We seem to be inquiring no longer about the truth of things, but about their *worth* or *goodness*, and particularly about the worth or goodness of a certain class of things, namely, human actions. In psychology we study human behavior *as it is*. In ethics we also study human behavior, but now from a wholly different point of view, namely, that of *approval* or *disapproval*.

At first we are puzzled by this new kind of question. Is ethics a science, an art, or a branch of philosophy? No doubt it is all three. Its unsolved problems make it a chapter in philosophy. If we could reduce human behavior to a set of practical rules for attaining a desired end, it would be an art. If we could gain an accurate knowledge of the laws of human behavior in relation to the well-being of society and the individual, it would be a science.

Ethics, however, as a practical science, seems to be far behind other practical sciences, such for instance as agriculture, or apiculture, or metallurgy, in respect to its stage of development. This is one of the strange anomalies of our civilization that we understand less about the relation of human behavior to human happiness than we do about the production of steel — or honey.

In most practical sciences, such, for instance, as medicine, there is a perfectly definite end to be gained, namely, the conservation of health. And in such sciences, both the end to be attained and the rules and regulations for attaining it are quite well understood. But in the case of that practical science called ethics neither the end to be gained nor the means of gaining it is wholly beyond dispute. Hence it presents a problem in philosophy. It seems strange, does it not, that while in all the lesser practical sciences, such as the ones mentioned, we know just what we wish to accomplish, in ethics, the practical science of human conduct in general, we do not know just what end we seek to gain. Some have said that what all men wish to attain is *happiness*, while others have said that it is not happiness, but *virtue*; while still others have thought that it is *self-realization*, or peace, or obedience to the *voice of duty* or to conscience, or to the *will of God*.

We are evidently engaged here in studying, not *behavior*, as in psychology, but good and bad behavior; that is, conduct. Matthew Arnold said that conduct is three fourths of life, which means, I suppose, that three fourths of the time our behavior is either good or bad. Hence, we have to find out what makes behavior good or bad.

When we were children our parents told us that some actions were *right* and some were *wrong* and that we "must not" do the wrong things, and "must" do the right ones. We discovered, however, that we were *free* to do the wrong things, if we chose, and often did so, and then some kind of punishment was apt to follow. In our early philosophical moods perhaps we asked ourselves why some actions were called right or good, and some wrong or bad; and possibly we were told that wrong was what God forbade and right was what he commanded. And this answer probably satisfied us for a while, but afterwards we began to inquire why God commanded certain things and forbade others.

Then also there is the question of *duty*, that curious feeling of obligation — the "ought" feeling. Even granting that there are certain actions that are right and others that are wrong, why *ought* I to do the right, and whence that strange feeling of duty? They used to tell me that it was the voice of conscience. But what is conscience? Is it an infallible guide that I should follow, and if so where does conscience get its authority?

How not to study this subject

Probably there is no chapter in philosophy so important as this one relating to the theory of conduct. It has more than a theoretical interest satisfying our thirst for knowledge; it bears directly on our own manners and morals. And yet it is very easy for the student to study it in a merely academic manner — and fail to see its practical bearing. He will cheerfully assent to the professor's conclusion that the highest good is service or love or righteousness or self-realization or duty, and straightway go out and pursue some other highest good without feeling the slightest need of making any mental readjustment at all.

But there is a way to avoid perfunctory study of this kind, and that way is for the student or the reader to try to think the problem through on his own account before listening to any "oracles" or reading any books on the subject. Never mind about the question of the Highest Good — just ask yourself, "What are the actual *bona fide* higher values in my own personal, present, or prospective life?"

Another way to see the practical bearing of this subject would be to imagine that a new community was to be started on some far distant island, and that you and I were delegated to draw up a constitution for such a community and plan a set of institutions for it and a system of education. We could not do all this without first getting pretty clearly in mind what we wished to attain. Offhand we should probably say that what we wished to attain was the happiness of the people. This general phrase might satisfy us until we began to reflect upon it carefully. Then we should find that it is not sufficiently definite. Simply to make all the people happy all the time would be an ideal that would probably not appeal to any social reformer.

The State Superintendent of Public Instruction stopped me

in the hall one day and said that he wanted someone to write a paper on the philosophy of education. After some questioning I found out that, having served certain years in his high office, he had finally come to the conclusion that it is useless to work over courses of study and methods of teaching until it is first clearly determined just what is to be accomplished for the young people. The philosophy of education is really the philosophy of life. Seen in this light the old problem of the highest good takes on a very practical aspect.

Do ants and bees have duties?

How shall we approach the difficult subject of human conduct? There have been many schools of ethical theory and many diverse views. How can we find our way through this tangle of opinion?

It may be helpful to simplify the subject by studying it in the form presented to primitive men living in simple communities; or it might be even better to go back to the life of lower animals, especially those living in social groups like the ants and bees. Do they have "duties," "moral obligations," and "moral laws"? Do they act "rightly" and "wrongly"? Do they have a "highest good"? Whether or not any of these terms may be applied to the behavior of these insects, they certainly exhibit in their instinctive actions a very high degree of *co-operation* toward a certain end; and that end is the *well-being* of the swarm or colony; and this well-being would seem to consist in the prosperous and continuous life of the species. These animals like all others seem to be concerned very much with three things, food, protection, and reproduction — in one word, *life*; not the life of the individual which is often ruthlessly sacrificed, but the life of the group; and not merely the life of the immediate group, but of the present and succeeding generations. Now, if the ants and bees had moral laws and punishments for the offenders and a sense of right and wrong, it is evident that these would all be directed toward this one end or highest good, the life of the species.

The behavior of the individual ants and bees is what from a human point of view we should call *good behavior*, because it is directed quite unerringly toward the well-being of the group;

and the reason why there is so little bad behavior is that animal behavior has been mechanized through the ages either by the action of natural selection or in other ways. This mechanized behavior we call *instinct,* and its action is so perfect that the well-being of the group is attained without the presence of laws and lawgivers and crimes and punishments, but of course at the sacrifice of the higher values which arise in a society of free individuals.

There is nothing, then, in the analogy of the bees and ants which will help us in the Theory of Morals except the very important fact that among these simple animals the *welfare* or *well-being* of the group or species is the end or goal of their activities, and that good behavior (instinct) is the condition of that well-being. If we could apply this to human society and believe that social well-being is the highest good, and that "good" or "right" conduct is that which conditions this well-being, and that all those *moral laws* which have been preached to us from our infancy are simply those rules of action which racial experience has found necessary for social welfare, why, then, the whole subject of ethics would be greatly simplified.

Life as highest good

Perhaps, then, life is the highest good, the *summum bonum,* which philosophers have long sought. At any rate, life is *good*; whether it is the highest good we may ask later on. All nature seems to strive toward life. The conative impulse, the will-to-life, the *élan vital,* the struggle for existence, which have confronted us so often, whether we were studying the origin and nature of life, the philosophy of evolution, or the philosophy of mind, seem now to offer us a foundation for the philosophy of conduct. Ethics would then be that practical science which considers the ways and means of *successful living,* just as agriculture considers the means of successful farming. Moral laws, in that case, would be the rules for successful living; and presumably the moral laws actually in vogue would be the rules which the experience of social groups has found necessary for successful living.

This conclusion would be, of course, altogether too simple to provide a theory of morals for human beings, but it might be useful as an introduction to get the matter clearly before us. The welfare of bees and ants is quite easily defined, but human welfare presents much more difficulty; you and I might not agree as to what successful living is.

Conduct among primitive men

Before we attack this problem it may help us to consider the situation in primitive human groups. Ants and bees do not have moral laws, nor duties, nor consciences, nor any moral sense. Neither do any animals, although among some gregarious types of mammals individual offenders against the common interest are killed or driven from the herd. Only man is a moral being, consciously reflecting upon right and wrong behavior, approving or disapproving, voluntarily choosing, and suffering regret for wrongdoing. In man behavior becomes rational, and with rational behavior or conduct arise morality, conscience, ethical judgment.

All these exist in primitive human society, mingled with many social instincts brought over from the subhuman inheritance. But in human society the actions of the individual are not wholly determined by instinct, although the social instincts are still present, as when the mother instinctively defends her child, or the war frenzy flashes through a community. Human actions become voluntary actions, determined by custom and authority. Morality now passes through the stage of social habits or *customs* made binding upon the individual by public approval or disapproval, by the favor or anger of tribal gods, and by the operation of physical force in the form of punishments administered by the tribal authorities. Something called public opinion arises, carrying approval or disapproval of certain actions. Pressure is brought upon individuals in the way of constraint or restraint to do or not to do certain things which are considered to be conducive or detrimental to the common good. Hence *conscience* arises, a kind of inner echo of the approval or disapproval of certain kinds of conduct by the group. Judgment is passed upon one's own conduct or that of others, as it is supposed to bear upon the common good. Hence arises *moral judgment*.

When all these things happen in a primitive community, then

morality has come.   Not all kinds of action are *moral* actions, but only the voluntary conduct of rational beings considered in respect to its *worth* in leading to a certain *end*.

When men live in communities many egoistic impulses have to be suppressed for the sake of the common good.   The sentinel in time of war stationed at his post to guard the camp must for the common good sacrifice his desire to sleep.   Thus *duty* arises, a feeling of constraint to act contrary to inclination, but for the common good.   The *sense of obligation* is now experienced by the individual, aroused by the force of approval or disapproval of public opinion, together with the dread of punishment either human or divine, or the hope of reward.   Under the sanction of law and authority the man says "I must"; but the "I must" becomes the "I ought" when the instinctive sympathy and love which belong to man's original nature are added to the external sanctions and the consciousness of public approval or disapproval. The sense of obligation may be defined as a certain compulsion in the form of public approval, in which I myself share, to act against my immediate selfish interests, when I feel myself free so to act or not.   Finally *character* appears, by which we mean the general reliability of an individual to act in conformity to duty, or to do the things which are considered right, and avoid those which are considered wrong.

It was in this way that man came to be a free moral agent.   It represented a mighty step upward in evolution when moral conduct took the place of social instincts.   A new set of values came to Mother Earth when rational beings began to reflect upon the worth of actions and freely to choose the higher values.   Then were born free personalities, having both rights and duties, perceiving differences in values and making free choices.   Then for the first time character was possible, that greatest of all great words.   Kant said that there is nothing in the Universe grander than the good-will — or, as we should say, character.

The evolution of morals

But the reader may ask, "How did it all come about?   How did the social instincts of gregarious animals change into the moral judgments of intelligent men?" When that brilliant speculation known as *Darwinism* burst upon the world, it was thought at first that its principles could be applied to ethics and would solve the old puzzle about the origin of man's moral nature. It was only necessary to suppose that moral action had survival value, and then, if by chance such action appeared as the result of variation, any persons or groups so furnished would have an advantage in the struggle for existence and so perpetuate moral traits. Probably few writers on ethics now would attempt to explain the coming of morality by the natural selection of small variations, for the development, though indeed slow, has been too rapid for that. We must substitute mutations for variations; and the mutations in the direction of morality would be difficult to explain — or at least more difficult than other evolution theories.

There has undoubtedly been an evolution of man's moral nature, but his moral nature has not been evolved out of the social instincts of the lower animals, because there is vastly more in moral character than in social instincts. It has been rather a growth in which new qualities and higher values have been slowly realized: it seems more like an "epigenesis" than like an evolution — a new birth, something achieved, a higher round of the ladder gained. Perhaps the only way that we can understand the evolution of the moral from the non-moral is to believe that there is some force at work, some driving force, or craving, or cosmic interest, which is struggling to realize these higher values.

The evolution of morals is taking place more rapidly than ever before at the present moment — and the method is through creative intelligence. When man begins to *think*, he can always think of a better way. Customs and moral laws are being constantly refined. When we got rid of human slavery, we saw that there were other forms of slavery which were also wrong, such as that exhibited in child labor in factories or the tyranny of capital over labor. Taking property belonging to another and taking human life are morally wrong; yet they were not thought to be wrong by primitive people, provided the one who suffered belonged to another tribe. But there came a time when theft and murder were wrong under any circumstances. Somebody's conscience told him that there was a higher law. Antigone in Sophocles' drama refused to obey the order of the King, because her conscience told her that there was a higher law. Jesus, Savonarola, Luther, and all our prophets and reformers have stood out against custom and tradition and proclaimed a better way. It is for this reason that the intuitional school of moralists has taught that conscience is a sort of God-given faculty, having immediate insight into right and wrong. Empiricists, on the other hand, have said that there is no such faculty, our higher knowledge coming from experience. But the situation is probably not well described by either of these schools. What we seem to have is a constantly enlarging insight into better methods, a more penetrating vision, a better judgment of values. In man we may call it rational thought; in the beginning we may perhaps call it the "power which makes for righteousness."

Partial summary

We seem, then, to have made thus far some progress in understanding the origin and meaning of certain of our ethical concepts. Right actions are those which conduce to social welfare. The social instincts guide the lower animals to this end. In man social instincts are replaced by free voluntary action, guided, but no longer infallibly guided, by social customs and moral laws, enforced by legal, social, or divine sanctions. In such a situation, reflective moral judgment, conscience, and duty necessarily arise. Gradually the social customs and moral laws are themselves refined by experience, and by the operation of reflective thinking and the insight of gifted leaders. And this whole movement from instinct to morality arises, we believe, as a part of the whole process of growth which we call *creative* or *emergent evolution*.

While we may be able to understand in this way what moral laws are, and how they have grown up, and what duty and conscience mean, and how they have arisen, there is one concept which we have repeatedly used in the discussion, but have not carefully defined — this is the concept of social welfare. Right actions are those which conduce to social welfare, but what is social welfare? So long as we are discussing swarms of bees or ants, flocks of birds or herds of animals, there is no great difficulty in defining welfare. It is the physical survival of the group or species.

But when we turn to human society, this definition of welfare is no longer adequate. Human beings have higher aims than mere physical survival. It is just here that the disagreement has arisen among the several schools of writers on the theory of ethics. It is the old problem of the Highest Good.

The Highest Good

What, then, are those higher values which are tne goal of human effort? If, as was intimated above, moral laws are the rules for successful living, what kind of living is successful living? If you or I had to draw up a constitution for a new social order or write a philosophy of education, what would we decide to be the *end* toward which our efforts should be directed? It is not sufficient to mention a number of virtues, such as temperance, courage, wisdom, justice, love, co-operation; or ideals, such as freedom, equality, opportunity; we must find, if possible, some general principle, which will serve as a criterion of social welfare. Several such principles, as we have seen, have been put forward in the history of ethical theory, namely, pleasure, happiness, self-realization, the activity of our highest powers, or merely obedience to duty. These may be embraced under three general theories relating to the *Ethical End* or *Highest Good*. First, the hedonistic theories regard pleasure or happiness as the end. Second, the functional theories regard self-realization or activity as the end. Third, the intuition theories regard unconditional obedience to duty as the end. These have all had a very important historical development, each represented by eminent scholars, ancient and modern.

Hedonism

Hedonism is from a Greek word meaning *pleasure*. In its simplest form it is the doctrine that pleasure is the highest good. In its more carefully developed form it teaches that this is happiness, especially the happiness of the greatest number. As such it is called *Utilitarianism*. A Greek philosopher named Aristippus, a disciple of Socrates, first proposed the view that pleasure is the highest good, and he had reference to the pleasure of the individual, not being interested in social welfare. As for pleasures, he held mere physical or bodily pleasures in the highest regard.

Epicurus, founder of the Epicurean school of philosophy, refined the theory and, while still making pleasure the highest good, emphasized mental rather than physical pleasures, and thought that in the end the greatest pleasure could be gained by freedom from fear and anxiety, and by studious avoidance of any cause of pain or worry. Epicurus himself lived a very simple and abstemious life and enjoined simplicity and virtue upon his disciples.

In modern times a much more serious attempt to construct an ethical philosophy on the basis of happiness was made by the eminent English thinkers, Hobbes, Bentham, and Mill. The theory of Jeremy Bentham (1748–1832) may be mentioned as the best expression of modern Utilitarianism. With Bentham, pleasure is still the highest good, not the pleasure of the moment, but of a lifetime; and not the pleasure of the individual, but of the greatest number. The latter qualification was an all-important one, marking the arrival of the social element in ethical theory. Bentham was interested in finding some universal principle which should serve as the basis of all legislation, and he found it in the principle of *"the greatest happiness for the greatest number"* — called the principle of utility. It is this which is the measure of right and wrong.

A still further refinement of Hedonism was made by John Stuart Mill (1806–73). In his little book, entitled *Utilitarianism*, will be found a clear and concise statement of his view. He accepts the principle of the greatest happiness for the greatest number, but he makes a very important modification of Bentham's doctrine in that he recognizes a difference in *quality* among pleasures, some pleasures being better than others. That there is such a difference seems to be true, but it represents the abandonment of the strict hedonistic ethics. Bentham had consistently denied any such qualitative difference, pleasures being measured quantitatively. Quantity being equal, the pleasures of art, poetry, or philanthropy are no better than the pleasures of the senses. This Mill denied.

"It is better," he said, "to be a human being dissatisfied than a pig satisfied; better to be Socrates dissatisfied than a fool satisfied." [1] Undoubtedly, but why? If we could think this through, we should find the ethical problem solved. Mill himself did not give a satisfactory answer to this question. He seemed to think that it is to be determined by the judgment of those best qualified to judge — by those who have had experience with both kinds of pleasure. However this difficulty may be met, the fact of the qualitative difference in pleasures seems to weaken the logical position of Hedonism. It introduces some other standard for right conduct than pleasure itself.

Hedonism has been weakened also by a better knowledge of the psychological motives of human actions. The desire for happiness is not the primary motive of action. We are creatures of impulse. By instinct, habit, or custom we crave not happiness nor pleasure, but specific things. We want a piece of land, a new car, a dance-date, a fur coat (or at least a fur collar), a position, a husband, or a wife. People want to exercise power, to rule, to succeed in business or in a profession, to make a lot of money, to gain praise or acclaim, to win in the election, to be noticed on the street, to be asked to join a fraternity or sorority, to write a book, to be an actor or movie star, to carry through some reform, to minister to the sick, to champion a great cause.

Furthermore, in our judgment of values we do not appraise happiness — certainly not pleasure — as the highest good. There are other things which we rank higher — genius, ability, devotion to ideals, heroism, self-sacrifice, public service, originality. Our biographies are not those of happy people. Jesus was a man of sorrows. Socrates was executed as a criminal. Lincoln fell a victim of a great cause. To be sure, we may say that we honor these men because they suffered for the happiness of others. But did they? Were they not martyrs to their efforts for specific things, to things we count good in themselves, righteousness, wisdom, freedom?

We assume that happiness usually accompanies the good life: but we certainly count as good many lives that are not happy.

---

[1] *Utilitarianism*, p. 14.

Socrates died in the quest of wisdom and knowledge. We may argue that wisdom and knowledge are not good unless they lead to happiness, which of course begs the question at issue.

We honor our heroes who died in battle, not because heroism is a *means* of happiness, but because death for one's country on the field of battle is accounted a deed of nobility. We honor our football heroes not because of their happiness, nor because they contribute to the happiness of the spectators, but because of their skill, their discipline, their devotion to their group and to their college. In their defeat they are unhappy; in their victory they are happy — but of that we take less account. We honor them because they display qualities which we rank as ideal. They did their best — and for that we praise them. In most of our experiences which we call good, we should probably say not that this is happiness but that this is life — real life. It is experience that we want, or struggle or adventure. I was talking with a young girl who had been an art student in a metropolitan city. "Isn't it wonderful," I said, "that in this safe country of ours, an attractive girl can go alone to a great city and nothing happen to her!" "Yes," she said, "that's just the trouble. Nothing ever happens!"

Interest and desire

But happiness is a very general term. Perhaps if it could be carefully defined or described we might indeed find it to be the highest good — and the promotion of it the final test of good behavior. But we must know what it means. Does it mean the satisfaction of desire? Referring to the list of things which we strive for, do we strive for them because we desire them? The good life has often been described as "the richest attainment of desire." Right actions would then be those which conduce to the greatest attainment of desire for the largest number of people in this and succeeding generations.

But difficulties appear. A conflict of desires speedily arises and different desires have a different worth. We approve of the satisfaction of some desires but not of all. Are we then to set up a standard for measuring the worth of our desires and what would such a standard be?

Some would prefer to use the word *interest*.[1] We are interested in everything we desire, but we do not desire everything we are interested in. The specific things for which we strive are objects of an intense and stimulating interest; for instance, the new coat, the new car, the new house, boy friend, husband, wife, business partner. We are *for* some things, and *against* others.

From this point of view, what we call *value* is that which we desire or are interested in. This is contrary to the theory long held in the history of thought that value or good is something objective and real, independent of our attitude towards it. We desire things, it is said, because they are good.

If value depends upon interest, the question of course arises — Why are we interested in things? What is the source and meaning of interest or desire? These are found in certain fundamental *urges*, or *drives*, or impulses; and the specific forms of these urges and drives arise from the interaction of the organisms with the environment through ages of evolution. Anything at all, for instance, connected with sex is apt to awaken a profound interest in both old and young, and this of course goes back to the primal need of perpetuating the life of the species.

It is evident however that in our modern fearfully complex and interwoven society there must be an almost infinite variety of interests — many of them conflicting. We must choose between them, and the basis of our choice will be, if this theory is to prevail, what we may call a *harmonized* life, yielding in the end a total of permanent satisfactions. Even a child soon learns that he must temper his desires by the lessons of experience. "Experience has taught us," quoting from Clifford Barrett, "that not everything which we *desire* proves on closer acquaintance to be *desirable*. 'When each desire has singed its wings and retired before some disillusion,' says Santayana, 'reflection may set in to suggest residual satisfactions that may still be possible, or some shifting of the ground by which much of what was hoped for may yet be attained.'"[2]

For instance, in choosing from the infinite variety of foods that

---

[1] Compare Ralph Barton Perry, *General Theory of Value* (Longmans, Green and Company, 1926). Also D. W. Prall, *Study in the Theory of Value* (University of California Publications in Philosophy), vol. III, no. 2.

[2] Clifford L. Barrett, *Ethics* (Harper and Brothers, 1933), p. 1.

may be offered, we find that a scientific knowledge of vitamins will add greatly to our total satisfactions, although we have at first no "interest" in vitamins. Our likes and dislikes were at some time a successful guide to life and health — but not now. An Antarctic explorer, providing for the great adventure, will not limit his choice of foods to the "likes" of his men. He will select what they ought to have. But who is to determine what they "ought" to have?

This does not mean that some other standard than interests is to be used, but that in conflicting interests a knowledge of their relative value in serving life as a whole is necessary. The men in the Antarctic expedition are "interested" in returning home in health and strength as well as in having foods which they like. Upon reflection they will *approve* of the things which promote their wider interests.

The satisfaction of human interests may therefore be a legitimate solution of the ethical problem, provided we mean organized or enlightened interests; and this does not necessarily involve the bringing in of any other criterion than interests themselves, but only such selection of them as may be approved after reflective thought. A young man will ignore many pressing desires for the sake of the satisfaction of the very imperative interests which will arise later. The organic relation which exists between youth and maturity exists also between the individual and society, and explains the puzzling problem of duties. In organizing my interests I find that one which is very serious and imperative is social approval — and not only social approval but social welfare. For I soon discover that I *need*, and therefore desire, the friendship, protection, and sympathy of my fellow men — and these I cannot have without the subordination of many of my own instinctive and personal interests. A man may rebel at any mention of the word *ought* or *duty*, and sneer at moral obligations or be little influenced by the exhortations of moralists, or the threats of punishment for the infraction of law; but if he is capable of thinking, he will see that the word 'ought' reduces to the word 'want,' providing his interests are sufficiently organized to include his present self, his future self, and the larger self of the great community. The real meaning of moral conduct is the response to larger and more remote situations.

> Virtuous action is conduct which responds to situations that are more extensive, more complicated, and take longer to reach their fulfillment, than the situations to which we instinctively respond. An infant knows neither vice nor virtue because it can respond only to what touches it immediately. A man has virtue in so far as he can respond to a larger situation.[1]

Mr. Lippmann contrasts the statesman with the politician as follows:

> The words of a statesman prove to have value because they express not the desires of the moment but the conditions under which desires can actually be adjusted to reality. His projects are policies which lay down an ordered plan of action in which all the elements affected will, after they have had some experience of it, find it profitable to cooperate. *His laws register what the people really desire when they have clarified their wants.* His laws have force because they mobilize the energies which alone can make them effective.[2]

Moral conduct does not, however, turn out to be merely far-sighted selfishness, and this because of the organic connection of the individual and society. A consistent theory of morals may therefore be based on the organization of interests, the satisfaction of which becomes the criterion of the good life.

The functional view

But, after all, I wonder whether we do not need a different set of terms for the description of the Good Life — other than happiness, pleasure, desire, interest, satisfaction. There is another way of approaching this study — and another theory of successful living. We may call it the functional view.[3] It has the prestige given it by the support of Plato and Aristotle, and is held by many modern writers. Plato said that man's highest good is a harmoniously developed personality, a condition in which every faculty

---

[1] Walter Lippmann, *A Preface to Morals* (The Macmillan Company), p. 224.

[2] *Op. cit.*, p. 283. The italics are my own.

[3] This theory has been given other names, such as perfectionism, self-realization, energism. All of these are misleading terms. The theory of self-realization has erroneously been used to encourage what is called "self-expression" — with sad results in American education.

functions in a perfect way without infringing upon any other faculty. The good man is one in whom appetite, reason, and courage work in harmony, no one of them being in excess.

Aristotle's book, called *Nicomachean Ethics*, is one of the great books of the world on ethical theory. Well-being, he said, is a functional conception. A good horse or a good sword is one that perfectly performs the functions of a horse or sword. The highest good is found in the normal activity of our highest powers. To Aristotle, man's highest activity is intellectual. He is a thinker, and the exercise of thought is what Aristotle ranks so high. God to him is essentially a thinker, the thought of thought — pure thought. Hence rational activity is Aristotle's notion of the highest good, expressed in scientific research, in philosophical thought, in the quest of truth.

In modern times the functional theory usually takes a somewhat different form. With our Northern and Western ideas we do not look upon reason as the only noble function of man, although we rank intellectual activity very high. We prize creative work of any kind, invention, exploration, initiative, adventure. We prize also, as indeed the Greeks did, artistic creation and the exercise of the faculty of appreciation, and religious activity, and wonder and worship. We think of congenial work and play, of recreation and sport, and of social relations of all kinds. The end in view is to be a *person*, and to exercise all the powers and enjoy all the privileges of a person, to develop all that is inherent in personality. In accordance with this principle, Everett in his book, entitled *Moral Values*, makes a table of values based on the idea of functional activity. He arranges them in eight groups as follows:

I. Economic Values	V. Character Values
II. Bodily Values	VI. Aesthetic Values
III. Values of Recreation	VII. Intellectual Values
IV. Values of Association	VIII. Religious Values [1]

Disregarding for the moment Everett's fifth class, called *character values*, his table is instructive, showing how bodily health and strength, sports and recreations, friends, the production and appreciation of works of art, rational thought, wonder and worship

[1] Walter Goodnow Everett, *Moral Values* (Henry Holt and Company), p. 182.

are all good in themselves, because they represent the exercise of our powers.

From this point of view, then, the good life is found in activity, rather than in the satisfaction of desires. We must find *something to do* — and something which we can do well, rather than something to eat or drink or see or hear or buy; and preferably it should be something demanding initiative, skill, pursuit, or mastery — or even something involving risk or danger. Two things, says Nietzsche, man wants — danger and play.

The story of man, whether told in poetry, sculpture, painting, or historical chronicles, throws great light on the kind of life in which he finds fulfillment. We find him engaged in some enterprise in which he can exercise his powers and his passion to excel — even his cunning. We find him at war, at the chase, at love making, at the shaping of works of art, at political intrigue, at song and revel, at worship and sacrifice, at study and contemplation. It is not happiness which he seeks or prizes, but in his search for specific things, he finds satisfaction — and, no doubt, happiness.

The man of the present, as well as the man of history, is a creator. He loves to fashion something requiring skill and ingenuity. He loves to plan, experiment, manipulate. He strives ever for some goal — to gain possession of something, to win a fortune, to attain to a position of honor or power, to win social prestige, to gain the favor of some woman. He loves novelty and excitement — gambling, for instance — at the race track, on the stock exchange, at the bridge table. He is a lover, seeking a mate; he is a thinker, philosopher, scientist, searching for truth; he is a pioneer, seeking new fields of endeavor; he is a worshiper, wondering at the beauty or power of Nature and God — seeking peace and harmony and forgiveness. He is a social being, participating in some kind of co-operative enterprise, craving praise when he succeeds and sympathy when he fails. He is a dreamer, picturing a world in which peace and justice and good will replace war and greed and inhumanity. And finally he is a thinker, devising, exploring, inventing — planning a better social order, a fairer administration of justice, and a better way of life. Happiness is not his aim, but fulfillment comes as a gift.

It is true of course that man as a conscious being is so constituted that pleasure accompanies the exercise of normal function; to be alive and well and strong is joy. But if we were entrusted with the task of forming a constitution for a new state, the end in view would be a society in which all men should attain, not to the satisfaction of their desires, but to the fulfillment of personality, as typified in activity, opportunity, justice, a square deal, a chance to work at fair wages, a chance to marry and have a home, means to educate their children, and leisure for enjoyment and self improvement. Hence, according to the functional view, it is *life*, rather than happiness or the satisfaction of desire, that is the highest good.

Character values

We recall, now, Everett's list of values according to the functional theory of the highest good. Certain "character values" hold the fifth place in that list. What are these character values and why do they appear in a series of values? They do not seem to be "activities" at all. The fact is that there is another side of human nature which we have thus far overlooked. The man of the past has been a man of *action* — but at the same time a man *disciplined* by the necessities of social life. Survival has depended upon co-operation with the members of his social group. He has learned the lessons of obedience, restraint, self-denial, and loyalty to his group or his chief. Thus another set of values, called character values, has appeared in his social relations. "Loyalty to the Great Community" has sometimes been taken to be the supreme value, as if the life of the community itself were the final Greatest Good. Many philosophers, both of the past and the present, have held that the State is an end in itself — and its safety, its integrity, and its glory, the Highest Good, something half divine.[1]

Now just what are these character values? Should they be put first in Everett's list as conditions of all values — or should they be put last in the list as highest of all? Evidently we have here to consider the relation of the individual to society.

Suppose we assume, for the sake of the argument, that the

[1] Compare the writings of Hegel, Bosanquet, Bernhardi, von Treitschke.

perfection of the individuals composing a community is the highest good. Since man is a social being and lives in communities, it is evident that he must contrive to get along with his fellow men before he can begin to realize any of his individual aims. Since his selfish interests come in conflict with the selfish interests of others, a set of social duties will arise, obedience to which conditions the very existence of society. Honesty, veracity, justice, regard for the lives and property of other men, regard for the wives and daughters of other men, are some of the duties which make life in a healthy social group possible. The fate of the individual is bound up with the fate of society. These social duties will be in the focus of attention, but this does not mean that they are themselves the highest values, only that they are indispensable to the realization of any values whatever. Hence, when one speaks of loyalty to the Great Society as the supreme good, this is because it is something which is absolutely fundamental. So vital are our duties to society that the word *character* has reference almost wholly to our social duties. Character values may therefore well stand at the head of any list of values — conditioning all the others. The order in Everett's table may thus be open to criticism.

This does not mean that social duties are instrumental values, or that prudential motives alone enjoin virtue, for men are bound together by sympathy, making of society an organic unity, each one sharing in the good or ill of all. Society is, indeed, the larger self, but it is of the individual self that we are speaking when we use the expression self-realization or self-development as the ethical end.

Various attempts have been made to formulate the highest good in accordance with this principle, bringing the individual and society into their proper relations. The following may serve as an example:

The end of all moral action is "a social order in which each member of the group may have a fair field for his activities and the fullest opportunity for self-development, without infringing upon the similar right of every other member of the group in the present or in future generations."

It is probable that in the years to come we shall have to put more and more emphasis upon character values; and the reason for this is that, as the world gets filled with people, as geographical expansion is no longer possible, as nations crowd one another in every continent, it becomes more and more difficult to live together in peace and harmony.   Nations jostle one another, and parties within a nation clash.   In times of war or civil strife or political turmoil there is little opportunity for the development of those other values which self-realization involves — intellectual, aesthetic, or recreational.   The only way that people or nations can live together in harmony is by the practice of the character values, co-operation, justice, respect for law, self-restraint, and self-control.

It seems, indeed, that a new set of moral values is coming into the foreground as a result of the modern social situation.   The values which have been preached to us in the past from every pulpit and platform are Liberty, Equality, Opportunity, Efficiency, Democracy, Organization, Science, Invention, and Discovery. We still believe in them heartily and fully, but the time has come when our attention must be focused upon other values which condition the existence and welfare of society itself, such as *Discipline, Self-restraint, Self-control, Respect for Law, Obedience to Law, Limitation of Desires, Temperance, Co-operation, Education.* The practice of these virtues has become urgent and imperative.

Character values as duties and moral laws

So supremely important are the character values that they come to us in the form of *duties*, not merely values — duties which we owe to society or to God.   And not only are they duties, but they are laws — moral laws.   Society itself, in its organized capacity as the State, enjoins them and enforces them with rigid sanctions; and God is represented as handing them down engraven plainly on tables of stone and as inflicting severe punishments for their infraction.   Thou shalt *not* steal or even covet thy neighbor's property, or do any murder, or commit adultery, or bear false witness.   They are the minimum conditions on which any society of men can exist and prosper.   They represent the boiled-down and concentrated experience of the ages as to the conditions of successful living in communities and thus become essential for the realization of all other values. Every man now and in succeeding generations demands a fair field for exercising his powers and developing his personality. This can only happen in a social order where justice prevails and where it extends beyond the narrow limits of one's own community to the whole of mankind. So fundamental are our *duties* to others, so ingrained by social if not biological inheritance, that they seem indeed like the very voice of God in the form of human conscience. This will enable us to understand the third theory of the highest good, which we may now consider.

Intuitionism

At first the theory of *Intuitionism,* or *Absolutism,* or *Apriorism,* as it is sometimes called, is a little hard to understand. We can see how happiness might be regarded as the highest good, or social welfare, or self-realization; but what can it mean to say that *duty* is the highest good? Duty, we supposed, was simply the obligation placed upon us for pursuing some moral value, and the moral value itself must first be determined. But Intuitionists do not speak primarily of value; they speak of right and wrong, and of conscience and duty. The human mind knows intuitively what is right and what is wrong, and duty must be done for duty's sake. There is in man a special "sense" or faculty or capacity, by which moral distinctions are immediately known. In all cases of doubt, follow your conscience; it is a God-given possession of every man. There is an inner appreciation of the moral quality of actions, a kind of moral taste, which needs no explanation and does not come from experience.

The philosopher Kant has given his authority to this ethical system. Kant's whole moral system was an emphasis upon duty. The practical reason expresses itself in the form of a *Categorical Imperative,* which we should call the *voice of duty.* By a categorical imperative Kant means a downright unconditional command. The will is self-legislative, issuing its orders categorically. Unconditional obedience to the moral law is demanded. It does not say *if* you would be happy, or *if* you would be perfect, or *if* social welfare is your end, you should do certain things.   It says simply, *Do right!*   Respect for the dignity of the moral law is the sole motive of moral action.   The moral law is absolutely sacred.

> Kant loves to dwell on its awful sublimity.... Absolute truthfulness, absolute respect for the rights and freedom of every one of your fellow men, with devotion to the cause of high-mindedness, of honesty, of justice, of simplicity, of honor — such is Kant's ideal, and so far as in him lay, he was always true to it.[1]

There is nothing then unconditionally good except a good will.

But it does not seem enough to say, *Do your duty.*   What is my duty?   Kant supplies a formula which is capable of application to every situation: *So act that the maxim of thy will may always hold good as a principle of universal legislation.*   Suppose that a sum of money were left in trust with me for a child.   Suppose that, under the stress of some great financial difficulty, I think of using this money temporarily for myself, to be paid back, of course, in a few weeks.   Is this right?   Simply apply the rule.   Would I wish this to become a general rule of action?

To this excellent rule Kant adds another equally wholesome: *So act as to treat humanity, whether in thine own person or in that of another, always as an end, never as a means.*   No child, no woman, no laboring man, can ever be treated as a means to one's own pleasure or profit.   The human personality is sacred.

Such is Kant's remarkable and lofty system of intuitional ethics. It is perhaps the view commonly accepted by mankind.   Do your duty, and do it because it is your duty.   Some years ago a great ocean liner, the Titanic, sailing west on her maiden voyage with a large passenger list including well-known and distinguished men, struck an iceberg and sank.   There were not lifeboats to accommodate all, and the men, helping the women and children into the boats, calmly remained on the decks and went down.   What was their motive for doing this?   No one even suggested any other motive than duty.   It was not for newspaper praise, nor reward in heaven, nor any other gain.   It was simply *the proper thing to do.*

No one questions either the grandeur or the practical working of Kant's ethical system, which exalts a stern uncompromising

[1] Royce, *Spirit of Modern Philosophy* (Houghton Mifflin Company), p. 133.

obedience to duty; but it may be possible to explain the almost instant and apparently intuitive character of our moral sense in other ways than by the postulate of the "autonomy of the will." The Empiricists would explain it as the result of individual or racial experience in living under a system of moral discipline. And as regards the *formula* above mentioned, so clearly practical in its application, it has been questioned whether, when I ask if I should wish the principle of my action to become a universal principle, some standard such as happiness or social welfare or the general good is not tacitly implied.

If one cannot quite accept Kant's rigorous Intuitionism, nevertheless there is an element of truth in this theory which other theories cannot ignore. When Kant proposes a practical rule for our behavior, namely: So act that thou shouldst wish that the principle of thine action might become a universal rule, we may by logical analysis find that this reduces to some more ultimate theory of the highest good; but in practice it is an exceedingly safe and wise rule of action, and seems to require no further analysis at all. The ethics of Kant represent a persistent emphasis upon the character values — upon good-will and social co-operation, and never since Kant's time has there been so great a need of this emphasis as at the present moment. If our civilization is to survive, we must learn this lesson of good-will and co-operation. We must not forget that first of all men have to learn to live together, and social classes have to learn to live together, and nations have to learn to live together. The world is getting very crowded, and the time has come for greater discipline, self-restraint, and co-operation. The lesson of co-operation is clearly our first lesson.

Sanctions

But what if we do not co-operate? Men are free agents, and the powerful motives of self-interest seem to conflict with the good of society — hence the moral laws will not always be obeyed. When they are not obeyed, what will happen? This is the problem of moral and social sanctions — more vital for human happiness than any other problem, philosophical, economic, political, or financial. It belongs in the field of social ethics and cannot be discussed here, but a brief reference to it may be made. Nothing could be more interesting and profitable than to try to think it through. Few people attempt this. Perhaps some have reasoned no further than the policeman's club and the possibility of escaping it. If I sin, the law will get me. But perhaps it will not get me. If so, all is well.

Next comes the sanction of public opinion, the disapproval of our fellow men, more powerful, no doubt, as a deterrent from evil than the laws of the State. But what will happen if an individual acts contrary to public opinion, or — and here is the graver question — what will happen if public opinion grows lax and the community no longer frowns upon the evil doer? "Everybody's doing it" removes the odium which was formerly attached to the evil deed. To meet these various cases and to provide what seems to be the absolutely necessary sanction for moral law, there has long been held a belief in a system of rewards and punishments in a future life. Often enough in this life we see the wicked prosper and the good man suffer. The eternal law of justice seems to demand that there be some compensation somewhere. It must be in a life after death. This was the well-known argument for the existence of God and for the immortality of the soul put forward by the philosopher Kant.

But the punishment for sin in a future life can act as a deterrent from evil only in case it is accepted as an article of faith, and even then it seems not always to be effective. So we must still press our question — What will happen in a community when offenders escape the law, when public opinion becomes lax, and when the belief in a future life has grown dim? The answer to this question is apparent. What would happen among gregarious animals if instinct failed? The group or the whole species would become extinct. What has happened among primitive men when social morale has failed? The group has been annihilated, or absorbed by some neighboring group in which morale has not failed. What will happen in our modern complex social groups if the laws of conduct which experience has found necessary for social welfare fail to be observed? Social dissolution must be the outcome. As long as the heart of society is sound, individual offenders may be cared for. When the whole social body begins to be corrupt, social organization will gradually fail.

The social outlook

This bears directly upon the possible future of our own civilization. History reveals no situation similar to that of our immense modern congested states. When in former times social morale failed, there were strong and virile people to the north to bring new blood and stern discipline. If social morale should fail now, if a disregard of the rules of healthy living should become general, would the dark ages which would follow have the seeds of a new and better era? I fear that the regeneration, although it would surely come, would be very slow. Perhaps there would intervene long centuries of social decadence with its accompanying poverty and hunger, dirt and disease, and infinite pain and suffering.

But social morale may not fail. There are regenerative forces at work in society now which were not known in former times. Just at present, to be sure, partly as a result of the World War and partly because of changing social and economic conditions and changing religious beliefs, social morale is low. We become weary of the daily chronicle of crimes, murders, rackets, and robberies. We are alarmed at the constant revelations of political corruption. We are disturbed by the apparent loss of the spirit of self-reliance among our people and the growing disposition to cast our burdens on the state or the federal government. We fear the danger of a decadent morality of sex, which may threaten the physical integrity of society. That a crisis has been reached in the moral progress of the world no one can doubt.

But, nevertheless, there are abundant encouraging signs. A new social conscience is arising, and there are visions of new values in the relations between individuals, and between individuals and society, and between social and political groups. There is a world-wide growing consciousness of the iniquity and uselessness of war, which will lessen its frequency from generation to generation, and will lessen the moral decadence which follows in its train. We are becoming conscious of the unity of mankind and of social groups — and this consciousness will gradually save us from the frightful costs of war and the disastrous consequences of hatred and suspicion among nations. And, furthermore, we are becoming conscious of the unity of the present generation with those to follow. We are beginning to understand that we cannot carelessly exhaust our forests, our coal mines, our oil wells, and our soils; but that our duty to our children and to their children extends to the conservation of all our material resources, and, what is still more important, to the conservation of our racial values, the physical and mental health of the race. The generations that are to come have the right to a sound physical and mental heritage. In a word, we are beginning to profit by the power of reflective thought, which is slowly but surely discovering a better way to live. Possibly we cannot depend in our democratic society upon great leaders to save the world; but eventually we may be saved through the influence of our great thinkers. Possibly we must depend upon universal education, which will show that in our crowded social groups self-realization for the individual can come only from that self-sacrifice and discipline which make co-operation possible.

However this may be, since natural selection has largely ceased to operate in human society, nothing will save us from social disaster except obedience to the older laws of honesty, veracity, chastity, and justice, and the newer law of love and co-operation enjoined by the conditions of our modern society.

> When all is said, there is nothing as yet to be changed in our old Aryan ideal of justice, conscientiousness, courage, kindness, and honor. We have only to draw nearer to it, to clasp it more closely, to realize it more effectively; and, before going beyond it, we have still a long and noble road to travel beneath the stars.[1]

Ethics and religion

But even if moral conduct is a kind of absolute value which Nature is trying to realize, still the actual working of the moral law seems, to one reflecting upon it as we have done in this chapter, to have a certain aspect of harshness. If you would be happy, you must be righteous. If you are unrighteous, you will suffer — or, if not you, then your children, your neighbor, or your social

[1] Maeterlinck, quoted by Drake, *The Problems of Conduct* (Houghton Mifflin Company).

group. I am afraid it is true that the moral law is, indeed, sometimes harsh. The laws of Nature and of God are unbending. The unfit have been swept from the stage to make room for the fit. That the unfit should perish to make room for the fit is in the end beneficent. Possibly God could have thought of some better way to create free, intelligent, and moral beings than through the slow process of evolution, than through error and its punishment — but no man has proposed this better way.

There is one means that has been found to soften somewhat the harshness of the moral law — and that means is religion. During all the ages religion has lightened the burden in some degree, not by annulling the consequences of unrighteousness, but by supplying motives to righteousness. The hard road of duty may be softened by love and loyalty. I fear that the law of consequences cannot be escaped; but what through stern duty may be onerous and difficult may, through willing loyalty, become a service of joy. Men do not like to be threatened and driven; but by love and friendship they may be readily led. Sometimes when they will not do right to escape evil consequences, they will eagerly do so out of loyalty, either to a great leader or to a great cause.

Impulsive motives are stronger than prudential motives. Tell men that the unrighteous shall perish and they will do unrighteousness still — even though they know that the consequences of wrongdoing are fatally sure, falling upon them, or their kin, or their social group; but once call out their spirit of *devotion* — to God, to Master, or to friend — to husband, wife, or lover — to church or party, even to club or fraternity — and they will undergo hardship and practice self-denial.

Religion teaches that the Universe is friendly — that God is love, and that deeper down than the law of competition there is the law of co-operation; that altruism is as primordial as egoism. It teaches that in our struggle for right the Universe in its spiritual depths is on our side — so that the struggle is not in vain. When these spiritual powers are incarnated or personified in a visible leader, devotion reaches its perfection, and great things may be done. When no such leader appears, then education is indispensable — *for the people must have either light or leader*.

In connection with this chapter read:

Durant Drake, *The New Morality* (The Macmillan Company).

Aristotle, *Nicomachean Ethics*. Translated by Robert Williams (Longmans, Green and Company), book I.

Further references:

Walter G. Everett, *Moral Values* (Henry Holt and Company).

John Dewey and J. H. Tufts, *Ethics* (American Science Series. Henry Holt and Company).

Edward Westermarck, *The Origin and Development of the Moral Ideas*. 2 vols. (The Macmillan Company).

John Dewey, *Human Nature and Conduct* (Henry Holt and Company).

John Stuart Mill, *Utilitarianism* (Longmans, Green and Company).

L. T. Hobhouse, *Morals in Evolution* (Chapman and Hall).

Josiah Royce, *The Philosophy of Loyalty* (The Macmillan Company).

Edgar S. Brightman, *Moral Laws* (Abingdon Press).

Clifford Barrett, *Ethics, An Introduction to the Philosophy of Moral Values* (Harper and Brothers, 1933).

W. M. Urban, *Fundamentals of Ethics* (Henry Holt and Company).

James H. Tufts, *America's Social Morality* (Henry Holt and Company, 1934).

Walter Lippmann, *A Preface to Morals* (The Macmillan Company).

Will Durant, "Our Morals" (*The Saturday Evening Post*, January 26, 1935).

H. W. Dresser, *Ethics in Theory and Application* (Thomas Y. Crowell and Company).

J. A. Leighton, *The Individual and the Social Order* (D. Appleton and Company), part IV.

CHAPTER XXIX

THE PHILOSOPHY OF ART

Objects of beauty

ON THE walls of certain caverns in Southern France there are pictures of animals painted by the men of the Old Stone Age. They display a considerable degree of artistic skill and were painted so that they have endured for probably more than twenty-five thousand years. Evidently a great deal of effort was expended upon them by the artists who made them, effort which was economically unproductive, providing no food or clothing, and ministering to no material needs. When asked to explain these pictures, we say that they possess a certain quality which we call *beauty*, and that they give to the beholder a certain kind of *pleasure*, which we call *aesthetic* pleasure. They belong to the sphere of *art*, and are thus quite outside the familiar field of economic enterprise, or love, or war, or moral and political institutions. They introduce us to a new field of philosophical inquiry, in which new problems appear.

If the reader is a college or university student and will let his thought rest for a moment on the buildings on his campus, he will at once recognize the fact that they differ in architectural merit, some, perhaps, being masterpieces of art and others having little or no merit of this kind. Furthermore, he will see that architectural merit is not judged on the ground of the practical utility of the building or its convenience for the purposes for which it was made, nor even its probable permanence and stability. It has or has not something else which we call *beauty*.

He will find also that he is constantly making the same judgment in respect to the music which he hears at oratorios, concerts, recitals, church services, dances, musical comedies. Some of it has the quality of artistic merit and some has not. He knows that the same is true of poetry and of paintings and sculptures and of landscapes and of human faces and of dress.

What is this elusive thing we call *beauty?* Almost all we know about it is that it gives us, or is in someway connected with, a peculiar and lasting pleasure, which we understand as *aesthetic pleasure.* We do not know what beauty is, nor how aesthetic pleasure differs from other kinds; but we do know that there is a supreme joy which we have felt in the contemplation of a beautiful building, painting, statue, landscape, a woman's face, tasteful dress, or in listening to music, or the poetry of Shelley or Keats, or in watching or participating in the graceful movements of the dance.

The science of aesthetics

Aesthetics investigates the meaning of aesthetic pleasure, the objective or subjective character of beauty, and the nature of beauty itself, and the origin and nature of the art impulse. All these questions have been discussed since the time of Socrates and many different answers have been given to them.

That aesthetic pleasures play a very important part in our lives, and that among normative sciences aesthetics may be comparable with ethics and far more interesting than logic is evident if we reflect how much oftener we hear the expression, *Isn't that pretty* or *beautiful!* than the expression, *Isn't that true,* or *good!* Personal beauty and personal adornment seem also to take more of our thought and attention than our moral endeavor, or the logical consistency of our discourse. It is no wonder that thinkers from the time of Socrates have wondered about beauty and what it is in objects that makes them beautiful.

It is evident that in aesthetic enjoyment we have a *value* which adds immeasurably to the richness of life. Music, poetry, drama, literature, painting, and sculpture are a refuge for the soul wearied with the daily cares of business or politics or professional duties. Our American cities may be ugly in their monotonous architecture, but there are few cities or towns in which, as we come and go, the eye is not rested by at least one beautiful building; while natural beauty awaits us everywhere, in wild and cultivated flowers, in fresh green lawns, in forest or ornamental trees, in waving fields of grain, in rivers, lakes, mountains, and sea, in the rainbow, in cloud effects, in the setting sun or the heavens at night, in the songs and motions of the birds and in their forms and plumage, in the gorgeous leaves of autumn or the fields covered with snow in winter, and in the human face and form.

Since beauty is so good to enjoy, the philosophical impulse in man must be very strong to cause him to break in upon his aesthetic pleasure to inquire what sort of experience it is, or to pick to pieces an object of beauty to find out in what its beauty consists, or to psychologize on the motives of the artist at work upon some great painting. Nevertheless, the human mind with its restless longing to penetrate to all knowledge has from the earliest times been asking and trying to answer these very questions. A course in the theory of art is indeed highly to be recommended. Quite apart from our interest in the theoretical questions, our own powers of appreciation may be greatly strengthened by such study, and the joy of life immeasurably enhanced by an initiation into a knowledge of the various sources of aesthetic pleasure.

Art periods in history

Lately the metaphysical aspects of the beauty problem have been less emphasized and increasing interest has been shown in the historical, sociological, educational, and psychological sides of the subject. One writer has said that there has been a continual slow decline in all the arts of Europe, except music, since the year 1500, and that music itself has been slowly declining since the death of Beethoven.[1] Perhaps not all those competent to pronounce judgment in such matters would agree with this critic. But if it be true, the question Why? involuntarily springs to our lips. Is it because of the lack of genius in our modern age, or because there is a lack of interest in art, or an undeveloped faculty of appreciation? There is certainly in America today a widespread interest in art, particularly in music and poetry and architecture. But if we speak of *relative* interests, comparing our interest in fine arts with our devotion to mechanical and useful arts and to the acquisition of wealth and the accumulation of externalities, and then compare in this way our own age with that of the great art periods of history, as in ancient Greece or

[1] F. S. Marvin, *Progress and History*, chap. IX. Article by A. Clutton Brock.

medieval and Renaissance Europe, the comparison is most unfavorable to us.

There would seem to be three conditions necessary to a great art period: First, deep feeling seeking expression. Second, genius to express it in appropriate form. Third, a sympathetic audience able to appreciate and enjoy the productions of genius. Probably we fail in all of these as compared with the people of the periods mentioned. But it is significant that there was a powerful religious motive back of the great architecture of the Middle Ages and to a very large extent of the great painting, music, and poetry of the Renaissance period. Religion and national feeling inspired also the work of the Greek masters. Their beautiful buildings were temples; their sublime drama originated in a religious service and had usually religious history for its theme, and gods and goddesses figured prominently in their sculpture, painting, and poetry. It will be one of the interesting questions which only the future can answer whether a great art period can spring from other than religious feeling, and if so what its powerful motive will be.

In fact, this introduces us to a special problem in aesthetics, which holds our interest at the present time more than the old theoretical discussion about the nature of beauty. This is the problem of the *art impulse*. Why do people compose music, write poetry, paint pictures, and model statues? We quickly see that the motives by which we explain other kinds of human activity will not apply here, namely, the hope of gain or fame or personal advancement. Products of art are too often economically unproductive, and when they are not so, few of us would believe that economic or selfish motives are adequate to explain the creative work of the artist. We see that such motives would not apply to the drama, poetry, or sculpture of the ancient Greeks, or to the art products of any great art period in history. So, then, let us consider this part of aesthetic theory first, the part, namely, which deals with the *art impulse*. Then in a second division we may consider some of the older and newer theories of *beauty*. Finally in the latter third of the chapter we may bring together some conclusions under the head of *aesthetic experience*.

I. THE ART IMPULSE

The fine arts

When intelligence and skill are expended in productive activity, we speak of this activity as *art*. If this activity is of such a kind as to lead to the production of objects of utility, we call it a *useful art*; if it leads to the production of objects of beauty, we call it a *fine art*. There is no difficulty whatever in explaining the presence, in a social group, of the useful arts, such as blacksmithing or shoe-making or weaving, since they serve the vital needs of the people. But so far as we can see, works of fine art serve no such need. And yet, not only at the present time, but as far back as we can go in the history of man, the creative work of the artist, whether in music, painting, poetry, sculpture, architecture, or decoration, is discovered in every social group. What is its explanation?

If it is a case of demand and supply, it is wholly unlike the operation of demand and supply in the economic world. We could not think of the creative activity of the poet or the musical composer as something done to meet a demand in the ordinary sense. Such activity is free and spontaneous, *the outgoing of some creative impulse*. It seems more like a form of *self-expression*. The artist has something to express, perhaps some deep emotion, for which ordinary language or gesture is inadequate. Language must be *embellished*, as in poetry, calling in the aid of rhythm and rhyme; or musical tones with their cadences and harmonies must be invoked. The artist or the poet or the musical composer is *impelled* by some insistent prompting to create something beautiful. The activity is spontaneous, instinctive — a kind of overflowing. The artist himself cannot explain the impulse. It seems to him like an inspiration.

The principle of social resonance

But art is something more than the expression of deep emotion. There is a social element in it, which is really its significant part. Art is fundamentally social. In our quest for an explanation of the art impulse, we must turn both to the psychologist and the sociologist. The potential artist, with his profound emotion or his great thought or his new vision, not only desires to give adequate expression to his mental state, but he demands the sympathetic expression and the sympathetic experience of his fellow beings.

The closest bonds of sympathy unite the members of a group. Each one shares the joys and sorrows of the others and each one wants others to share his own newfound joy — as many others as possible. The child, almost as soon as it can talk, cries, "Oh, mamma, come and see." We run to our friend to have him share in some new beauty that we have found. No friend being present, we may even beg a stranger to share with us some gorgeous sunset or grand Alpine scene.

We may think, therefore, of the artist as impelled to give expression to some overmastering emotion, or, indeed, to some overmastering thought, in such a way as to gain a kind of *social resonance* through the sympathetic participation of his fellow men in his new possession. The art impulse has thus been called "the pursuit of social resonance," [1] and the principle may be applied not only to the musical composer, the poet, the painter, and the sculptor, but to the man of the Old Stone Age, painting his picture of the bison on the walls of his cavern, or to the savage beating his tom-tom.

But it is something more than mere sympathy which the artist asks and receives from his fellows; it is actual and active participation in his feelings, moods, and creative work. The organic unity between the members of society is much more intimate than we used to think when first we spoke of sympathy. The psychology and physiology of sympathy are better understood now. Sympathy extends to actual bodily movements, and when the outer movements must be inhibited, it extends to incipient movements — muscular innervations or motor images. We wish to dance when we see others dance, but if we cannot dance with our whole bodies, we dance with parts of them, the sympathetic strains and tremors being felt in our legs and arms as we watch the dance. Hirn recalls the instance of the dancers brought into court for causing a disturbance, who, when asked to give an exhibition of the suspected performance, compelled both judge and jury to yield to the temptation, the sitting being dissolved in a

[1] See the excellent account in Hirn's *Origins of Art*, especially chaps. VI, VII, VIII.

wild dance carnival. Much of the pleasure in the enjoyment of art forms is now thought to be due to faint, incipient, and possibly subconscious movements, perhaps of the eye, perhaps of the muscles of the limbs or trunk. I shall refer again below to this "internal imitation." The artist, therefore, gains an actual sympathetic response from his fellows, his own emotion being enhanced by this social diffusion.

The art impulse is thus a kind of extension or enlargement of one's personality. We love to extend our personalities by means of a cane, or high-heeled shoes, or a tall hat, or by furs and feathers; but the kind of enlargement on the part of the artist that we are studying here is different. It is a social enlargement, the instinctive need to have others think and feel with us; and the artist's audience is not limited to his circle of friends or to his fellow townsmen, but extends to all the world and to posterity.

Art and morals

This principle of *social resonance*, I think, may explain the old difficulty about the relation of aesthetics to ethics. Are there moral lessons in works of art? Does the artist aim to instruct or to edify? Is poetry written to teach a lesson? Is there any such thing as didactic poetry? Lucretius, for instance, is reckoned among the great poets of Rome. His *De Rerum Natura* seems to have been specially, if not deliberately, written to set forth a materialistic philosophy and to free men's minds from fear.

I think we must answer that, while the relation between art and conduct is very close, true art cannot have any primary moral purpose; its purpose is to please, not to instruct. Goethe said that to require moral ends in art means its destruction, although any true art will have moral consequences. The artist is never a preacher or a teacher — he is just a *sharer*. He has a divine thought, a profound emotion, and his only wish is to share it with you and me. The relation of teacher to pupil is a lesser one; the motive of the artist is higher. Hence it follows that art is a great moral influence; it is the expression of our spiritual ideals, and the power of the artist for good is without limit. Greek art, at its best, was distinctly moral. It carried a great lesson, but never in the form of a lesson.   It brought harmony and temperance and courage and justice; but it did not teach them.

Art and social morale

Art is thus the great harmonizer, the pacifier, the reliever.   It relieves social tension, and conduces to peace and good-will.   Works of art are not objects of desire.   We love to have others share in our aesthetic joy, so that the eternal strife over mine and thine, as it pertains to houses and lands and material goods, is abated in times of aesthetic enjoyment, and life is lifted to a higher plane.   The soothing effect of music upon us as individuals is familiar, but it produces social harmonies as well as harmonies of soul.

Hence we can understand the social importance of art.   It has been from the earliest times of primitive man a socializing agency, integrating the people, uniting them in the bonds of social sympathy.   It has strengthened social morale to an unknown degree.   Unfortunately, the socializing and moralizing influence of art has probably never been so slight as it is today, perhaps not because of lack of activity in artistic production, but rather because of the relative lack of interest in it as compared with other forms of human activity.   The actual moral life of the people is not touched by the influence of art as it has been at other periods.[1]

The play motive in the art impulse

By many writers, notably by the poet Schiller and the philosopher Herbert Spencer, the creative impulse of the artist has been likened to the play instinct of children, being free and spontaneous and having no direct life-serving end.   We work because we must in order to gain something that we need — food, shelter, clothing; we play just because we wish to play.   Our overflowing

[1] In this I have in mind the accepted list of fine arts.   But there are certain forms of art, if we may so call them, that are widely cultivated now, which have both a moral and a social influence in the highest possible degree, such, for instance, as popular music, the modern dance, the moving pictures.   Concerning the moral influence of these more or less degraded forms of art I cannot speak here; but the socializing power of them is certainly very great.   The modern automobile has a degree of beauty as well as efficiency, and has a socializing influence of unknown power, a universal theme for conversation, and a means of social intercourse.   At the risk of shocking the cultured reader, I might even refer to a certain artistic effect of the bright and attractive filling-stations that have sprung up in every city, town, and village throughout the land, replacing many an unsightly edifice.

energy needs an outlet of some kind. So it is with art, which is the simple outgoing of our creative powers finding expression in activity beyond the requirements of our daily life. This is well illustrated in Dr. Edman's interesting description of the emergence of the fine arts:

> In the sharp struggle of man with his environment, those instincts survived which were of practical use. The natural impulses with which a human being is at birth endowed, are chiefly those which enable him to cope successfully and efficiently with his environment. But even in primitive life, so exuberant and resilient is human energy that it is not exhausted by necessary labors. The plastic arts, for example, began in the practical business of pottery and weaving. The weaver and the potter who have acquired skill and who have a little more vitality than is required for turning out something that is merely useful, turn out something that is also beautiful. The decorations which are made upon primitive pottery exhibit the excess vitality and skill of the virtuoso. Similarly, religious ritual, which, as we have seen, arises in practical commerce with the gods, comes to be in itself cherished and beautiful. The chants which are prescribed invocations of divinity, become songs intrinsically interesting to singer and listener alike; the dance ceases to be merely a necessary religious form and becomes an occasion of beauty and delight.... Repeatedly we find in primitive life that activity is not exhausted in agriculture, hunting, and handicraft, or in a desperate commerce with divinity. Harvest becomes a festival, pottery becomes an opportunity for decoration, and prayer, for poetry. Even in primitive life men find the leisure to let their imaginations loiter over these intrinsically lovely episodes in their experience.[1]

The imagination supreme

Finally it is in the imaginative work of the artist that the creative power of the human mind attains its perfection. In a preceding chapter we have compared the creative agency which is at work in evolution to an artist "with inexhaustible resources of imagination." Whatever this agency is, its supreme achievement is the human mind — an achievement supreme because the mind itself is creative of still higher values, and this power is seen at its best in imaginative work in the fine arts, where even the beauties of nature are surpassed. In the study of ethical values we have

[1] Irwin Edman, *Human Traits and Their Social Significance* (Houghton Mifflin Company), pp. 333, 334.

seen how that marvelous power which we call *rational thought* has discovered higher and ever higher standards of conduct; but in all such creative work of thought, as also in scientific discovery and in mechanical invention, the imagination is an active factor. Sometimes we speak of it as insight or vision. Whatever we call it, imagination is supreme in the work of the artist, where it seems like inspiration.

I have spoken of the art impulse as if it belonged only to the artist. But both the art impulse and the creative power of thought and imagination are common to all minds, differing only in degree. Most of us have at some time tried our hands at poetry, or modeling in clay or artistic designing, drawing, or painting; while the creative imagination is manifest, even in day-dreaming or in telling stories or in the writing of fiction. When these powers common to all are most highly developed and accompanied by a high degree of technical skill, we have *genius*; then appears the great poet, painter, sculptor, architect, or musical composer

II. THEORIES OF THE BEAUTIFUL

Art from the observer's standpoint

We have tried to see just what art is from the standpoint of the artist, the creator of an object of beauty. We must now inquire what it is from the standpoint of the beholder. What sort of experience is aesthetic experience? The obvious answer is that it is the sort of experience which we have in the contemplation of beauty of any kind, in nature or in art. So the final question comes, What is beauty? — and it is this part of the aesthetic problem which has been so much discussed and which has led to so many different answers. We know what beauty is until we are asked. Then we do not know.

The older theories of beauty were metaphysical, in contrast with our modern theories, which are psychological. The metaphysical theories considered beauty as something real and objective — perhaps a kind of essence or entity, or at least some objective aspect or quality of things. The ancient Greeks hardly thought of explaining beauty as a certain kind of feeling existing only in the mind of the beholder.

Historical

Plato in certain of his Dialogues seems to hold a peculiarly metaphysical theory of beauty, as if it were a reality in itself, a kind of eternal and unchanging essence or "form," any individual beautiful object being said to participate in this essential beauty. When in other places he speaks of harmony, proportion, and symmetry as constituting beauty, he still thinks of them metaphysically as objective qualities of things.

For he who would proceed aright in this matter should begin in youth to visit beautiful forms; and first, if he be guided by his instructor aright, to love one such form only — out of that he should create fair thoughts; and soon he will of himself perceive that the beauty of one form is akin to the beauty of another; and then if beauty of form in general is his pursuit, how foolish would he be not to recognize that the beauty in every form is one and the same! And when he perceives this he will abate his violent love of the one, which he will despise and deem a small thing, and will become a lover of all beautiful forms; in the next stage he will consider that the beauty of the mind is more honourable than the beauty of the outward form. So that if a virtuous soul have but a little comeliness, he will be content to love and tend him, and will search out and bring to the birth thoughts which may improve the young, until he is compelled to contemplate and see the beauty of institutions and laws, and to understand that the beauty of them all is of one family, and that personal beauty is a trifle; and after laws and institutions he will go on to the sciences, that he may see their beauty, being not like a servant in love with the beauty of one youth or man or institution, himself a slave mean and narrow-minded, but drawing towards and contemplating the vast sea of beauty, he will create many fair and noble thoughts and notions in boundless love of wisdom; until on that shore he grows and waxes strong, and at last the vision is revealed to him of a single science, which is the science of beauty everywhere....

He who has been instructed thus far in the things of love, and who has learned to see the beautiful in due order and succession, when he comes toward the end will suddenly perceive a nature of wondrous beauty (and this, Socrates, is the final cause of all our former toils) — a nature which in the first place is everlasting, not growing and decaying, or waxing and waning;... but beauty absolute, separate, simple, and everlasting, which without diminution and without increase, or any change, is imparted to the ever-growing and perishing beauties of all other things. He, who from these ascending under the influence of true love, begins to perceive that beauty, is not far from the end. And the true order of going, or being led by another, to the things of love, is to begin from the beauties of earth and mount upwards for the sake of that other beauty, using these as steps only, and from one going on to two, and from two to all fair forms, and from fair forms to fair practices, and from fair practices to fair notions, until from fair notions he arrives at the notion of absolute beauty, and at last knows what the essence of beauty is. "This, my dear Socrates," said the stranger of Mantineia, "is that life above all others which men should live, in the contemplation of beauty absolute,... the divine beauty, I mean, pure and clear and unalloyed, not clogged with the pollutions of mortality and all the colours and vanities of human life — thither looking, and holding converse with the true beauty simple and divine." Remember how in that communion only, beholding beauty with the eye of the mind, he will be enabled to bring forth, not images of beauty, but realities (for he has hold not of an image but of a reality), and bringing forth and nourishing true virtue to become the friend of God and be immortal, if mortal man may.[1]

A still more spiritual theory of beauty was held by Plotinus, the Neo-Platonist (A.D. 205–70), who thought that beauty is the pure effulgence of the divine Reason. When the Absolute expresses itself or shines forth in its full pristine reality, it is beauty. The artist is the "seer," who can see the divine beauty.

Hegel's theory is an instance of a more modern metaphysical view. All nature is a manifestation of the Absolute Idea. Beauty is the Absolute Idea shining through some sensuous medium. It is a kind of *disclosure* of spirit. Art, religion, and philosophy are for Hegel the highest stages in the development of spirit.

> The art-products of the world register the insight of the human race into Beauty, and the nations of the world have left their profoundest intuitions and ideas thus embodied. Art gives to phenomenal appearances "a reality that is born of mind"; and through Art they become, not semblances, but higher realities. It is thus that Art breaks, as it were, through the shell, and gets out the kernel for us.[2]

Schopenhauer's Theory of Beauty, also metaphysical, is very striking. The Absolute Will, which is reality, objectifies itself directly in the Platonic Ideas, or, as we should say, in the idea, type, species, genus — and indirectly in individual things. Any-

---

[1] Plato, *The Symposium.* Translated by Jowett (Oxford University Press).
[2] William Knight, *The Philosophy of the Beautiful*, part I, p. 71, discussing Hegel.

thing is beautiful in proportion as it realizes or approximates to the type. In moments of pure contemplation, when we put aside all desire and deny the "will-to-live," we are able to see this ideal beauty. The common man is two thirds will and desire, and one third intellect; the artist is two thirds intellect and one third will, and hence is able to see through the outer husk of things to the ideal beauty lying back of phenomena. It is the artist, therefore, rather than the scientist, who knows reality. The artist ceases to ask about the "why" and "when" and "where" of things, and regards only the "what." That art is the lowest which is most encumbered with matter. This is architecture. Then comes sculpture and painting and poetry, and finally music, the highest of the fine arts, in which there is an immediate objectification of the Absolute. The composer reveals the inner nature of the world, and expresses the deepest wisdom in a language which his reason does not understand.[1]

Another type of metaphysical theory is that of Ruskin, who believed that beauty in objects is found in certain qualities, such as unity, repose, symmetry, purity, and moderation, which typify divine attributes.

A recent subjectivistic metaphysical theory is that of the Italian philosopher, Benedetto Croce, who says that beauty is wholly mental, not belonging to physical objects. Aesthetic creation is the mind's most primitive and elemental form of activity. Croce calls it "expression"; but by this he does not mean the translation of a mental concept into some outer physical form. Aesthetic activity is a spiritual act, by which we convert mere impressions into intuitions. It is pure intuition.[2]

An entirely new direction was given to aesthetic inquiry by Kant, whose penetrating mind seemed to get at the heart of so many philosophical problems. Kant represents the beginning of the modern scientific and psychological study of aesthetic theory. In his third great critique, *The Critique of Judgment*, Kant says that the mind has a third faculty beyond that of the reason and the will, namely, that of feeling. The peculiar characteristic of aesthetic

---

[1] Arthur Schopenhauer, *The World as Will and Idea*, vol. I, p. 336.
[2] See Benedetto Croce, *Aesthetic*. Translated by Douglas Ainslie. See H. Wildon Carr, *The Philosophy of Benedetto Croce*, chaps. III and IX.

feeling or aesthetic pleasure is that it is *disinterested*.   This marks
it off from all other pleasures, which have an element of desire,
involving personal or vital interests.   Sugar, for instance, is not
beautiful; it is agreeable.   We have to possess it in order to enjoy
it.   Likewise a moral act is not beautiful; it is *good*.   We approve
of it and therefore have an interest in it.   The beautiful, on the
other hand, is always the object of disinterested satisfaction,
separate from all desire.   Beauty, however, although it is mental,
is objective, since it is always the object of a judgment, in which
we say, "This thing is beautiful," thus regarding beauty as a quality
of objects, not a merely subjective taste.

The play theory of art

We have seen above, in studying the art impulse, how the creative activity of the artist has been likened to play.   But the play
theory applies equally well to the beholder, and has proved to be
a valuable help in understanding aesthetic pleasure.   A suggestion
made by Kant and followed up by the poet Schiller was later developed by Herbert Spencer [1] into the so-called *Spieltrieb*, or play-
impulse theory.   The word *play* may be applied to all those human
activities which are free and spontaneous and pursued for their
own sake alone.   The interest in them is self-developing and they
are not continued under any internal or external compulsion.   The
word *work* on the other hand, includes all those activities in which
by means of sustained voluntary attention one holds oneself down
to a given task for the sake of some end to be attained other
than the activity itself.   Work involves mental stress, strain, effort,
tension, and concentration.   Play, being the spontaneous expression of vitality itself, involves none of these, but is pleasurable in
a high degree.   Now, when this playlike activity involves the two
higher senses, sight and hearing, and our higher mental powers
and even our emotions, says Spencer, the conditions are fulfilled
for the acquirement of aesthetic pleasure, which arises in the use
of overflowing and surplus energy.   "The aesthetic excitement is
one arising when there is an exercise of certain faculties for its own
sake apart from ulterior benefits."

[1] *Principles of Psychology*, vol. II, part IX, chap. IX.

In the contemplation of beauty, therefore, in its many forms, the eye and the ear and the mind are at play, and the accompanying pleasure is aesthetic. To take a single example, the perception of unity in variety is one of the most constant of mental functions, daily exercised in real life. When, now, this function is performed for the mere love of it with no serious end, the affective tone accompanying it is of the aesthetic kind. Thus, unity in variety is found in every work of art, be it a musical composition, painting, statue, or poetic masterpiece. We all love to see unity in variety, particularly to discover it. It satisfies and rests us, bringing to the mind what someone has called a kind of "domestic peace." In a musical composition a peculiar pleasure follows the discovery of a recurrent theme, lending a unity to what first seemed a mere diversity.

It has even been suggested that the pleasure which we find in elementary colors and tones and in tone and color harmonies may be likewise explained by the play theory. We greatly enjoy bright colors, such as red, orange, and yellow, in the sunset, rainbow, cultivated flowers, and autumn leaves, as well as in painting, decoration, and dress. The eye delights to use its sensory powers, merely for the sake of using them, and, as Grant Allen has suggested, surrounded as we are with grays and greens and blues from street and lawn and sky, the eye revels in the enjoyment of the brighter colors when opportunity offers. The play theory of aesthetic pleasure is again illustrated in the dance, when harmonious and balanced movements provide the needed exercise to the overnourished and underworked muscles and motor centers of the body, while the "realized expectation" of the rhythm and the music add to the aesthetic joy.

The play theory of art has withstood adverse criticism fairly well since the time of Schiller and Spencer. We now know that play is not so much the overflow of surplus and unexpended energy as it is that outflowing of energy which is the expression of life itself. But this revision of Spencer's theory strengthens rather than weakens its force as applied to art production and aesthetic pleasure. Art is not a kind of child's play or pastime for idle moments, any more than play is a kind of activity *left over* after one's work is done.

Our modern industrial society has given us an exaggerated notion of the relative importance of work in life as a whole, so much so that certain social reformers have proposed the absurd theory that only industrial workers should be entitled to citizenship. The child does not play because "surplus" energy needs to be expended; he plays because he is a child and play is his spontaneous activity.[1] So the natural life of a man is not work in the sense of drudgery, but some kind of spontaneous creative activity in which, to be sure, he produces something. He may produce something useful, in which case we call his activity work, or he may produce something beautiful, when we call it art. The latter is equally with work a part of real life, but in freedom and spontaneity it resembles play.

Empathy

The word *empathy* has been used to denote the sympathetic motor attitudes which the observer assumes in the presence of objects of beauty. This word was suggested by Titchener for the German word *Einfühlung*, used by Theodor Lipps, who writing at the beginning of the century first gave currency to the *Einfühlung* theory. A clear account of this theory may be found in Langfeld's book, *The Aesthetic Attitude*. He says:

> When we listen to a song, we have a tendency to move in time to the rhythm, and to repeat the notes with accompanying tension in the throat. In silent reading, the tendency to movement often goes over into actual movement of the lips or muscles of the larynx. The act of unity itself, fundamental to experience, is conceived in motor terms as a bringing of things together. It will rightly be objected that in many instances of perception there is no consciousness of such movement, not even of the faintest tendency toward such imitation of facial expression as that just described. The answer is that these motor sets may be, and in fact most frequently are, subconscious. The object observed, whether through the eye, ear, or another of the senses, arouses the memory of former movements, which are so revived that they form a nervous pattern; that is, the nerve paths going to the necessary muscle groups are opened, and those to opposed muscle groups are closed, and this pattern, which is ready on additional stimulation to produce actual movement, is sufficient to give us our perception of space, weight, form,

[1] See the author's *Psychology of Relaxation* (Houghton Mifflin Company), chap. II, "The Psychology of Play."

smoothness, delicacy, and many of our other experiences. Accordingly one must for the most part explain this tendency to movement in physiological rather than psychological terms.[1]

Almost anyone may become conscious of these motor attitudes by thinking vividly of a man rowing a boat, or dancers gliding about a room, or an automobile skidding around a corner. As you think of these movements, you can feel your own tendency to move in your arms, trunk, or legs. But now these same motor attitudes are assumed, not only in mental imagery, but in perception, and in the perception, not only of moving objects like dancers, but of buildings, statues, and paintings, and even of music. In aesthetic contemplation we are wholly unconscious of these movements, so that they become for us, not subjective phenomena at all, but qualities of the beautiful object. We cannot say that they are "projected" into the object; they are simply felt to be there; they belong to the object, and at once glorify it with all the rich meaning of our own former experiences. The thing becomes beautiful because it is clothed with a meaning drawn from our own active life; the object is vitalized. For instance, a Doric column of a Greek temple gets its meaning and its beauty partly from the unconscious motor set of our own organism as we have the tendency firmly to brace our feet as if to support a great weight. The pleasure in the experience seems to consist in the successful balance of forces and is interpreted as the quality of beauty in the object.

It would seem that the Theory of Empathy is a valuable contribution to our understanding of the philosophy of art. It seems clear that in the contemplation of a work of art, these motor tendencies are, indeed, present, and that they add to our understanding and appreciation of the object of beauty. They give it a strange life and vitality. But Empathy alone would seem to furnish a philosophy of appreciation rather than a philosophy of aesthetic pleasure. The source of pleasure in the empathetic experience is not quite apparent.

There is, however, one aspect of the Theory of Empathy which is important. We remember that in speaking of the art impulse

[1] Herbert Sidney Langfeld, *The Aesthetic Attitude* (Harcourt, Brace and Company), pp. 110, 111.

we found that the primary motive of the artist is to widen and in-
tensify his experience by sharing it with all mankind. He desires
a social response to his own emotion or great thought. Certainly
this is attained in the highest degree if the observer goes through
with him empathetically his very motions as he worked upon his
art production. Sympathy could go no further than this. The
Theory of Empathy may thus in part explain that peculiar and
essential social solidarity which it is the function of all art to
promote.

The element of repose and unity in harmonious functioning has
been emphasized by Ethel D. Puffer in her admirable book, *The
Psychology of Beauty,* "The beautiful object possesses those qualities
which bring the personality into a state of unity and self-com-
pleteness." She says:

> A thoroughgoing analysis of the nature of the aesthetic experience in
> its simplest and most sensuous form has given us a principle — the prin-
> ciple of unity in harmonious functioning — which has enabled us to
> follow the track of beauty into the more complex realms of ideas and of
> moral attitudes, and to discover that there also the law of internal rela-
> tion and of fitness for imitative response holds for all embodiments of
> beauty. That harmonious, imitative response, the psychophysical
> state known on its feeling side as aesthetic pleasure, we have seen to be,
> first, a kind of physiological equilibrium, a "coexistence of opposing
> impulses which heightens the sense of being while it prevents action,"
> like the impulses to movement corresponding to geometrical symmetry;
> secondly, a psychological equilibrium, in which the flow of ideas and
> impulses is a circle rounding upon itself, all associations, emotions, ex-
> pectations indissolubly linked with the central thought and leading
> back only to it, and proceeding in an irrevocable order, which is yet
> adapted to the possibilities of human experience; and thirdly, a qui-
> etude of the will in the acceptance of the given moral attitude for the
> whole scheme of life. Thus is given, in the fusion of these three orders
> of mental life, the perfect movement of unity and self-completeness.[1]

III. THE AESTHETIC EXPERIENCE

Psychological aspects

While, perhaps, we cannot yet say that a science of the beautiful
has replaced the older "theories," I think we may be greatly en-

[1] Ethel D. Puffer, *The Psychology of Beauty* (Houghton Mifflin Company), pp. 285, 286.

couraged by the progress that has been made in unraveling the skein of puzzles which formerly comprised the "problem" of beauty. *Beauty* is a name that we give to certain qualities of objects by virtue of which they give rise in us to certain peculiar pleasures which we call *aesthetic*. Such pleasures are disinterested, universal, and permanently pleasurable, even in revival in memory.[1] In speaking of aesthetic pleasures as universal, we mean nothing more than that they are objectified, thought of not at all as agreeable feelings of our own, but as qualities of objects which would give pleasure to all. In aesthetic contemplation the self is forgotten. There is a kind of absorption in the beautiful object, a feeling of complete unity, freedom, and completeness.[2]

Under what conditions, then, do those pleasures which are permanent, universal, and disinterested arise in the human mind. Pleasure, as we remember, is the affective tone which accompanies mental and physiological processes when they are normal and healthy, when life is at full tide, when all goes well, and the vital strivings of the individual are being realized. When we were studying the mind in a former chapter, we discovered that the elementary things in our soul life are profound impulses or desires, *conations*, as we call them — perhaps the will-to-live. In his striving after life, full and free, the individual finds the environment sometimes friendly, sometimes hostile. To its friendly contacts nature has added something which we call *pleasure* — a new and wonderful value.

It is evident, then, that the conditions under which those peculiar, permanent, universal, and disinterested pleasures, which we call *aesthetic*, arise, are those in which there is a complete harmony between the individual and his environment. The situation will then be one of perfect *adjustment* of the individual to his surroundings. There will be a feeling of unity and repose, and this will come only after all material wants have been satisfied, in moments of pure spontaneity, when some part of the personality is at play and its pleasures are wholly disinterested.

[1] Compare Marshall's *Aesthetic Principles*, chaps. I and II.

[2] See the short, clear account in the article entitled "The True, the Good, and the Beautiful from a Pragmatic Standpoint," by Montague, in the *Jour. of Phil., Psych., and Sci. Meth.*, vol. VI, p. 233.

Thus we see that beauty is not anything belonging to objects in themselves apart from the perceiving subject; neither is it anything which belongs alone to the subject; it depends upon the relation of the object perceived to the perceiving organism, and the relation is of the kind which we may characterize as a harmony and adjustment brought about by the fact that there is something in the object which calls into play the harmonious and restful functioning of mind and body under circumstances free from selfish or personally interested motives.   As Kallen says:

> The object, when apprehended, awakens the active functioning of the whole organism directly and harmoniously with itself, cuts it off from the surrounding world, shuts that world out for the time being, and forms a complete, harmonious, and self-sufficient system, peculiar and unique in the fact that there is no passing from this deed into further adaptation with the object.   Struggle and aliency are at end, and whatever activity now goes on feels self-conserving, spontaneous, free. The need of readjustment has disappeared, and with it the feeling of strain, obstruction, and resistance, which is its sign.   There is nothing but the object, and that is possessed completely, satisfyingly, and as if forever.   Art, in a word, supplies an environment from which strife, foreignness, obstruction, and death are eliminated.   It actualizes unity, spirituality, and eternity in the environment; it frees and enhances the life of the self.   To the environment which art successfully creates, the mind finds itself completely and harmoniously adapted by the initial act of perception.
> In the world of art, value and existence are one.[1]

Let us see whether these principles could be applied concretely to the work of the artist.   We recall that the aim of the artist is to attract by pleasing.   In its very simplest form perhaps it is nothing more than an impulse to expend in the regular practice of some mechanic art, perhaps in the making of a basket or an earthen pot or a bow and arrow, a little of the artisan's abounding energy in making it not only useful, but *attractive*.   He will *embellish* his product — and becomes thereby the artist.

Now, the artist perhaps knows little of psychology or physiology, and possibly does not reason about the sources of human pleasure; he proceeds quite instinctively and empirically.   But *it is as if*

[1] Horace M. Kallen, "Value and Existence in Philosophy, Art, and Religion," in *Creative Intelligence* (Henry Holt and Company), p. 439.

he had a keen insight into the motor mechanism of the human subject, the structure and functioning of the organs of sense and the inner working of the mind, and thus knew how to fashion his work of art in such a way as to bring about in the beholder that peculiar absorption, detachment, and "distance," that state of unity in repose, that self-conserving, spontaneous, and harmonious functioning of the whole organism which constitutes aesthetic experience. It is as if he knew how to play upon the mind and motor mechanism of the human subject in such a way as to cause precisely those permanent, disinterested, and universal pleasures which we call *aesthetic*.

The artist seems to do all this intuitively. His knowledge, if not instinctive, is at any rate empirical. He has discovered, first, that he may gain the end in view by the use of *bright colors* or *pure colors* and *color harmonies*, by *pure tones* and *tone harmonies*, and by *cadence, rhyme,* and *rhythm*. With the results of his discovery of rhythm, he would be particularly well pleased, for he would find that in the dance and in music and poetry it would exercise a fascination that no one could resist.

As he proceeds to more elaborate works of art, he would find that *unity in variety* is a never-failing source of pleasure, as well as *symmetry* and *proportion*. He would discover that there are certain forms and certain lines and curves that are universally pleasing. He would find that in painting and sculpture the representation of familiar objects in nature, particularly animal bodies and the human form and face, yields the kind of pleasure that he seeks. In poetry he would learn how his hearers are charmed by the narration in metric form of scenes and events from their own lives — their lives of war and love and even of industry, with all the joyous parts extolled and all the hardships forgotten.

Finally he would see that, in depicting scenes of natural beauty and animal and human forms and human faces, the greatest pleasure arises, not from a slavish imitation of nature, but by a kind of "representation," in which the imagination of the beholder has a part to play, or even by a kind of idealization, in which the essential and significant elements are intensified, or perhaps delicately exaggerated. Thus the genius of the artist puts upon canvas a sunset more exquisite than any actual sunset, or paints a Madonna more beautiful than any actual face of woman. Now, the psychologist or the philosopher in reflecting upon all this is able to explain to some extent the causes of the peculiar pleasure awakened in each of these several ways. Some of these explanations have been indicated in this chapter; some are still to seek.

Resumé

Summarizing in the briefest way what we have learned, we may say that art is a social phenomenon springing from the creative impulse in the mind of the artist, an impulse to give expression in creative form to some profound emotion or great thought, which he wishes to share with other members of his group or with all mankind. And instinctively he grasps the means of making his fellow men his sharers. He appeals directly to their love of color, to their love of harmony, to their love of unity and proportion. He appeals to the play impulse, to the joy of harmonious functioning of every organ and every faculty. He appeals to the deep need which every man feels for moments of repose, of rest from his eternal striving, the need for intervals of perfect adjustment in a life of restless striving for an adjustment which striving never brings. The artist comes to the beholder with a gift — the gift of repose and harmony and a feeling of unity and completeness. Such an experience as this is *aesthetic experience*. It gives *aesthetic pleasure*, which we might better call *aesthetic joy*. And to the object of contemplation the beholder ascribes a quality which he calls *beauty*. Therefore works of art, which call forth these sentiments, are beautiful. Objects of nature may also arouse these aesthetic feelings. Shall we say in this case that Nature is the artist, impelled likewise by an art impulse, aspiring to self-completion in both beauty and its appreciation? Is Nature, too, trying to express herself, to express ever some great thought or feeling, aiming to bring into being works of beauty and also enjoyment of them? This latter question we cannot answer, but in aesthetic contemplation we know that a peculiar unity and sympathy arise between Nature and man.

This is an imperfect summary of our imperfect knowledge of the aesthetic experience. But it may be useful as an approach to further study of this engaging theme. Particularly in music has it proved difficult to formulate the psychological grounds of its strange emotional effects.[1]

The mystery of music

Even if the aesthetics of harmony, melody, and rhythm could be understood, there is still a deep unexplained residue of aesthetic pleasure in music. One subject which awaits experimental inquiry is the question to what extent the "mystical" overtones and their varied combinations may awaken forgotten memories, racial or individual, of emotions engendered in social intercourse through *the human voice*, dimly suggesting distant scenes of love or war or social enterprise.

Psychological explanations of the aesthetics of music failing, many metaphysical ones have been suggested. Some have thought that through the medium of the ear we are in more immediate communication with the very heart of reality than through the eye, which limits us to surface phenomena only. Music, said Schopenhauer, is entirely independent of the phenomenal world, ignores it altogether, and could in a sense exist if there were no world at all. Thus music is a universal language, intuitively understood, and loses some of its inner meaning when accompanied by words. The world is "embodied music":

> The unutterable depth of all music by virtue of which it floats through our consciousness as the vision of a paradise firmly believed in yet ever distant from us, and by which also it is so fully understood and yet so inexplicable, rests on the fact that it restores to us all the emotions of our inmost nature, but entirely without reality and far removed from their pain.[2]

Beauty as ideal value

There is still another puzzling question which should be mentioned. Since we speak now not so much of beauty as of aesthetic

---

[1] The almost intoxicating effects of rhythm have been partly explained. See the instructive article by Carl E. Seashore entitled "The Sense of Rhythm as a Musical Talent," in *The Musical Quarterly*, vol. IV, no. 4, pp. 507–15.

[2] Schopenhauer, *The World as Will and Idea*. Translated by R. B. Haldane and J. Kemp, vol. I, p. 341.

pleasure, the whole treatment seems too psychological, too sub-jective. Is there, then, no beauty in itself? Was Plato wholly wrong? Were not the wild flowers, which blossomed on the prairies ages before the advent of man, beautiful before the eye came to see and appreciate them? Did the rainbow just begin to acquire beauty when the first man saw it?

Again, if beauty is subjective, depending upon the awakening of certain peculiar kinds of pleasure, then it would appear that any object will be beautiful in proportion as it awakens pleasure of this kind. But this seems to be inconsistent with the fact that good taste in art is the result of education and a cultured environment. If a person does not enjoy good music (that is, music which ap-pears to us to be good), or if he cannot appreciate the work of the great masters (that is, masters who are commonly reputed to be great), we say that he has poor taste, assuming that there is some *norm* or *standard* of beauty which this person cannot appre-ciate. Chandler in a recent article [1] attempts to meet this difficulty by saying that the standard of beauty is found in the judgment of those of richly developed experience; but this seems to imply some goal toward which the development is tending.

Perhaps this difficulty may be met if we consider that beauty is after all *a value*, let us say an ultimate value — or even, if you choose, an "eternal value" to be realized through a process of evo-lution. The notion of beauty arises only in a total situation repre-senting a relation between certain qualities of objects, such as colors, tones, symmetry, unity, proportion, on the one hand, and on the other, a highly developed and exceedingly complex human organism with a mind in which has developed the capacity of entering into peculiar relations with those qualities and extracting therefrom a peculiar joy, which we call *aesthetic pleasure*. Beauty, then, would be a new *value* attained through creative evolution; an end for which all the separate factors in the total situation are indispensable.

If we accept this view that beauty is a value, and, together with moral good, perhaps the highest value that we know, there would

---

[1] Albert R Chandler, "The Nature of Esthetic Objectivity," *Jour. of Phil., Psych., and Sci Meth.*, vol. XVII, p. 632.

be, I think, three ways of interpreting this highly idealistic theory. We might consider these moral and aesthetic values as "novelties," but novelties of supreme worth, which in the age-long progress of evolution have finally *appeared*. They were not foreseen by any mind, human or divine, nor planned, nor desired, nor willed. But they are here, and they are good; and it is not impossible that other still higher values may be forthcoming in the future. This method of interpretation would be, I suppose, dear to the heart of the Pragmatist, and it is a view that must certainly make a deep appeal.

A second view would regard moral and aesthetic values as ends toward which Nature has been consciously striving. They have been willed, foreseen, *envisaged* by some cosmic mind or will of God. They are "ideas" as well as ideals. Such a view would be welcomed by all schools of personal or theistic Idealism, and is again a view appealing with great power to many of us.

A third theory would regard these moral and aesthetic values as the product of a creative evolution which is in the nature of a process of *realization*, beauty being one of the values to be realized. Beauty, then, like justice, and others of the "eternal values," would be an end in itself, which has actually been a factor in determining the means of its realization, the various steps in the evolutionary program being *indispensable* to this end, and a certain *control* over the whole world movement being exercised by the values themselves. We should then have to think of the world, not as a series of events in a time order in which antecedents alone were causes — a convenient notation for our work in the physical sciences — but as a process of realization, in which events in the time series would be regarded as indispensable conditions for the realization of the ideal values. In this manner of thinking, God as the totality of values would again be the creator of the world, but rather as an alluring than as an efficient cause. Such a view would be both idealistic and teleological; but the latter term would be used in a sense somewhat different from its older meaning. In Santayana's words, "the whole of natural life, then, is an aspiration after the realization and visions of Ideas, and all action is for the sake of contemplation."

In connection with this chapter read:

Irwin Edman, *Human Traits and Their Social Significance* (Houghton Mifflin Company), chap. XIII.

Further references:

Herbert Sidney Langfeld, *The Aesthetic Attitude* (Harcourt, Brace and Company).
DeWitt Henry Parker, *The Principles of Aesthetics* (Silver, Burdett and Company).
W. T. Stace, *The Meaning of Beauty* (The Cayme Press, 1929).
C. J. Ducasse, *Philosophy of Art* (Dial Press, 1929).
C. E. Spearman, *Creative Mind* (D. Appleton and Company, 1931).
E. F. Carritt, *What Is Beauty?* (Oxford, 1932).
George Santayana, *The Sense of Beauty* (Charles Scribner's Sons).
Henry Rutgers Marshall, *Aesthetic Principles* (The Macmillan Company).
Aristotle, *The Poetics*.
S. Alexander, *Art and Instinct* (Oxford, 1927).
H. H. Powers, *The Message of Greek Art* (The Macmillan Company).
Irving Babbitt, *The New Laocoön* (Houghton Mifflin Company).
M. H. Bird, *Study in Aesthetics* (Harvard University Press, 1932).
Ethel D. Puffer, *The Psychology of Beauty* (Houghton Mifflin Company).
Edward Howard Griggs, *The Philosophy of Art* (B. W. Huebsch).
Arthur Schopenhauer, *Selected Essays of Arthur Schopenhauer* by E. B. Bax (George Bell and Sons), "On the Metaphysics of the Beautiful and on Aesthetics," 274–318.
Yrjö Hirn, *The Origins of Art* (The Macmillan Company).
D. W. Prall, *Aesthetic Judgment* (Thomas Y. Crowell Company).
John Dewey, *Art as Experience* (Minton, Balch and Company).

INDEX